Texas Women on the Cattle Trails

Number Thirteen:
Sam Rayburn Series on Rural Life
Sponsored by Texas A&M University–Commerce
M. Hunter Hayes, General Editor

TEXAS WOMEN ON THE CATTLE TRAILS

EDITED BY

Sara R. Massey

TEXAS A&M UNIVERSITY

College Station

Library of Congress Cataloging-in-Publication Data

Texas women on the cattle trails / edited by Sara R. Massey. — 1st ed.
p. cm. — (Sam Rayburn series on rural life ; no. 13)
Includes bibliographical references and index.
ISBN-13: 978-1-58544-543-1 (cloth : alk. paper)
ISBN-10: 1-58544-543-6 (cloth : alk. paper)
1. Cowgirls—Texas—Biography. 2. Cowgirls—Texas—History—19th Century.
3. Ranch life—Texas—History—19th Century. 4. Frontier and pioneer life—Texas.
5. Cattle drives—West (U.S.)—History—19th century. 6. Texas—Biography.
7. Texas—History—1846–1950. I. Massey, Sara R. II. Series. F391.T4 2006 976.4'05—dc22
2006001539

Contents

Illustrations

Series Editor's Foreword

IT IS FITTING THAT in *Texas Women on the Cattle Trails* Sara R. Massey should bring together accounts of the diverse experiences that the sixteen women who constitute the subjects of this book embody. Misrepresented by many legends and hindered by restrictive nineteenth-century social ideals, these women refute the patronizing roles that their era prescribed. Instead of the "Angel in the House," the image popularized by the British poet Coventry Patmore, these "Cowgirls and Cattle Queens" grappled with the forces that would transform a state and a nation.

Popular culture is rife with images in movies and television of men battling odds, nature, Native Americans, laws and other codes of the Wild West, and one another while moving cattle to market. For many people, the myth has become reality. As Massey and her fellow contributors to *Texas Women on the Cattle Trails* show, however, there exists a far deeper historical account than the tales of male determination, courage, and vigor. Like their subjects, the contributors to this volume traverse a wide range as it were of experiences and concerns carrying many historical and cultural implications. Together, they offer a variety of astute perspectives that produce a new understanding of the history of not only East Texas or the Lone Star state as a whole but of modern history and culture.

Massey and the other contributors to this volume write in an engaged and energetic style, bringing these events to life for contemporary readers by transcending the various myths that surround much of this history. Readers can fully appreciate the quotidian and remarkable events alike through the biographical narratives this book presents, seeing these women and their surroundings as they were. As these accounts demonstrate, this was a period when storms, rabid skunks, disease, and other factors could pose more problems and hazards than cattle rustlers, trail bosses, or indigenous groups. Moreover, Massey's editorial acumen in her selection and organization of contributors and texts enhances these biographies without the imposition of personal bias. As a result of the multifaceted efforts by its editor, authors, and narrative subjects, *Texas Women on the Cattle Trails* provides as a vital addition to the Sam Rayburn Series on Rural Life.

Begun in 1987 under the auspices of Texas A&M University Press, with James A. Grimshaw Jr. as General Editor, the Rayburn Series has had a single purpose: to elucidate the many dimensions of rural life in and around East Texas. The series has a necessarily broad scope in revealing the many aspects of rural life in the region. Previous volumes have examined New Deal cotton programs, a railroad ministry, outlaws, civil disputes, and prairie grasslands, among other aspects of rural life. Although these volumes engage with the history of the region, they remain equally concerned with the present and future as with the past. *Texas Women on the Cattle Trails* is a welcome addition to the series.

—M. Hunter Hayes, General Editor

Texas Women on the Cattle Trails

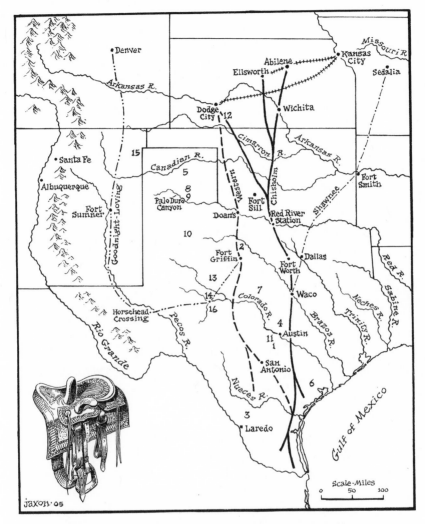

KEY TO MAP: 1. Kate Medlin 2. Bettie Reynolds 3. Amanda Burks
4. Hattie Cluck 5. Molly Bugbee 6. Margaret Borland 7. Minta Holmsley
8. Molly Goodnight 9. Cornelia Adair 10. Anna Slaughter 11. Lizzie
Williams 12. Viola Anderson 13. Mary Bunton 14. Alma Miles
15. Willie Matthews 16. Bennie Miskimon

Figure 1.   Map courtesy Jack Jackson.

Preface

The history of Texas that we like to recall is primarily the story
of vigorous men impelled by strong wills and sustained by brave hearts
to carry their aspirations, ideals, and convictions to positive ends.
J. EVETTS HALEY, 1943

THE HISTORY OF TEXAS, as historian J. Evetts Haley has noted, is one that fo-
cuses on white males, who have traditionally dominated not only the history of
Texas but that of the Western United States as well.[1] Nowhere are the men more
visible and dominant than in the cattle drives that took place from the end of the
Civil War in 1865 to the great freeze and drought of 1885–1886, which abruptly
ended the most profitable of the cattle ventures, although it did not end the cattle
industry as such. Histories of the cattle drives have focused on the men—the dangers they faced, the challenges they overcame, and their ultimate success in profit-
ing from the sale of cattle in the markets of the northeastern United States. As with
most Western history, however, recent historians have begun to focus on the role of
women in this industry. As a habitually excluded group, where were the women?
Did they participate in the cattle drives? If so, to what extent? What was their role,
if any, in this burgeoning industry?

This book brings together the biographies of sixteen women who participated
in the trail drives of Texas during the nineteenth century. Presented in order according to the date these women made their first cattle drive, the stories, many drawing heavily on the words of the women themselves, define their participation in the
cattle drives through detailed descriptions that provide insight into their experiences on these ventures. The cattle drives and the cattle industry had an impact on
the lives of these women that was far different from that of the urban environment
or the farms from which many of them came. These case studies are most note-
worthy for their complexity and diversity. No one generalization can be made
about this group of women. Some of them married quite young, while others were
past thirty. Some had large numbers of children, while others had none at all.
Some joined the cattle trails by choice, and others out of necessity. Some went
along to look at the stars, and others to work the cattle. Some made money and
built ranching empires; others went bankrupt and were forced to live frugally.
Some were well educated; others had the most basic of educations. Some traveled

extensively, whereas others rarely left Texas. Each story is as distinct and different as the women themselves.

Since the 1970s, historians, in particular women historians, have expressed a growing interest in explaining the role of women in all aspects of the development of Texas and the West. Historians of women's studies, in a desire to be more in-clusive of the women traditionally left out of Western histories, have, over the last thirty years, provided a new view of Western women as integral participants in the creation of the West. Women, who had received little or no mention in earlier his-tories, have been moved to center stage to become sentimental stereotypes with ro-mantic lifestyles. From nonexistent or unimportant, women have frequently been elevated to a "rhetorical, mystical importance approaching sainthood."[2] On the one hand, there has been a tendency to conveniently categorize them as "gentle tamers, sunbonneted helpmates, hell-raisers and bad girls."[3] Other scholars, using heroic metaphors, have labeled them independent trailblazers, assertive crusaders, and courageous trendsetters. Western women's history has moved beyond these out-dated interpretations to include a more realistic view of the women who peopled the West.

These sixteen chapters provide a more nuanced view of these women of the West. The stories indicate that for the most part they were ordinary people doing the best they could in difficult and often harsh frontier conditions. They did not see themselves as living in remarkable times or participating in particularly ro-mantic lifestyles. They perceived their lives as no more unusual than those of the many other women crossing the continent in wagon trains or facing the dangers of settling on the Western frontier. The stereotypes and categories no longer fit, and we find that their lives are more fascinating, more varied, and more vital than the interpretations provided in earlier Western histories.

The women of the nineteenth century were born into an era that, for better or worse, has been named for Queen Victoria. By the 1870s the ideal Victorian lady was passive, childlike, unreflective, sacrificing, and dependent. The father of a family had total authority, both legally and morally, and he made decisions for his wife and children. The laws required that a woman defer to male authority and to her husband's decisions as she had done earlier with her father and brothers. A woman was expected to adapt and mold herself to her husband's requirements. In return, women were often placed on pedestals and shielded from coarse language and un-pleasant facts. A woman's duty was to bear children, care for the home, and abide by her husband's wishes.

The women in these chapters did not intentionally fly in the face of the estab-lished norms of the Victorian era. The circumstances they faced in their daily lives, however, often caused them to act in ways that were contrary to these societal norms. These women were undoubtedly familiar with the rigid codes and severe modesty presented in generally available works such as *Godey's Ladies Magazine* and *Frank Leslie's Weekly Newspaper,* but when death intervened or their own best interest or the safety of their families was at stake, they ignored society's strictures. This was particularly true of their attitudes toward the dominant males in their lives. When a husband proved to be incompetent or a ne'er-do-well, the woman quietly took up the burden of making financial decisions. In cases in which a woman entered the marriage with a substantial fortune, she could influence her husband's decisions, although the pressure might be exerted privately. Widowhood could bring debt and the problems of survival, and both women and men often remarried to ensure economic support and to provide for their children.

In Texas, the laws that were adopted from the Spanish community property system allowed women some flexibility. The Texas laws allowed women to own land and town lots in their own names. When a husband went bankrupt after an unsuccessful trip up the cattle trail, a wife's land or possessions could keep the family solvent and provide the necessary credit to get another stake. Examples abound of cattle brands registered for wives and children, and these permitted husbands to expand their acreage and cattle operations, benefiting the whole family.

Owning cattle meant finding markets, and the cattle drives in which these women participated were a necessary part of living in the West. The cattle drives, although we know them best from the romanticized versions of novels and the silver screen, had their origins in the centuries-old Spanish traditions of moving livestock from winter to summer pastures and driving them to markets in Spain and, later, New Spain. The earliest drives in Texas took place during the American Revolution, when Spanish general Bernardo de Gálvez called on the missions to supply beef for his troops in Louisiana, where, in support of George Washington and the American colonists, he fought the British. During the years of the Republic of Texas and with the arrival of statehood, Anglos adopted the free-range methods of ranching from their Mexican neighbors in South Texas. During the early years of Texas statehood, the rangy animals were gathered up from the thickets, branded, and herded to local markets in San Antonio or Galveston, where they were sold for hides and tallow. The meat was bartered for other needed supplies.

The first attempts at trail drives to sell cattle in the beef-hungry Northeast began shortly after statehood was granted. In 1846 Edward Piper drove one thousand longhorns to Ohio, but the trail proved too long to be profitable. Others herded cattle over the Shawnee trail and through swampy marshlands to points on the Mississippi River or to Gulf ports for shipment north. During the years of the gold rush, if beef could be trailed to California through Indian lands, the potential for profits was enormous. As many of the entrepreneurial would-be cattle barons found, however, the Indians appreciated the cattle even more. During the Civil War, Southern troops depended on herds of Texas beef that were brought across the Mississippi.

At the end of the war, Texans faced depression and financial hardship. People had little money and little hope, and as Texas rejoined the Union, Texans saw a potential for profit from the cattle running wild in the brush country and bottomlands that had been abandoned—because the owners would never return from the war. As one of the early cattlemen described it, they had to find a way to "connect the four-dollar cow with the forty-dollar market."[4] Railroads had begun to crisscross the country in the years following the war, and if the cattle could be moved to the railheads in Kansas and Colorado, a healthy profit seemed guaranteed. The stories of these sixteen women clearly illustrate that driving cattle—whether to California, up the trail to the railheads, or from pasture to pasture—was no easy task. The women faced the rough terrain, swollen rivers, encounters with Indians, and the fickleness of nature with whatever determination they could muster. Some faced the trials heroically, whereas others panicked and hid, but for all of these women, going up the trail was the adventure of a lifetime.

For those looking back into history, these women's stories convey the message that ordinary lives can provide a clearer, more accurate record of the past. The women portrayed here may not have been heroines in the traditional sense, but their lives, taken as a whole, show the reality of the Western experience for them. Much more than isolated images, they instead illustrate the broad spectrum of the personalities and experiences found on the cattle trails. Their stories are communicated by the women's own words left behind in diaries, letters, and journals, as well as in interviews with newspaper reporters and family members. In some cases the only remnants of their lives are now found in secondary sources, but for all of them, their words still resonate for readers today. Their stories are filled with prairie fires, rattlesnakes, and stampedes, but these women also took time to look at the stars and enjoy the flowers. They may have been ordinary women, but to those of us who follow their trails, they were, indeed, cattle queens.

Sara R. Massey
October 2006

NOTES

1. The quote by J. Evetts Haley at the beginning of this chapter is from *George W. Littlefield: Texan,* vii.

2. Mary Ann Irwin and James F. Brooks, eds., *Women and Gender in the American West,* 10–11.

3. Ibid., 12.

4. "Butler, William G." *The New Handbook of Texas Online.*

Introduction: Cowgirls and Cattle Queens

Joyce Gibson Roach

THERE ARE THREE LEGENDARY FEMALE FIGURES of the frontier.[1] One is Pocahontas, whose story became imbued with myth during the childhood of America. Says scholar Charles Larson, "She has come to represent too many differing aspects of our country's nascence, and at this late stage it is almost impossible to separate truth from myth. She has been called 'the first lady of America,' 'a daughter of Eve,' 'a child of the forest,' 'an angel of peace,' 'a Madonna figure,' and the 'great Earth Mother of the Americas.' In a way, of course, she is all these and more—an Indian princess, one of our few claims to royalty."[2]

The second is Sacajawea, whose story springs from the adolescence of America, when the westward movement began in earnest. She followed right on Pocahontas's heels, assuming the mantle of royalty as the interpreter and guide for the Lewis and Clark expedition into the mysterious forests and along the mighty waters of the Pacific Northwest.

The third figure appears under the label of Pioneer Woman, whose statues on courthouse squares still testify about how hard it was on the womenfolk to go West, walking much of the way in sturdy shoes and dressed in calico and wearing sunbonnets, with a passel of children beside them. They, too, ventured into an unknown region made even more ominous because it seemed to be an unending stretch of nothing—brooding, terrifying, tangible—the solid wall of space called the Great Plains. These pioneers were heroic in their roles as helpmates and praised as the real civilizers of the frontier. The word "saintly" was sometimes applied to them, and certainly the ennobled Pioneer Woman became the symbol of female dedication to establishing and preserving family in the Great American West.[3] Many names of pioneer women come to mind, but no single name of national memory represents her.

There is also another group that falls under the designation of Pioneer Women. Its members ascended the realm of myth, and they did not enter into our national psyche walking as did the other three, but rather came riding. Their past is traceable, but few people knew about their origins until long after that wildly romantic

Figure 2.   Cowgirls of the American West, A. J. Fimbel Saddlery, Victoria, Texas,
c. 1905–1910. Courtesy of the estate of Mary Ellen O'Connor, Goliad, Texas;
Institute of Texan Cultures at the University of Texas–San Antonio.

word "cowgirl" entered the country's vocabulary. Buffalo Bill introduced them full blown into the Wild West arena under the name of *vaqueras,* women who could rope and ride as well as men, but the appellation was changed to cowgirls to complement cowboys. Sarah Wood Clark, Wild West historian, says that cowgirls were the "creations of Wild West exhibitions, which were conceived as educational programs accurately depicting episodes of the westward expansion and exhibiting varied styles of horsemanship."[4]

Along with their historical time and place, cowgirls were put on public display for all the world to see. However, their models did not remain in one location, nor were their images static. Rather, the exhibitions were transported from place to place, and the heroines were constantly invigorated with action and interaction. The protagonists, both male and female, were reinvented as the enclosure traveled. Each one was a "built West" that was portable and pliable.[5] No one had to go West or anywhere else to find the cowgirl, and she did not have to wait for modern history or interest to discover her. The public witnessed her birth, something that cannot be said for the women mentioned earlier.

The idealized Western male and female were spirited away from the ranch and transported not only by horseback but also by wagon and eventually by train and ship. Local, regional, national, and international audiences viewed them at a time when the thirst for a national identity was great.[6] The first invitation to females went to Annie Oakley, not a Westerner at all, let alone a ranch female, who made her debut in the Wild West shows and made shooting and riding females noticeable and acceptable.[7] It was the Miller's 101 Show, featuring Lucille Mulhall, who had learned her ranch skills on her daddy's spread, that fleshed out the image. Rodeos continued to shape and refine the definition of a cowgirl. Tad Barnes Lucas, who came from a Nebraska ranching background, brought that portrait to full flower. Filling in the ranks, however, were many women without any Western experience who learned to be cowgirls right there in the "built West."[8] And, at this point, cattle—the only reason for ranching in the first place—were largely left out of the composed picture. Horses—horse-and-rider is a better image—made the transition and remained the most evocative symbol of cowboy and cowgirl life.

Thus, a nation hungry for an identity—and starved for heroes and heroines and myths and legends not from Europe but of their own—looked at and embraced the Constructed West as theirs, taking it to be the Real West, complete with the lore that surrounded it, heroine and hero included. The history of cowgirls is now well documented in articles, books, exhibits, photographs, and documentaries. Every year, local and national rodeo queens are chosen—complete with crown—and this queen of national and international reputation is always splendidly mounted on a horse worthy of a royal rider.

The story of the progenitors of cowgirls is not so well known except in entangled tales of all kinds about ranch women involved in cattle and horse enterprises, Wild

West shows, rodeos, riding organizations, clubs, competitions, show business, and other venues. It is time to start at the beginning—when women first made a home on the range. To use a phrase from the cattle country, it is time to cut the herd and look more carefully at those early prototypes.

These early women of the range were easily distinguishable. They rode horses and mules either sidesaddle or astride or made skilled use of horse- or mule-drawn wagons and buggies. They did not walk to do their work. Their clothing became distinctive—always important to the female myth—and their skills differed from other frontier household duties because horses and cattle entered into the home-making routine. Women also became proficient in the use of cowboy equipment such as ropes, spurs, branding irons, knives, whips, and even weapons, including pistols and rifles.

These predecessors needed a kingdom, and they have one. For our purposes, we are able to give a site-specific name to the West we are interested in—the Cattle Frontier West. Henry Nash Smith, in his seminal work, *Virgin Land,* refers to the entire region as the Garden of the World because it was the newest untouched paradise with God's plenty everywhere if only one could get to it, get hold of it, and keep a little or a lot of it. This promised land, guaranteed by God and Manifest Destiny, soon swarmed with men and women bent on learning to manage the Garden, of course, but some of them chose the grasslands—the plains and prairies—as their special province: the cowlot of the Garden.

In the beginning, around the mid-1800s, their domain ran along or near the border country of Texas, New Mexico, Arizona, and California. There, as in other parts of the West, the female myth received little notice. Rather, it was the Western male that received nearly all of the attention. As one historian observes, the West was "a place where the dominant popular culture suggests that white women were civilizers, women of color were temptresses or drudges, and men of color were foils for the inevitable white male hero, who is, after all, the true subject of the history of the 'American West.'"[9] Other clichés further characterize the role of the white female: (1) Few women were to be found in the West, (2) the place was hell on women and horses, and (3) all of the women on the range "gave themselves to competitive housewifery."[10]

There is nothing to dispute historical data, which inform us that women on the frontier, whatever their roles, were of three kinds—two brunettes and a blonde. The brunettes were Native Americans and Hispanic (of Spanish descent or Mexican ethnicity). They had centuries of experience in living with and managing horses in the cowlot of the Garden, but it was the blonde, whether she actually had golden hair or merely a fair complexion, whose story dominated Western female history until recently. This was the case regardless of the role she played, whether we think of her as Anglo, Anglo-Celtic, or Caucasian or by any other label that separates her from the brunettes and despite the fact that she was very much a latecomer to our

part of the Garden. Even later, African Americans have significance and are accounted for in Western history, of course, but the trio were dominant, with the
Anglo ranking first, at least as far as historical writing was concerned.[11]

So who was she, this mounted heroine who dressed distinctively, disregarded the
dictates of the Victorian mores of the culture into which she was born, lived in an
untamed and magnificent setting occupied by unpredictable "savages" and wicked
wildlife, and was prone to aberrant natural phenomena? These women, unnoticed
and unheralded, were born into the most unlikely time for female change—the
Victorian era. There were already models for the Victorians that addressed recre-
ational and leisure riding for females, which sometimes included shooting for sport.
Proper dress and behavior, however, were dictated well before the Victorian age,
although these women took them to a new level. Certainly, it was the English who
provided the examples of female riding and clothing that the Americans adopted.
However, it was the Moors who, when they invaded Spain in the eighth century,
decreed that women had a legitimate place in equine affairs. They also brought
horses and introduced the business of breeding, training, and riding in general.
This may well be the Moors' greatest gift to the Spanish. According to Moorish
custom, to travel by horse, a woman would sit in a kind of basket attached to the
side of the horse. She was covered with fabric from head to toe—reminiscent of
the garment that Moslem women wear today.

Ordinary European females, meaning those not found at court, have ridden
astride since the fourteenth century. The illustration of Chaucer's *Wife of Bath,* for
example, shows a bold, sassy gadabout riding in the fashion of the day. In Europe,
female royalty and other aristocratic women, however, rode sidesaddle from the
same time period and—in the Moorish tradition—wore enough clothing to cover
the rider and a good part of her mount as well. It is said that Catherine of Aragon,
the youngest child of Ferdinand and Isabella of Spain, brought the first sidesaddle
to England when, around 1501, she became entangled in the affairs of the Tudors.
The connections are easy to make: The Moors conquered Spain, bringing with
them their horse culture, which Spain completely absorbed; Spain got rid of the
Moors and purged itself of foreign influences with the Inquisition; and then the
greatest explorer, at least for our purposes of horse business, Christopher Columbus (followed by men such as Hernán Cortés), sailed forth; and the conquistadors
transported their horse culture to the New World.

About the same time, Spanish royalty, who were responsible for sending the conquistadors on their way, also sent Catherine to England to marry; she of course took
along the art of horseback riding, as well as the sidesaddle for highborn females.
Spain, looking for glory, God, and gold, continued to invade the New World and
eventually established itself in South, Central, and North America, using horses to
accomplish its aims. Several centuries later, on the Atlantic side, the Revolution-

ary War deposed England in 1776. The patriots, who were predominantly English themselves, knew what other Englishmen knew about horses, including the place of women on horseback. Exploring and laying claim to the Great American West began, and the entire cultural baggage of horse and horsemanship of the Spanish, Moorish, and English traditions eventually converged in the borderlands of the Southwest—the cowlot. All of this took place over a mere seven centuries or so.

Many people on the cattle frontier learned to ride almost immediately. At first the female figures, complete with cumbersome riding habits, rode sidesaddle, but soon they were riding astride, a method unheard of for women at that time. On the early ranching frontier, it was on the cattle ranges along the borders with Mexico that the methods and traditions of horsemanship and ranching adopted from the Spanish took place.[12]

Highborn Spanish females coming from Mexico to the Southwest of the New World rode sidesaddle out of necessity or for recreation. A few even supervised ranching enterprises on their own, presumably riding sidesaddle, although it would be interesting to know whether they departed from tradition. The best-known example is Doña María del Carmen Calvillo. Descended from a Canary Islander, she inherited her father's land near Floresville and operated one of the early large cattle ranches. Riding a white stallion, maybe astride, she made treaties with Indians, with whom her relationship was so good that she was never attacked. When Santa Anna's army was defeated at San Jacinto in 1836, the retreating army camped at her ranch on its way back to Mexico. Her life story, complete with murder and tales of ghosts, is, for the Mexican people, replete with legends.[13]

And there were others: Doña Rosa Hinojosa de Ballí was, by 1798, one of the largest landowners in the Rio Grande Valley of South Texas. Padre Island was named for her son, a priest. María Rita Valdez ranched in Southern California in the late 1900s, and it was for her ranch, Rancho Rodeo de las Aguas, that Rodeo Drive was named. Other women of note were doña Manuela Montes, doña Josefa de la Garza, doña Estancia Sambrano, and doña María Feliciana Durán.[14]

The vaquero institutions of Mexico, based on the Spanish model, provided an example for the cowboy, and the vaquera was part of that nineteenth-century scene at about the same time that Anglo women were getting into the saddle in the Southwest.[15] One observer has noted that, "while women did not compete for wages, women vaqueros were common according to eyewitnesses. As early as 1840, a Spanish visitor to California confirmed that, while many women rode special mounts, gentled for them and for the trail, some women were as at home in the fields as their husbands, even to the extent of throwing a steer like a man."[16]

In the late 1860s William Brewer described two women vaqueros: "I washed my clothes . . . and as I was in the midst of it, along came two women, one young and quite pretty who were assisting vaqueros. . . . The wife and daughter of the ranchero came out to assist in getting in the cattle. Well mounted, they managed their horses superbly, and just as I was up to my elbows in soapsuds, along they came, with a herd of several hundred cattle, back from the hills."[17]

Bruce Shackelford, an authority on Mexican history, folklore, and culture, says that some highborn Spanish women rode astride behind the men for hunting—hawking—and were known to ride astride when out of the company of men. Ordinary peon women, as they were called, rode astride to work with their men.[18]

Kathleen Mullen Sands, author of a book on *charreada,* the Mexican rodeo, states that, "with the development of ranching and the civil wars in Mexico, women took on roles as stock handlers, couriers, and fighters, adopting a much more active riding style in the process."[19] Such a statement is valuable in anticipating what happened when Anglo women entered the ranching frontier of the Southwest and took on similar roles. Necessity and practicality set in, and, for all we know, those Mexican vaqueras may well have served as models.[20]

Before the arrival of the Spanish, Indians thrived everywhere in the Americas, but they did not have horses until the conquistadors introduced them to the New World. One of the more dramatic Spanish *relaciones* (accounts) is the story of Hernán Cortés transporting horses to the New World in 1519. Hanging in slings on the deck of a ship to keep them from falling overboard, mares and a few stallions endured the legendary voyage from the West Indies. Horses of special breeding were brought for the express purpose of establishing stations for maintaining, breeding, training, and riding in order to control the Spaniards' unbounded and unexplored kingdom. Of all of their many advantages, including guns, the Spaniards were most afraid of the native people getting hold of mounts because they were well aware that such animals would put them on equal footing and make them impossible to catch and subdue. Apparently the natives recognized that truth, too. Within fifty years of the horses' arrival, almost every tribe from the Southwest all the way to Canada had acquired them. Further, they established a distinct horse culture of their own, which included their women.

Moreover, they borrowed something from the Spanish in the type of riding equipment. Nineteenth-century Navajo saddles copied the seventeenth-century Spanish models. For instance, George Catlin noted in his journals that he was met by a Comanche war chief wearing Spanish spurs and that the mount's bridle made use of a Spanish ring bit.[21] There is no doubt that Indians struck fear in the hearts of both the Mexicans and the Americans that poured into the border country after 1848, when the Treaty of Guadalupe Hidalgo was finalized. Certainly, the *Norte Americanos,* as they were called, saw Indian women riding bareback and astride.

Many women of various tribes, especially of the Plains, rode well. Some were designated as warrior women. The Comanche, who were given the label "lords of the southern Plains" because of their remarkable expertise on horseback, included their women in that formidable designation.[22]

One of the better-known stories, among whites at least, concerns Tabbe (perhaps Tave) Pete, a female shaman of the Comanche. In 1849 or 1850, Mexican officials came across the woman, describing her as a "generaless and prophetess" who traveled on horseback with her two grandsons, Tabetoi and Mague, throughout the border regions.[23] Mexicans in the Davis Mountains described her as an ancient crone who had great influence with the Comanche. Her son was Tave Tuk, also known as Bajo el sol, a courageous Comanche war chief. Tabbe Pete was so old, they said, that, when she rode, she tied up her lower jaw with a thong that went under her chin and over her head to keep it from flopping against her throat.[24]

During the early nineteenth century, some of the first Anglo females—cavalry wives, daughters, and female kin—came to the Southwest riding sidesaddle. They rode in the Victorian mode copied from Europe, particularly England, that had firmly entrenched itself in the East and the South. Riding schools that taught women of the elite to ride were available in the East. Groomsmen, stablemen, and even riding instructors working on plantations in the South likewise taught riding to the family, women included. Stories of women following the troops and traveling hundreds of miles by wagon or riding sidesaddle over rough terrain and in harsh weather to arrive at posts and camps in Indian Territory are remarkable because such women were riding for transportation, not merely for recreation, although they did that, too. These military females fit the model of the riding elite, although some of them were not from the upper crust socially.[25] They rode in the style first used only by royalty and their court in Europe, which dictated the pattern from at least the fourteenth century and influenced the tradition that followed in the United States, where the moneyed gentry freely rode in the manner of royalty. In this book, Cornelia Adair's story is an example of how this Eastern mindset was transported to the high plains of Texas in the 1870s.

Beginning in the mid-1800s, a variety of women came to the ranching frontier—not just a select few, but all kinds. One scholar, Anne Patton Malone, has observed that not all of the women on the Texas frontier fit the profile of young, refined Anglos. Backgrounds, experiences, and expectations differed. They ranged from cultured, educated women to poor white females who had none of these advantages. "Most," Malone says, "fell into the middle range socially, economically, and in their emotional reactions to frontier conditions." And, of course, not nearly all of them came to ranch, but those who did were still a mixed group.[26]

Malone underscores the idea that "The Victorian social system was powerful and reached even into the frontier regions. But frontier experiences created challenges to the Code, and incongruities developed. The women who had been inculcated from infancy with the feminine ideals of the Victorian Code [of subservience and obedience] and then found many of the precepts obsolete or inappropriate on the Texas frontier were often torn and bewildered—even traumatized—by the experience."[27] Nowhere was the inappropriateness of riding sidesaddle while swathed in countless yards of a riding habit in order to work on the range more evident than on the cattle ranches. It was at this point that the majority of women on the range frontier, regardless of their class, needed a mount and not for bounding after the hounds or leaping over Victorian fences.

Ranch women developed their own version of how things should be—*had* to be. With regard to the use of horses, the cattle range differed dramatically from the farming frontier. A farm wife walked behind a horse or mule. Looking at the rear end of either animal will certainly limit anyone's horizons, man or woman. Until the last thirty years or so, the unromantic nature of a farmwoman's life was emphasized, especially in nonfiction. Walter Prescott Webb, in *The Great Plains,* commented on the hard life, and nothing much was written to dispel the image of women's drudgery and constant toil. In recent years fiction has managed to soften and even romanticize the life of these farm women. Still, they are usually portrayed as characters walking, not riding.

Most ranch women did not walk, at least after they established themselves on a ranch. There they got to ride and see the world from the back of a horse. It makes all the difference to work above the ground—it still does. Thus their lives have been much easier to romanticize. The world has always idealized the horseman. J. Frank Dobie, Texas' eminent folklorist, has said, "no man by taking thought can add to his stature, but by taking a horse he can."[28] The venerable Dobie might not have agreed, but everybody knows by now that the same is true for women of the range.

When women began to ride like the men—astride, clothespin-style, astraddle, cross-seat, which were all sexually evocative words to the Victorians—they made adaptations in clothing, but it was done in transitions from the long, full riding skirt to a shortened version that was sewn up the middle to form voluminous legs, to still shorter and more tailored divided skirts of leather or heavy cloth, to trousers or jodhpurs. Boots, hats, shirts, and gloves were borrowed from the men with concessions to individual touches of femininity such as scarves and bows in the hair.[29]

What kind of work did they do? They ran the households and bore children; rode and broke horses; herded, branded, castrated, doctored, and went up the trail with cattle; made deals with buyers and sellers of cattle and horses; held off bandits and marauding Indians with guns, knives, and whips; succored their neighbors, if they had any—and that's about all. We know that some women did all of these things, some did a few of them, and some did none of these things.

One woman who performed every kind of such work (a lot of it while on horseback) is Alice Stillwell Henderson, who ranched—and even taught school—in the rough, lonely expanses of the Big Bend country along the Rio Grande. Alice's family helped settle Brewster County in the Bend. In 1890, after she was married, she and her husband established a ranch on Maravillas Creek. Her home was a typical cow camp—no house, just a tent for shelter. There she made do. Their nearest neighbor was Jim Wilson, who lived thirty miles away.

Most of the stories about Alice center around her intimate involvement with ranching, which in the Big Bend meant riding constantly to reclaim cattle from bandits across the border. One of the most dramatic stories concerns the time she crossed into Mexico to retrieve her husband's rifle. The incident, which involved the Mexican police, was part of the larger difficulty Texas cattlemen encountered in the form of border bandits. Alice's husband, Billy, had been forced to leave the area because of some trouble with the Mexican police. During the dilemma, whatever it was, Billy's cattle and Winchester rifle were confiscated. He asked his wife to recover both possessions for him.

Alice wasted no time. Riding her horse at a dead run, she did not stop until she reached Rancho Conejo in Coahuila, where some fifty men, under the command of a Captain Rivera, were camped. She entered their building, took her husband's rifle, and dashed away. The astonished *rurales* went after her—and might have caught her—except that she came across a fresh mount belonging to Ed Lindsay, who just happened to be leading a wagon train across the path of the pursued and the pursuing. Alice took the horse at gunpoint and rode on. She recovered the rifle, but it took her longer to get the cows, which were stolen from her side of the Rio Grande.[30]

The stalwart helpmate had four brothers, and, with their help over the next two years, Alice was able to get back two thousand of the livestock. She bought a ranch in the Davis Mountains some 130 miles from the border and drove the cattle back in small bunches. The police did not approve, but they could do nothing about the fearless Alice and her kin on the other side of the border.

Although bandits were accustomed to raiding Texas ranches across the Rio Grande, they often found they had bitten off more than they could chew when they tangled with the Hendersons. On one occasion, bandits raided the Henderson herd, taking food, saddles, and other equipment as well. After instructing Alice to ride to the Wilson camp for help, Billy headed for the river in hot pursuit of the rustlers. Canyons, rocky trails, plants with dangerous spines, and the blackness of night barred the way, but Alice finally reached the camp after riding all night. Along with Alice, Jim and his two hands made the long ride back. They left Alice at her base camp to rest after her long ordeal, while they went on to help Billy recover the cattle. Alice had no more than settled in before five bandits rode into her camp. She was not unprepared, however, and, by her own methods, persuaded them to surrender their weapons. She held them at gunpoint all that long day until the men returned with the stolen herd.[31]

Little is known about Alice's physical appearance. Most remember her character, which they describe as "enduring and splendid." It was said that "every man and woman who knew her, though women were mighty scarce over her range, respected her."[32] Hallie Stillwell, Alice's kinswoman, who led a flamboyant life of her own in the Bend, remembered that Alice rode astride, wearing men's trousers and a man's hat. When she rode to town, however, she marked the occasion by slipping a divided skirt over the trousers, which she pushed down into her boot tops. She was reputed to be a lady at all times, and, even riding as she did most of the time with her brothers and other men, she was respected. Although she made trips by herself from Mexico leading a pack horse, she had no fear of making camp alone.[33]

This intrepid lady was very fond of a large Mexican sombrero that she always wore on the trail. Returning from a cattle-retrieving expedition into Mexico, Alice and her brothers had a large bunch of cattle pointed toward Texas when darkness prevented them from continuing. They made camp and started a fire, leaving no guard with the cattle since they were certain they were not being followed. It was one of the few mistakes the family made, but they paid dearly for it. During the night, bandits attacked, taking everything, and the group was forced to run for cover. While they were making their getaway, a bullet clipped the chinstrap on Alice's sombrero. She might have lost everything else, but Alice was not about to lose her beloved hat, too. She stopped in a hail of lead to retrieve it.[34]

Alice Stillwell Henderson faced life's obligations in a man's way, yet those who knew her said that, even "when called upon to face loneliness, danger, cold steel and blood, she remained a womanly woman."[35]

Alice herself was interested in another frontier woman whose exploits were well known in the Bend. This was Sally Skull. It is claimed that Alice wrote a book on Sally's life, but the manuscript was lost before it could be published. One cannot but wonder what Alice saw in Sally's life that was any more remarkable than her own.

From the stories that compose this book, a different kind of woman emerges. Many were capable of cowboy work, especially in handling horses. Pushing aside their fears, they were assertive and self-assured in their own world—although often misunderstood and harshly judged outside their realm—and definitely independent since they did not always have a man around to make the decisions or judgment calls. Importantly, many, if not most, were empowered by their men, not held back by them. Some emerged as capable in their own right, standing in no man's shadow. Some remained in the role of helpmate, although being one might entail the kind of help Alice Stillwell Henderson gave. And, yes, a rare woman turned out to be wild, fierce, dangerous, and not to be trifled with. Of those, some had menfolk who backed them, yet some of the men backed up from them. They were not all alike, but all of these women lived in a place so remote and so vast that many of them never saw home again after claiming their place in the Garden's cowlot.

Few of these remarkable women left behind tales of their lives. Many died without anyone outside the local area knowing even their names. The little information about them that escaped usually found its way into the early newspapers of the day or was grist for the pulp dime novels. Early fiction, posters, advertising, photographs, musical compositions, art, drama, and books told the world all it needed to know about Western females, and only a little of it alluded to life in the

Figure 3.   This image was identified as Sally Skull by family
descendents in C. F. Ballard, *The Family History and
Genealogy of Cecil Raymond Ballard and Maurice (Bradford)
Ballard, 1734–1975* (Seguin, Tex.: Country Printer, 1979).
Courtesy of Mary Ellen Thoms, Beeville, Texas.

Built West of the rodeos and Wild West shows. Most media described what was
presumed to go on in ranch country, and, truth to tell, a lot of it actually took place.
The modern venues of television and film expanded the coverage. Exhibits and
specials in written and visual form testify to the elevated place occupied by these
genuine models, who came to be called cowgirls, although the label never quite fit.
It is an interesting twist of history that what amounted to entertainment businesses of all kinds—Wild West shows, rodeos, circuses, stage shows, nightclubs,
and vaudeville—stood by waiting to display a version of such women to the nation and rest of the world. I will be forever grateful to those who, within the con-

fines of an enclosed, encapsulated Built West canonized these frontier women as cowgirls, thereby nourishing the growth of a legendary icon in America.

The real emancipation of women began well before Susan B. Anthony marched and carried signs declaring that women, too, were created equal. Genuine freedom began when some unnamed, obscure woman of the border regions looked at the world from atop a horse and realized how different and fine the view was, how far she could go, and who she might become. Challenging the centuries-old ways of riding and dressing in order to ride astride, unencumbered, and to take on a new role was as far reaching in its implications for the female world in frontier times as "the pill" was for women in the late twentieth century.

One vision remains constant after all these years—the image of horse and rider, indivisible. For many people, cowgirls exist in memory—a figure on horseback, a genuine American heroine and icon, internationally adored. She is part of our heritage, and every generation, from the West or not, has a right to claim her. Mounted on a splendid horse, she managed her part of the Garden of the West, whether on the range or in the reenactment inside a created venue. Today she still rides the ranges or participates in rodeo arenas or as a member of horse groups of all kinds, reminding us of a distant time and place. Because she is ahorseback, she always seems to be a little above us, someone to look up to, a figure moving elusively away. As she rides into the future, the shadow of the past is ever with both her and us. She retains that touch of royalty—whatever and wherever the next Garden turns out to be, which may well be on the pages of this extraordinary book.

NOTES

1. The title of this chapter is adapted from the title of C. L. Sonnichsen's book *Cowboys and Cattle Kings.*

2. Charles P. Larson, "The Children of Pocahontas," 24.

3. Blaine T. Williams, "The Frontier Family: Demographic Fact and Historical Myth." Williams examines the role of women and family during the Texas frontier days.

4. Sarah Wood Clark, "Beautiful Daring Western Girls: Women of the Wild West Shows," 6–7.

5. David M. Emmons, "Constructed Province: History and the Making of the Last American West," 437–59. Emmons describes the concept of a generic West occurring in more than one place and constructed by the groups who occupied it and invested it with their myths.

6. Buffalo Bill took the first Wild West show to London in 1887. That exhibition included Annie Oakley, but the first rodeo tour did not take place until 1924. For an artistic and factual account of the first rodeo tour abroad, see Charles Simpson, *El Rodeo.*

7. Glenda Riley, "Annie Oakley: Creating the Cowgirl," 32–47. Riley discusses Oakley's role in giving a positive portrayal of cowgirls to Victorian audiences; see also Glenda Riley, *The Life and Legacy of Annie Oakley.*

8. Some of these women left the ranch completely to pursue a life in the spotlight. Some, however, never did leave, while others led double lives on the range as well as in the arena.

9. Susan Lee Johnson, "'A Memory Sweet to Soldiers': The Significance of Gender in the History of the 'American West,'" 495–517.

10. Phillip Aston Rollins, *The Cowboys,* 35. The clichés are verified by many other sources, such as diaries, memoirs, narratives, and books.

11. A few African American women participated fully in ranch life. In the 1850s Henrietta Williams Foster, known as Aunt Rittie, worked with cowboys on the ranches of the Texas Coastal Bend. According to Louise O'Connor, "She worked cattle bareback with the men and she would go out in the cow camps with the different cow crowds. . . , She rode sidesaddle and bareback on her white horse. She wore those old long dresses and rode astraddle. She could throw calves and do anything else a man could and maybe better." See Louise O'Connor, "Henrietta Williams Foster, 'Aunt Rittie': A Cowgirl of the Texas Coastal Bend," 67–72. Johanna July was a Black Seminole. Born in Mexico in 1857 or 1858, she came to Eagle Pass around 1871. In Mexico, Johanna learned about cattle and horses from her father. Of women on horseback, she had seen Indian women riding astride and Mexican women riding sidesaddle. Johanna rode both ways. Breaking horses became her forte. See Jim Coffey, "Johanna July: A Horse-breaking Woman," 73–84.

12. It is historically fair to point out that the same changes were going on in Wild West shows. Sarah Wood Clark says, "The issue of femininity was consistently broached in conjunction with two issues—riding style and mode of dress. As women became increasingly involved in the more risky equestrian occupations, they abandoned the sidesaddle, adopted the cross seat or astride riding style and made appropriate changes in attire. Riding astride was not well accepted by the general public. Having been considered unladylike since the fourteenth century, the cross seat defied social conventions and was certainly shocking to audiences who had probably read physicians' warnings that many forms of exercise, including horseback riding, were potentially harmful to women's reproductive systems. Again, publicity for the Wild West shows patiently explained the cross seat in terms of comfort for horse and rider, practicality, safety and health." See Clark, "Beautiful Daring Western Girls."

13. Sara Massey, "The Other Cowboys," 2.

14. In *Texas Women: A Pictorial History: From Indians to Astronauts,* Ruthe Winegarten mentions these women but gives little information about them.

15. See Sandra L. Myres, "The Ranching Frontier: Spanish Institutional Backgrounds of the Plains Cattle Industry," for an excellent discussion of the subject.

16. Don José Arnas, "Recuerdos," 1878, 28, Bancroft Library, University of California–Berkeley, cited in Nora E. Ramirez, "The Vaquero and Ranching in the Southwestern United States, 1600–1970," Ph.D. diss., Indiana University, Nov. 1970, 69.

17. William H. Brewer, *Up and Down California in 1860–1864* (Berkeley: University of California Press, 1966), 285–86, cited in ibid.

18. Bruce Shackelford, e-mail to author, Oct. 10, 2003.

19. Kathleen Mullen Sands, *Charrería Mexicana: An Equestrian Folk Tradition,* 11.

20. Vaqueras came closer to the idea of early ranch women before they were labeled cowgirls, but, again, proximity to the border makes the comparison more notable. The Mexican tradition of charreada, forerunner to the rodeo, included women only in precision drills, riding sidesaddle and dressed in ruffled dresses known as *escaramuza.* Games of skill on horseback were pleasant pastimes on Anglo ranches, too, and there might yet be unrevealed stories

about men and women of both cultures mingling and participating in each other's events along the border.

Later, a few Hispanic women (or possibly Anglo women dressed up like "Mexican senoritas," as they were billed) appeared in Wild West shows, indicating that the Manipulated West took notice of female riding traditions of other races on the western frontier.

21. George Catlin, *Letters and Notes on the Manners, Customs, and Conditions of the North American Indians,* vol. 2, letter no. 41 (The Great Comanche Village), 53–56. Plate number 157 illustrates this event.

22. One special story dear to the hearts of Texans concerns Cynthia Ann Parker, a white child who was taken captive by the Comanche in 1836. She became thoroughly acculturated into Indian life, married a war chief, and had two sons and a daughter. The recounting of her recapture takes note of the fact that she was a superb horsewoman who carried her infant daughter on the horse with her when trying to escape.

23. Thomas Kavanaugh, *Political Power and Political Organization of Comanche Politics, 1786–1875.*

24. Carlysle Raht, *Romance of the Davis Mountains.*

25. An excellent source is Patricia Y. Stallard, *Glittering Misery: Dependents of the Indian Fighting Army.* Another account of a woman's life in the cavalry is found in the diaries of Elizabeth Custer, wife of George Armstrong Custer; see *Civil War Memories of Elizabeth Bacon Custer, From Her Diaries and Notes,* edited by Arlene Reynolds (Austin: University of Texas Press, 1994).

26. Ann Patton Malone, *Women on the Texas Frontier: A Cross-cultural Perspective,* 1. It is interesting to note that the word "cowgirl" was defined in *Webster's Ninth New Collegiate Dictionary* in 1885 as "a girl or woman who tends cattle or horses." The designation put females in the yeoman, working, or lower class, as though she were a milkmaid or someone who slopped the hogs. The definition makes no mention of riding horses.

27. Malone, *Women on the Texas Frontier,* 1.

28. J. Frank Dobie, *The Mustangs,* 43.

29. *Bloomingdale's Catalog* of 1886 featured riding habits for sidesaddle but no other kind of female riding attire. The *Sears Roebuck Catalog* of 1897 had two pages of sidesaddles but offered no dresses for riding. Obviously, women on the range used their husbands' stock saddles. A photograph in Sarah Wood Clark's booklet "Beautiful Daring Western Girls" shows a "Woman's astride saddle with padded seat and 'squaw roll,' made by R. T. Frazier, Pueblo, Colorado, ca. 1900" (16). A squaw roll seems to be some kind of padding at the front of the saddle. It is doubtful that such saddles were manufactured in any quantity. Again, the women of the range and of Wild West shows and rodeos probably used men's saddles.

30. Reminiscences of E. E. Townsend, Alpine, Tex. Unpublished document from the files of Mody C. Boatright, location unknown. Author's notes in Joyce Roach Papers, Special Collections, Alkek Library, Texas State University–San Marcos.

31. O. L. Shipman, *Taming of the Big Bend: A History of the Extreme Western Portion of Texas from Fort Clark to El Paso,* 103.

32. J. Frank Dobie, *Some Part of Myself,* 176.

33. Letter from Hallie Stillwell, Alpine, Tex., to Joyce Roach, Mar. 12, 1971.

34. Shipman, *Taming of the Big Bend,* 104.

35. Ibid., 101.

PART 1

THE EARLY CATTLE DRIVES, 1868–77

Catherine (Kate) Malone Medlin

MRS. JARRET MEDLIN

Patricia A. Dunn and Sara R. Massey

T HIS IS THE STORY OF KATE MALONE MEDLIN, a woman with four children who, after surviving the privations of the Civil War, joined a wagon
train driving a herd of cattle from Texas to California in 1868. The gold prospec-
tors working the minefields of northern California wanted "beef on the hoof," and
they were willing to pay good money for it. Getting the cattle to California, however, was no easy chore.

Kate's story begins in Missouri. In 1836 her mother, Mary Ellen "Polly" Harris
(1818–56), was from Tennessee and married Perry Malone (1814–1907), a Ken-
tuckian. They settled in Lexington, Platte County, Missouri, and began their family with Anna Eliza, who was born on August 22, 1837, and Catherine ("Kate"),
who arrived in 1839. The Malones added four more daughters to their family before they left for Texas: Elizabeth H., Margaret G., M. Clementine, and Martha M.[1]

Hall Medlin, Kate's future father-in-law and a local Platte County patriarch,
had decided to move to the new territory of Texas. "The Platte County settlers
were unusual . . . as they had little property among them, and yet they were well
enough to do. All seem to be on an equality, and the sole object in living was to do
all they could for the comfort and satisfaction of one another and to make their
way into a better world."[2] Medlin took a group to Texas in the fall of 1844.

After a difficult journey from Missouri, on which they encountered hostile Indians and had to cross swollen rivers, the Medlin family settled in the Peters
Colony, which included territory that became Collins, Grayson, Denton, and Tarrant counties. Hall Medlin and his extended family soon moved to Grapevine
Springs, where they began the Hallford (Holford) Prairie settlement (later called
the Missouri Colony) in what became Denton County, Texas.[3]

In 1845, Hall Medlin sent his brothers back to Missouri to convince others to
join them in Texas. The Malones, along with the Andrew Harris family and John A.
Freeman, a Baptist minister and his family, departed Platte County for Texas. Kate
was seven years old when she climbed into the wagon, joining her family on their
journey. The "twelve ox wagons containing related family members and the men

on horseback crossed the Red River by ferry—stopping briefly to visit [Medlin] relatives in East Texas and purchase supplies the 1st of November."[4] Kate's family settled along what later became the Denton and Tarrant county line.[5]

Most of the early settlers began farming with a small cotton patch or started a ranch and went into the cattle business. The 1850 census for Denton County shows that Kate, along with four sisters, enrolled in a subscription school during the two-to-three-month summer season. Over the next five years the Malone family increased, with Rachel M., Oliver G., Richard, Sarah (Sophrona) P., and John H. Now Kate had ten siblings, which included only two younger brothers.[6]

Shortly after the Malones and the other Medlin families arrived, Denton County was formed out of Fannin County.[7] It encompassed nine hundred square miles in the Grand Prairie and Eastern Cross Timbers region of North Central Texas. Led by Hall Medlin, the area became a mustering place for the extended Medlin families during the latter half of the 1840s. In addition to Hall, his brothers, sisters, and mother, another group of Medlins arrived and settled in what was called "the Medlin settlement." All of the Medlins were staunch Baptists who took their religion very seriously. Along with the Malones, Hall and his relatives were charter members of the Lonesome Dove Baptist Church, founded in 1846.[8]

As the communities developed, disaster began brewing in Kate's family. Shortly after her mother gave birth to Kate's youngest brother, John, the family's attention focused on Kate. In 1855 Kate, at seventeen, had attracted the interest of a local German, who asked to marry her. When Kate's mother, Polly, refused the offer, the infuriated man shot Polly and mortally wounded her. Kate's father rushed to his wife's defense, wrestled the gun from the man, and beat him over the head with the gun, breaking the man's neck and killing him.[9] Left with a large family, Malone was relieved when Kate married Jarret Medlin, the second son of Hall Medlin. Jarret and Kate's wedding ceremony took place in 1857 at the Lonesome Dove Baptist Church, and within three years the couple had two children: John Lewis, age two, and Sarah, age one.[10]

Meanwhile, Hall Medlin, the family patriarch, had acquired three tracts of land in Travis, thirteen miles northwest of Austin, which his son Jarret and a man named Gibson had surveyed in 1851. Following the death of his second wife, Hall married again. He then decided to move with his third wife, Catherine Bradford, and both of their children to Travis County.

Although Hall and his family moved to Travis County, Jarrett and Kate remained in Denton. By 1859, rumblings of war and secession were beginning, and daily life became difficult for the young couple. Money was scarce, so all exchanges were made by bartering tallow, wheat, beeswax, and food. All the while, the Indian raids continued.[11] Because the times were so hard, Jarret and Kate decided to move and join Hall and the rest of the Medlin clan, who were living in Hays and Travis counties. Kate's sister Anna married Joseph Bradford (the son of Hall's third wife) and with their children moved south as well, hoping for a safer, calmer life.[12]

However, restless and discontent, Jarret's father decided to try his luck at prospecting in California. While Kate and Jarret, along with Kate's sister Anna Eliza, remained behind in Hays County, in 1859 Hall sold some of his land in Travis County, went back to the Denton area, where he put together a wagon train of family members, and set out for California. The large wagon train included Perry Malone and his motherless family, as well as the now ordained Rev. John Freeman and his family. They arrived safely in San Bernardino, California, where some of the group settled.

Jarret found work as a teamster driving oxen, but the young couple found the people in Hays County just as embroiled in support of the secessionist effort as those back in Denton. Between 1861 and 1865 Hays County, with its well-established cattle industry, had several men, including the neighboring Day brothers, who transported beef for the Confederacy, but Jarret had other plans.[13] The young men of the county rapidly signed up for military service, mustering several companies. A short six years after Kate's marriage, both Jarret and his older brother Marion, who lived close by, enlisted in the Confederate Army. Left at home now with their three small children (John, Sarah, and Alice) and pregnant once again, Kate assumed responsibility for the welfare of their small family. In Jarret's absence she gave birth to their fourth child, whom she named after both her father (Perry Malone) and her father-in-law (Hall Medlin): Perry Hall.

The war was hard on the women of the county, who were kept busy spinning and weaving their "own dresses; they looked awfully coarse and ugly, as many of us had never woven any cloth, much less worn such shoddy looking goods. We girls wasn't [sic] the kind to give up; as fast as we would get one web of our common looking cloth out of the loom we would get another ready."[14] Jarret never returned home, however, and Kate found herself a young widow with four small children. It was later reported that he had died of measles and exposure.[15]

At the end of the Civil War, Jarret's father, Hall Medlin, who was still in San Bernardino prospecting for gold, decided that, if the family was ever to make any real money in California, it would be in cattle: "The discovery of gold in California, and the consequent rush of fortune-seekers thither, created an abnormal demand in that Territory for the necessaries of life. The fabulous prices ruling in that district market for beef induced a few enterprising parties to brave the difficulties and dangers of incidents to a drive of fifteen hundred miles through an almost unknown country to that land of promise."[16]

Hall returned to his sisters' families in Hays County and proposed another cattle drive to California, inviting his oldest son, Marion, his in-laws, and his close relatives to join him. As a widow with young children, Kate knew her family's future rested with her in-laws and thus hinged on traveling to California, where the rest of her family now lived. Her journey with the Medlin wagon train began in Hays County on April 15, 1868, and ended a very long eight months later in Los Angeles. Forty-one people, including women and children, set out on the cattle drive.[17]

Women braved the dangers of the unknown frontier for many reasons. Kate and others like her wanted to better their own lives and those of their children. "I made the start to California with great hopes. It was like starting to fairyland, and I thought I had counted the cost and could see what the hardships and trouble would be but I soon found I had no idea what was coming, but still braved the storm. I thought when I arrived in California with my money and got to my relatives, it would be all right with me."[18]

Kate also said, "It was a long and hard journey from Hays County, Texas, to Los Angeles with oxen, for our teams consisted of three and five yoke to a wagon. Our train was made up of seven of these strong canvas covered wagons, and we started April 15, 1868. Once out into the frontier of Texas amid the cattle range, we stayed there long enough to gather enough stock to bring with us, which took until the 3rd of May. Then we started for California with our string of seven wagons."[19]

The Hall Medlin wagon train left Texas with eighteen hundred cattle and 150 horses, with few men and numerous women with children. Hall Medlin and the adults knew that they did not have enough men, arms, or ammunition to last the whole journey but planned to stop at a fort or town to replenish their supplies and acquire the necessary gun power to ensure their protection from any dangers that might arise on the trip. Having selected a captain and given him decision-making authority on the trail, they set off heading west to California. As they neared the cutoff for a fort where they planned to get provisions and ammunition, the captain, expressing assurance for their safety, decided not to go to the fort but rather to continue on to find sufficient grass and water for the livestock. Hall Medlin, Kate, and the others went along with the captain and thus were not equipped with the needed guns, ammunition, and food for the ordeals that lay ahead.[20]

Because she had never traveled this far west, all of the territory they passed through was unfamiliar to Kate. Like most women of her time, she traveled only when moving from one location to another for economic reasons or to visit neighbors. As a widow with small children in her care, Kate had worked hard back home in Hays County, but on the trail to California even more was expected of her. After seeing to her children, she cooked for the several men (cowhands) her father-in-law had hired to help with the livestock. Along with the cooking chores, it was also Kate's job to gather firewood. As she walked beside the wagon, she collected wood and stored it with the cooking pots in a cowhide fastened under her wagon. The group covered about ten miles a day, and Kate walked most of it picking up wood.

When the wagons stopped for water, Kate and the other women washed clothes and replenished the water barrels. In an interview with a *Los Angeles Times* reporter in 1907, Kate described herself as "small, weighing only ninety-eight pounds, strong and able to work hard all day, and all night, if necessary. I had done all kinds of hard work all my life. I tell you, the women of California don't know what hard work is. We women of Texas had worked both indoors and outdoors when needed, which was often during the Civil War."[21]

The journey was a very difficult one. The first serious obstacle that Kate and the wagon train faced on the trail was the Staked Plains of Texas. To cross this area, cattle, horses, and people had to travel eighty miles without fresh water. All of the wagons were equipped with large water barrels attached to the rear, and Kate's wagon had a forty-gallon barrel, but everyone knew the cattle would have trouble surviving the arid stretch. To help them, the wagon train traveled in the cool of night, when the stock could better endure the trek. Water from the barrels was given to the horses, enabling them to stay alive. It took three days and nights to reach the Pecos River. The cattle suffered from lack of water, and hundreds of them were lost before they completed the eighty miles:

> Four miles before we came to the river we came to mud holes. There had been some water here a few days before, but there was another train ahead of us whose stock had drunk it dry, and the water was so full of alkali it poisoned such a large number of animals you could almost step from one dead one onto another. They had died in such numbers, some before getting out of the water. When our cattle reached the mud holes they plunged into the mud and got enough [water] to kill many of them. They were by this time uncontrollable for want of water, and were close enough to smell it. Our men rode out ahead to hold them back from the river as the bank was very steep and high and the stock would crowd one another off into the water, which was full of quick sand, but at last the men had to give the road to the cattle as they were so wild that they ran over anything in their way.[22]

At the Pecos River the Medlin party encountered another wagon train resting from its own ordeal of crossing the plains, but instead of stopping, the Medlin captain decided to continue up the north bank of the river. As they proceeded, they encountered a group of cattle herders traveling without families. Now aware of the dangers ahead, the Medlin captain arranged to travel behind the herders for the extra protection they offered. Everyone was warned to be extra vigilant of their surroundings as they proceeded through the Pecos River country. For several days they traveled many miles along the river until they reached another fork in the road, where an argument ensued. The captain indicated that the wagon train should take the road toward the mountains, but two men in the party disagreed, so the herders left the wagon train and headed toward the Hondo River country. Already short of men, the Medlin train was now left with only thirteen men, one a mere fifteen years old: "So we started on to our doom and I felt as though we were going into trouble as we had heard that the Indians had taken a large herd of cattle only three days before. This, our Captain did not believe, but I did, as we could see fine beef cattle along the roadside. The Indians had secured them from the train ahead and had let them scatter out on the range to feed."[23]

On the third night after leaving the fork in the road, Indian fires were seen in the mountains, but the Medlin train continued, always on guard in anticipation of an attack. For several tense days they traveled on, but then tragedy struck—in the form of mud. Kate's sister Anna and her family were also traveling with the train. Anna's husband, Joseph Bradford, was injured while straining to lift a wagon that had become mired in the mud. Joseph and others had been helping to lift the wagon so that the other men could slip a piece of wood underneath the wheel and thus prevent it from becoming more deeply buried, but the extreme strain injured him. With Joseph in pain and unable to drive his family's wagon, Kate's driver took over Anna's wagon, and a Spanish vaquero started driving Kate's wagon.

They traveled on, but Joseph went downhill quickly. The captain sent riders ahead to hold the cattle, and those in the wagons made camp. The stopping place was Independence Springs—a low place with running water and high mountains all around: "It was 12 o'clock when we got to water, so we got dinner as quickly as we could and then as usual caught up some fresh oxen to drive and turned out the ones we had been driving to rest. They were thus engaged out among the herd when suddenly our men came running along the side of the mountain screaming Indians."[24] Kate and the other women knew they had to protect the children, as well as themselves, but they were short of guns, ammunition, and men: "Now you can't imagine, nor can I tell you my feelings at the time, my children were my first thought and my heart sank as I saw no help, no one near and so few men, short of guns and ammunition but I said I would fight until they killed me. Some of the women began to wring their hands and cry. I said, 'What is the use of crying, it will not help matters any.' But they said, 'Oh, they will kill us!' I told them that crying would not keep them from killing us. So I quickly placed my children and my sister's children in my wagon and put my feather beds around them, as I had heard that bullets would not go through feathers. The Indians had a few guns and plenty of bows and arrows."[25]

Kate and the other mothers lifted their children into the wagons for protection and tied the oxen to the wagons to stop them from running off and leaving them without transportation—if they were fortunate enough to survive. Determined to defend and protect her children, Kate grabbed her old Enfield rifle, but the men told the women to make bullets for their few weapons. Giving up her Enfield, Kate and the women hurriedly molded bullets for the different firearms. The six-shooters used a pointed bullet, while the other weapons used round ones. The women melted lead and then poured the hot metal into molds and, after a quick cooling, passed the bullets to the men, who were reloading as fast as possible. Indian arrows were flying around the women, and the gunfire kept up until sundown, when the Indians left at last. They had made off with more than half of the Medlins' already depleted herd. The men wanted to try to recover them, but the decision was made for them to stay, protect the camp, and guard the remaining cattle.

By morning, everyone was exhausted from trying to stay alert all night and praying there would not be another attack. Dawn arrived—along with the Indians, who began rounding up the remaining cattle while the helpless travelers looked on. As the hours passed, the Indians kept circling; no one could leave the encampment. About noon, Kate and the others noticed that a young Indian woman with a long spear in her lap was sitting astride their captain's captured horse. She headed directly for their camp, singing a song. As she came within twenty feet of the wagons, one of the men raised his gun to fire at her, but someone said, "No, don't shoot her."[26] "If we had killed the young squaw that would have opened the war. But thank God, who was protecting us, no one shot her. The Indians came closer and closer, I could stand on my wagon wheel and count 60. I did count that many, but later more came."[27]

Kate and the other women again loaded the guns while the men fired. In the midst of the attack, Kate's brother-in-law Joseph died from the peritonitis and infection that had set in from his injury. Some of the men quickly dug a grave within the wagon corral and buried him, while the few remaining men continued to shoot at the Indians. All day long the Indians kept the camp surrounded: "We waited there all day in terrible suspense and when evening came the Indians said for us to go on now, that they were friends to us but at the next watering place the Apaches would be there and kill all of us. The Indians wanted to make friends with us and buy tobacco but we knew it was to get the advantage of us and get in nearer to the wagons and families, so we kept them back. At sundown, they went again into the mountains, as they never fought at night. We waited 'till [sic] about eight o'clock and then started again on our journey."[28]

That evening, the wagon train left Independence Springs and, heeding the Indians' warning, did not stop at the first watering hole. The wagons slowly moved on through the night over rugged trails and around huge boulders. At dawn they exited the canyon on a mesa and then stopped to allow the women to fix breakfast while the stock rested. About 3:00 P.M., the wagons began moving again, traveling through the night until daybreak as usual. It was July 4, 1868, when the Medlin train corralled the wagons at an old fort with crumbling adobe walls. There they made camp and spent a week resting and recovering their strength after the grueling trek.

While they were at the old fort, another group arrived and brought the news that the Indians had dug up Joseph, scalped him, and rammed a spear through his body. Seeing the abandoned saddles and wagons along with the grazing cattle, the new arrivals thought the Medlin train had been taken prisoner by the Indians. Composed of twenty-two well-armed men but no women or children, the new-comers were in much better shape than the members of the Medlin train. Still, even with all of their manpower, half of their cattle had been stolen by the Indi-ans. The group had also encountered the dreaded Apaches and engaged in a fero-cious battle—until they killed the chief, thus ending the conflict. The warriors had then collected the chief's body and left the battleground. The men from the wagon train then recovered their cattle, herded them over the rugged terrain, and arrived at the old fort.

When rested, the Medlin train proceeded to the town of Franklin ahead of the other trail herd. Kate and her family had had a punishing trip so far, but now the horses and oxen were giving out, and their food was gone. The Medlins had planned to sell some of the livestock for needed supplies at Franklin, but, with the cattle stolen, they had nothing to trade: "Now we were out of everything to eat, as we started with just enough, just what we thought would last us, just bacon and beans with dried fruit as a diet. We thought we could sell enough stock when we reached Franklin but when we reached there we were beggars. We asked for food, but they investigated our case first and gave sparingly. We stayed there 14 days and tried to get help to go back and get our stake. They told us that there were 700 warriors in the Guadalupe Mountains which we had just passed through and we were lucky to be living."[29]

Kate and the other women remained in Franklin until the second train arrived, bringing part of the Medlin herd, which they had recovered from the Indians. They then sold some of the returned livestock for food and supplies and at last continued on their way to California. At that point, only three wagons were in ac-ceptable condition to withstand the trip, and the weather had turned hot—so hot that it was again necessary to travel mainly at night.

For adults like Kate and the others, the trip was an exhausting one, but for the children, it was terrible. The youngsters rode in the wagons the whole time to keep from getting lost or hurt, and they quickly got tired of being cooped up. Be-cause rattlesnakes were common on the trail, the youngsters were not allowed to wander far; during the night hours they were not permitted to roam at all for fear they might lose their way. One day Kate's daughter Sarah was walking by the side of their wagon. While attempting to climb back inside, she fell underneath the front wheel, which ran over her, breaking her leg and thigh. Hall Medlin had to sell one yoke of oxen, worth $25, to pay for a doctor in Yuma to set her thighbone. Forced to wait for six days until Sarah was past the danger of infection, Kate was further delayed.

The Hall Medlin wagon train at last reached California in November of 1868.

Figure 4.   Marion Medlin General Store and Saloon, Los Angeles, c. 1872. From
Trek to Texas by Pearl O'Donnell Foster.

They had begun the cattle drive with eighteen hundred cattle and 150 horses—a
sizeable operation that had had the potential to make them all very wealthy. With
the loss of most of the cattle, however, the Medlin wagon train was instead a financial disaster. The survivors considered themselves lucky merely to have reached
their destination, and Kate and her four children were thankful they were alive.
The family settled in the Los Angeles area near Kate's father, Perry Malone, who
by then was a deacon in the Azusa Church and had moved from San Bernardino
to Los Angeles along with Kate's other brothers and sisters.

In 1869, a few months after their arrival in California the preceding autumn,
Kate, as was common at the time, married her late husband's older brother, Marion. He became a successful businessman by running a general store with lodgings
and a saloon, although some of his Baptist relatives had reservations about the latter. Kate's children, John Lewis, Sarah, Alice, and Perry, along with her sister Anna
and her children, remained in Los Angeles. When the *Los Angeles Times* interviewed Kate in 1907, she was sixty-seven years old, without a gray hair on her head
and known in the neighborhood as a "plucky old lady."[30] Her father died that year,
and her children had all settled in California and Arizona. John Lewis, better known
as J. L., had become a constable at Needles, Arizona, and a successful miner. Sarah,
who had been hurt on the trail, had married a man named Leggett and moved to
Naco, Arizona. Alice, too, had married and settled in Searchlight, California. Perry
Hall, the youngest son, remained near his mother in Los Angeles. Meanwhile, Hall
Medlin, with his restless nature, returned to Hays County, Texas, with his wife
Catherine sometime after 1871 and died there in 1883.

Figure 5.   Marion Medlin, second husband of Kate Medlin.
From *Trek to Texas* by Pearl O'Donnell Foster.

For Kate, driving cattle to California had not been the financial success that Medlin had hoped for. The men, women, and children on the wagon train had suffered and survived by using the skills they had learned on the Texas frontier. It was the attempt to drive cattle to a profitable market that made their trip different from that of most of the wagon trains bound for California. Kate had learned the importance of cattle as a marketable commodity. Other women would later accompany herds of livestock to California, but Kate Medlin can be credited with being the first documented woman to help do so. She lived through it all to tell her story as a woman of Texas on the cattle trail.

NOTES

1. Pearl O'Donnell Foster, *Trek to Texas,* 119–20; U.S. Bureau of the Census, 1850, Denton County, Texas, 108.

2. Foster, *Trek to Texas,* 124, from E. F. Bates, "A History of Denton County," 1918.

3. In 1950 a high lookout in Denton named Medlin Point had a tree with a tomahawk buried in the fork of its trunk. The area was purchased by the city and made into a park.

4. Foster, *Trek to Texas,* 25.

5. U.S. Bureau of the Census, 1850, Denton County, 108.

6. Ibid.; Foster, *Trek to Texas,* 119–20.

7. In 1960 the city of Denton had a Malone Street.

8. Foster, *Trek to Texas,* 124.

9. Ibid., 120.

10. U.S. Bureau of the Census, 1860, Hays County, 11.

11. Clarence Allen Bridges, *History of Denton, Texas, from Its Beginning to 1960,* 96, 100.

12. Joseph Bradford was a son of Catherine Bradford, who also traveled with her husband on the wagon train.

13. Kate and Jarret lived in the same area as another cattle woman, Lizzie Johnson, and her family.

14. Mrs. Ermine Redwine, in Emanuel Dubbs, *Pioneer Days in the Southwest, 1850–1879,* 297.

15. Foster, *Trek to Texas,* 125.

16. James Cox, ed., *Historical and Biographical Records of the Cattle Industry and the Cattlemen of Texas and Adjacent Territory,* vol. 1, 35.

17. "Kate Medlin's Story," *Los Angeles Times* (Jan. 6, 1907).

18. Ibid., 4.

19. Ibid., 2. The *Los Angeles Times* reporter met with Kate Medlin at Kate's home on West Forty-fifth Street in Los Angeles.

20. Bruce Shackelford, e-mail to Sara R. Massey, Dec. 11, 2003. The fort referred to is Fort Concho, in present-day San Angelo, and the wagon train members traveled a stretch of what became known as the Goodnight-Loving Trail along the route of the Butterfield Overland Mail.

21. "Kate Medlin's Story," *Los Angeles Times,* 3.

22. Foster, *Trek to Texas,* 129.

23. Ibid.

24. Ibid., 130.

25. Ibid.

26. "Kate Medlin's Story," *Los Angeles Times,* 5.

27. Foster, *Trek to Texas,* 131.

28. Ibid.

29. Ibid., 132.

30. "Kate Medlin's Story," *Los Angeles Times,* 9.

Lucinda Elizabeth (Bettie) Matthews Reynolds

MRS. GEORGE THOMAS REYNOLDS

Bruce M. Shackelford

B ETTIE MATTHEWS MADE WHAT WAS PROBABLY the longest trip over the western cattle trails that any woman ever made. She saw a wild country full of buffalo and an endless prairie transformed into a settled area of large fenced ranches stocked with cattle. She saw drillers strike oil on the land around the ranches, ensuring prosperity for generations to come. Probably no other woman in history has experienced both so much of life on a trail drive and the creation of the U.S. cattle industry as Bettie Matthews Reynolds.[1]

Bettie Matthews was born in Louisiana on November 10, 1851, and named Lucinda Elizabeth Matthews.[2] She was the daughter of Caroline Spears and Joseph Beck Matthews, who came to Texas by way of Louisiana in the early 1860s.[3] J. B. Matthews was originally from Alabama, and the Matthews family settled in Stephens County, Texas, where they developed friendships with their neighbors and future in-laws, the Reynolds family. In 1847 B. W. and Anne Campbell Reynolds came to Texas, where they settled for thirteen years in Shelby County before moving on to Stephens County in the 1860s.[4] Their son George Thomas was born in Montgomery County, Alabama, on February 14, 1844, and at sixteen he helped his father with the cattle and found work riding for the Pony Express from Palo Pinto to Weatherford. Relationships between the two families led to marriages and later relationships that continued into the twenty-first century.

Bettie's father, J. B. Matthews, was the first appointed grand juror in Buchanan County, Texas. Like almost everyone else in the area west of Fort Worth, Matthews raised cattle. Bettie's mother, Caroline Matthews, was described as a woman who did more to spiritually, morally, and socially uplift the community than almost anyone else.[5] Bettie grew up in "a land of bright skies, glorious sunsets and most brilliant starlight; a land where the hills and plains are gay with lovely wildflowers in the springtime, and where we have the everlasting hills unto which we may lift up our eyes. It is a land where the cries of the coyote and the hoot owl and an occasional scream of a panther break the nocturnal stillness."[6] This pastoral description leaves out the main source of danger and disharmony for the new settlers—

Figure 6.   Bettie Reynolds. From James Cox, *Historical and
Biographical Record of the Cattle Industry and the Cattlemen of
Texas and Adjacent Territory, 1894.*

virtual war with the Comanche and Kiowa tribes. Of all of the newly settled lands
in Texas, Buchanan County and the region west of Fort Worth were nearest to the
indigenous people of the plains. Violence was continual between the two cultures,
with innocent victims on both sides, as well as outright vicious killings commit-
ted by both the settlers and the native tribes.

Because settlers often left as rapidly as they had arrived, permanent dwellings
in the area were a rarity.[7] Nevertheless, the Matthews family stayed on, and Bettie
grew up in a house made of log walls with sod roofs and dirt floors. Here the first
permanent bonds began between the neighboring Reynolds and Matthews families. In 1862 Susan Reynolds, then fourteen, married a local youth, Sam Newcomb.
Susan's bridesmaid was her eleven-year-old friend, Bettie Matthews, and the wedding was held on Bettie's birthday. Bettie's future husband, George T. Reynolds,
the bride's brother, also attended the ceremony. Early marriages were common on
the frontier. Susan's sister Sallie described the reason: "In those early days girls were
married very young, too young entirely. There were reasons for this, however, one
being the fact that a pioneer life tends to develop boys and girls, maturing them

earlier, and another being the high ratio of young men to young women. In a new country there are many unattached young men who come with the spirit of adventure seeking their fortunes, while the girls are not so plentiful and therefore are much sought after."[8]

On October 13, 1864, almost two years after Susan Reynolds's wedding, several hundred Comanche and Kiowa warriors attacked the Elm Creek Valley in Texas, which was northwest of the Reynolds and the Matthews ranches. A number of men, women, and children were killed, as well as at least five U.S. Army soldiers. Several women and children were kidnapped and held for ransom. The settlers learned to rely on their own resources, and their response to the violence was to "fort up." Families and neighbors gathered together and constructed houses in groups, often surrounded by a stockade, creating a siegelike atmosphere. The Matthews family, along with thirteen-year-old Bettie, retreated to Fort Owl Head. The Reynolds family moved to Fort Davis, on the east bank of the Clear Fork River, near the county line between Stephens and Shackelford counties.[9] Although the families organized these forts for protection, the time spent with other neighbors was also a welcome change from the loneliness of ranch life.

Over the next couple of years, both families worked hard to build their cattle herds and stave off Indian attacks. Then the Matthews and the Reynolds families moved again. Bettie Matthews moved with her family to a small village called Picketville, in Stephens County. As the Reynolds family moved from Fort Davis to what they called the "Old Stone Ranch" in Throckmorton County, Texas, George maintained contact with Bettie. The stone house on the ranch was originally built by troops stationed at Fort Phantom Hill for their commanding officer, Capt. Newton Givens.[10] The fort was abandoned in 1854, and the house stood empty for a number of years before the Reynolds family moved in.

Bettie and George married at the Matthews home in Picketville on July 15, 1867. Lucinda Elizabeth Matthews was fifteen years old, and her husband, George, twenty-three. Their wedding temporarily broke the mood of living under siege. Over a three-day period, people cautiously arrived from throughout the Clear Fork region, with some coming more than seventy-five miles.[11] Several members of the Reynolds family traveled to Picketville for the wedding, while George's mother remained at home getting things in order for the new bride and preparing for festivities there. Bettie brought a handsome dowry to the marriage. Her father gave the couple two hundred head of cattle to add to George's growing herd.[12]

The marriage of Lucinda Elizabeth Matthews and George Thomas Reynolds was a time to dispense with the worries of conflict and work and to celebrate the joining of the two families. The bride and groom arrived at the Stone Ranch on the third day after the wedding, having ridden for two days from the celebration in Picketville. They arrived with a party of at least ten friends and relatives. "They were all on horseback and came riding in by twos."[13] Fiddlers played through the night, accompanying the dancing couples. The family provided large washtubs of coffee to go with the cakes made specially for the occasion. The next day the guests returned home as they had come—on horseback. The event is best described by George's sister Sallie and clearly depicts the women's method of transportation: "I am sure that they must have been exceedingly tired after the dancing and the horseback rides, though young women were quite used to the saddle in those days, that being the most convenient way they had of going about. They rode sidesaddles exclusively. A woman thought nothing of taking a small child behind her saddle and another in her lap, and riding several miles to visit a neighbor. I've done it many times in my early married life."[14]

Bettie, called "Sister Bettie" by her sister-in-law Sallie Reynolds, moved into the Stone Ranch with her husband, George. The house contained some furnishings at that time. Members of the family found a number of household goods, including almost a full set of dishes packed in a wooden box stored in a nearby rock quarry. They also found other hidden items, including a cowbell, an ox yoke, and a small coffin containing the body of a baby. The coffin was buried, but the baby was never identified.[15]

Bettie's mother-in-law slept in the room where the long dining table stood (the table accommodated twelve to fifteen people).[16] At one end of the room was a wide fireplace, where the women did the cooking using cast-iron pots. In the evening the family gathered around the hearth, the women "sewing, knitting, or mending," while the boys molded bullets. On some evenings they roasted pecans and cured buffalo tongues over the open flames.

Less than two months after Bettie and George Reynolds married, the U.S. Army opened a new post nearby, Fort Griffin. The garrison was established to deal with the continuing "Indian problem" that so affected the area. Later, in the fall of 1867, George's father moved the family to a newly built house closer to Fort Griffin, leaving the Stone Ranch house. The presence of the U.S. Army gave a sense of security to the Reynolds clan, which now included Bettie. At the fort, the officers and their wives added a new social dimension to the settlers' lives. George and his brother William worked as freighters hauling lumber to Fort Griffin.[17]

Violent confrontations between the Comanche raiders, the ranchers, and the cowboys continued during the 1860s and 1870s. White settlers' atrocities against the Indian people were well known, and, in return, no one was spared the "cold-blooded cruelty" of the Indian attacks on the settlers.[18] The favorite booty of the Comanche raiders was livestock, especially horses. The ranchers felt compelled and fully justified in taking whatever action they believed was necessary to protect their herds and retrieve stolen animals. Whether Indian or white, killing was considered justified for horse stealing, except that a white rustler usually received a trial, whereas an Indian thief was dealt with as an enemy fighter and killed upon capture. These were dangerous years for anyone traveling or working in the area. The number of deaths was not high by the standards of war, but the violent nature of the encounters caused everyone anxiety.

In 1868, two of the Reynolds sons, George and William, decided to take their cattle up the trail to market again. In the late 1860s a triad of cattle trails left Texas: the Chisholm Trail, the Western Trail, and the Goodnight-Loving Trail. None of these were new to travelers, especially the Goodnight-Loving Trail, which started about sixty miles west of Fort Worth and ran west by southwest toward Fort Concho and ultimately back northwest to Fort Sumner, New Mexico, and then north to Denver, Colorado. Following the route of the old Butterfield Overland Mail of the late 1850s and early 1860s, the route was known among cowboys as one of the worst ways to "go up the trail." In fact, George Reynolds, with his brother and one other cowboy, had led several hundred cattle along the same trail a year before ranchers Charles Goodnight and Oliver Loving made their first trip in October of 1865.[19]

Within a year of Bettie's marriage, her husband, George, and his younger brother, William, old hands on the cattle trail, formed a partnership that became the basis for Reynolds Cattle Company. Their new brand, the "Long X," is still in use today. The first to leave with a small herd of cattle, William then joined Goodnight and Loving. The drive turned out to be a legendary trip, during which Oliver Loving was wounded by Comanche raiders and later died at Fort Sumner, New Mexico. William helped Goodnight bring the body of his partner and friend back to Texas for burial.[20]

Soon after William left with Goodnight, George began organizing another cattle drive, which Bettie joined. He put together a herd of 700–800 cattle, and, with Bettie's dowry of 200 more, the total came to almost 1,000 head. Profit could be made only by driving the livestock to market in New Mexico and Colorado. The group set out on the Goodnight-Loving trail, and, although it was not new to George, it was still a demanding trip. Bettie and George, George's younger brother, Benjamin (or Bennie), a cousin named McLean, and about a dozen cowboys made up the trail crew. Both Bennie and McLean were advised to go west for medical reasons—Bennie for his general health and McLean for tuberculosis. Bennie also added his own cattle to the herd.[21]

Bettie's role on the trail included responsibilities uncommon for a young woman. For the journey, Reynolds acquired a military ambulance to use as one of several wagons, and Bettie drove the wagon almost the entire trip. The Civil War ambulance was her responsibility, as well as her traveling home, for several months. The ambulance had a covered passenger compartment and resembled the coaches used by the Butterfield Stage Line in the late 1850s and early 1860s. Inside the compartment were three long seats. George removed two of them to make more room, and he and Bennie installed a bed for Bettie where the two seats had been. Bettie and her sister-in-law sewed pockets for toilet articles, hairbrushes, and other personal items onto the inside of the compartment's curtains. They mounted a shelf on the side of the wagon and tied a barrel to it to hold water. Ambulance and passenger coaches were pulled by four (or more often six) mules or horses. Bettie controlled the large team with skill, strength, and her knowledge of horses.[22]

The party of travelers said their good-byes and started out on the morning of July 9, 1868. The first day's drive was to the Old Stone Ranch, where the group spent several days loading supplies. They then headed the herd southwest, toward the ruins at old Fort Phantom Hill.[23] After following the trail to Fort Concho, they turned westward up Centralia Draw to reach Horsehead Crossing on the Pecos River. This leg of the trip turned out to be an arduous, waterless ordeal. In late July and August, when sixteen-year-old Bettie and her party crossed the area, temperatures often passed the 100-degree mark, with a pounding sun shining more than fourteen hours a day. The soil was alkali, and every breeze blew the fine white powder into a rider's eyes, ears, nose, throat, and clothing. They had no place to escape the dust.

Once the middle tributary of the Concho River, just west of Fort Concho, ran dry, there was no drinkable water for the thirsty cattle or travelers until they reached the Pecos. Although there was water on the trail, it was poisonous and caused sickness and death when drunk. The water of the Pecos River itself was not much better. The banks of the river were steep, and the water was salty to the taste. Rattlesnakes only added to the problem; they were one of the few animals that easily survived the desert environment. The final problem was other people. In addition to outlaws, Comanche, Kiowa, and Apache raiders traversed the region on a regular basis. For the Comanche, the main raiding trail into Mexico ran through the same area that Bettie and the rest of the cowboys traveled.

Good planning and proper supplies made the trip across the dry *llano estacado,* or Staked Plains, as the area was known, less of a problem, and George Reynolds had planned well. Other drives often lost at least one cowboy by the time they reached the ruined chimneys of Fort Phantom Hill. The Reynolds party fortunately encountered no problems all the way to Horsehead Crossing. They also avoided any confrontation with the Comanche until they reached the Pecos River. Instead of fording the Pecos at Horsehead Crossing, as most herds did, the group continued up the east side of the river, made camp, and bedded down the cattle. Late at night, Indian riders assaulted the camp, taking six horses. The cowboys on night watch rode into camp to wake the sleeping crew, but the horses were already gone. In the excitement George Reynolds put his pants on backward, and his younger brother, Bennie, lost his gun. Rightly deciding that he could not chase Indians without a weapon, Bennie returned to bed. In the moonlight, Bettie hid anxiously under the ambulance with the tubercular McLean, while George and the other men chased the raiding party. The men soon returned—without the stolen horses but still alive and well. Had they chased the raiders farther, they would have risked everyone's lives if they had run into a larger band of Indians.[24]

After this incident the trail drive went on full alert, and everyone kept a look-out for the Indians. Using a small telescope he always carried, George spotted a party of about 150 warriors at a distance from the herd. Bettie approached him with a request: "The little wife begged her husband's promise to shoot her if he saw she would fall captive to the Indians."[25] The cowboys moved the herd as rapidly as possible to keep the Indians at a distance. Fear continued to grip the trail crew, however, and everyone, including Bettie, stayed up all night keeping watch.

The crew pushed the herd hard, and on the second day following the night raid, they arrived at Fort Sumner, New Mexico, where they fell under the protection of the U.S. Army. Exhausted from the tension, the travelers collapsed into sleep, leaving the cattle unguarded. When they awoke the next morning, all of the cattle were gone. The cowboys quickly found the livestock, however, which had wandered off looking for grass in the barren country.

When the herd reached Bosque Grande, New Mexico, George's father sold his portion of the cattle, as well as those of the other Texas ranchers.[26] He took the profits in cash, buttoned the money into a canvas money belt, and put it under his shirt. Along with two other men, he then headed back to Texas. Bettie once again climbed into the wagon, following George and the crew with their herd into northern New Mexico near Red River Station, where they decided to spend the winter. The Reynoldses took their meals at a place called a "stage stand," where stagecoach drivers and passengers were fed. Here they met friends from Texas, Tom Stockton and his wife, Etta Cuington, who had come over the trail the previous year. George and Bettie spent their first New Mexico winter in the company of the Stocktons. At winter's end the Reynoldses drove their herd into Colorado and then turned west. At the end of the trail in California, Bettie and George finally sold their herd at what was said to be "an extremely good profit."[27]

With the cattle sold and the crew dispersed, Bettie and George Reynolds decided to travel and enjoy themselves before returning to Texas. San Francisco became their home for most of the year, and they made occasional trips to Sacramento. On the return trip to Texas, the couple visited Salt Lake City, Utah.[28] Bettie and George arrived back at the Texas ranch in late fall of 1870. They had been on the trail and traveling the West for more than two years. For family members, they brought gifts from California, and Bettie, "dressed handsomely in costumes made by city dressmakers, seemed a grand lady indeed."[29] The young couple, Bettie now eighteen, and George twenty-six, told endless stories of their adventures. Soon after their return, Bettie's family arrived to greet them. The Matthews family had not seen their daughter for more than two years, and they moved into the tenement house behind George and Bettie's ranch home. The two families lived together on the ranch for several years.

The cattle drive to California was Bettie Reynolds's first trip away from Texas but certainly not her last. She worked tirelessly with her husband and his brother

Will to build a cattle empire under the Long X brand. Theirs was a life of cattle and cattle drives. In 1871 Bettie and George took to the trail once again. George and his brother Will rounded up the livestock and hired a crew for another drive to Colorado, with California again as the ultimate market. For the first part of the journey, Will Reynolds took charge of one herd. He was helped by his brother Bennie and a one-armed drover, while Rice Derrett worked as trail boss of a second herd. Bettie and George Reynolds made their own way to Colorado, including one stretch on a train. For the first segment of the trip, they used the ambulance wagon that Bettie had driven on the trail in 1868, but this time Bettie rode as a passenger with her husband. The wagon was driven by a Frenchman called, in the finest Texas fashion, "Frenchie."

Frenchie drove Bettie and George, along with George's brother Glenn and Bettie's brother Bud, to Fort Gibson in the Indian Territory. Even though the trip seems insignificant in comparison to Bettie's earlier trip, the distance they covered in the wagon was more than 350 miles. At a fast pace of 25 miles a day, the trip lasted around fifteen days. After bumping along the trail in the daytime, the group spent most of their nights in the open. In 1871 Indian Territory was still a lawless place, and the Indian Wars were still being fought across the southern Plains by the U.S. Army, a circumstance that would seem to warrant a cancellation of the trip by today's standards. Nevertheless, the Reynoldses arrived at their destination without incident or any record of complaint. They then boarded a train that eventually took them to Kit Carson, Colorado, west of present-day Colorado Springs. From Kit Carson, Bettie and George Reynolds went south, again by wagon, to the north bank of the Arkansas River. Their trip ended in Colorado, while the crew herded the cattle westward through Nevada and on to California.

Bettie and George scouted the area and came upon a valley just south of the location of the 1864 massacre by Gen. John M. Chivington of more than 160 Cheyenne men, women, and children, who were under the leadership of Chief Black Kettle.[30] At a place called the "Point of Rocks," George and Bettie selected a spot for their home and ranching operation. To the south, the site overlooked the Arkansas River and a valley. To the north were miles of native grass prairies for grazing cattle. Owned by the U.S. government, the land was divided into 160-acre tracts "with small easy payments."[31] All of the government land was unfenced and open to free-grazing livestock until an actual landowner came to the area to occupy it. Will Reynolds drove a herd of longhorn cattle from Texas to stock the new ranch. Line camps were established around the perimeter of the grazing lands, with cowboys, called line riders, keeping the cattle on the Reynoldses' ranch lands.[32]

Bettie lived as a ranch wife at the remote cattle operation. The nearest store was twelve miles away from the Point of Rocks ranch house. In the fall of 1871 George's sister Susan arrived in Pueblo, Colorado, with her son, Gus, to visit them. The first winter in Colorado was a memorable one filled with all kinds of trouble for the

Reynolds family. Both George and Gus were seriously ill. George's brother, Will, fell down a flight of stairs into the cellar. He was badly cut and couldn't work for a period.[33] The rest of the winter proved agreeable to the family, and by spring 1872 George and Will were buying and selling herds of cattle.

The year 1872 brought another change to the Reynolds family. George's father, Barber Watkins Reynolds, decided to sell the Texas ranch and move the family to Colorado, where most of the Reynolds family now resided. In 1874 Bettie and George made a trip to Texas and brought back Bettie's cousin, Susan Matthews.[34] That was another long journey made in a wagon to the train station, then by train to Indian Territory, again by wagon to Texas, and back again. By the next year, 1875, the ranching area of southeastern Colorado was changing. The Santa Fe Railroad established a railhead at the newly formed town of La Junta, Colorado, just across the Arkansas River from the Reynoldses' ranching operation. At that time, the area was experiencing a severe drought, and things looked better back in Texas. In 1875 the Red River Wars, fought by the U.S. Army against the Comanche and Kiowa raiders, at last ended, opening the area to safer ranching. Professional buffalo hunters also entered the area. The nearest town, called "the Flats," was visited by everyone from Pat Garrett, then a buffalo skinner, to the famous woman poker player, Lottie Deno. In November of 1875 George, Bettie, and the rest of the Reynolds family boarded the new train and headed back to Texas. The railroad now went as far as Denison, where they disembarked. George and Bettie boarded a wagon and went on to the ranch owned by Bettie's parents, near Fort Griffin. The Texas that Bettie and George Reynolds came home to had changed from the wilderness ranch country they had left a short four years earlier to a civilized ranching community.

George and Will got busy restocking the ranches, taking annual cattle drives into Wyoming, Utah, Nevada, Montana, Nebraska, the Dakotas, and Canada.[35] After a year on the ranch, in July 1876, Bettie and George, along with several other family members, traveled to Philadelphia, Pennsylvania, for the Centennial Exposition—another trip by train and wagon. Over the years Bettie made extended stays in relatives' ranch homes to help with the children and elder family members. In the 1880s Bettie traveled to Massachusetts, in addition to short visits to Fort Worth, Texas, and Kansas City, Missouri.[36]

By the 1880s Bettie and George were wealthy, respected cattle ranchers. They owned ranches in Haskell, Shackelford, and Throckmorton counties, which formed the basis of their company. In 1893, along with a group of family members, the couple attended the World's Columbian Exposition in Chicago. After the holiday Bettie and George boarded a train for South Dakota to visit one of the Long X cattle ranches of another Reynolds brother. The Reynolds brothers' ranching empire now included thousands of cattle spread across several states, but Reynolds Bend on the Clear Fork of the Brazos River was still home for Bettie and George. George established a bank in nearby Albany, and in 1884, with Will, formally in-

Figure 7.   Bettie and George Reynolds with Betty Cantelou, early 1900s.
Robert E. Nail Archives of the Old Jail Art Center, Albany, Texas.

corporated the Reynolds Cattle Company, making it a family enterprise. The couple
often spent winters in the nearby town of Albany, Texas, where George became actively involved in banking and politics. Bettie was well known for her charity work
and general socializing in the area.

Bettie and George had no children of their own, but she raised the daughter of
her cousin Lulu Matthews Cantelou, named Betty, whom they formally adopted.[37]

The family maintained a lifelong religious affiliation, and, with their extensive cattle operations in Jeff Davis County, George was a founder of the Bloys Camp Meetings, held annually at the turn of the century.

Bettie and George built a true cattle empire. When George died in Fort Worth, Texas, on March 5, 1925, at eighty-one years of age, the Reynolds Cattle Company held almost a half million acres of ranch land in Jeff Davis County in far west Texas, Shackelford, Haskell, Throckmorton, and several other counties as far north as the Texas Panhandle, with additional ranches across the west. He was buried in Albany, Texas, with Bettie inheriting his estate.

Ten years later, in 1935, Lucinda "Bettie" Reynolds died and was buried alongside George, her husband of fifty-eight years. The estate was inherited by their adopted daughter, Betty Reynolds Cornell.

In 1868 Bettie was one of the first women to make the trip from Texas to Colorado over the old Goodnight-Loving Trail and on to California, the first of many such trips for her. For the cowboys it was just one more cattle drive, but, for Bettie and George Reynolds, the 1868 drive marked the beginning of a ranching empire, and for all involved, the journey was one of a lifetime of adventures as pioneer Texans.

NOTES

1. Many of the stories related here are documented in several books, including *Interwoven: A Pioneer Chronicle* by Sallie Reynolds Matthews; *Cattle Kings of Texas* by C. L. Douglas; *The Trail Drivers of Texas,* edited by J. Marvin Hunter; and *Historical and Biographical Record of the Cattle Industry and the Cattlemen of Texas and Adjacent Territory,* edited by James Cox, to name a few. The most accurate telling of the stories is in *Interwoven,* which was written by the younger sister of George Reynolds, Sallie. I have used this as the main source since it contains fewer discrepancies. Where stories appear that are not told in *Interwoven,* I have cited the source.

2. Matthews, *Interwoven,* 13.

3. Ibid., 10.

4. Cox, *Historical and Biographical Record,* vol. 1, 339.

5. Matthews, *Interwoven,* 11.

6. Ibid., 9.

7. Ibid.

8. Ibid., 13–14. Ten years prior to the marriage, the 1850 Texas census indicates the average marriage age was 22 for women and 26 for men; see Blaine T. Williams, "The Frontier Family: Demographic Fact and Historical Myth," 17.

9. Ibid., 17.

10. "Old Stone Ranch," *The New Handbook of Texas Online,* http://www.tsha.utexas.edu/handbook/online (accessed Oct. 15, 2005).

11. Ty Cashion, *A Texas Frontier: The Clear Fork Country and Fort Griffin, 1849–1887,* 76, 249.

12. Matthews, "Reynolds, George Thomas," *Interwoven,* 40.

13. Ibid., 41–42.

14. Ibid., 42.

15. Ibid., 30. The original owners were paid by Barber Watkins Reynolds for the items found and the furniture that was left in the house.

16. Ibid.

17. Douglas, *Cattle Kings of Texas*, 24.

18. Ibid., 88.

19. Prior to the trail drive of Goodnight and Loving, the route that eventually became the Goodnight-Loving Trail was used by drover James Patterson in 1864 and by George Reynolds in 1865. Thus the trail has undoubtedly been misnamed. See Charles Kenner, "The Origins of the 'Goodnight' Trail Reconsidered," 390–94.

20. Matthews, *Interwoven*, 57.

21. Douglas, *Cattle Kings of Texas*, 187.

22. Ibid.

23. The U.S. Army post on the Clear Fork, better known as Fort Phantom Hill, was a noted landmark and was frequently used as a camp by drives over the Goodnight-Loving Trail.

24. Matthews, *Interwoven*, 59.

25. Ibid., 60.

26. Bosque Grande, New Mexico, is now the city of Roswell.

27. Matthews, *Interwoven*, 61.

28. Ibid.

29. Ibid., 74.

30. The Cheyenne band had been part of a resettlement program to teach the tribe farming. As a result of the slaughter, now called the "Sand Creek Massacre," the Cheyenne fled, finally to western Indian Territory. On Nov. 20, 1868, while peaceably camped on a snowy fall morning, the Cheyenne camp was attacked by U.S. 7th Cavalry troopers under the leadership of Gen. George Armstrong Custer. Chief Black Kettle was slain, as well as a number of women and children at the so-called battle of the Washita.

31. Matthews, *Interwoven*, 80.

32. Ibid., 86.

33. Ibid., 94.

34. Ibid., 176.

35. *The New Handbook of Texas Online,* http://www.tsha.utexas.edu/handbook/online (accessed Oct. 15, 2005), s.v. "Reynolds Cattle Company."

36. Ibid., s.v. "Old Stone Ranch."

37. Ibid., s.v. "Reynolds Cattle Company."

Estelle Amanda Nite Burks

MRS. WILLIAM FRANKLIN BURKS

Lisa A. Neely

Range women are strong, sturdy, delightful types.
They've always had to struggle against the unknown—
changing economies, not to mention loneliness—
the common traits of remote living. They take
justifiable pride in meeting every challenge.

ELIZABETH MARET[1]

ESTELLE AMANDA NITE BURKS WAS SUCH A WOMAN. Though her life was filled with tragedy, adventure, and success, Miss Amanda, or Aunt Mandy as she became known, met challenges head on, drawing strength from her faith and pioneer spirit. Because her life was such a testament to the American frontier, it was memorialized both in text and on the big screen. Even the members of the Old Trail Drivers Association recognized her place in history when they elected her queen of their organization. They said she was "the only woman who ever personally drove a herd of cattle out of Texas to meet the new railroad."[2] Despite all of her accomplishments and recognition, the "famed 'Cattle Queen of Cotulla'" always remained a true Texan at heart.[3]

Amanda was born of pioneer stock in Houston County, Texas, on February 8, 1841. Her parents, John Edward, a native of North Carolina, and Lucy Stepp Nite, from Oglethorpe County, Georgia, had arrived in Houston County in 1835 from Tennessee, led by their blind faith and courage, to seek a better life. They traveled overland in a covered wagon drawn by a team of four horses, with the threat of Indians always on their minds. When they arrived in Houston County, like nearly all of the pioneers of that time, they had no fortune. Their funds for starting a new life, $1,800 in gold, were stolen during their trip. As time passed, their hard work and perseverance paid off, and by 1838, with 4,605 acres they were among the largest landowning families in Houston County.[4] As Amanda grew, she learned the rudiments of riding and eventually became almost fearless in the saddle. She learned not only how to handle a horse but how to break one as well. Her solid frontier upbringing prepared her for the disappointments in life that lay ahead.[5]

It must have been predestined that Amanda Nite would one day marry William

Figure 8.   Amanda Burks when married, October 14, 1858.
Courtesy of Louisa S. Franklin, Cotulla, Texas.

Franklin Burks, for they were truly kindred spirits. Bud, as he was called, was born on the White River, near Little Rock, Arkansas, on June 11, 1839, the son of Simpson and Phoetna Jones Burks from Tennessee. They lived in Arkansas for a number of years before moving to Texas, where they settled in Angelina County. While living there, William received his formal elementary education. As a lad, he began driving and selling cattle in the county.[6] William's sheer determination and pioneering instinct set into motion events that placed him essentially at the doorstep of Amanda Nite, his future bride.

Stories handed down through the Baylor and Bell families, William's nieces and nephews, recount that eighteen-year-old William traveled from his home in Jonesville to Crockett, Texas, on business in 1857. While there, his friend, Jim Nite, invited him to attend the Christmas ball at the Crockett Female Seminary. At the dance, Jim introduced William to his sixteen-year-old sister, Amanda. Whether they ever stood under the mistletoe is not known, but apparently it was love at first sight, for within a week they were engaged. William refused to leave town until Amanda agreed to marry him. She did, and less than a year later, on October 14, 1858, they married.[7]

The couple moved to Shawnee Prairie in Angelina County, near William's parents' home in Jonesville, and started ranching and raising horses. Life was good for them, and Amanda was soon pregnant. On September 23, 1859, their son, John, was born. Tragically, on June 8, 1860, their nine-month-old baby died. John Burks was buried in the Jonesville Cemetery and, according to some records, was the first person interred there.[8] William and Amanda took the loss hard.

The following year brought a series of events that would cast the shadow of the Civil War across the country. Whether the issue of slavery was morally or ethically correct, by 1860, slave labor was an economic necessity. In Texas alone, the assessed value of all of the slaves in the state was $106,688,920.[9] William and Amanda Burks were among those who owned slaves. From records that survive, it appears that they owned "two faithful negro [*sic*] servants, Uncle Ike and the negro girl 'Liza,'" whom Amanda "raised."[10] William bought six-week-old Eliza for Amanda in New Orleans in 1861 for $1,500.[11] On February 1, 1861, Texas voted to secede from the Union.

As the first battles of the Civil War raged, happiness came again to the Burks home on July 1, 1861, with the birth of their daughter, Lucy. The Burks family at this time included William's younger sister, Rhoda (seventeen), his half-brothers, Bob (fourteen), Mark (thirteen), and John (eleven), and his half-sister, Margaret (nine). It is unclear why William's siblings came to live with him and Amanda except for the fact that they arrived in 1860, shortly after William's stepmother, Unity Burks, passed away. They continued to live with William and Amanda even though their father, Simpson, eventually remarried.[12]

Even though Angelina County voted against secession in 1861, many of its men volunteered for service in the Confederacy. William Burks, an ardent Confederate, joined Capt. John Duff Brown's Company D, 22nd Texas Infantry of the Confederate States of America, mustering into service on March 31, 1862.[13] The following week, on April 6, 1862, William wrote Amanda from Crockett, Texas, where she had been born. In that letter, he told her that he had "seen all of your connections," her relatives, and that he was spending time with her mother, who will "send for you this summer if Bob does not bring you out."[14] This letter and the other few that survive describe in detail the events of the war that William experienced.

In the weeks that followed, William greatly missed Amanda. On April 6, 1862, he wrote that he expected to be home soon. "I think I can get a furlow [*sic*] to come home before I go off," "I think I will be sure to come by home when we start," and "I will see you sure before I leave for good."[15] His optimism, though, quickly changed to despair. In subsequent letters he wrote, "there is no chance to get a furlow [*sic*] to come home,"[16] "I don't think I will be home until the war is over, no man can get a furlow [*sic*] not even the captains,"[17] "I do not know whether I will ever see you again or not,"[18] and "If I never get home again rais [*sic*] the baby up as good as you can & teach her to [be] honest & truthful."[19] By the end of the war, William was again optimistic that he would see his wife again, but the years and the distance between them were difficult. "Manda I want you to come and see me this summer wherever I am. I don't know where I will be but I want you to come to me wherever I am,"[20] and "I would like to see your face out here do you think you would come to me if I was to write to you? I think you would come."[21]

Amanda was left to take care of her family's home and property while her husband was away at war. Believing she needed guidance in such matters, William wrote letters to her that are full of advice. He talked about their crops, stock, and the family's general well-being. Regarding the crops, William instructed her to "have them negros [*sic*] work sharlott [*sic*] in particular tell Pall to work & to stay in the field all the time for unless he does he wont [*sic*] make anything."[22] "I want you to go to see Jerry Stark and let him have the cotton bales that is behind yet & take up my notes that he has."[23] "I have not got any paper if I had I would write to Mr. Stevens about making a crop and then bringing my cotton out next Fall or Summer. If he can I want you to get him to bring out this Summer all my cotton and he can make more money on one load of cotton than he can in making two crops."[24] Concerning their livestock, William said, "I made arrangements to get that rone [*sic*] horse broke to plow."[25] "I want you to have our hogs attended to & if there is any nast [*sic*] in the river bottom get bob [*sic*] to take them to it."[26] "I want you to write to me how our horses are doing & our cattle too for I am thinking we are going to have a might hard winter."[27] Finally, when discussing his family's welfare, William continuously wrote, "do the best that you can."[28] He also made suggestions: "Make the children mind you,"[29] and "keep the children together if you can but if you see you can't get them to a good place if you can. Talk to them and try to get them [to] do right and if they won't do right whip them and make them."[30]

Sometime in 1864, William became a member of Col. John Salmon "Rip" Ford's command and found himself in Nueces County. While there, he "was greatly impressed with the possibilities of stock raising in that particular section."[31] "This is the best country I have ever seen in my life. Stock is just as fat as it can be. I wish you could just see this country and see how you like it."[32]

During the war, the Burkses' home flourished under Amanda's resolute determination, and, in the latter part of 1864, William managed to come home on an extended furlough. When he returned to his outfit, Amanda accompanied him on the first day's ride. They left their four-year-old daughter, Lucy, in the care of William's sister, Rhoda. When Amanda returned on February 6, 1865, she found Lucy had suddenly taken ill and died. Amanda's kindly neighbors prepared the tiny body for burial.[33] Grief overwhelmed William and Amanda, who had now lost two children, and they never fully recovered from their loss.[34]

In April 1865 Amanda made the first of many trips across the Texas plains. On one particular journey, accompanied by her brother-in-law John, she visited her sister, Martha Ann "Mat" Nite Richardson, who lived in Greenwood, Louisiana. Years later, Amanda wrote that she could not "remember anything of special interest except that we were caught in hard rains & crossed in swollen streams."[35] By the time she wrote her reminiscences of this trip, it is obvious she was accustomed to such dramatic events of nature.

Shortly after Amanda's return to Jonesville, the family prepared to move to "the golden west of which we heard so many wonderful stories."[36] The war was over, and carpetbaggers had moved into the area. Fearing that William might lose his temper and kill one of the Yankees, the family decided to relocate. Returning home from a cattle drive to St. Joseph, Louisiana, William wrote, "I will call your attention to one thing and that is to be ready to move as soon as I get back home. I intend to move if I don't only get out of the county. . . . This country is the worst torn up of any Place you ever saw. There is no Regularity about anything here. . . . We can move as Far as Goliad Co. if not Further."[37] The family left Angelina County on October 1, 1866, bound for Mexico. Amanda later said this was the darkest day of her life, having to leave behind her two babies in the Jonesville Cemetery.[38]

The Burkses headed south with two wagons, one with six yokes of oxen hitched to it, and the other pulled by four horses. Uncle Ike, their former slave, who had remained with the family after emancipation, and Mark, William's half-brother, drove the two wagons loaded with the family's bedding and trunks. One of the wagons also contained their "bank account of $2,200 in gold."[39] Apparently the Burkses survived the war better than most Texas families. William, Amanda, and William's siblings Rhoda, John, and Bob rode along on horseback, driving their thirty-five head of horse. Their trip to a new home took approximately six weeks. Amanda later recalled, "We had merry times around our campfires at night and the slow process we were making didn't bother us for every thing took time in those days."[40] They traveled past Crockett, Bryan, present-day Cuero, and then Goliad.

Before they reached their "new home" in Mexico, the Burkses decided to settle in Banquete. When they reached San Patricio, William left them and rode to Corpus Christi to rent a house for them in Banquete. The family arrived at their new homestead on November 16, 1866. The house they moved into had been used as a hospital during the war, and the Burkses heard many tales of ghosts that supposedly inhabited the place. Soon they bought 151 acres close by for $1,500 from the Coleman, Mathis, Fulton Pasture Company. Part of the land was bounded by the left bank of the Banquete Creek, and another part was bounded by the El Diezmero land grant, which was held by Vicente de Herrera.[41] There the Burkses built their home "of five rooms, quite a mansion in those days."[42] They even had "a fine garden & raised all kinds of vegetables alltho [*sic*] we were told it was an impossibility."[43]

Shortly after their arrival in Banquete, William established his stock business and began making drives across the state into Louisiana to sell his horses and "beeves."[44] While William was away, Amanda once again found herself in charge of their homestead. His letters to her from the stock drives between 1867 and 1870 are filled with much the same kind of advice that he had given her during the war. Again, some of the topics he emphasized related to their crops, stock, and the family's well-being, but underlying these messages is his anxiety at being separated from her once more.[45] William's longing may be the reason he asked his wife to join him on the trail drive to Kansas in 1871.

Before Amanda's trip in 1871, "Few women are known to have gone up the trail from Texas, as cattle driving demanded the extreme in human endurance, and it was judged by cowmen and frontier women alike as 'no place for a lady.'"[46] Home was where women were supposed to be, safe and not worrying about anything except "sick children, cattle rustlers, and ornery steers."[47] In the Burkses' household, this ideology soon changed. In the early spring of 1871, William rounded up his cattle. "He topped out at a thousand head of the best to take to market."[48] Another trail boss, Jasper "Jap" Clark, also prepared his own herds. Because of the hazards they might encounter on the journey, they decided to trail the two herds together. The drive began in April, with ten cowboys assigned to each herd, along with their respective cooks. The cattle were road branded at Pintas and started up the trail. The herds had been gone only a day when Amanda received word from her husband that he wanted her to join him on the drive. He instructed her to bring either Liza or Nick, their former slaves, along to tend to her needs while on the trail. He further suggested that she choose Nick since he would be of more assistance to her.[49]

Nick packed Amanda's buggy and hitched two good brown ponies to it. They overtook the herds in a day's time. While on the trail, Nick tended to Amanda's every need. He prepared her meals, put up her tent and took it down, and was supposed to drive her buggy, but because the herds were moving so slowly, the buggy and horses usually followed the herds without anyone driving them. Amanda later recalled that she "would find a comfortable position, fasten the lines, and take a little nap."[50] As was the custom, the herds were driven only about ten miles a day or less. By taking a slow pace, the cattle were able to graze and fatten along the trail, thus they were still in good condition when they reached the railheads in Kansas. This leisurely pace went on for weeks and months except when the herds encountered the timber country. Then the cattle were driven straight through without stopping so that they did not scatter and get lost among the trees, causing a delay.[51]

While on the trail, Amanda witnessed firsthand many of the horrors that her husband had written about through the years. Though nothing was said out loud, "the female presence [on a trail drive] was looked upon as a bad omen by most trail hands, perhaps because cowboys in the main were over-protective of their womenfolk. Also when the herd was ready to move on, having to extricate a lady from her newly-found patch of wild flowers or plums was as hard as punching cattle."[52] This maxim was tested several times before the end of the drive.

The night before they reached Beeville, the Clark herd stampeded. The animals scattered so far that the Burkses' herd was "way up-state" before Clark and his crew caught up with them.[53] By the time the herds reached Central Texas, the weather had started to turn bad. Frequent lightning and hailstorms overtook them. One evening, near Bosque County, Amanda witnessed the severity of these storms. When the hail began to pelt them, William drove her buggy into a sheltered part of the timber. He unfastened the traces and handed her the reins while he hurried back to help the other men control the frightened herd. Seeking shelter under the buggy top, Amanda tried to hold the horses as the hail increased. The rain poured down in torrents. Sitting there cold and alone, Amanda later admitted that this was "the only time of all the months of my trip that I wished I was back on the old ranch at Banquette [*sic*]."[54] Hours later, William joined her. It was now 1:00 in the morning. The storm had been so severe that he and the other cowboys had big blood blisters on their hands that the hail had caused.

Weeks drifted by, and the herds eventually arrived at Fort Worth. They camped there while waiting for the swollen Trinity River to subside. Amanda later recalled how amazed she was to see fifteen different herds milling along the banks waiting to cross. As the Burks and Clark herds crossed into the Indian Territory, the men kept guard, watching for Indians and cattle rustlers, which they had been warned about. Though the Indians never attacked them, a few came into their camp to trade. Rustlers were a different story, however. While alone in camp one afternoon, Amanda was surprised when she saw two men approach and start throwing rocks at the grazing cattle. Realizing they meant to stampede the herd, she shouted at them to stop. Fortunately, some of the drive's cowboys rode up just then, and the rustlers hurried away. On another occasion, Indians were supposedly to blame for stampeding the herds. Amanda recalled years later that watching the frantic cowboys trying to slow the wild flight was a "horrible, yet fascinating sight."[55] After a week of hard work, the cattle were gathered, separated into their respective herds, and again moving northward.

Prairie fires were another problem that Amanda witnessed firsthand on the trail. She later exclaimed that she felt as if they were being "pursued by fire during our entire trip."[56] The worst fire occurred, however, because of Amanda's own ignorance. While the cook was off getting water, Amanda, instead of building a fire in a gully, started one that burned straight across the prairie for at least fifty miles.

When the investigators arrived the next day to find out who had caused the conflagration, they soon learned that it was Amanda. After that, nothing more was said about the incident, except that one man remarked that he was glad that he had not struck the match.[57]

While on the trail, Amanda periodically saw wild plums growing. More than once she asked her husband to stop for a while so that she could pick some. William, not ready to halt, told her there were troublesome Indians in the area. Not wanting to verify their existence, Amanda kept her buggy moving along. When they arrived at the Canadian River, though, Amanda again asked to stop for a while, for she saw red, blue, and yellow plums and just had to have several. She asked one of the cowboys to help her gather some of the fruit. Because Amanda was the only woman in camp, the men rivaled each other for her attention, so the cowboy happily obliged. As he and Amanda picked the fruit, they wandered farther and farther away from her buggy. When they headed back to it, Amanda panicked when she thought her horses had run away. The cowboy tried to reassure her and insisted that they just walk a bit farther. Sure enough, they found the horses standing in the exact spot where she had left them. That night she ate plum pie and quickly forgot about the afternoon's scare.[58]

As the herds made their way through the "northern part of the Territory," the cattle slowed and were taken off the trail to graze and fatten for a time. Amanda went on ahead until she reached a stream. There she saw Jap Clark at a distance, motioning for her to stop. Unfortunately, she misunderstood his gesture and thought that he meant for her to go on. Amanda plunged her horses and buggy into the swollen creek. Somehow she and the rig made it across even though one of the horses stumbled and fell. The crossing was so bad, though, that the embankment had to be dug out and slopped before it was safe for the herds. Needless to say, Amanda was teased relentlessly that evening "because of this alleged attempt to break my neck."[59]

Amanda's adventures continued in much the same manner until they reached Kansas. Unfortunately, when the Burks and Clark herds arrived in July of 1871, the price for cattle was low. Because of this, William decided to winter them on the Smoky River. Worried about Amanda's health, William took his wife into Elsmore to stay at one of the hotels. A few days after William left her there, however, she witnessed another fire. This time one of the hotels had caught fire, and several of the residents were injured. Needless to say, Amanda quickly returned to the "safety" of the cow camp.[60]

Kansas winters, however, were not to William's liking, so, before the heavy storms of the season set in, he decided to sell the cattle and "leave for Sunny Texas as soon as possible."[61] Amanda recalled that "He met with no discouragement of his plans from me, for never had I endured such cold."[62] William and Amanda left Kansas in December, dressed "as if we were Esquimaux."[63] They took their friends

Figure 9.   Amanda and W. F. Burks when they went up the trail in 1871.
Courtesy of Louisa S. Franklin, Cotulla, Texas.

back home a "bucket of frozen buffalo tongues as a souvenir."[64] The trip home was not nearly as eventful as the trail drive and took a lot less time. The Burkses left Kansas by rail and traveled via St. Louis to New Orleans, where they booked passage on a ship to Corpus Christi by way of Galveston and Indianola. In later years, when asked whether she had any regrets about her experience on the trail drive of 1871, Amanda replied no, "for what woman, youthful and full of spirit and love of living, needs sympathy because of availing herself of the opportunity of being with her husband while at his chosen work in the great out-of-door world?"[65]

Though this was Amanda's only trip up the trail with her husband, it was by far not the last that William took. He continued to sell cattle and horses for another five years—through 1876. During these drives, William began to see the fencing of the open range. When he returned home to Banquete after the 1876 drive, he decided it was time for the family to move someplace where the country was still open. The Burkses had lived in Nueces County for approximately ten years. Though they were good years for William and Amanda, joy and sorrow do go hand in hand. William's half-brother Bob and his half-sister, Margaret, had passed away while living there.[66]

William left Banquete searching for the ideal land. When he reached La Salle County, he met a survey party running a line. Stopping to speak to them, he saw what he was looking for: "beautiful country; great-wide expanses of prairie bordering a wooded stream and shady lakes."[67] He asked the surveyors who owned the land on the other side of the lake. One of the men told him it was vacant. William immediately filed on it, and the Burkses' new home, La Motta, was established.[68]

When William told Amanda about her new home, she was eager to see it. He had found a place that offered an abundance of wood and water, for she "was always grumbling about the scarcity of both at Banquette [sic]."[69] The family dismantled the old homestead at Banquete and moved the lumber to build their new house at La Motta. After the sheep were sheared, they were driven to La Motta, and in November 1876 William, Amanda, and Rhoda moved into their new home. Unfortunately, along with the beauty of the wide-open space also came the dangers of thieves and wild animals. The Burkses had to be constantly on the lookout since their livestock was prey to both two-legged and four-legged bandits. Amanda tied a dog to the chicken coop to prevent wild animals from eating the fowl.[70] Forty-six years later, in 1922, she was still having trouble with panthers.[71]

The Burkses' new home was not their nirvana, however. William never fully recovered from the effects of the Civil War, during which he had contracted tuberculosis; he now spent most of his days in bed. His health declined rapidly, and, on January 27, 1877, six weeks after they arrived at La Motta, thirty-seven-year-old William Franklin Burks passed away. His sister, Rhoda, rode to Guajoco to get a neighbor to help Amanda bury him. This was the beginning of La Motta Cemetery. When William died, Amanda and Rhoda were alone at La Motta, as all the ranch hands had returned to Banquete to drive the remaining horses and sheep to the new homestead.[72]

Even on his deathbed, William was concerned about Amanda and her welfare. He spent his last few hours giving her instructions about their property. He advised her to sell the horse stock and buy more sheep because he felt that she could handle this type of farm animal better. Honoring her husband's wishes, Amanda did as he instructed.[73] Never one to run from fear, Amanda faced the unknown head on.

That fall, she began selling off the large herd of horses that grazed at La Motta. She sold some of the first polo horses that left Texas to James Gordon Bennett of Long Island, New York. A few years later, she sold the remaining horse stock for the unheard-of price of fourteen dollars per head to the Dull Brothers on a neighboring ranch. Her brother-in-law John returned from Louisiana to help manage the ranch, relieving her of some of the burden. Tragically, only a year later, John was ambushed and killed at a saloon in Wahooka. Amanda had sensed something was wrong that evening when John's riderless horse wandered back to La Motta. She and Rhoda once again buried a family member in their private cemetery.[74]

Even in the face of all of these difficulties, Amanda refused to leave the ranch. When word came that one hundred Mexican *banditos* were plundering and murdering in the area, Amanda held firm at La Motta until the danger passed. In 1878 the last Indian raids in the area occurred, during which many people were killed and hundreds of horses were stolen. Although the Indians crossed the Nueces River just above La Motta, for reasons unknown they did not molest Amanda's property.[75]

In the midst of the tragedy and danger that seemed to engulf La Motta, a ray of sunshine peeked through. In May 1877 Rhoda, Amanda's sister-in-law and companion, married John W. Baylor in Tilden, Texas. Amanda escorted the couple to Tilden, and when John asked whether Rhoda could sit next to him in the front of the buggy during the trip, Amanda firmly replied, "No, wait until after you are married!"[76] John had a sheep ranch nearby, where he lived with Rhoda, and was a great help in managing the vast La Motta Ranch. He and Rhoda were blessed with three children: Willie, Mary, and Jack, but Rhoda died while her children were very young, and John passed away two years later. As she had in years past, Amanda was left to raise someone else's children. This time, however, as they grew, because of "Auntie Amanda's" age, she became very dependent upon them.[77]

Amanda's sheep ranch continued to grow, as did industry in the rest of La Salle County. For a time, sheep ranching became an important part of the county's economy. In 1870, 5,000 head grazed on the prairie grass. By 1880 that number had jumped to 36,714. By 1890 the number topped out at 50,560.[78] As the sheep operation at La Motta expanded, Amanda made biannual trips to Corpus Christi to sell her wool to the brokers. She traveled in her buggy with a driver, a female companion, and an outrider. The trip took several weeks, and they often encountered

Figure 10.   Amanda Burks (on right, turned sideways) and Rhoda Burks Baylor,
Amanda's sister-in-law (left of Amanda), at La Motta with bags of wool on
wagon in background. Courtesy of Louisa S. Franklin, Cotulla, Texas.

problems similar to those she had experienced on the 1871 trail drive. After each
trip to sell the wool, Amanda returned to La Motta with enough provisions to last
six months, and on one trip she purchased lumber to expand her house.[79] Amanda
continued this twice-yearly trip selling wool until 1882, when the International and
Great Northern (IGN) Railroad was built, and the town of Cotulla was established.

Joseph Cotulla, a Polish immigrant who had moved to the area in 1868, donated
land for the town that would bear his name. Learning in the early 1880s that the
IGN intended to run its tracks through the county, Cotulla worked to bring the
railroad to the town site that he was attempting to develop. In 1881 Cotulla donated 120 acres of land to the railroad, and by 1882 a depot had been constructed
and town lots sold. With the railhead close by, Amanda now only had to travel to
Cotulla, approximately twenty-five miles away, to ship her wool and buy provisions.[80] To ensure the town's success, Amanda bought a building that was used for
many years as a stage stand near old Fort Ewell and had it moved in 1890 to serve
as the first courthouse in La Salle County.[81]

During the 1880s and 1890s, Amanda expanded La Motta to encompass 33,000
acres. She also owned the 10,000-acre Los Pintas Ranch in Webb County.[82] Because
of the sharp drop in wool prices, a severe drought, and the brush that was taking
over the prairie grass, Amanda decided to sell her sheep stock and again began raising cattle. She also bought sixty thousand board feet of lumber from Perkins Mill
in Lake Charles, Louisiana, and shipped it to Cotulla, where it was hauled over-

land to La Motta. With the lumber, the modest home that she and William had built years ago was enlarged and turned into modern ranch headquarters.[83]

A neighbor and good friend of Amanda's was J. Frank Dobie. As a teenager, he met Amanda while visiting his uncle, Jim Dobie, at his Olmos Ranch adjoining La Motta. Jim Dobie and the Burkses had known one another when the latter lived near Banquete.[84] When J. Frank Dobie began writing, he used some of the stories Amanda shared with him about her life in the brush country. Unfortunately, his writing style did not please her. She once told him that she was not happy that he changed her story from the way she had told it to him. Dobie replied that he had to change it so that his book would sell. Somewhat taken back, Amanda replied that she was never going to tell him another story unless he wrote it the way she related it.[85] Dobie respected her wishes and later wrote that she was "a remarkable representative of frontier womanhood."[86] Some of Dobie's stories about Amanda are in his books *Cow People* and *Coronado's Children.*

In her later years, Amanda received many honors. On November 26, 1923, at the ninth annual meeting of the Trail Drivers Association held in San Antonio, one newspaper reported that "Mrs. Amanda Burks has been unanimously elected Queen of the Old Time Trail Drivers Association."[87] Members of the Texas and Southwestern Cattle Raisers Association, of which Amanda was a member, recounted that the Burkses were "true pioneers of Texas, and of the cattle industry, and this industry owes much" to them.[88]

When Emerson Hough immortalized Amanda Burks in his 1923 novel, *North of 36,* her name became a household term. As a working journalist, Hough traveled around the American West at the close of the nineteenth century. In his novels he attempted to identify the West with the ideals of the American past. *The Covered Wagon* (1922) and *North of 36* did just that.[89] In researching the material for *North of 36,* Hough learned about Amanda Burks and her 1871 trail drive with her husband. Many people believed that the lead character, Taisie Lockheart, in both the book and the subsequent film of the same name, was based on Amanda. When asked in an interview whether she thought the book accurately depicted the ways of the old trail drives, Amanda replied, "I have read that great and truthful book. On many pages, I saw evidence of Mr. Hough's careful examination of our records. 'North of 36' seems to me as true a work of fiction as can possibly be."[90] When asked specifically whether the heroine, Taisie Lockheart, was based on her life, Amanda replied, "How could anyone lay claim to such an honor without the author's authority? . . . Some of our experiences were very similar."[91]

When the film *North of 36* was remade in 1938 as *The Texans,* the producers shot footage at La Motta. Paramount Production Company of Hollywood, California, turned La Motta into a virtual movie lot. During the filming, a slew of Texas officials visited the ranch to officially welcome the Paramount executives to La Salle County and Texas. Hundreds of sightseers were turned away at the ranch gates every day. As befitting Amanda's story, Virginia Bell Sturges and Amanda Bell New-man, Amanda's great-nieces, and Frank Newman, a great-nephew-in-law, were used either as stunt doubles for the movie stars or as extras. One can only imagine what Amanda thought about all of the fuss going on at her beloved La Motta.[92]

Amanda never ceased to mourn the death of her husband. Until the day she died, she refused to wear anything but black, white, or a combination of both. Oc-casionally she added a bit of lavender to her dress. In her later years, as her eyesight failed, one of her nieces or a nurse would help her dress. As they did so, Amanda always asked what color they were dressing her in just to make sure it was appro-priate. Amanda was very religious and never allowed card playing in her home; she also frowned on hunting or fishing at the ranch on Sundays. Her views on the im-portance of education were well known to many, and, as a tribute to the "famed 'Cattle Queen of Cotulla,'" Cotulla's two-story brick school, built in 1909, was re-named the Amanda Burks School in her honor shortly before her death.[93]

During the last years of her life, Amanda was confined to her home because of a fall that broke her hip, but she nonetheless continued to run La Motta. Even when bedridden, she made the decisions about her ranch and did so until the day she died.[94] Estelle Amanda Nite Burks died at home on her much-loved La Motta Ranch on September 15, 1931, at the age of ninety. The prosperity of La Motta Ranch was solely the result of her management. Having outlived her husband, William Franklin Burks, by more than fifty-four years, she was laid to rest beside him in the family cemetery at La Motta. It was reported shortly after her death that "In her there was tenderness with strength; refinement with courage; contempt for a coward, but pity for the weak; intolerance for the indolent, but charity for the poor. She dared, but with charming modesty that disarmed her foes. She was truly a gentle-woman."[95]

NOTES

1. Elizabeth Maret, *Women of the Range: Women's Roles in the Texas Beef Cattle Industry,* xi.

2. Curtis Dunham, "La Salle Woman Queen of Trail Drivers." The Trail Drivers Associa-tion was organized in 1915 under the leadership of George W. Saunders to preserve the memories of the old trail drivers for posterity. See Ron Tyler, ed., *The New Handbook of Texas,* vol. 6, 544.

3. C. L. Douglas, *Cattle Kings of Texas,* 188.

4. "Death Takes Woman Who Managed Ranch for Half Century," *Cotulla Record,* Sept. 18, 1931, in Marion Day Mullins, comp., "Houston County Texas Tax List: 1838." In Ray H. Nelson, contr., "Republic of Texas 1846 Poll Tax List for Houston County," the surname Nite is spelled as Night. In Sandy Tubbs, trans., "Houston County, Texas, 1840 Tax Roll," John E. Nite (1805–1849) is assessed $1.62 and $4.25 in taxes. In Sandy Tubbs, trans., "1850 Houston County, Texas Census," Lucy Nite (1807–1865) is listed as the head of the household, along with Amanda (eleven), John D. (twenty-three), James M. (twenty), Calvin J. (eighteen), Lucy J. (twelve), Martha A. (six), and Sam H. (three). Of note is that Amanda's age is listed as

eleven, not nine, as it should be with an 1841 birth date. John Edward Nite and Lucy Stepp were married on May 29, 1826. John was stabbed to death, leaving Lucy with three children under the age of ten: Amanda, Martha Ann, and Samuel Houston. Both John and Lucy are buried in the Glenwood Cemetery in Crockett, Tex. Louisa Franklin, interview with Lisa Neely, Cotulla, Tex., Aug. 22, 2003; Louisa Franklin and Margaret Sturges (great-great-nieces of William and Amanda Burks), e-mail correspondence with Lisa Neely, Sept. 14, 2003.

5. "William Franklin Burks," *New Encyclopedia of Texas,* vol. 4, 2441.

6. Simpson D. Burks was born in 1812 in either Tennessee or White River, Deshay County, Arkansas. Phoetna Jones (1820–1845) was born in Jefferson County, Tennessee, and died at Old Royal, White County, Arkansas. They were married in 1838 in White County, Arkansas; see "Burks," *The New Encyclopedia of Texas,* 2441, and Franklin, interview, Aug. 22, 2003.

7. William and Jim "both liked horses, and that may have been what drew them together." Franklin, interview, Aug. 22, 2003.

8. Louisa Franklin, "Letters of William F. Burks," 1–2. Other sources state that Martin William Jones, the founder of Jonesville, Angelina County, Tex., was the first person buried at Jonesville Cemetery, when he was interred in 1887; see Tyler, *The New Handbook of Texas,* vol. 3, 997.

9. T. R. Fehrenbach, *Lone Star: A History of Texas and the Texans,* 307.

10. "Amanda Burks, East to West," manuscript fragment, n.p., n.d., 1.

11. Family stories relate that William bought Eliza on the slave block in New Orleans when he was on one of his horse-selling trips. She stayed with Amanda until she was approximately twenty years old; see Franklin, "Letters of William F. Burks," 15; also Franklin, interview, Aug. 22, 2003.

12. Family stories report that, when William's stepmother was on her deathbed, she "gave" her children to William and Amanda to raise; see Franklin, "Letters of William F. Burks," 2. Also see Franklin, interview, Aug. 22, 2003. Texas delegates voted 166 to 8 in favor of secession; see Tyler, *The New Handbook of Texas,* vol. 2, 121–26.

13. Franklin, "Letters of William F. Burks," 2. Angelina County was the only county in East Texas and one of only a handful of other Texas counties to reject secession; see Tyler, *The New Handbook of Texas,* vol. 1, 180–82. John Duff Brown (1823–1908) was a physician who volunteered for the Confederate Army, first with Ebenezar B. Nichols's regiment in Galveston and then with Company D of Thomas Neville Waul's Texas Legion. Waul's Legion comprised twelve companies of infantry, six companies of cavalry, and a six-gun battery of field artillery, with a complement of two thousand men; see Tyler, *The New Handbook of Texas,* vol. 1, 764–65, and vol. 6, 852.

14. William F. Burks, letter to Amanda Burks, Apr. 6, 1862. Bob is William's younger half-brother, who was living at the Burks home.

15. Ibid.

16. Ibid., Sept. 10, 1862.

17. Ibid., Oct. 26, 1862.

18. Ibid., Oct. 9, 1862.

19. Ibid., Oct. 5, 1862. The baby he refers to is his daughter, Lucy.

20. Ibid., Mar. 19, 1865.

21. Ibid., Mar. 30, 1865.

22. Ibid., Apr. 6, 1862.

23. Ibid., Sept. 10, 1862.

24. Ibid., Mar. 19, 1865.

25. Ibid., Apr. 6, 1862.

26. Ibid., Oct. 9, 1862.

27. Ibid., Nov. 13, 1862.

28. Ibid., Sept. 10, 1862; Oct. 5, 1862; Nov. 13, 1862; Dec. 10, 1862.

29. Ibid., Oct. 9, 1862. The children he refers to are his five siblings, who came to live with him and Amanda.

30. Ibid., Dec. 10, 1862.

31. "Amanda Burks, East to West," manuscript fragment. During the Civil War, Col. John Salmon Ford (1815–1897) led the 2nd Texas Cavalry, with a command in the Rio Grande district; see Tyler, *The New Handbook of Texas,* vol. 2, 1073.

32. Burks, letter to Amanda Burks, Mar. 30, 1865. William is referring to Houston County.

33. "Death Takes Woman," *Cotulla Record.*

34. Franklin, "Letters of William F. Burks," 12–13.

35. "Amanda Burks, East to West," 2.

36. Ibid., 4.

37. Burks, letter to Amanda Burks, Aug. 21, 1866.

38. Franklin, interview, Aug. 22, 2003. Though no surviving correspondence indicates that Amanda ever returned to visit her children's graves, William did so on his stock drive in 1867; see Burks, letter to Amanda Burks, July 22, 1867.

39. "Amanda Burks, East to West," 5.

40. Ibid., 6–7.

41. Nueces County, deed records, book M, 174–75. Formed in 1871, the Coleman, Mathis, Fulton Pasture Company was at one time one of the largest cattle companies in Texas.

42. "Amanda Burks, East to West," 10.

43. Ibid.

44. Franklin, interview, Aug. 22, 2003; Burks, letter to Amanda Burks, Nov. 21, 1868.

45. Johnye C. Sturcken, "Amanda and William Franklin Burks: A Nueces County Partnership," 1.

46. Ann Fears Crawford and Crystal Sasse Ragsdale, *Women in Texas: Their Lives, Their Experiences, Their Accomplishments,* 128.

47. Candice Savage, *Cowgirls,* 5.

48. J. Marvin Hunter, comp. and ed., *The Trail Drivers of Texas,* vol. 1, 296.

49. Ibid.

50. Ibid.

51. "Death Takes Woman," *Cotulla Record.*

52. Sue Flanagan, *Trailing the Longhorns: A Century Later,* 83.

53. Hunter, *Trail Drivers of Texas,* 298.

54. Ibid.

55. Ibid., 300–301.

56. Ibid., 301.

57. Ibid., 301–302.

58. Ibid., 302–303.

59. Ibid., 303.

60. Ibid., 304.

61. Ibid., 304–305.

62. Ibid., 305.

63. Ibid.

64. Ibid.

65. Ibid.

66. "East to West: Reminiscences of Mrs. Amanda Burks, Pioneer Woman and One of La Salle's Largest Ranch Owners," *Cotulla Record,* May 3, 1924.

67. Ibid.

68. "Death Takes Woman," *Cotulla Record.*

69. "East to West," *Cotulla Record.*

70. Ibid.

71. "Juan Rodriquez Kills Big Panther on La Motta Ranch," *Cotulla Record,* Dec. 6, 1922.

72. Annette Martin Ludeman, *A History of La Salle County: South Texas Brush Country, 1856–1975,* 144. Tuberculosis is an infectious disease that usually attacks the lungs but can also infect almost any part of the body. On Nov. 13, 1862, William first wrote about the widespread sickness and death he saw in camp. At that time, he said that he had "enjoyęd fine health since I left home." On March 19, 1865, he began complaining about his "Breast which has been troubling me very bad. I have not slept some for several nights on account of my Breast and Lungs"; see Burks, letters, Nov. 13, 1862, and Mar. 19, 1865. Ten years later, William knew something was wrong with his health. He wrote, "I have never recovered my health entirely yet my cough is bad and sometimes I have fever. I am really not able to get about by rights. But I keep a going." William F. Burks, letter to Amanda Burks, Dec. 21, 1875.

73. Ludeman, *A History of La Salle County,* 144.

74. Ibid., 145.

75. "Death Takes Woman," *Cotulla Record.*

76. Ludeman, *A History of La Salle County,* 145.

77. Ibid.

78. Leffler, "La Salle County, Texas, History," 3.

79. Ludeman, *A History of La Salle County,* 145; Franklin, interview, Aug. 22, 2003.

80. Leffler, "La Salle County, Texas, History," 3.

81. "Queen of Trail Dies Age 92," n.p., n.d.

82. Sturcken, "Amanda and William Franklin Burks," 10.

83. "Queen of Trail Dies." Around 1950, when La Motta was sold by the descendants of William and Amanda Burks, the original two-story house was torn down, and the lumber was taken into Cotulla, where another family house was built. Today Margaret Sturges, William and Amanda's great-great-niece lives in that house; Franklin, interview, Aug. 22, 2003.

84. Johnye C. Sturcken, "Amanda Nite Burks, Willie Baylor Bell, and J. Frank Dobie: A Brush Country Friendship," 1. Folklorist J. Frank Dobie (1888–1964) was born on a ranch in Live Oak County, Texas, and his ranching heritage became an early influence on his character and personality. Through his writing, he went on to become an avid spokesman of Texas and the Southwestern culture; see Tyler, *The New Handbook of Texas,* vol. 2, 662–66.

85. Franklin, interview, Aug. 22, 2003.

86. Sturcken, "Amanda Nite Burks," 4. J. Frank Dobie's book *Cow People* records the fading memories of a bygone Texas from reminiscences of the cow people themselves.

87. Dunham, "La Salle Woman."

88. "Burks," *The New Encyclopedia of Texas,* vol. 4, 2441. The Texas and Southwestern Cattle Raisers Association is the oldest and largest organization of its kind in the United States. It was formed in 1877 under the name Stock-Raisers Association of North-West Texas. Cattlemen in Oklahoma, New Mexico, and the Indian Territory were invited to join. Today it has more than seventeen thousand members, predominately in Texas, representing 2.5 million cattle; see Tyler, *The New Handbook of Texas,* vol. 6, 417–18.

89. Emerson Hough (1857–1923), like Amanda Burks, was born of pioneer stock. His father, Joseph Bond Hough, was the prototype for many of his fictional heroes and a pattern for his own life. See Carole M. Johnson, "Emerson Hough's American West," 1–2. *The Covered Wagon* chronicles the largest wagon train ever to cross the valley of the Platte River. Produced by Paramount Studios, the movie was filmed in Utah and Nevada. The film starred, among others, J. Warren Kerrigan, Louis Wilson, Ernest Torrence, and Alan Hale; see Paul Brenner, "The Covered Wagon"; also "J. M. (Monty) East, Native Texan, Won 'North of 36' for Houston; Has Been Picturesque Figure in Films." Filmed in the wake of *The Covered Wagon, North of 36* used many of the same actors and actresses. Much of the movie is devoted to "actuality" footage of a real-life cattle drive. Also produced by Paramount Studios, *North of 36* was filmed near Houston, Texas. This silent film starred, among others, Jack Holt, Louis Wilson, Noah Beery Sr., and David Dunbar; see Hal Erickson, *"North of 36"*; also Kevin Brownlow, *The War, the West, and the Wilderness,* 381–86.

90. Dunham, "La Salle Woman," 544. The "records" that Amanda Burks referred to are the personal narratives found in J. Marvin Hunter's two-volume book, *The Trail Drivers of Texas,* published in 1924.

91. Dunham, "La Salle Woman," 544.

92. Ludeman, *A History of La Salle County,* 132–33. *The Texans* starred, among others, Joan Bennett, Randolph Scott, May Robson, Walter Brennan, and Robert Cummings; see Hal Erickson, *"The Texans."* Walter Stephenson, Chisel Earnest, Jones Lansford, Buck Jenkins, Harry Sheeran, and Marcellus Talbott, all friends of the Burks family, were also extras in the movie.

93. Franklin, interview, Aug. 22, 2003.

94. William Britt (great-nephew of William and Amanda Burks), telephone interview by Lisa Neely, Aug. 20, 2003.

95. "Queen of the Trail," 128.

HARRIETT ("HATTIE) L. STANDEFER CLUCK

MRS. GEORGE WASHINGTON CLUCK

Bill Stein

O N AUGUST 24, 2000, IN THE GROWING and prosperous city of Round Rock, Texas, on the north edge of Austin in Williamson County, an eight-foot-high bronze sculpture called "The Pioneer Woman" was unveiled. It was the first completed piece of a proposed installation of eighteen to twenty pieces collectively titled "Crossing the Brushy at the Round Rock." The sculpture was meant to commemorate the cattle drives that marked the area's history. Considerably larger than life, the statue depicted Harriett L. ("Hattie") Cluck, a woman who lived in Williamson County for most of her life. Her inclusion in the work was not strictly a bow to recent impulses to include women in public monuments devoted to history. Hattie Cluck actually went up the Chisholm Trail.[1]

Cluck, the daughter of James Stuart ("Jimmie") Standefer and Caroline Randal Standefer, was born April 14, 1846, in Cherokee County, Alabama, a rural area in the northeast part of the state. Her paternal grandfather was Israel Standefer, who came to Texas in 1841, secured a land grant in 1843, represented Milam County at the convention that drafted the proposed constitution of the State of Texas in Austin in the summer of 1845, and served as Milam County's first chief justice. Shortly after Hattie's birth, her parents moved the family, which included at least eight (and possibly as many as ten) children, to Texas. Her father recorded his cattle brand in Williamson County on October 8, 1849. In or around 1851 her parents, then in their midforties, had their last-known child, another daughter, whom they named Susan. In their first few years in Texas, the Standefers apparently struggled to make a living and opened their home as an informal inn to travelers. By 1860 they owned a ranch of more than one thousand acres, on which they raised cattle, corn, and a few swine. They did not raise cotton, and they did not own slaves.[2]

The rising prominence of the Standefer family afforded them an invitation to events surrounding the inauguration of Sam Houston as governor of Texas on December 21, 1859. Hattie Standefer, then thirteen, went to the inaugural ball, wearing a small black cape that she preserved forever after. When Salado College, in neighboring Bell County, opened the following year, Hattie Standefer enrolled as

Figure 11. Harriett and George Cluck. Courtesy
of Mary Judith Griffin, Georgetown, Texas.

a student. In these same years, she attended a dance at which she met a young man named George Washington Cluck. Born December 18, 1839, he was a bit more than five years older than Hattie. Like her, he was from a large family and was one of at least eleven children of James Madison Cluck and Allie Docia Vandergriff Cluck, who moved their family from Tennessee to Texas around 1855. Sixty years later Hattie remembered "how full of fun and how nice he acted about everything" at the dance.[3]

There is no record of the date of the dance at which George Cluck met Hattie Standefer, but it seems likely that it was after the outbreak of the Civil War. If so, Cluck's father, who died on January 22, 1861, was already dead. His death and the demands of the war diminished the Cluck family's previously substantial household. Two of George's brothers, John and Joseph J., joined the Confederate Army. They enlisted in the Williamson Grays, a unit mustered into service at San Antonio on October 24, 1861, designated Company C, 7th Regiment, Texas Mounted Volunteers, and made up part of the brigade under the command of Brig. Gen. Henry Hopkins Sibley. Shortly after mobilizing, they invaded New Mexico. David F. Standefer, Hattie's older brother, was in the same company. Although George Cluck was twenty-one years old when the war broke out and apparently in good physical condition, he seems to have avoided serving in the military during the war. He was certainly in his home county on June 25, 1863, when he married Hattie Standefer. The bride had turned seventeen a little more than two months earlier. Little more than a year later, on August 5, 1864, the couple had their first child, a daughter, Allie Annie Cluck. She was followed two years later on August 14, 1866, by a son, George Emmett Cluck, and on February 16, 1869, by a second daughter, Harriet Minnie Cluck.[4]

Before the war, George Cluck had gotten into the cattle business, registering his brand in Williamson County on November 30, 1859. A decade later, nearly everyone in the county who engaged in agriculture raised cattle, and only about half of them also cultivated crops. With the free-range land still open and, consequently, no costs for grazing or water, ranchers who sold their cattle locally made handsome profits. But those who could provide beef to more distant markets made small fortunes. Cluck was surely aware that, in 1868 and 1869, Williamson County cattleman Dudley Hiram Snyder had driven large herds to Fort Union in New Mexico and Abilene, Kansas, and returned each year with considerable money. And so he began planning a cattle drive of his own.[5]

In April 1871 Cluck and another rancher rounded up their cattle and united their herds for a drive to Abilene. Besides Cluck, fourteen other men went on the drive. So did Hattie Cluck and her three children, the oldest of whom was six, the youngest barely two. That she went, and that her children went, was at least unusual and probably unprecedented. Many years later she remembered that she went along because, for her husband, "there was nothing else to do with me and

Figure 12.   The Cluck family embarking on their 1871 cattle drive.
Courtesy of Mary Judith Griffin, Georgetown, Texas.

the babies but to take us with him. He took all he had in the world with him, and we wanted to be together no matter what happened." Her granddaughter, Mary Judith Griffin, amplified the story, saying that George Cluck tried to keep his wife from going on the trip, "but she told the men to get out the wagon and put it in the line of the cattle," and when Cluck came out, "she was in the line, ready. So they went." According to Griffin, George Cluck already knew that his wife was in the early stages of her fourth pregnancy.[6]

Hattie Cluck was not an imposing physical specimen. Three descriptions of her, admittedly made when she was sixty, indicate that, if anything, she was diminutive. One person described her as "rather slender, about medium height and weight, with a strong face, features larger than ordinary, with brownish hair." Another said she "had a matronly appearance" and "was not very vigorous looking." A third characterized her as "a medium sized lady, rather spare made." Her granddaughter, who knew her at an even more advanced age, remembered that "she was small; she never weighed more than 100 pounds."[7]

The trail drive was long and arduous, but no more so than journeys commonly made by other women and children at the time. The trip was certainly no more difficult than the one she had made as a child with her family from Alabama to Texas more than twenty years earlier. While it would be too much to say that she had no role in the cattle drive, her presence was superfluous. She was not a cowboy or a cook. She shot neither intruders nor game, and she did not provide medical care for anyone who was injured or ill. She spent her days, dreary and dusty as they must have been, riding in a wagon and caring for her children. She did, however, have two harrowing experiences, which she remembered until the end of her days.

The first difficulty was a rough crossing of the rapidly running Red River. Upon seeing the strong current, Hattie and her three children abandoned the wagon in

which they had ridden so far and made the crossing on horseback, carried or conducted across by George Cluck or one of the cowhands. Other cowboys guided
the wagon across, with logs strapped to each side for buoyancy. Elsewhere on the
trail, the Clucks encountered a group of men who apparently intended to rob
them—and kill them, if necessary. Having seen the group approaching and fearing they were bent on some hostile purpose, Cluck and the fourteen other men on
the drive gathered around Hattie's wagon. There the two groups met. The out-
siders demanded some of the Cluck cattle. George refused and let it be known that
he and his men were willing to defend the herd with their guns. Hattie may have
picked up a shotgun. In any event, the would-be bandits decided against pressing
the issue and rode away.[8]

Those two incidents aside, the trip was routine, even tedious. If Hattie Cluck
had any difficulty with her children on the trail, she never alluded to it. The Clucks
arrived in Abilene with their herd virtually undiminished and quickly sold it. Because they did not yet own a ranch or a home and had taken all their children along
with them to Abilene, they had no compelling reason to return to Texas. With
Hattie now far along in her pregnancy, the Clucks decided to stay in Kansas, at
least for the time being. Their fourth child, Euell Standefer Cluck, was born there
on October 17, 1871.[9]

The Clucks may have stayed in Kansas for more than a year. Certainly they returned to Texas no earlier than the spring of 1872. While in Kansas, George bought
and sold cattle, and several lawsuits were filed against him apparently as a result of
these transactions. In the same months, local farmers, angered by the considerable
damage to crops caused by the numerous Texas cattle and hoping to end Abilene's
days as a destination for trail drives, formed the Farmers Protective Association of
Dickinson County. It may have been the increasingly hostile feelings toward Texans and their cattle or the desire to flee the civil actions against him and not simply
the increasing viability of their infant son that prompted the Clucks' departure
from Kansas. They were back in Williamson County by October 25, 1873, when
they registered a second cattle brand, this one under Hattie's name. By then, a national depression triggered by the so-called panic of 1873 had begun to severely
curtail the cattle market. If George had been contemplating a second cattle drive,
he quickly abandoned the idea.[10]

On December 3, 1873, the Clucks bought a ranch, a 329-acre tract known as the
Floyd Farm, about twelve miles southwest of Georgetown on the road between
Austin and Burnet, for $2,000. They moved to the ranch and constructed a log
cabin to house the family. Little less than a year later, on October 24, 1874, they
acquired an adjacent tract of 640 acres for only $300. Perhaps reflecting a strain on
their finances, on November 13, 1874, the Clucks sold an undivided half interest
in the 640-acre tract for $575. Four years later, on August 6, 1878, they reacquired

Figure 13.   Harriett and George Cluck with their family.
Courtesy of Mary Judith Griffin, Georgetown, Texas.

that interest at a tax sale, paying less than seven dollars for it. Finally, on April 22, 1884, the Clucks sold 100 acres for $200. Thus they were left with 869 acres, for which they had paid a total of $1,532, or $1.76 per acre—a great bargain. On their ranch, which was located on Running Brushy Creek, the Clucks prospered, raising cattle, engaging in other conventional agricultural pursuits, and selling stone from a quarry on their land.[11]

As the Clucks worked out the configuration of their ranch, the area around them grew in population and began to develop. A post office named Running Brushy, with Joel Sutton as postmaster, was installed on February 27, 1874. George Cluck prevailed on Sutton and presumably others to donate money to create a school, the Running Brushy School. Cluck himself conveyed one and a half acres on the edge of his ranch for the site and, at least for a time, allowed the teacher to live on his ranch. When Sutton moved away shortly afterward, Hattie Cluck was named to replace him as postmaster, and the post office was moved into the Cluck home. She was appointed on December 22, 1874, and served until the post office was discontinued on July 29, 1880. In 1881 the recently created Austin and Northwestern Railroad planned a track through the area, paying the Clucks $600 for a right-of-way across the ranch, the right to use stone from the ranch for construction, and the right to use water from Running Brushy Creek for its operations. The following year, the track, which connected Austin to Burnet, was constructed, and a new post office, called Brueggerhoff, was installed. On August 25, 1887, that bulky, unpopular name was changed to Cedar Park.[12]

In the same period, George and Hattie Cluck had six more children: Clarance Andy, born February 7, 1874; John Ollie, born May 30, 1876; Julia Maude, born October 7, 1878; David Albert, born May 5, 1881; Alvin Blain, born July 24, 1884; and Thomas Edison, born September 5, 1889. Hattie Cluck was forty-three years old when her last child was born. By then, her first child, Allie, was twenty-five and had been married for nearly eight years. Still, the Clucks added another child to the family, informally adopting the son of George Cluck's brother John, Joseph Matison Cluck, born February 9, 1878. Hattie Cluck's mother died on April 19, 1887; her father, October 28, 1889. Except for two lawsuits the Clucks filed in the first decade of the twentieth century against the railroad, which crossed their land, little else interrupted their regular and tranquil lives for the next thirty years. George Cluck died at five o'clock on the afternoon of August 23, 1920, a Monday. Left a widow, Hattie Cluck lived quietly, making quilts, reading popular detective stories and Westerns, writing poetry, dreaming up plots for plays, and collecting Indian arrowheads, which she excavated from a productive site on her ranch less than two hundred yards from her home.[13]

When she was in her eighties, Hattie Cluck ascended to celebrity. Rising interest in the history of the trail drives, prompted in part by the formation of the Old Time Trail Drivers Association at San Antonio on February 15, 1915, finally engulfed her in 1930. That year, and again in 1931, 1932, 1935, 1936, and 1937, she was profiled in newspaper and magazine articles and one book. On April 20, 1930, a three-paragraph article prompted by the recent celebration of her eighty-fourth birthday, "Pioneer Resident Counts Incidents of Early History," appeared in the *Waco Sunday Tribune–Herald.* Though Cluck still lived in Cedar Park, many of the members of her immediate family lived in Waco. The article mentioned her grandfather Israel Standefer and reported that, at her birthday party, she told stories about Indian warfare and the Sam Houston inaugural: "She [c]laims to have been the first white woman to go over the trail, made only three days behind Custer and his soldiers, who were massacred by Indians."[14]

The confused attempt to associate Cluck's life with Custer's Last Stand, which occurred five years after she made her trail drive, was modified by Lorraine Barnes in her considerably longer article in the *Austin Statesman,* "Aged Central Texas Woman, Once a Fighter of Indians, Reads Tales of Adventure." Barnes informed her readers that, on their trail drive, the Clucks came across ashes that were "mute testimony" that, one day earlier, in what was "clearly a forerunner of the famous Custer massacre which took place a few years later," Indians had attacked some travelers and burned a wagon. Barnes had been drawn to Hattie Cluck's story by a recent celebration of her birthday and obviously interviewed Cluck. She more definitely stated that Cluck was "the first white woman to ride up the famous old Chisholm Trail" but indicated that Hattie was not entirely sure when the drive occurred. Cluck was pictured holding a nineteenth-century rifle. In Barnes's account, when the Clucks were on the trail, they had a skirmish with a group of Indians. She attributed a quote to Hattie that describes her role in the skirmish: "I had to load the guns for the men and keep handing them out."[15]

On October 9, 1932, the *Austin Sunday American–Statesman* published a longer article about Cluck, this one written by Irma Brown Cardiff, "Cedar Park Woman Tells of Adventures of Early Texas Days." Cardiff interviewed Cluck and related, for the first time, the stories of Cluck's meeting with her future husband and of the difficult crossing of the Red River. She also provided some details about the family's time in Abilene and Cluck's activities since her husband died. The article mentions Indians, but, in Cardiff's account, the bandits who accosted the Clucks on the trail were white men, and no gunfight ensued. Happily, at this point, George Armstrong Custer drops out of the story. Cardiff hedges a bit on the question of Cluck's primacy on the trail, opening her piece with "If ever a white woman took the Chisholm Trail from Texas to Kansas before she did, 86-year-old Mrs. Harriett Cluck said she never had heard of it."[16]

Having been interviewed three times in three years, Hattie Cluck was left alone by reporters and historians for the next three. Even so, another short account of her life appeared in print in 1935. This one, "She Was a Pioneer," was produced by history writer Alfred E. Menn and published in the semimonthly magazine *Farm and Ranch*. Menn extracted his information from the Cardiff article and apparently no other source. Perhaps he intended to interview Cluck but could not find her. Between 1933 and 1936 she left her home of at least sixty years and moved in with her daughter Julia Maude Friedsam, who lived in Waco.[17]

The state's centennial year, 1936, saw the publication of two more pieces on Cluck, each written by Thomas Ulvan Taylor, long-time dean of the department of engineering at the University of Texas–Austin and an avocational historian. One of Taylor's pieces, "The Stork Rides the Chisholm Trail," appeared in the magazine *Frontier Times;* the other, "The Stork Travels the Chisholm Trail," is contained in a book produced by *Frontier Times.* Taylor, who surely made contact with Hattie, presented her story in a sensationalized manner that now seems comical. In Taylor's accounts, the Clucks encountered both white bandits and Indians. Hattie loaded guns for the cowboys, who were so "nervous and white under the gills" that she offered to stand and fight in their place if, as he had her say, "'any of you boys are afraid to fight.'" At the Red River, Hattie Cluck is similarly dauntless, planning the crossing for the timid men in the outfit. As one can tell by his titles, Taylor devoted considerable attention to Cluck's pregnancy, which had not been mentioned by previous writers. In both pieces he stated definitely that Cluck was "the first white woman" to participate in a cattle drive along the Chisholm Trail and mentioned a rifle and a fiddle owned by the family. In the magazine article, he greatly amplified the story of how the Clucks met at a dance and added some information about the fates of the three youngsters who went on the trail drive. The book included photographs of the three children, taken when they were adults, and of George and Hattie. Taylor's works, published in readily available and regularly accessed sources, brought Cluck enduring prominence.[18]

On March 1, 1937, Hattie Cluck was visited by James Britton Buchanan Boone Cranfill. Besides being a leader in the Baptist church in Texas in the late nineteenth and early twentieth centuries, as well as the nominee of the Prohibition Party for U.S. vice president in 1892, Cranfill was a journalist. More than a month later, he published another treatment of Hattie Cluck's life, "Mind My Babies and I'll Fight These Rustlers; That's Cry of Texas Woman on Chisholm Trail," in a Dallas newspaper. Cranfill, who stated that Cluck was "the first Texas woman to ride up the trail," described her as a bronco-busting crack shot, compared her courage to that of Joan of Arc, declared her to be intellectually brilliant, described her bearing and appearance as regal, and called her "the queen of the Chisholm Trail." In Cranfill's account, the Clucks did not meet Indians, only the white bandits. At that encounter, however, Cranfill had Hattie playing her most central role, holding a shotgun and described by her husband as "one of the best shots that ever came out of Texas." Here again she engineered the hazardous crossing of the Red River. Building on Taylor's mention of a fiddle, Cranfill added a fresh twist, an anecdote involving poker, night watches, and a Cluck cowboy who was an accomplished musician, a man he calls Buchanan Boone. It can only be regarded as suspicious that the cowboy-fiddler bore Cranfill's seldom-used third and fourth given names.[19]

Hattie Cluck died at her daughter's home in Waco, closely attended by her granddaughter, Mary Judith Friedsam, on March 2, 1938, at the age of ninety-two. She had outlived all three of the children who went on the trail drive with her nearly sixty-seven years earlier. Her body was returned to Williamson County, and, the day after she died, she was buried next to her husband in the Cedar Park Cemetery. Her obituary, on page 5 of the March 4, 1938, issue of the *Williamson County Sun,* did not mention the cattle drive. She continued to crop up in historical writing.[20] In 1989 Thompson's research on the Cluck family led to the erection of a state historical marker for the Cedar Park Cemetery.[21]

Near the end of her long life, Hattie Cluck, who until then must have regarded herself as rather commonplace, saw herself depicted as a frontier heroine by accomplished historians and writers in increasingly substantial media. Along the way, her biographers, who evidently believed that women were more historically interesting if at some point in their lives they had acted like men, transformed her from a rather passive participant in a half-forgotten trail drive into a bold, shotgun-toting, decision maker on an Old West adventure. Whether she was the first white woman to go up the Chisholm Trail or not is of little consequence. If she was, as is certainly possible, it was mere happenstance. She made no conscious effort to overcome any perceived barriers, and nothing she did induced other women to follow her example. Except for her trip up the Chisholm Trail with a cattle drive, she led a conventional life. If she had not made that journey, other women certainly would have. However, before Hattie Cluck, it seems, no woman ever had.[22]

NOTES

1. Julie Allison, "Preserving Spirit of Chisholm Trail: Pioneer Woman Remembered by Family and Community"; Round Rock, Texas, city council minutes, May 11, 2000; Denise Williams, "Generous Gifts Ring in the New Year for Chamber." The sculpture is the work of Jim Thomas. Commissioned by William H. Peckham, owner of a Round Rock travel agency, the statue was initially installed in front of the travel agency's building. Though Peckham heeded the suggestion of local historian Karen Ruth Thompson to model the sculpture on Cluck and even though many photographs of Cluck exist, he stipulated that it be made to look like his wife, Mary Sparks Peckham.

2. Cluck Family Bible Records; "Mrs. Harriett Cluck Dead"; Israel Standefer Bible records; *Biographical Directory of the Texan Conventions and Congresses 1832–1845,* 175; *Journals of the Convention Assembled at the City of Austin on the Fourth of July, 1845,* for the Purpose of Framing a Constitution for the State of Texas, 378; Williamson County, Texas, *Mark and Brand Records,* vol. 1, 206; U.S. Bureau of the Census, 1850, schedules 1 and 2, Williamson County, Tex.; U.S. Bureau of the Census, 1860, schedules 1, 2, and 4, Williamson County, Tex.; U.S. Bureau of the Census, 1870, schedule 3, Williamson County, Tex.; Noah Smithwick, *The Evolution of a State, or Recollections of Old Texas Days,* 291–92. In all cases except that of Hattie's father (where the Standefer family Bible is used), the spellings of the names of the Cluck family used herein are those given in the Cluck family Bible. The Cluck Bible calls Hattie's father James Stewart Standefer. Smithwick reports that Standefer bought "slaves, investing all his savings thus, only a short time before the war." Here his memory failed him, however. Neither the 1860 census nor the Williamson County tax rolls from the Civil War period indicate that Standefer owned slaves; see U.S. Bureau of the Census, 1860, schedule 2, Williamson County, Tex.; Williamson County tax rolls, 1860, 1861, 1862, 1863, 1864, 1865.

The Standefer children listed on the 1850 census are John B., seventeen; Elizabeth, fourteen; Mary A., eleven; Benjamin, eleven; David, nine; Jemima, eight; Julia A., six; and Harriett, four. The household included six other people as well, two of whom seemingly were also the children of James S. and Caroline Standefer: twenty-two-year-old William R. Standefer and sixteen-year-old Naomi (spelled this way in the census) J. Champion. The latter was the wife of John Champion, who was also a member of the household. The death date of Naomia (spelled this way in the family Bible) Jane Champion, Dec. 24, 1862, is recorded in the Cluck family Bible. Her son, Nathan D. Champion, later went to Wyoming, where he was killed in a famous standoff during the celebrated Johnson County war on Apr. 9, 1892; see Howard R. Lamar, ed., *The New Encyclopedia of the American West,* 577–79. The Standefers of Williamson County, Texas, are often confused with another family named Standefer or Standifer, which is associated with Bastrop County; see, for instance, John Holland Jenkins, ed., *Recollections of Early Texas: The Memoirs of John Holland Jenkins,* 267, and the latest edition of Smithwick's *Evolution of a State,* 264. Smithwick mentions "Jimmie Standefer" as his "nearest neighbor," clear evidence that the man to whom he is referring is James Standefer of Williamson County, for their households appear next to each other on the 1850 census of Williamson County.

3. *Waco Sunday Tribune–Herald,* Apr. 20, 1930; *Round Rock Leader,* June 12, 2000; Thomas Ulvan Taylor, "The Stork Rides the Chisholm Trail," 52; *Austin Sunday American–Statesman,* Oct. 9, 1932; U.S. Bureau of the Census, 1860, schedule 1, Williamson County, Tex.; Williamson County death records, book 2, 11–12. The surviving records of Salado College do not confirm that Hattie Standefer was a student; see Earl Vandale Collection, Center for American History, University of Texas–Austin. The date the Cluck family moved to Texas is inferred from the birthplaces of their children. The 1860 census reports that their eight-year-old daughter Angeline was born in Tennessee, and their five-year-old daughter Sallie in Texas. For an account of Hattie's encounter with George Cluck at the dance, which differs considerably from that in the *Austin Sunday American–Statesman,* Oct. 9, 1932, see Taylor, "The Stork Rides the Chisholm Trail," 51.

4. Cluck Family Bible records, Cluck Family file; *Compiled Service Records of Confederate Soldiers Who Served in Organizations from the State of Texas;* Martin Hardwick Hall, *The Confederate Army of New Mexico,* 238. The Williamson County company saw little or no action during the New Mexico campaign. Neither David F. Standefer nor either of the Clucks were wounded or killed during the fighting, though Joseph J. Cluck was captured at an engagement at Donaldsville, Louisiana, on June 28, 1863. A man named Riley J. Cluck also served in the Williamson Grays during the war, but no evidence has been discovered that he had any relationship to George W. Cluck.

5. *Mark and Brand Records,* Williamson County, vol. 1, 132; *Texas Almanac for 1871, and Emigrant's Guide to Texas,* 159; John Marvin Hunter, comp. and ed., *The Trail Drivers of Texas* (1925), 724–26.

6. *Austin Sunday American–Statesman,* Oct. 9, 1932, including first quote; *Round Rock Leader,* June 12, 2000, second quote. Thomas Ulvan Taylor states that the second herd on the Cluck drive belonged to Dudley H. Snyder; see Thomas Ulvan Taylor, *The Chisholm Trail and Other Routes,* 158. However, though it is of course possible that two herds with different destinations set out together, it has been elsewhere reported that Snyder took a herd to Wyoming in 1871 and, for that matter, in 1872 and 1873; see Hunter, *Trail Drivers of Texas,* 726. Snyder's papers, part of the collections of the University of Texas, shed no light on this matter; see Dudley Hiram Snyder Papers.

7. Statements of John G. Townes, James A. French, and J. B. Martin in Williamson County District Court records, civil cause file 5818/5819: *George W. Cluck v. Houston and Texas Central Railroad Company; Round Rock Leader,* June 12, 2002.

8. *Austin Statesman,* Apr. 15, 1931; *Austin Sunday American–Statesman,* Oct. 9, 1932. Hattie's role with guns or rifles on the trail drive became significantly glorified as the years passed.

9. *Austin Sunday American–Statesman,* Oct. 9, 1932; Cluck Family Bible, Cluck Family file. It is the birth of Euell Cluck that confirms that the family made the trail drive in 1871. When Hattie Cluck was interviewed in 1931, she did not seem quite sure of the year, as the article states that "It must have been in '71, she reckons." The 1880 census confirms that Euell Cluck was born in Kansas; see U.S. Bureau of the Census, 1880, schedule 1, Williamson County, Tex.

10. *Austin Sunday American–Statesman,* Oct. 9, 1932; Taylor, "The Stork Rides the Chisholm Trail," 53; Lamar, ed., *The New Encyclopedia of the American West,* 183; *Mark and Brand Records,* Williamson County, vol. 1, 48. Unhappily, neither official documents of the lawsuits, which were allegedly filed against George Cluck in Kansas, nor indeed any other official records of the Cluck family's activities have survived. According to Jeff Sheets, director of the Dickinson County (Kansas) Heritage Society, the county's records were destroyed by a fire in 1882. Sheets graciously searched through other sources, including local newspapers, but found no mention of the Clucks.

11. Deed records, Williamson County, book 14, 451; book 15, 536; book 18, 643; book 33, 504; book 34, 145; Williamson County District Court records, civil case file 5405: *George W. Cluck v. Houston and Texas Central Railroad Company; Austin Statesman,* Apr. 15, 1931; *Austin Sunday American–Statesman,* Oct. 9, 1932.

12. Deed records, Williamson County, book 24, 36; book 27, 382; Williamson County District Court records, civil cause file 1456: *Joel Sutton v. George W. Cluck;* U.S. Bureau of the Census, 1880, schedule 1, Williamson County, Tex.; Jim Wheat, comp., *Postmasters and Post Offices of Texas, 1846–1930,* 200, 264, 1297; *Austin Statesman,* Apr. 15, 1931; Charles P. Zlatkovich, *Texas Railroads: A Record of Construction and Abandonment,* 61. In his lawsuit, Sutton stipulated that he had given ten dollars for the school, contingent on a promise by Cluck that his money would be refunded if he left the area within a year; since Sutton had left less than a year later, Cluck should be made to keep the promise.

13. Cluck Family Bible, Cluck Family file; Taylor, "The Stork Rides the Chisholm Trail," 55; *Waco Sunday Tribune–Herald,* Apr. 20, 1930; *Austin Statesman,* Apr. 15, 1931; *Austin Sunday American–Statesman,* Oct. 9, 1932; Williamson County District Court records: civil case file 5404: *George W. and Harriett L. Cluck v. Houston and Texas Central Railroad;* also civil case file 5818/5819: *George W. Cluck v. Houston and Texas Central Railroad.* In the first lawsuit, the Clucks contended that the railroad had illegally used water from their ranch; in the second, that they were improperly removed from a passenger train.

14. Hunter, *Trail Drivers of Texas,* 4; *Waco Sunday Tribune–Herald,* Apr. 20, 1930.

15. *Austin Statesman,* Apr. 15, 1931. In the article, the statement that Cluck was the "first white woman" to go up the trail is somewhat ambiguous since it is listed as one of "the distinctions claimed" by Cluck. The caption of the photograph, however, makes the explicit claim.

16. *Austin Sunday American–Statesman,* Oct. 9, 1932. The same picture of Cluck and the rifle, which was published in the *Austin Statesman* in 1931, accompanies the Cardiff article.

17. Alfred E. Menn, "She Was a Pioneer," 28.

18. Taylor, "The Stork Rides the Chisholm Trail," 51–55; Taylor, *The Chisholm Trail and Other Routes,* 157–62; Ron Tyler, ed., *The New Handbook of Texas,* vol. 6, 221. The quoted version of the remark attributed to Hattie is taken from Taylor's book; in the magazine article, the word "boys" is omitted. Taylor apparently wrote each of his pieces on Cluck in August 1936 since he explicitly states this in the *Frontier Times* article. In the book, he reports that Cluck was "four score and ten years and four months," which would be her correct age in August 1936.

19. *Dallas Morning News,* Apr. 25, 1937; Harry Leon McBeth, *Texas Baptists: A Sesquicentennial History,* 93; Joseph Nathan Kane, *Facts about the Presidents,* 147. The Center for American History, University of Texas–Austin has collections of documents for both J. B. Cranfill

and Thomas Ulvan Taylor, but neither collection contains any material about Hattie or their work on her.

20. See, for instance, Thomas Ulvan Taylor's 1939 article "An Airplane Trip over the Chisholm Trail"; Wayne Gard's 1954 book, *The Chisholm Trail;* Clara Stearns Scarbrough's 1973 volume, *Land of Good Water: Takachue Pouetsu, A Williamson County, Texas, History;* Lorena Eillyer Fox's 1981 article "Hattie Standefer Cluck"; and Karen Ruth Thompson's book from 2000, *Historical Williamson County, Texas: A Pictorial History, 1848–2000.*

21. *Williamson County Sun,* Mar. 4, 1938; *Round Rock Leader,* June 12, 2002; Taylor, "The Stork Rides the Chisholm Trail," 55; Taylor, "An Airplane Trip over the Chisholm Trail," 467, 469; Gard, *The Chisholm Trail,* 155–56; Scarbrough, *Land of Good Water,* 202–203; Fox, "Hattie Standefer Cluck," 43–44; Thompson, *Historical Williamson County, Texas,* 138. It is some measure of her fame to note that Hattie was mentioned by Anderson Jones, a former slave, who was interviewed on Feb. 11, 1941, as part of the slave narrative project of the Federal Writers' Project of the Works Progress Administration; see George P. Rawick, ed., *The American Slave: A Composite Autobiography,* Supplement Series 2, vol. 6, 2069.

22. It seems likely that there were two women on the Chisholm Trail in 1871, Amanda Burks and Hattie Cluck, and thus—until future researchers can dispute this claim—they must share the honor as the first white women to go up the trail.

Mary ("Molly) Catherine Dunn Bugbee

MRS. THOMAS SHERMAN BUGBEE

Allan O. Kownslar

ONE AFTERNOON IN JULY OF 1871, eighteen-year-old Mary ("Molly") Catherine Dunn was sweeping the yard at her family's home when a thirty-year-old cowboy named Thomas Sherman Bugbee rode up. He had come to borrow an axe. The two talked for a while and discovered a common interest in riding horses. Thomas asked Molly whether he could take her riding sometime, and she accepted his offer. Unable to think of a way to prolong the conversation, the smitten Thomas rode back to his nearby cattle herd, completely oblivious to the fact that he had forgotten to ask about borrowing an axe. This was the beginning of a one-year courtship and a fifty-three-year marriage between the couple that later built cattle empires in Kansas, Oklahoma, and Texas.

Mary Catherine Dunn was of English and Irish ancestry. Her mother, "Mitty" Nancy Catherine Straughn, of English descent, married Thomas Dunn, an Irish merchant. Their home was in Leon, West Virginia, where Molly was born on December 4, 1852. Her father died when Molly was a young girl, and Mitty remarried to Henry Thompson, a salt maker. The family then moved to Gallipolis, Ohio, and later to Racine, Ohio, where Molly apprenticed for two summers to a milliner. She developed an allergy to the sulfur used in cleaning hats and had to quit her formal schooling but by then was quite skilled in reading, writing, and mathematics. The Thompsons moved again, this time settling in West Columbia, Ohio, before making their last home in Peace (now Sterling), Kansas. It was there Molly first met Thomas Sherman Bugbee.[1]

The shy cowboy came from a long, distinguished line of New Englanders. His maternal ancestors made him a ninth-generation descendant of Richard Warren, a signer of the 1620 Mayflower Compact. Seven generations of his ancestors from that line lived in Massachusetts until Bugbee's maternal grandparents, Daniel Sherman (1785–1864) and Mary Greenleaf (1785–1830), moved to Perry, Maine. There they had a daughter, Hannah, born April 9, 1813, who, twenty years later in the local Congregation Church, married John Brewer Bugbee, a farmer four years older than she. Their second son was Thomas Sherman Bugbee, born January 18, 1841,

Figure 14. Molly and Thomas Bugbee with family. Courtesy
of the Panhandle-Plains Historical Museum, Canyon, Texas.

in Perry. Contrary to what some authors have claimed, Thomas was not the great-grandson of Roger Sherman, a signer of the Declaration of Independence. Instead, he was the great-grandson of Thomas Sherman, who married Betsy Keith. Their son was the Daniel Sherman who married Mary Greenleaf, and it was their daughter, Hannah Sherman, who married John Brewer Bugbee, the union that resulted in our cowboy.[2]

With the beginning of the Civil War in 1861, the three sons of Hannah and John Brewer Bugbee enlisted to fight for the Union. Thomas, the middle son, enlisted on October 4, 1861, in the 10th Maine Infantry but soon transferred to the 29th Maine Infantry, where he was honorably discharged on October 14, 1864.[3]

Once back in Maine, Bugbee decided his future lay west of the Mississippi River. With his brother George, he set out for Saint Joseph, Missouri. Once there, the two men worked their way toward Idaho by driving ox teams in a train of ninety wagons. Thomas and George left the wagon train at Salt Lake City and made the five-hundred-mile journey to Silver City, Idaho, by horseback, traveling only at night to avoid encounters with Indians. Once in Silver City, George decided to go on to California, and Thomas began a two-year stint mining gold. He managed to save enough money to purchase a team of oxen and a wagon for hauling lumber to the miners. He made about $20 a day and, by living frugally, saved about $3,500.[4]

Determined to better himself financially, Thomas, along with two friends, Cornelius Shea and George Miller, conceived the idea of buying cheap cattle at $11 a head in Texas and driving them to Idaho, where they were selling for $45. The three friends set out for Texas and arrived in Fort Worth in January of 1869. This marked the beginning of Bugbee's venture into the cattle business.

Making several profitable cattle drives from Texas to Idaho, Thomas first met Mary Catherine Dunn in Kansas in July 1871. At the time, he had with him eight other men and 650 head of cattle. Their courtship included rides on the prairie. According to Helen Francis Bugbee:

[Thomas] ordered a fine saddle all the way from California—for a beautiful, big black horse and he had sent for a new suit of clothes for himself. So he could appear before the rosy-cheeked maiden (Mama).

The saddle and clothes happened to come while Tom was away from camp, so his mischievous cousin Henry Bugbee dressed up in the suit, put the saddle on the grand black horse, and called on the pretty little girl. She knew to whom the new luxuries belonged but neither mentioned it, and later she welcomed her lover in his new glory just as if she had never seen them before. On her 19th birthday, Dec. 4, 1871, her lover proposed and she accepted. He presented her with a gold pen with an ebony handle while they were on a horseback ride.

In the spring he had to move his herd about thirty five miles beyond the settlement for grass. On August 13, 1872, this lover came to claim his bride and they were married on this date at Peace (Sterling), Kansas, by a justice of peace in the first house built in the settlement. The guests at the wedding were the bride's mother, Miss Mitty Thompson, Mr. Ninde and Miss Kate Ninde. The bride wore a gray poplin dress. She had no trousseau. She had sent to the city for a gray face veil and a pair of gloves, and these did not arrive until after the wedding. The wedding gifts were a watermelon and a cantaloupe. After the wedding the couple drove forty-five miles in a buggy to Great Bend, Kansas, where they were to join the herd of cattle, which the groom had started to drive to Colorado. Mama stayed at the Great Bend Hotel for a week while Daddy had to go back after some horses that had strayed away.

With five hired men and Daddy, this little bride drove seven hundred and fifty five cattle to western Kansas. When they started on the trail Mama wouldn't ride in the chuck wagon with dirty Frank the cook so she made Daddy ride in the wagon with her and Frank ride the horse. Mama had her trials trying to cross the plains with her cowboy husband. On the first day out from Great Bend she lost her sunbonnet, which had been tied to the wagon bows, so in the heat of the day they had to go back and find her bonnet. No sooner had they found the bonnet than she caused another delay. Tired out, she sat on the sack of flour, and the sack burst and the flour spilled. This detained the wagon till it was dark, so they made camp. So glad to reach camp and tired from her long ride, she jumped to the ground as soon as the wagon stopped. But alas! More trouble. The cattle weren't accustomed to women in light dresses jumping from wagons, so they stampeded.

Sleeping on the ground out of doors was a new experience for Mama. In order to keep away from the cattle Mama and Daddy made their bed under the wagon. The day had been very hot and just as they had settled for the night mama felt something drip, drip, drip, on her head. She investigated and found the bacon had become so hot that it had turned to grease; this was dripping on her head. In the morning she had a shampoo in the river and the next night they slept with their heads at the other end of the wagon. Imagine her horror when she again felt something dripping on her hair—this time it was the molasses keg that was leaking. Both times Daddy escaped unmolested.

After a long hard drive they arrived at Colorado only to find that the land Daddy wanted [had been] taken by another. So they went back to Kansas. Mama was driving the wagon alone while Daddy was counting the cattle. He told her to drive back to the place where she had mended his pants. She remembered mending the trousers but had promptly forgotten what part of the trail they had camped on. Not wishing to display her forgetfulness, she started driving back. She didn't know where. Suddenly she came across a rattlesnake in the road so she entertained herself for a while throwing chunks of wood out of the wagon at it. Having exhausted the wood supply and the snake very much alive, she was in a ponder. The snake wouldn't let her get the wood, and she hated to go on without it. Daddy seeing that the wagon had stopped hastened up to see what the trouble was. He killed the snake, reloaded the wood and started her off again. By this time he was able to go on ahead and stop where he wished to camp. Mama followed and never let on that she had forgotten where he had wanted her to go.

This trip lasted from August 20 till Sept last [i.e., last day of September] when they settled about four and one half miles from Larkin Station, Kansas [extreme western Kansas], here they dug out the side of a hill and with rocks built them a one room house. Later they added another room. On August 19, 1873, their eldest child was born, Ethel Hannah. Mama's mother was staying with the family at the time of the baby's birth. Daddy and Mama lived in this section for almost four years. They had to move across the river on account of the prairie fires.

In the fall of 1874 they moved to Syracuse, Kansas, where their second child, Thomas Everett, was born on August 30, 1875. When he was but an infant and Mama was alone with him and Ethel, a terrific waterspout marooned them in their home. Mama and the children were forced to get in the garret [loft] and the water flooded the house until workmen had to get them out. This little house was made up of seven houses [rooms]. . . . Grandmother Thompson returned to Ohio and [because they feared trouble with Indians] the Bugbees moved to Texas in October 1876.

They drove a herd of cattle and got lost on the way [they also lost about half of the herd and many of their belongings in the flooded Cimarron River]. Later, for three days they were without water [after some of the remaining cattle panicked and broke both water barrels tied to one of the wagons]. This trip took them from October 9 to November 26.[5]

At the beginning of their cattle drive to Texas, Molly had placed a wooden door in one of the two freight wagons. She wanted a door rather than a buffalo hide for an entrance to their new Texas home. Thomas objected, saying its weight and size would take the place of needed supplies in the wagons, so he tossed the door aside. After he left, Molly quietly placed the door in another wagon. Later he discovered the door and again discarded it. Undeterred, Molly had one of the trail hands secretly tie the door underneath a wagon so that Thomas would not spot it again.[6]

In late November the Bugbees managed to reach the Canadian River, and, after finding their remaining cattle, which had again stampeded, they settled near Adobe Walls in Hutchinson County, Texas. There they built a large dugout that was to be their home for several years. If Molly's treasured door was not among the items lost in the Cimarron River, we can assume that it became part of the dugout. Aside from that possible luxury, the shelter had a back wall dug into the earth. Pickets daubed with mud formed the front. The rest was made up of a dirt roof with wooden supports and tow sacking used to cover the dirt ceiling, dirt-packed floors covered with buffalo hides for carpet, and windows of thin deerskin over the openings. The walls were whitewashed by baking gyprock, crushing it, and mixing the particles with water to form a sort of plaster. Lighting, heating, and water for household use always entailed much work.[7]

The dugout home served as headquarters for the Bugbees' Quarter Circle T Ranch, the second oldest ranch in the Texas Panhandle. Molly Bugbee also had the dubious distinction of being the second Anglo female to settle in the area (Ellen O'Loughlin was the first; she had come with her husband, Tom, and two sons to Wheeler County in 1875). Molly's other female neighbor, seventy-five miles away, was Mary Ann Goodnight, wife of Charles Goodnight, on the JA Ranch. She arrived in the area a year later, along with Cornelia Adair, a visiting partner at the ranch.[8]

At the time, luxuries in that area of Texas were nonexistent. For needed supplies, Thomas Bugbee had to make a two-hundred-mile, ten-day round-trip by wagon to Dodge City, Kansas. When merchandise stores began to appear in the Texas Panhandle, they might as well have displayed a "for men only'" sign since

there was nothing in stock that a woman might want to buy. No frontier mercantile store sold women's hats, so women made their own bonnets, washing and iron-
ing them when necessary. Washing clothes in itself was an ordeal, for dirt walls and
floors were omnipresent on the High Plains, and the dirt-laden wind was a dreaded
and never-ceasing presence. Boiling clothes in lye soap failed to remove the dingy
hue caused by the silty waters of the nearby ponds and springs, and it was not until wells were drilled and windmills pumped water from deeper strata that a bright
wash hung from the clothesline.[9]

Refusing to be defeated by the isolation or the harsh physical environment of
the plains, Molly, again joined by her mother, "sewed, cooked, canned dried fruit
from the riverbanks, milked, churned, made preserves, and built a little pen to
keep chickens for a change occasionally from beef. They extended the warmest
hospitality to cowboy or traveler, and the Bugbee dugout became a favorite stop
for excellent food, careful attention, and a jovial atmosphere."[10]

According to Helen Francis, "Molly Bugbee, who was a fine rifle shot, could
stand in her door and kill buffalo as they grazed near or came thundering by. They
were so numerous that they were exceedingly troublesome, and for two years men
were regularly hired to drive buffalo off the range." Helen added that, a few years
later, "at a point on the north side of the Canadian River, some Portuguese stone
masons who happened to be some of the 'hands,' with Mrs. Bugbee's help, built
the 'Stone House.' It had five rooms and was comfortable and adequate. Hooked
rugs made by Molly from worn-out red flannel underwear covered the floors. The
third child, Ruby, was born there on April 10, 1879 [Ruby died from the bite of a
rabid skunk in 1888]. We can little realize the hours of anxiety for Tom and Molly
both—babies arriving in a world where the nearest doctor was seventy-five miles
away and even helpful neighbors a good two days journey."[11]

Nevertheless, Molly managed while Thomas gradually built up the cattle herd.
In 1881 he received an offer of $175,000 for his cattle. While Thomas favored sell-
ing the herd, Molly convinced him to wait for a better offer. A year later, and after
a storm destroyed Molly's spring-fed milk house and devastated much of the surrounding landscape, she told Thomas it was time to sell the cattle. He then sold
their twelve thousand head of Quarter Circle T cattle for $350,000 to the Hansford
Cattle Company. The sale completed, the family made a trip to California to visit
Thomas's brother George, then in the sugar business, and his sister, Mary. It was
the first of many trips the Bugbees took during their marriage; later destinations
included Alaska, Hawaii, China, Japan, the Philippines, and South America.[12]

Now eager to live in a more populous area, the Bugbees built a large home surrounded by 10 acres of fruit trees outside Kansas City. They also operated an 800-
acre farm in Bonner Springs, Kansas, and went into partnership with William
States on a 6,000-acre cattle ranch near Dodge City, Kansas.[13]

Five children were born to Thomas and Molly during the fifteen years they spent in their Kansas City home: Mary Bliss (1883), Kate Alymer (1886), Stella (1889), John Sherman (1891), and Helen Francis (1895). Thomas and Molly also had six other children—nephews and nieces—living with them while the youngsters received their formal education.[14]

Between 1882 and 1897 Thomas Bugbee also became involved with numerous other ranching and farming ventures. One was a partnership with Orville Howell Nelson of the Shoe Bar Ranch in Briscoe, Hall, and Donley counties, Texas. Bugbee bought Nelson's share of the Shoe Bar in 1886 and, with L. C. Coleman, formed the Bugbee-Coleman Cattle Company. They expanded the Shoe Bar to 450,000 acres, leasing out 340,000 acres of the total spread.[15] Another of Bugbee's business ventures was the Charles W. Word–Thomas Bugbee Cattle Company, with 225,000 acres of land that they leased at two cents an acre in the Cheyenne-Arapaho country of Indian Territory.[16]

When Coleman died in 1894, Bugbee sold his interests in the Shoe Bar to A. J. Snyder and in 1895 did the same with the 54,000-acre 69 Ranch in Knox County, Texas. Two years later he procured the twenty-section T5 Ranch in Donley, Hall, and Armstrong counties in Texas, to which he added twenty-five sections sold by the Goodnight Ranch in 1899; the combined acquisition was called the T5 Ranch. These would be Bugbee's final ventures in the cattle business.[17]

In 1897, with Tom away from home on cattle business much of the time, Molly decided the family should leave the Kansas City residence and live closer to his work in Texas. She sent Tom a telegram, which had to be delivered to him by horseback messenger in the Panhandle. This message said simply, "Get us a house. Family coming to Texas."

Molly took a collapsible house to augment the three rooms of the only dwelling available in Clarendon, Texas. She packed up her five young children and journeyed to meet her husband. For some time the Bugbee home was so crowded that the piano had to sit on the front porch, but in 1898 the big house on Bugbee Hill was built and became Thomas and Molly's last residence.[18]

As Molly raised the family and tended the home, Thomas increased his involvement in other professional and civic activities. In 1912 the Bugbees converted the T5 Ranch to a family corporation, the Bugbee Live Stock and Land Company, with Thomas Jr. as its manager. When he died a short five years later, in 1917, the family sold its cattle but kept the property, and John Sherman, the youngest son, took over as manager.[19] Helen Francis remembered that the death of her eldest brother was a tragedy for the entire family, especially her father. He said that he was living then on "borrowed time," in "the sense that the family circle was broken."[20]

After a long life of eighty-five years, Thomas Sherman Bugbee died of a stroke at his Clarendon home on October 18, 1925. In his will Bugbee left $1,000 to a half-sister, Sarah W. Kane. He further directed that "the residue of my estate, both real and personal, shall be divided share and share alike between my children who are living at my death, and in the event that any of my said children shall die before my death and leave child or children of their own, then the share of such of my said children shall descend to their children. It is my will and desire that no more of my said estate shall be sold than is necessary to pay expenses and the benefits herein made, and that my property be kept together as long as practical and that my wife and children shall share the revenue and benefits of the same so long as it may be done without injury to the estate."[21] The executors of his estate were Molly; John Sherman, his youngest son; and W. H. Patrick, his son-in-law. Since Texas was a community property state, Molly, aside from being one of his executors, owned half of the Bugbee estate.[22]

Molly Bugbee outlived her husband by a little more than three years, dying at age seventy-six on December 19, 1928. A newspaper account of her death noted that she "was extremely active to a few years past, but had been troubled to some extent with rheumatism and had not left her home for any great length of time recently. A fall received some years past further added to her infirmities and kept her more closely at home than was ordinary for the past two years. She was alone in her home at the time of her death and was found by her youngest son, John Sherman Bugbee, when he returned from his day's work in the late afternoon."[23]

Besides her son and daughters, Molly Bugbee's survivors included fifteen grandchildren. L. C. Swan, rector of the local Episcopal church, conducted the final rites at the Bugbee home before Molly was interred next to her husband in the Bugbee mausoleum at the Clarendon Citizens' Cemetery.[24] Molly Bugbee left no will, and Donley County did not record a death certificate for her.[25] It is possible she had by then turned over her holdings to the estate for her son John Sherman to administer, but more likely, according to Texas law, her surviving children inherited all that she owned.

Perhaps the best tribute to Molly and her husband is the one written by their daughter Helen Francis: "To rise from the dugout to the big house on the hill, or from the covered wagon following the trail of a few straggling cattle to the ownership of teeming acres and herds numbered by the thousand head is a feat worthy to adorn a tale; but we honor Tom and Molly Bugbee and all other pioneers like them, not only for their daring and energy, which extended the boundaries and developed the resources of a great nation but also for those other qualities of integrity, big-heartedness, and firm upright nobility of character—fundamental ideals for any people who desire to endure."[26]

NOTES

1. Helen Francis Bugbee, "Story of Thomas Sherman Bugbee and Mary Catherine Dunn Bugbee." Since the 1915 manuscript by Helen Francis Bugbee, often noted in this chapter, was

a first draft intended only for family members, it has been edited for punctuation and typographical errors. Scholars are extremely fortunate in that Helen Francis Bugbee, who later married H. G. Officer in 1915, recorded a detailed history of her parents.

2. Peggy M. Baker, "A Woman of Valor: Elizabeth Warren of Plymouth Colony"; Annie Arnoux Haxton, *Signers of the Mayflower Compact*, 32; Linda Ashley, letter to Allan Kownslar, June 5, 2003; Bugbee, "Story of Thomas Sherman Bugbee and Mary Catherine Dunn Bugbee"; cemetery records, Perry, Maine; Frederick Wallace Pyne, *Descendants of the Signers of the Declaration of Independence: The New England States*, 2d ed., vol. 1, 395–401; Kip Sperry, "New England Sources at the Genealogical Library in Salt Lake City," 237; Robert S. Wakefield, "Family of Richard Warren," vol. 18, part 1, 1–2, 7–8, 26, 33, 130; and Kenneth L. Willey, ed., *Vital Records from the Eastport Sentinal* [sic] *of Eastport, Maine, 1818–1900*, 126–27, 143, 205, 291. A detailed genealogy of Thomas Sherman Bugbee's descent from Richard Warren is available from the author.

3. Bugbee, "Story of Thomas Sherman Bugbee and Mary Catherine Dunn Bugbee." After Bugbee's release from the Union Army, he paid a visit to his home in Perry, where he voted for Abraham Lincoln in the presidential election. Soon after, he went to Washington, D.C., where he worked as a streetcar conductor. He soon quit that job and headed back home. By coincidence, he left Washington, D.C., on the same night John Wilkes Booth assassinated President Lincoln. Bugbee, who had a physical similarity to Booth, was arrested by two detectives while traveling through Boston. They thought he was Booth, but Bugbee fortunately managed to convince them of his actual identity by showing them his Union Army discharge papers.

4. Ibid.

5. Ibid.

6. Laura Vernon Hamner, *Short Grass and Longhorns*, 55–57.

7. Ibid., 57.

8. Pauline Durrett Robertson and R. L. Robertson, *Cowman's Country: Fifty Frontier Ranches in the Texas Panhandle, 1876–1887*, 129.

9. Ann Fears Crawford and Crystal Sasse Ragsdale, *Women in Texas: Their Lives, Their Experiences, Their Accomplishments*, 116.

10. Robertson and Robertson, *Cowman's Country*, 129.

11. Helen Francis Officer, "Sketch of the Life of Thomas Sherman Bugbee, 1841–1925," 16.

12. Ibid., 16–17, 21; Hamner, *Short Grass and Longhorns*, 60.

13. Hammer, *Cowman's Country*, 129; Officer, "Sketch," 18.

14. Officer, "Sketch," 18.

15. Hamner, *Short Grass and Longhorns*, 196.

16. Bugbee, "Story of Thomas Sherman Bugbee and Mary Catherine Dunn Bugbee"; C. L. Douglas, *Cattle Kings of Texas*, 212–14; Lester Fields Sheffy, "Thomas Sherman Bugbee," 133; Hamner, *Cowman's Country*, 62–63, 195–98, 201; Hobart Ebey Stocking, "Thomas Sherman Bugbee," 62.

17. Hamner, *Cowman's Country*, 62.

18. Officer, "Sketch," 20.

19. "Thomas Sherman Bugbee Is Buried," obituary.

20. Officer, "Sketch," 22.

21. Thomas Sherman Bugbee, last will and testament.

22. Ibid.

23. "Pioneer Woman Buried Sunday: Resident of Clarendon since 1897, One of First Women in Panhandle."

24. Ibid.; "Mrs. T. S. Bugbee Dead at Home."

25. Tina Hagler, deputy clerk, Donley County, Tex., letter to Allan O. Kownslar, May 19, 2003.

26. Officer, "Sketch," 22.

Margaret Heffernan Dunbar Hardy Borland

MRS. ALEXANDER BORLAND

Phyllis A. McKenzie

IN 1873 MARGARET HEFFERNAN BORLAND DROVE a herd of her own cattle up the Chisholm Trail from Victoria, Texas, to the booming cow town of Wichita, Kansas. Accompanying her on the cattle trail were her daughter, who was about to turn nine years old; her sons, ages fourteen and sixteen; her granddaughter, barely six; several hired hands; and a black cook.[1]

Margaret's singular feat capped a lifetime of squarely facing the vicissitudes of fortune. Raised near the epicenter of the Texas cattle industry, she survived the maelstrom of the Texas Revolution. She was widowed three times and witnessed the deaths of most of her children.

The rigors of the 1873 trail drive can only be imagined, for no participant was ever interviewed about it. Margaret died a month after safely reaching Wichita but before she sold her cattle. She left no diary and no letters, hardly anything in her own handwriting except for her signature. Flickers of Margaret's story are tucked away in courthouse records, census listings, newspaper obituaries, bills of sale, and a few rare passages from people who knew her—most notably her son-in-law Victor Rose, who wrote "Some Historical Facts in Regard to the Settlement of Victoria, Texas" in 1883. From these barest of threads, an outline her life emerges.

Margaret's parents, John and Margaret Heffernan, were natives of Tipperary in the south of Ireland. At some point in the early 1820s, they sailed across the Atlantic Ocean with their small daughter, Mary. They settled first in New York City, where Margaret, their second daughter, was born on April 3, 1824.[2] According to family lore, John Heffernan plied a trade making candles and struggled to provide a living for his family since conditions were tough for Irish immigrants in New York in the 1820s. When a man named John McMullen came to the city with tales of abundance and opportunity in Texas, the Heffernans were among the families who signed on to join his colony.[3]

McMullen worked as an empresario, or land agent, in the era when Mexico had newly won its independence from Spain. Texas formed the northernmost section of this vast young nation. Concerned with protecting its borders, Mexico invited

Figure 15.   Margaret Borland, daughter of John Heffernan, c. 1872.
Courtesy of Celeste Brown, Victoria, Texas; Institute of Texan
Cultures at the University of Texas–San Antonio.

empresarios to bring in settlers to occupy the territory. The government promised each family a league of land (4,428 acres, including 177 acres of premium farmland), ten milk cows, one cart, and a yoke of oxen. In return, the families needed to bring their tools and enough additional supplies to sustain themselves for one year. They were required to use the Spanish language for official business and to practice Catholicism, the state religion.[4]

In October 1829, after a five-week voyage, the brig *New Packet* docked in Copano Bay near present-day Bayside, Refugio County, Texas. Among the colonists on board was the John Heffernan family.[5] Daughters Margaret and Mary, ages five and nine respectively, scampered ashore to explore the land that was to become their home.

Soon after disembarking, the immigrants gathered their possessions and trudged inland twelve miles to the nearest settlement, Mission Refugio. Here they took shelter within the thick walls of an abandoned stone church, where they were joined by another boatload of Irish brought by McMullen's partner, James McGloin.[6]

Many of the immigrants had doubts about staying in Texas after they perceived how truly isolated they were. Their anxiety increased when a group of Lipan Apaches appeared, demanding gifts.[7] Sickness pervaded those in the mission, sapping their energy and causing death. Much of the time, Mary and Margaret were confined in the church.

In April 1830 McMullen led some of the immigrants from the mission to their allotted lands along the Nueces River drainage. The Heffernans were among the families moving to the countryside.[8] The settlers began to make homes for themselves, building jacales (huts), clearing fields, and grazing stock. In addition to ranch lands, each family living on the Nueces received a plot in the newly established town of San Patricio de Hibernia. They named their community in honor of Ireland's patron saint and joined together to erect a picket church.[9]

In October 1831 a Mexican land commissioner arrived. He provided John Heffernan and eleven other fortunate settlers with titles to the lands they were occupying.[10] Possession of a land title gave Margaret's parents the right to build a permanent cabin on their property. They planted crops such as corn, beans, squash, yams, and melons. The family increased in size with the birth of two sons, John Jr. around 1830 and James in 1834.[11]

In 1834 empresarios McMullen and McGloin brought a new shipload of immigrants to San Patricio directly from Tipperary County, Ireland. Arriving in this group were John's brother, James Heffernan, and his family.[12] The Tipperary immigrants brought fresh, welcome news of the old country. Margaret and her siblings now had an aunt and an uncle to enliven family gatherings and five young cousins as playmates.

When a new land commissioner came to San Patricio in June 1835, he granted a league of land to the James Heffernan family and an additional league of land to the John Heffernans.[13] This grant enlarged the holdings that John had received in

1831. He now owned almost nine thousand acres for the bargain price of less than $200 in fees.[14]

On coming into possession of their lands, the Irish experimented with a variety of crops, but both the terrain and the colonization contracts favored ranching. Herds of wild cattle and horses, descendants of animals brought by early Spaniards, freely roamed the prairie. It is said that the Texas cattle industry began in the heart of the Irish area around 1840.[15]

In the Irish colony, Spanish was the official language for business and commerce, and the Heffernan children grew up speaking it fluently.[16] San Patricio residents appreciated the protection of nearby Fort Lipantitlán and were on cordial terms with the Mexican soldiers who garrisoned it. The Heffernans, like other Irish immigrants, counted Mexican families among their neighbors and friends.

Disease was a constant concern. Colonists froze in alarm at signs of cholera, for a person could die within a few hours of first having diarrhea or other symptoms. This disease, transmitted by ingesting contaminated food or water, arrived in America from India in 1833 and killed scores of Irish who immigrated to Texas in 1834.[17] Other diseases such as yellow fever were transmitted by mosquitoes. Settlers noted that the illness was most prevalent during hot, humid summers near the coast. Epidemics of yellow fever broke out in Texas at least seven times before the Civil War.[18]

Colonists were ever mindful of their vulnerability and isolation. From spring through fall, they dreaded the moon's stark illumination on certain nights that they called "Comanche moon."[19] The Comanche were one of the few tribes who moved after nightfall, and, indeed, raids happened most frequently in the full of the moon. To protect their livestock, families piled brush into a fence surrounding their back door, with no entryway except through the house. "About the full of the moon, or whenever an Indian raid was anticipated, the horses, oxen and milk cows were kept in this enclosure."[20] The danger from Indians was very real, as was the threat of disease. Both would return to scar Margaret's life.

As Margaret reached adolescence, the winds of war were gathering in Texas. On September 20, 1835, a Mexican warship appeared on the horizon at Copano Bay, bringing five hundred troops under the command of Gen. Martín Perfecto de Cos.[21] The head of the Mexican government, Antonio López de Santa Anna, had dispatched Cos on a mission to disarm Texas. Word of the ship's arrival spread quickly through the Irish colonies, causing considerable consternation. After meeting with the Irish empresario, Cos turned his army toward San Antonio. On October 9 a contingent of Anglo Americans stormed the fort at Goliad and overcame the small garrison that Cos had stationed there. Reinforced by Irish volunteers from Refugio, the rebel group then marched to Fort Lipantitlán. Receiving the fort's surrender on November 3, they discovered a number of Irish colonists fighting on the side of Mexico.[22]

During this tumult the John Heffernan family was living in San Patricio. John's

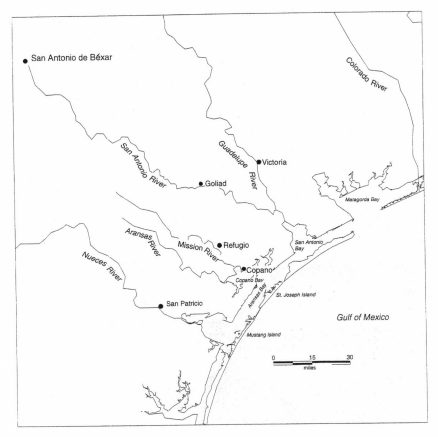

Figure 16.   Area map of Irish colonies. Courtesy of Graham Davis, Bath, England; Texas A&M University Press, College Station, Texas.

name appears neither on the lists of Irish combatants at Goliad and Lipantititlán nor on the muster of volunteers storming San Antonio de Béxar in December.[23] Quite likely the Heffernans, like many other San Patricio colonists, lay low and bided their time, attending to personal business like raising crops and tending livestock, quietly watching the course of events. Whatever one's individual preferences, allegiances were subject to rapid turnover. Just ten days after the battle of Lipantitlán, the commander of Goliad reported that all of the people in San Patricio had allied themselves with the Texan cause.[24]

In December, the Irish colonies received the heartening news that General Cos had been driven from San Antonio. On December 10 Texas volunteers assailed his position and prevailed upon him to withdraw south of the Rio Grande. Among the successful attackers were at least eight volunteers from the Irish colonies.[25]

The euphoria in Texas following Cos's departure proved to be the lull before the storm. Santa Anna determined to punish the defiant Texans himself. Shortly after the beginning of 1836, he led an army of 6,000 across the Rio Grande and headed for San Antonio to retake the town. Gen. José Urrea, an extremely competent strategist, took a right wing of nearly 1,000 men northward on a route paralleling the Texas coast.[26] His goal was to recapture Goliad and take control of the Gulf of Mexico. The Irish colonies lay directly in Urrea's path.

Amid rumors and rising panic, the provisional government of Texas called for a gathering of delegates at Washington-on-the-Brazos. The Irish colonies were still divided in their loyalties. Chosen to represent San Patricio at the convention was empresario John McMullen. John Heffernan and several other San Patricio citizens signed a petition protesting the selection process.[27] This document, dated February 1, is the last to show John Heffernan still alive.

Sometime in the weeks that followed, John Heffernan, Margaret's father, died a violent death along with her Uncle James and James's entire family. In an interview years later, Margaret's sister, Mary, recalled that traumatic event:

> My uncle, James Heffernan, still lived on the Poesta when the war broke out. My father's family lived in San Patricio. My father and a cousin, John Ryan, went to James Heffernan to assist him in laying by his crop, so that they could all join the command of Gen. [actually Colonel] James Walker Fannin Jr. at Goliad.
>
> The day before they finished plowing, they were attacked by Mexicans and Indians while at work, and all were killed. The Indians then went to the house and killed the family of James Heffernan, which consisted of his wife and five children.
>
> The first intimation of the sad fate that had befallen these early settlers was received by relatives and friends at San Patricio when they found at their cowpens one morning the cows of James Heffernan, which he had taken from there to his home on the Poesta. . . . The party of men went to investigate. They found the men dead in the field. They had been dead several days. The body of the eldest son of James Heffernan was lying between the field and the house, while the bodies of Mrs. Heffernan and the four younger children were found at the house. The remains were collected and placed in one large box and were buried near the scene of the murder.[28]

Shocked and shaken, Margaret's mother struggled with grief and the logistics of survival. She was now solely responsible for the safety of her hapless family—daughter Mary, who had turned fifteen years old; Margaret, eleven; and the little boys, ages five and one.[29]

As the Mexican army approached, alarm swept through the Irish colony. Many of the men had departed to enlist in the Texas forces at Goliad. Women from San

Patricio gathered their possessions and fled with their children. This marked the beginning of the Runaway Scrape, a massive evacuation of people throughout South Texas in search of safety. The Runaway Scrape continued through March and into April 1836, as people struggled to stay ahead of the Mexican troops. Most of the refugees headed north and east, where Gen. Sam Houston mustered the Texan army.

The movements of the Heffernan family during this period are difficult to trace. At some point Mrs. Heffernan and the children joined the exodus of fleeing settlers. Victor Rose describes their grim journey: "Bereft of their natural head and support, . . . loading their earthly possessions into a cart, the unfortunates set their faces toward the rising sun, following like a funeral procession the snail-like cart on foot."[30]

However, there is some evidence that the Heffernans stayed in San Patricio during the war and did not depart until *after* the Texan victory at San Jacinto on April 21, 1836.[31] They were definitely in their home in San Patricio when retreating Mexican troops came through in May.[32] If they indeed remained in the colony during this time, they experienced a whirlwind of insecurity and conflict and saw disaster cut down neighbors and friends, whom they knew well.

On February 27 the Mexican general, Urrea, appeared at the gates of San Patricio. Arriving at night in a cold rainstorm, he quickly took possession of the town. The general considered killing all of the captured male combatants but relented after an Irish priest protested "that it was barbarous and inhuman, and that those prisoners he knew to be as loyal to the country as Santa Anna."[33] Urrea stayed in San Patricio for two weeks, provisioned his troops, and then turned down the road toward Refugio. On March 2 at Washington-on-the-Brazos, delegates from throughout Texas issued a clear declaration of Texas independence. The Alamo in San Antonio fell to Santa Anna on March 6, 1836; all of the male defenders died, including at least eight volunteers from the Irish colonies.[34] Wherever Margaret and her family may have been at this time, the unfolding of events brought uncertainty and stress.

Urrea caught up with Colonel Fannin outside Goliad and procured the surrender of the Texan forces. Fannin and his men were imprisoned in the Goliad fort. Their numbers swelled to 407, with the addition of more captives from the storming of Victoria. Acting under Santa Anna's orders, Urrea authorized the execution of the male prisoners. On March 27 they were marched to the outskirts of town and shot.[35] Local lore has long held that Margaret and her sister were present at Goliad and avoided execution by speaking Spanish so fluently that the soldiers believed that they were Mexican children.[36] This story, for all its appeal, seems dubious on several grounds: (1) There is no document indicating that Mrs. Heffernan ever left San Patricio for Goliad;[37] (2) surviving photographs of Margaret and Mary show them to be fair skinned and light eyed and thus not likely to have been mistaken for Mexican children; (3) Urrea's soldiers did not execute children at Goliad, only adult men serving in the Texas forces. Any child who was there would not have been in danger.

Perhaps this story was an embellishment created after the Texas Revolution, when Irish loyalties were called into question, and subsequently passed down to future generations with the full force of a family legend. On the other hand, it *is* possible that the Heffernan family sought refuge in the Goliad fort, hoping to find safety with the Texan forces. Certainly the children spoke Spanish, given their upbringing in Mexican Texas.

Urrea had emerged victorious from all of his military engagements. However, the mass executions had alienated the settlers, shattered their allegiance to Mexico, and galvanized support for the Texan cause. "Remember the Alamo! Remember Goliad!" became rallying cries. On April 21 Santa Anna fell into the hands of Gen. Sam Houston's forces at San Jacinto. To secure his release, he agreed to recognize the independence of Texas and to withdraw all of the Mexican troops south of the Rio Grande.[38] News of the Texan victory at San Jacinto filtered back to the scattered refugees of the Runaway Scrape. They began to return home, but many found their property in ruins: Fields had been laid bare, cattle driven off, and storage bins emptied.

Mrs. Heffernan and the children were ensconced in their house at San Patricio when the retreating Mexican army crossed the Nueces on May 30. Officer José Enrique de la Peña, famous afterward for his diary describing Davy Crockett's execution, lodged in their home for the night. The family hosted him with dignity despite their recent personal loss. Peña was impressed by their graciousness and especially noticed sixteen-year-old Mary. He wrote the following in his diary on May 31: "I was quartered in the house of John Stefferman [Heffernan], a man who had unfortunately been murdered by the Indians last April together with his brother, the brother's wife, five nieces and nephews, and a cousin. Mistress Margaret was left with four orphaned children, among whom one's attention is drawn to Miss Mary, whose amiability and misfortune touched my sensibility."[39]

From 1836 to 1845 Texas existed as an independent nation. During this period the region of the Irish colonies faced continual turmoil. The Mexican government did not accept the independence of Texas and sent armies to reclaim the territory. The Nueces River demarcated the disputed boundary between Mexico and Texas—an irritant to officials and opportunists alike. The town of San Patricio, situated squarely on the Nueces, became a lightning rod for conflict.

Both Mexican and Texan troops preyed upon the larders of the Irish and stole their cattle. Bandits raided as well. Continuing incursions marked the Irish region as a dangerous place to live. Whether or not the Heffernan family remained in San Patricio during the war, they certainly left for awhile afterward. In October 1836 the Texas government advised settlers to move away from the Nueces and San Antonio rivers for their own protection.[40]

The Irish received this news with dismay. To leave meant abandoning everything they had worked hard to achieve. A number of settlers, however, did withdraw elsewhere, at least for a time. Mrs. Heffernan took the children to the Brazos River just south of Houston, where they settled on a strip of land and raised food. Two early chroniclers of county histories noted the family's activity: "The family of Mrs. John Heffernan continued to live in San Patricio until after the battle of San Jacinto, when General Sam Houston ordered all settlers on the frontier of Mexico to go either east or into Mexico. Mrs. Heffernan, with the rest of the family, went east, locating at Brazoria."[41] After the battle of San Jacinto, they returned to the Brazos and made a crop of corn, that indispensable staff of life to the early Texan colonists.[42]

The family stayed in Brazoria for at least two years, for they were still living there in 1838.[43] "Finally," reports Victor Rose, "they were able to return to their deserted home."[44] However, the widow and children may have moved instead to Victoria, a town in the Irish area about twenty-five miles from Goliad. Margaret's mother, who never remarried, died in Victoria in 1849.[45]

Even in unsettled conditions, the children grew up to establish independent homes and lives. During her family's sojourn in Brazoria, Mary Heffernan, then seventeen, was courted by Hiram Riggs and accepted his proposal of marriage. After their wedding in 1838, the couple moved to Goliad, where they farmed for six years. Afterward they settled in Corpus Christi. Until his death in 1855, Riggs worked as a merchant to support his family. Mary lived a long life and parented nine children. She died in 1903 at the age of eighty-two.[46]

Young Margaret also reached the threshold of adulthood. Five years after her sister wed, Margaret married a man named Harrison Dunbar in August 1843. Little is known about him except that he was a resident of Victoria. The 1840 census shows that he owned thirty head of cattle.[47] In 1844, shortly after the birth of their daughter, Mary, Harrison Dunbar was killed in a pistol duel on the streets of Victoria.[48]

Barely twenty years old, Margaret found herself both a widow and a single parent. Economic security was a difficult prospect for a woman alone in the Republic of Texas. More uncertainty loomed: Texas was moving close to annexation with the United States, a move likely to provoke war with Mexico. Social relations were fluid and unpredictable. Margaret was probably grateful for the opportunity to marry again very soon—to Milton Hardy in October 1845.[49]

Margaret's second husband, born in 1816, was the eldest child of the family and had four younger sisters. In 1822 Milton's parents had moved from Tennessee to Texas with their small children. Like Margaret's family, they were caught in the upheaval of the Texas Revolution. In spring 1836 the Hardy family, with a toddler in tow, joined the Runaway Scrape, fleeing the advancing troops and the destruction they were wreaking upon the countryside. Milton's father died near San Augustine in May. In the autumn of that year, his mother gathered her offspring and returned

Figure 17. Mary Heffernan Riggs, daughter of John Heffernan and sister of Margaret Heffernan. Courtesy of Celeste Brown, Victoria, Texas; Institute of Texan Cultures at the University of Texas–San Antonio.

to their deserted farm on the Navidad River. She planted a corn crop the following spring and registered her own cattle brand in 1838.[50]

As a young man, Milton distinguished himself as a civic leader. He served as a Victoria city council member in 1840.[51] The census of that year shows him owning 2,912 acres of land and five lots in town.[52]

Following their marriage, Margaret and Milton Hardy settled upon land near the DeWitt county line. About a year later, in early 1847, Margaret gave birth to a baby girl, Eliza. The following year their daughter Julia was born. Eliza did not survive long, nor was she the only child whom the couple lost in infancy.[53] But Julia grew strong and healthy, as did Margaret's daughter from her previous marriage, young Miss Mary. Around 1852 Margaret bore another robust baby, a little girl whom they named Rosa.[54]

During this period ranchers in Texas, with an eye toward producing income, embarked on an array of business ventures. Herds of wild cattle and horses wandered—sometimes thundered—through the region. Cattle belonging to many different owners grazed together on open lands, and settlers distinguished their animals by brands. Surrounded by more animals than they could eat or use, ranchers searched for outside markets. The expected war with Mexico, which did indeed come in 1845 and 1846, brought a temporary demand for cattle to feed the U.S. troops. However, most of this conflict took place in Mexico. Some stockmen trailed herds to New Orleans, a difficult journey through swamps. By 1848 it was possible to send animals by steamship from Texas to New Orleans. However, stress and fear caused the cattle to lose weight in transit. With profits low, this method of shipment never became popular. In 1846 a Texas stockman drove a thousand longhorns to Ohio, the first known cattle drive northward out of Texas.[55]

Margaret's husband Milton occupied himself managing stock in this crucible of Texas ranching. Besides his business endeavors, he showed a strong inclination for legal affairs. In 1847 Hardy wrote a will calling for the manumission of his slave, Louisa, and her children upon his death. He bequeathed all of his land and three-fourths of his personal property to daughter Eliza, his only child at the time. To Margaret, "my dear and beloved wife," he left the remaining one-fourth of his property.[56] In 1852 Milton filed claim on the estates of John and James Heffernan, Margaret's father and uncle, who had died during the Texas Revolution. Hardy sought compensation for Margaret and her siblings for "the amount of property destroyed and lost by the Mexican and Texian armies, in AD 1836 during the Revolution of the late Republic of Texas."[57]

These efforts were stopped short when Hardy contracted cholera. The disease progressed with characteristic swiftness, and Milton Hardy died on August 24, 1852.[58] The couple's young son, William, died in the same epidemic.[59] Hardy's considerable estate included twelve hundred head of stock cattle, several tracts of property, and four slaves.[60]

Margaret was left to support her three little girls, ages eight, four, and less than one year. Little is known about how she managed during the next few years. Margaret's youngest sibling, James, who helped with her ranching operations in later years, perhaps lent a hand since he participated in settling the Milton Hardy estate.[61] Margaret's other brother, John, had married in 1847 but died a year later, as did his young wife. They left behind an infant son, who shared his name. Young John was apparently taken into Margaret's household, for he was living with her at the time of the 1860 census.[62]

The slave, Louisa, was not freed as Milton had stipulated. Instead, she remained with the family and would be known as "Mammy" to Margaret's children born in her next marriage.[63] On February 11, 1856, Margaret married Alexander Borland, one of the richest ranchers in Victoria County.[64] A Methodist minister officiated at this ceremony, perhaps an indication that Margaret no longer adhered to the Catholic faith of her youth.[65]

Borland, born in North Carolina in 1818, had established himself in Texas as a stockman. In 1860 Alexander and Margaret Borland possessed eight thousand head of cattle, the largest herd in Victoria.[66] Some of these animals may have been Margaret's inheritance from either her father or Hardy, for in later years she consistently used the "H" brand in her ranching operations.[67] The 1860 census shows the Borlands owning $14,500 worth of real estate, $28,000 in personal property, and twelve slaves.[68]

Their ranching enterprise prospered, particularly in the years preceding the Civil War. To work their cattle, the Borlands hired several ranch hands, including a German laborer and Margaret's younger brother, James, now a competent stock handler in his twenties. Margaret's orphaned nephew, John, an adolescent living with the family, also assisted with ranch chores.[69] In 1858 Alexander Borland participated in Victoria's first annual livestock exhibition, an event organized by the Gulf Coast Fair Association.[70]

Margaret had much experience rearing daughters, but her role was soon to change. The couple became parents to three boys in quick succession: Alex Jr., born in 1857, Jesse in 1859, and Willie in 1861, all of whom survived their early months apparently in good health. There is no record of any Borland child dying in infancy. In June 1864, two months after her fortieth birthday, Margaret gave birth to one more daughter, Nellie.[71]

With steady income Margaret was able to bring some fine furnishings into her home, including a pianoforte, walnut furniture, a marble-top bureau, a baby buggy, linens, and a full set of china.[72] She managed the burgeoning household with quiet dignity. Victor Rose has described Margaret's earnest nature: "She had, unaided, acquired a good education; her manners were ladylike, and when fortune smiled upon her at last in a pecuniary sense, she was as perfectly at home in the drawing rooms of the cultured as if refinement had engrafted its polishing touches upon her mind in maidenhood."[73]

The family began to hear tales about experimental trail drives from Texas to Missouri and beyond. By the mid-1850s such drives were no longer newsworthy. Cattle fetched high prices in the Midwest, several times the rates in Texas, but the Borlands resisted any temptation to undertake this kind of expedition. Besides the ever-present danger from Indians and acts of nature, drovers from Texas encountered fierce opposition in the Midwest. Settlers there feared the introduction of a malady called "Texas fever," which might infect their herds. Vigilante committees sometimes blocked Texans at gunpoint and turned them back toward home.[74]

The Civil War abruptly shut down markets for Texas cattle from 1861 to 1865. Scarcely any livestock left the state after New Orleans fell to Union forces early in 1862.[75] Alexander Borland, age forty-three at the war's outbreak, felt little compunction to join the Confederate Army. He continued to run his ranch and raise livestock and even bought a neighbor's plantation in 1862.[76] The majority of the ranchers in the area, however, were ardent secessionists, who quickly enlisted. They left their cattle largely untended for the duration of the war. Herds ran wild. Texas longhorns developed their legendary characteristics during this period: They grew leaner and meaner and quite capable of defending themselves with their formidable horns.[77] At war's end, some five million wild longhorns roamed the Texas terrain, providing the Borlands with broad and continuing opportunities to enlarge their herd.[78]

Margaret's daughters Mary, twenty-one, and Julia, seventeen, watched the steady stream of veterans returning from the war. Soon they each had a beau. In March 1866 Julia married Victor Rose, the dashing young son of a Victoria plantation owner. Victor had been wounded multiple times in the service of the Confederacy and nearly starved in an Ohio prison before his father sent a slave, who smuggled supplies to him.[79] In May 1866 Mary married A. B. Peticolas, a tall, dignified lawyer born and educated in Virginia. Peticolas produced detailed sketches of scenes he had witnessed in the Civil War. He liked to play chess and handcraft fine furniture.[80] By year's end both young wives were expecting their first child.[81]

Sometime in the first half of 1867, the Borlands opened a cattle market in Victoria, and the government levied a special tax for its operation.[82] After the Civil War, hide and tallow factories sprang up in towns and ranches near the Texas coast. With seemingly endless herds of wild longhorns, coastal factories purchased animals cheaply. Through Rockport, they extracted hides and tallow for export and discarded the meat.[83] Perhaps the Borland market operated in this manner, rendering products for export. More likely it served the local area with a handful of hired workers.

Winter's end found Margaret's husband weak from a lingering illness. Borland could afford to pay for the finest medical care available, and in the spring of 1867 he departed for New Orleans to consult with "the eminent surgeon, Dr. Stone." Alexander Borland never returned, however, and died within the confines of that city.[84] After her husband's death, Margaret, a widow for the third time, moved her family from their ranch into the town of Victoria.[85] Management of the business operations fell to her. During the summer she paid for a wagon repair and employed two men to work as butchers.[86]

The summer of 1867 was one of the hottest in memory and ushered in a new wave of illness upon the Texas shores. By July reports began to surface of yellow fever in the coastal towns.[87] Few diseases evoked more dread. The fever inflicted a miserable death on up to 85 percent of the people who contracted it.[88] Mexicans knew it as *vomito negro* for the copious dark blood clots that victims would vomit—a dire signal that death was at hand.[89]

Yellow fever is a viral disease transmitted by mosquitoes. Not understanding the cause, people suspected shortcomings in hygiene and sanitation. They placed barrels of tar and whiskey outside their homes and burned the mixture in the hope that the smoke would clear the air of toxins. Local governments took care to quarantine ships, smoke bags of incoming mail, and pour lime down sewers. In infected towns, mule-drawn carts meandered through the streets, collecting victims' blankets and clothing for burning.[90]

Reports from the coast doubtless disturbed Margaret, for her sister lived in Corpus Christi. But the pestilence also visited Victoria soon enough. By September it struck in force, felling nearly all of Margaret's family at the same time.[91] During earlier epidemics, the standard treatments for yellow fever had involved bloodletting, purging, and administration of mercury. By 1867 new treatments were in vogue, recently introduced from France. Doctors recommended gentler actions such as taking warm baths, drinking medicinal teas, and vigorously rubbing the patient's body.[92] Margaret probably employed some of these measures in her ministrations to her family. She nursed everyone as best she could, purchasing a mattress, pillow, and pillowcase, carefully separating the linens needed to care for the sick. Her purchase receipt notes that these items were "used by her in the epidemic of 1867."[93]

Despite her best efforts, Margaret was unable to halt the terrible toll. The first to die was fifteen-year-old Rosa, described by her brother-in-law as a "most promising young girl."[94] In the households of the newlywed daughters, Mary Dunbar Peticolas sickened and died, followed a few hours later by her infant son, Malcolm.[95] Julia Hardy Rose succumbed in the year of her nineteenth birthday, leaving behind a six-month-old daughter.[96] Her husband, Victor, barely survived, and he decided to place his little girl under Margaret's care.[97]

Margaret had now lost all of the children from her first two marriages, the three daughters whom she had once guided and protected as a single parent. Nor did the disease spare the boys. Margaret kept vigil over the bedside of her youngest son, Willie, "a bright, intelligent little fellow of six."[98] Willie grew steadily weaker, and on September 29 Margaret paid the city sexton four dollars for digging his grave.[99]

In November, with the arrival of cooler weather, the yellow fever at last ran its course. New outbreaks of illness subsided, then ceased. Only three of Margaret's seven children were still alive: Alex, ten; Jesse, eight; and Nellie, three. Her baby granddaughter, Julia Rosa Rose, had also survived. Margaret's brother James stayed to help in the household, as did nephew John, now a nineteen-year-old laborer.[100] Victor Rose admired Margaret's resilience and compared her to steadfast women warriors of antiquity: "Mrs. Borland had much of the heroic in her composition, and under the same circumstances would have enacted the part of a Semiramis, or Philippa of Hainault."[101]

After the devastating loss, the group came together to face the challenge of running a ranch and managing a huge herd of livestock. A number of receipts survive that record the day-to-day operations on the ranch. James Heffernan supervised a crew of at least nine ranch hands who worked for Margaret. In 1868 they received wages for "gathering beeves of the 'H' brand," "prairie branding," "work on prairie gather[ing] stock," "collecting beeves," "driving beeves," and "branding 'H' stock." Provisions were purchased in bulk. Wagons rolled in bringing hefty bags of cornmeal, flour, sugar, coffee, bacon, salt, corn, and potatoes. Margaret continued to operate the market, issuing disbursements "for rent of market space," "for services rendered in market," and "for beeves butchered."[102] In the spring of 1868 Margaret paid her brother and another ranch hand for "one month collecting horses."[103] These were probably wild mustangs that still roamed the prairie. During the same period she purchased seven stock horses to add to her herd.[104]

Victor Rose commended the long and loyal service of James Heffernan, of whom he wrote the following: "Brother of the foregoing, he attended for many years the large cattle interests of his sister, Mrs. Borland, and contributed in no small degree to the honest accumulation of the fine property possessed by her. . . . Though he had golden opportunities for the advancement of his own fortunes by illegitimate practices, so often availed of at the time so as to create scarce an [sic] comment, he surrendered his trust finally a very poor man."[105]

The 1870 census shows Margaret owning real estate valued at $1,500 and other property (mostly cattle) worth $16,386. This was a lesser estate than she had owned with her husband ten years earlier but was still a considerable holding for the post–Civil War era. The census identifies the following people living in the household:

> Margaret Borland, 45, stock raiser
> Children Alex, Jesse, and Nellie
> Granddaughter Julia Rose
> Nephew John Heffernan, 22, stock keeper
> Mariah George, 13, mulatto, domestic servant
> Calvin Pease, 20, mulatto, stock laborer
> Riley Mackey, 23, black, stock laborer[106]

Margaret's children conducted their own business transactions from an early age. In 1870, when Alex was thirteen years old, Margaret presented him with a red roan horse. The following year Alex traded the horse to his cousin John Heffernan for two mares.

Both of the mares later produced colts. Lacking a brand of his own, Alex branded the colts with his mother's H brand and added them to his own small herd.[107]

On at least two occasions Margaret bought out small-time operators in the region who needed to liquidate their assets. In 1872 she purchased a herd of 200 cattle from a local couple at $4.75 per head and another 30 animals from a husband and wife willing to take $4 per head. These sales represented the owners' entire stock.[108]

At one point in the early 1870s, Margaret is said to have managed more than ten thousand cattle.[109] However, cattle prices in Texas remained pitifully low. More and more Margaret thought wistfully about a trail drive north. With the right timing and planning, such an endeavor could bring a considerable portion of her stock to market. Margaret knew people who drove herds to Kansas and returned with success stories and busting pocketbooks, eager to head out again.

In 1867 an Illinois cattleman named Joseph McCoy opened the Chisholm Trail leading from South Texas to Abilene, Kansas. McCoy's idea was to drive cattle to railheads following a route outside of settled areas (and quarantine lines). Each subsequent year cattle drives doubled in volume, from 35,000 animals the first season to 600,000 four years later. Low rail-freight prices in 1870 allowed drovers to obtain profits of as much as $25 per animal.[110]

Rail lines pushed southward through Kansas, opening new towns as shipping points. By 1872 Wichita had emerged as the leader. The town lay one hundred miles closer to Texas than Abilene did, a boon for weary drovers on the trail.[111] Great potential earnings beckoned at trail's end, but profits were by no means guaranteed. When Texas herds arrived in Kansas in 1871, the bargain rail rates of the previous season had disappeared. Many drovers decided to winter their cattle in Kansas in hopes of getting a higher bid for their stock. During the winter of 1871–1872 a great blizzard swept down upon the Great Plains, and tens of thousands of wintering cattle from Texas froze to death.[112]

The brutal winter thrust its hand far south into Texas, and cattle carcasses dotted the prairie near Margaret's ranch. Roving bands of skinners scoured the area seeking free hides. Newspapers reported 200,000 cattle deaths in Texas and more than 25,000 skinned carcasses in Goliad alone.[113]

When early spring of 1873 rolled around, Margaret weighed her options and decided to drive a herd up the Chisholm Trail. Cattle were selling for $23.80 per head in Kansas compared to $8 in San Antonio.[114] Although neither she nor her ranch hands had ever trailed so far, they understood how to handle cattle and provide for themselves. Hundreds of Texans had successfully taken the trail before them, including an occasional woman. Margaret's experience was distinct in that she would be *in charge;* as boss and organizer, she would be responsible for the well-being of the entire group.

Margaret set about planning logistics and making assignments for the journey. With no one at home to care for the children, she decided they had to go along. Alex, sixteen, and Jesse, fourteen, were old enough to work as "waddies," general trail hands to keep the herd moving. Margaret's nephew, John Heffernan, was then twenty-five and thus old enough to be a "ramrod," or supervisor. The number of hired hands is uncertain, but half a dozen or so would have been needed to manage their market herd of more than one thousand animals.[115]

The little girls, Nellie, age eight and a half, and Julia, barely six, were too young to work the herd, but they had definite chores and knew the rules for staying safe. A black cook (perhaps one of the household employees listed in the 1870 census) also accompanied the group.[116]

The Chisholm Trail began in South Texas with several feeder lines that merged north of San Antonio. Heavy rains in 1873 caused streams to swell. At Waco an impressive new suspension bridge charged a fee of five cents per head to pass. Drovers generally avoided the charge by swimming their cattle across the Brazos River, but in the wet year of 1873, the Borlands may well have opted for the bridge.[117]

The team pushed northward through country that was new to them. When they reached Fort Worth, a newly built stage station offered a welcome respite and a chance to send and receive mail.[118] From there the trail led to the Red River station, overlooking a mighty river that formed the boundary with the Indian Territory (Oklahoma). In Indian Territory the Chisholm Trail meandered across rolling lands with plenty of grass and timbered streams. How the Borland team coped with the various challenges is unrecorded, but they drove steadily north. A trail drive typically covered ten to twelve miles per day—a leisurely pace that allowed the cattle to fatten and graze their way to market.[119]

Margaret may have sold some animals to Indian agents along the way, but she entered Kansas with the bulk of her herd intact. After more than two months on the trail, the Borland crew reached their destination and pulled into Wichita, Kansas.[120] Wichita was then at its peak as a shipping center. Gates, chutes, and runways were newly built to receive cattle from Texas. Facilities included a holding area by a creek where the owners stayed with their animals while awaiting permission to cross the Arkansas River Bridge. During the 1873 season, more than four hundred thousand Texas cattle streamed into Wichita.[121]

Prominent Texans had erected a two-story hotel called the Texas House to accommodate themselves and the cattle buyers. Margaret, however, checked into a more modest lodging. The *Wichita Beacon* noted on June 4 that "Mrs. T. M. Borland of Texas, with three children, is stopping at the Planter house. She is the happy possessor of about one thousand head of cattle, and accompanied the herd all the way from its starting point to this place, giving evidence of a pluck and business tact far superior to many of the 'lords.'"[122] As in earlier circumstances, Margaret's grace and manners impressed the people she met. A newspaper column remarked that she had "become endeared to many acquaintances here on account of her lady-like character."[123]

While waiting to sell her cattle, Margaret shopped at Jake Karatofsky's newly opened store, billed as the finest establishment west of Kansas City. Its fancy plate-glass show windows were the talk of the town. There Margaret purchased a chemise and skirt for herself.[124] However, the hours weighed heavily as the group pondered how to sell their cattle and return home. Few buyers could be found in Wichita that season, for Texas cattle were a glut on the market. Purchasing agents around town were looking mainly for young, robust animals to stock new ranges, not scraggly longhorns intended for market. Some drovers contemplated wintering their cattle in Kansas in hopes of finding better prices in the spring, but the Borland crew had other worries.[125]

In Victoria on June 25, 1873, J. L. Cunningham signed a receipt acknowledging an allowance of "one hundred dollars in currency to bear my expenses to Kansas to take charge of Mrs. Borland's cattle and business there, in case it is necessary."[126] On June 27 daughter Nellie turned nine years old, but there was little mood for celebrating.[127] At the end of the trail in Wichita, Margaret was sick.

Her ailment has been variously described as "congestion of the brain" and "trail driving fever."[128] Perhaps it was a form of meningitis.[129] Its manifestations included agitation and delirium. Margaret Borland died on July 5, 1873, at the age of forty-nine. The *Wichita Beacon* reported, "We regret to announce the painful news that Mrs. Borland, the widow lady who came up with her own herd of cattle about two months ago, bringing with her three little children, died at the Planter house Saturday evening with mania, superinduced by her long, tedious journey and over-taxation of the brain."[130] Victor Rose stated simply, "It is believed that this journey and the attendant responsibilities proved too severe for her mental and physical resources, as she died soon after reaching the long looked-for goal, and before she had sold her cattle."[131]

Margaret was surrounded by loyal supporters to the end. The newspaper noted, "Her affairs are in the hands of her own kin and also her children. Everything was done by relatives and friends to smooth the rapid current of dark rolling river."[132] The team of comrades sprang into action to make the necessary arrangements. A Mrs. Martin headed directly to Wichita's New York Store and purchased nine yards of silk for sewing the shroud. John Heffernan bought a coffin on July 7 and settled the medical account on July 8. The itemized apothecary bill listed a number of medicines, glycerin, brandy, and bedpans.[133]

On July 8 Margaret's body was loaded for shipment to Victoria.[134] Soon afterward, the children arrived home safely. In time, Alex and Jesse erected a handsome marker over their mother's grave in Evergreen Cemetery, Victoria:

Our Mama
Margaret Heffernan Borland
Born Apr. 3, 1824
Died July 5, 1873
Gone, but not forgotten[135]

Writing in tribute to his mother-in-law, Victor Rose assessed her life: "Educated in the school of adversity, and an intimate acquaintance of trials, Mrs. Borland was a woman of resolute will and self-reliance; yet she was one of the kindest mothers."[136]

During the autumn months of 1873, the Victoria courts met to consider the fate of Margaret's orphaned children. The court determined that "Alex and Jesse are over fourteen years of age and able to realize something from their labor."[137] Consequently, it set aside a smaller fund for their maintenance than it did for their sister, Nellie. Alex, shouldering adult responsibilities at the age of sixteen, was summoned to give sworn depositions in court. He chose J. E. J. Moody to be guardian of himself and his brother, Jesse.[138] In the final settlement, Margaret's estate was divided equally among her three children, Alex, Jesse, and Nellie, and one grandchild, Julia Rose.[139]

Margaret's cattle, which were left in Kansas, never produced the hoped-for profit. In the financial panic of autumn 1873, the livestock market crashed. Many drovers had borrowed against their herds while waiting for prices to rise. When the debts were called in, they had no choice but to put their animals on the market. Cattle sold for as little as a dollar per hundredweight. Nearly every drover who trailed cattle in 1873 suffered a severe financial loss.[140]

Industrial products and political developments were hastening the end of the cattle drives. By 1880 barbed wire, patented in 1874, had become cheap and readily available. Farmers fenced their lands, ending the open range that had supported the cattle kingdom. Railroad tracks led from Texas to St. Louis and Chicago as early as 1873. Quarantine lines against Texas livestock moved westward. After 1875, Wichita and other towns in the eastern half of Kansas were completely closed to the Texas cattle trade.[141]

For a few years starting in 1876, a new trail offered some promise. The Western Trail snaked northwest out of Texas to Dodge City, Kansas, pushed north through Nebraska, and ultimately turned west to the Dakotas, Wyoming, and Montana. With the defeat of the Sioux Indians, markets for Texas cattle opened in Indian agencies and mining camps of the northern Rockies.[142]

In 1883 Alex and Jesse Borland were listed as livestock dealers in Victoria, but they took the Western Trail shortly afterward. Alex made a career of working on the range and was often seen astride his favorite Appaloosa pony. He died in Kansas in 1915.[143] Jesse joined his friend John Kendrick in trailing herds to Wyoming. Kendrick, after settling there, eventually became governor of that state. It is said that Jesse Borland taught the future governor how to read and write. Jesse, like his brother Alex, worked with cattle all his life. He died in South Dakota in 1925.[144]

Margaret's brother James did not outlive her for long. James Heffernan married Susan Higdon of the Garcias settlement in Victoria County, and the couple had several young children when he died around 1880.[145] Nephew John Heffernan married a woman from Mississippi and secured a job with the railroad in Cuero,

Texas. At the time of the 1880 census, he lived there with his children, ages one, four, and five. Victor Rose noted of him in 1883 that "He was for a number of years a reliable and efficient conductor on the line of the GWT&P railway; and is at present, it is believed, still in the employ of that company."[146]

Margaret's granddaughter, Julia Rose, was taken in by an aunt and uncle named Jones, who had recently arrived from South Carolina. William Jones established himself in Victoria as a farmer. In 1880 Julia was living with them and their five little girls.[147] Margaret's daughter Nellie remained in Victoria nearly all her life. Her guardians enrolled her in Nazareth Academy, a Catholic boarding school. After graduation, she taught in Victoria public schools. She married twice and gave birth to six children, four of whom lived to adulthood. Nellie Borland Wood-Kreisle became a leading Victoria clubwoman and was active in the Daughters of the Republic of Texas and the Daughters of the Confederacy. She sponsored historical markers and cared for Victoria's Memorial Square, planting trees and flowers. In her 1929 obituary, the *Victoria Advocate* explained her antiquarian zeal: "Because of the part her grandparents and parents played in the war for independence, she displayed a deep interest in the early history of Texas."[148] None of Margaret's four grandchildren through Nellie had descendents. With the extinction of that lineage, Margaret's story comes to a close.

Texas history fits like a glove over the history of Margaret Borland. Margaret was *there* at events that forged Texas into a state of mythic proportions. She was a child on the first boatload of Irish colonists to reach Texas shores. Her family lived in the heart of the war zone during the Texas Revolution, and her father died violently during that tumultuous period. She adjusted to dramatic change wrought by the Mexican War, the Civil War, and the coming of the railroads.

Margaret parented at least nine children whose names we know and possibly others who remain anonymous.[149] Most of her progeny died young, and she outlived three husbands. She witnessed the birth of the Texas cattle industry and rode up its most famous trail. Yet we search in vain for her feelings, her own words describing the momentous events she experienced.

Margaret's story was not entirely lost, for Victor Rose wrote a version just ten years after her death. Her story remains like a half-hidden nugget in the lore of the West. She was valiant, but her lasting influence was slim. Margaret Borland lived earnestly and respectfully as a wife, mother, business operator, and cattle drover. Always a lady, she casts but a faint shadow on the vast plains of history.

NOTES

1. The trail drive took place in the spring of 1873, reaching Wichita by early June; *Wichita Beacon,* June 4, 1873. Sources for ages of children: Daughter Nellie Borland was born June 27, 1864, from her obituary in the *Victoria Advocate,* Mar. 31, 1929. Sons Jesse and Alex were ages 1 and 3 in the U.S. Bureau of the Census, 1860, Victoria Co., Tex.; ages 11 and 13 in the 1870

census. Granddaughter Julia Rosa Rose was six months old when her mother died in the autumn of 1867, as recorded by Victor M. Rose, "Some Historical Facts in Regard to the Settlement of Victoria, Texas," 131. Further evidence of Julia's birth in 1867 comes from U.S. censuses of Victoria County: Julia was age 3 in the 1870 census and age 13 in the 1880 census. Source for participation by hired hands and a black cook: Sue Flanagan, *Trailing the Longhorns: A Century Later*, 83.

2. The Heffernans' origin in Tipperary County is noted by Camp Ezell, *Historical Story of Bee County, Texas*, 13. Mary was born in Ireland, and Margaret in New York, according to Rose, "Some Historical Facts," 130; thus, the Heffernans immigrated sometime between their daughters' births. Mary's birth date of around 1820 can be determined from the U.S. Bureau of the Census, 1880, Corpus Christi, where she provided her married name: Mary Riggs, widow, age 60, born in Ireland. Mary died in 1903 at age 82, according to Ezell, *Historical Story of Bee County*, 9. Margaret's birth date of April 3, 1824, is engraved on her tombstone in Evergreen Cemetery, Victoria, Tex. It is consistent with her age of 25 in the U.S. Bureau of the Census, 1850, Victoria Co. (Margaret Hardy, wife of Milton Hardy), and 45 in the 1870 census (Margaret Borland, head of household). In both documents Margaret lists her birthplace as New York.

3. John Heffernan is identified as a candle maker in the *Victoria* (Texas) *Advocate*, Sept. 28, 1934, cited in Mary Margaret Bierman, "A History of Victoria, Texas, 1824–1900," 72; also in Roy Grimes, ed., *300 Years in Victoria County*, 377, and in C. Richard King, "Margaret Borland," 321. In 1829 the Heffernan family came to Texas with other colonists on the brig *New Packet*, whose passenger list is reproduced in full in William H. Oberste, *Texas Irish Empresarios and Their Colonies: Power and Hewetson, McMullen and McGloin*, 47–48.

4. Mexican officials looked with favor upon Irish immigrants, whom they could expect to be devout Catholics; see Graham Davis, *Land! Irish Pioneers in Mexican and Revolutionary Texas*, 32, 78. For the terms of the colonization agreements, see Oberste, *Texas Irish Empresarios*, 3–4, 19, 99–100, 130; Ezell, *Historical Story of Bee County*, 5, 7.

5. For the arrival of the colonists in October, see Davis, *Land!* 83. The ship's manifest for the brig *New Packet*, Oct. 26, 1829, is cited in Oberste, *Texas Irish Empresarios*, 47–48. The manifest lists thirty-five passengers, including "John Heffernan, wife and four children." The Heffernans did eventually have four children, but sons John and James were born after the family's arrival in Texas; see Rose, "Some Historical Facts," 130. If there were indeed four children at the time of landing, the names and fates of these additional siblings are unknown.

6. Davis, *Land!* 84.

7. Ibid.; Oberste, *Texas Irish Empresarios*, 52.

8. John Heffernan was one of a few settlers to receive a confirmation of his land claim when a Mexican inspector came in 1831. In all likelihood, these first titles were granted to settlers who had been living on the property for some time and had established a homestead.

9. Rachel Bluntzer Hébert, *The Forgotten Colony, San Patricio de Hibernia: The History, the People, and the Legends of the Irish Colony of McMullen-McGloin*, 25–26; Grace Bauer, *Bee County Centennial, 1858–1958*, 5, 7.

10. Hébert, *The Forgotten Colony*, 25–26; John Brendan Flannery, *The Irish Texans*, 37; Oberste, *Texas Irish Empresarios*, 60, 127, 131. All of these scholars identify John Heffernan as one of the colonists who received land in 1831.

11. Rose notes that both John and James were born in Texas. If true, that would date their births after the family's arrival in Texas in October 1829 ("Some Historical Facts," 130). John Jr. married in 1847 and died soon after the birth of his only child (marriage records, Victoria Co., vol. 1, 1838–1870; Rose, "Some Historical Facts," 132). To have been old enough to marry in 1847, John must have been born not long after the family landed in Texas, almost certainly by the close of 1830. James's birth date of 1834 is extrapolated from his age of 26 years in the U.S. Bureau of the Census, 1860, Victoria Co., Tex.

12. Flannery, *The Irish Texans*, 37.

13. Hébert, *The Forgotten Colony*, appendix A, 430; Davis, *Land!* appendix 2, 247; Ezell, *Historical Story of Bee County*, 7.

14. For a breakdown of assessments per league of land, see Oberste, *Texas Irish Empresarios*, 121–22.

15. Ezell, *Historical Story of Bee County*, 18, citing Mrs. I. C. Madray.

16. Grimes, ed., *300 Years in Victoria County*, 377; Flanagan, *Trailing the Longhorns*, 83.

17. Facts about cholera's history and treatment come from Davis, *Land!* 170. Symptoms, progression, and mode of transmission are described in "Summary of Infectious and Communicable Diseases Manual," 16th ed., http://www.tulsa-health.org/assessment/appendix_c.pdf (accessed Nov. 13, 2005), 304.

18. Discussion of yellow fever from Davis, *Land!* 171.

19. Flannery, *The Irish Texans*, 53.

20. Patrick Burke reminiscences, quoted in Oberste, *Texas Irish Empresarios*, 146–47; also quoted in Davis, *Land!* 181, and in Ezell, *Historical Story of Bee County*, 11.

21. Flannery, *The Irish Texans*, 69; Oberste, *Texas Irish Empresarios*, 151–52.

22. Consternation and meeting between Cos and empresario in Oberste, *Texas Irish Empresarios*, 152; Goliad and Lipantitlán engagements, 154–56. Reports of Irish colonists fighting on the side of Mexico: Ira Westover to Sam Houston, Nov. 15, 1835, quoted in Oberste, *Texas Irish Empresarios*, 158; J. H. Jones to James W. Fannin, Nov. 12, 1835, quoted in Hébert, *The Forgotten Colony*, 37.

23. For these lists, see Oberste, *Texas Irish Empresarios*, 154, 170; Flannery, *The Irish Texans*, 70.

24. Flannery, *The Irish Texans*, 66.

25. Oberste, *Texas Irish Empresarios*, 170

26. The numbers in Santa Anna's forces are cited at the *New Handbook of Texas Online*, s.v. "Texas Revolution," by Eugene C. Barker and James W. Pohl, http://www.tsha.utexas.edu/handbook/online/articles/view/TT/qdt1.html (accessed Sept. 9, 2003), 4; in Adrian Anderson et al., *Texas and Texans*, 226. The size of Urrea's army is from Davis, *Land!* 121.

27. Oberste, *Texas Irish Empresarios*, 183n39.

28. Mary Heffernan Riggs in Mrs. I. C. Madray, *A History of Bee County*, 1–2. This out-of-print account is reproduced in Oberste, *Texas Irish Empresarios*, 145–46, and in Ezell, *Historical Story of Bee County*, 7–8. Dating the deaths is difficult. Rose states that John Heffernan was killed just before the invasion of Santa Anna, which would mean autumn 1835 ("Some Historical Facts," 130). Mary's account mentions plowing, which normally takes place in early spring. The preponderance of evidence points to an early spring date, particularly in view of the citizens' petition signed by John Heffernan on Feb. 1. If the brothers were planning to join

Fannin at Goliad, their deaths must have occurred between Feb. 1, 1836, when Fannin landed at Copano to take command of Goliad (as stated in Oberste, *Texas Irish Empresarios*, 189), and Mar. 20, when he surrendered. A Mexican officer who stayed at the Heffernan home in May garnered the impression that the killings took place in April. For his account, see José Enrique de la Peña, *With Santa Anna in Texas: A Personal Narrative of the Revolution*, 186. Perhaps the plan to join Fannin was an embellishment added after Texas independence, when Irish loyalties were questioned and colonists tried to justify their actions during the war.

Also problematic is the question of who was responsible for the deaths. Mary says it was "Indians and Mexicans"; Peña says it was "Indians"; Rose says it was "Mexican assassins." Flanagan says that John Heffernan was "slain in the 1836 Texas Revolution by General José Urrea's advancing forces" (*Trailing the Longhorns*, 83). Mexicans acting in official capacity did not normally kill noncombatants, especially Irish colonists, whom they considered citizens of Mexico; see Davis, *Land!* 145. Considering all of the foregoing and relying on Mary as the primary source, I find the most probable cause of their deaths to be an Indian raid on the James Heffernan homestead shortly before Urrea's army reached San Patricio on February 27.

29. For the children's ages in early 1836, see notes 2 and 11.

30. Rose, "Some Historical Facts," 130.

31. Ezell states that "The family of Mrs. John Heffernan continued to live in San Patricio until after the Battle of San Jacinto" (*Historical Story of Bee County*, 9).

32. Mexican officer José Enrique de la Peña secured lodging with the family in San Patricio the night of May 30. Peña's diary is unclear whether he stayed with the Heffernans May 29–30 or just May 30. He describes this encounter in his diary, *With Santa Anna in Texas*, 186.

33. "McGoin's Historical Notes," in *Lamar Papers*, vol. 5, edited by Glulick and Allen, 382, quoted in Hébert, *The Forgotten Colony*, 119.

34. Flannery, *The Irish Texans*, 74.

35. Ibid., 75; Davis, *Land!* 139–45.

36. The anecdote of the Heffernan children passing for Mexicans is told in Bierman, "A History of Victoria, Texas, 1824–1900," 73. It is repeated in Grimes, ed., *300 Years in Victoria County*, 377, as well as in King, "Margaret Borland," 321, and Flanagan, *Trailing the Longhorns*, 83. Both Bierman and King cite Rose ("Some Historical Facts," 130–31) as their source, but the story does not appear in the reprint edition of Rose (1961). Flanagan's research included an interview with Corinne Wood, granddaughter of Margaret Heffernan Borland, who perhaps repeated a tale passed down in her family.

37. Ezell claims that Mrs. Heffernan and her children remained in San Patricio until after the battle of San Jacinto on April 21 (*Historical Story of Bee County*, 9). If his information is correct, the family neither joined the Runaway Scrape nor fled to Goliad for protection.

38. Davis, *Land!* 149; Oberste, *Texas Irish Empresarios*, 238; Flannery, *The Irish Texans*, 84.

39. Peña, *With Santa Anna in Texas*, 186. My attention was first drawn to this connection by Hébert, *The Forgotten Colony*, 120. Mary Heffernan's narrative in Madray, *History of Bee County*, has long been considered the only record that an Indian raid was responsible for the deaths of John Heffernan and the James Heffernan family; see Flannery, *The Irish Texans*, 80. In fact, Peña's diary provides an independent confirmation that this attack took place.

40. Flannery, *The Irish Texans*, 78–79.

41. Ezell, *Historical Story of Bee County*, 9.

42. Rose, "Some Historical Facts," 130–31.

43. Ezell, *Historical Story of Bee County,* 9.

44. Rose, "Some Historical Facts," 131.

45. Death of Mrs. Heffernan: Charles Spurlin, e-mail correspondence to Phyllis McKenzie, May 27, 2003; John Heffernan, estate, Victoria Co. probate minutes, vol. 3, 199. The obituary of Margaret's daughter Nellie says that "after the Battle of San Jacinto, the Heffernans returned to this section [Victoria Co.] to make their home." For the obituary, see "Mrs. Kreisle Passed Away Friday Night," *Victoria* (Texas) *Advocate,* Mar. 31, 1929.

46. Details of Mary's life are from Ezell, *Historical Story of Bee County,* 8–9.

47. Marriage date from marriage records, Victoria Co., vol. 1, 1838–1870. Census statistic from Gifford White, *The 1840 Census of the Republic of Texas* (Austin: Pemberton Press, 1966), 200, cited in King, "Margaret Borland," 322.

48. Dunbar's death in a pistol duel soon after birth of his daughter is told by Grimes, ed., *300 Years in Victoria County,* 377, and by King, "Margaret Borland," 322. Mary's birth year is on her tombstone in Victoria, Tex.

49. Marriage date of Oct. 16, 1845, in marriage records, Victoria Co., vol. 1, 1838–1870.

50. Information about the Hardy family comes from Rose, "Some Historical Facts," 137–38; from "Vignettes of Victoria County—Hardy, Mr. and Mrs. William, extracted from *Victoria Advocate,* Historical Edition, May 1968," 4–5; and from King, "Margaret Borland," 322.

51. "Victoria County, Texas, City Council Members," http://www.viptx.net/vcgs/citycouncil.html (accessed Oct. 18, 2005), 1.

52. White, *The 1840 Census of the Republic of Texas,* cited in King, "Margaret Borland," 322.

53. Eliza's existence is noted by Milton Hardy's will, dated Feb. 26, 1847, Victoria County probate minutes, vol. 2, 178–79. Julia was two years old in the U.S. Bureau of the Census, 1850, Victoria Co., and eleven in the 1860 census. This indicates a birth date in midyear or later 1848. Rose says, "Of this marriage were born several children, all of whom died in infancy except two daughters" ("Some Historical Facts," 131). A young son, William, died in 1852, according to "Notes on Early Residents of Victoria—Milton Hardy, excerpted from the 88th Anniversary Edition of the *Victoria Advocate,* Sept. 28, 1934," 1. If other Hardy babies died besides Eliza and William, their names and dates are unknown. In the 1850 census, Julia is the only Hardy child listed in the household.

54. Rosa's birth date is problematic. The U.S. Bureau of the Census, 1860, Victoria Co., lists her as eight years old, indicating birth in 1851 or 1852. Victor Rose says she was "in her thirteenth year" when she died in autumn 1867, which would mean birth in 1854 or 1855 ("Some Historical Facts," 131). His understanding of Rosa's age cannot be correct, even though he knew her as a sister-in-law. Rosa's father, Milton Hardy, died Aug. 24, 1852, according to Rose himself (138). Rose states elsewhere (131) that Milton Hardy died in 1855, but the 1852 date is confirmed by probate proceedings, which began in Dec. 1852; see "Estate of Milton H. Hardy," Victoria County probate minutes, vol. 2, 178–89. It seems likely, then, that Rosa was born in 1852.

55. Flanagan, *Trailing the Longhorns,* 11; *New Handbook of Texas Online,* "Cattle Trailing," 1.

56. "Estate of Milton H. Hardy," Victoria County probate minutes, vol. 2, 178–89.

57. "Estate of John Heffernan," Victoria County probate minutes, vol. 3, 199–200. When

Milton Hardy filed on the estates of John and James Heffernan, he apparently confused which man was Margaret's father and which was her uncle.

58. Rose, "Some Historical Facts," 138.

59. "Notes on Early Residents of Victoria—Milton Hardy," 1, cites a *Victoria Advocate* memorial edition stating that Hardy died of cholera in 1852 (see note 53) and "his two little children, William and Eliza, died in the same epidemic." Eliza was born before Feb. 1847. Neither Eliza nor William appears in the 1850 census of the Hardy household. Their absence from the listing of family members suggests that Eliza died *before* the 1850 census and that William was born *after* that year.

60. "Estate of Milton H. Hardy," Victoria County probate minutes, vol. 2, 178–89.

61. Ibid. James Heffernan bought oxen and other property at the estate auction.

62. Marriage date 1847 from marriage records, Victoria, vol. 1, 1838–1870. Heffernan's early death is recorded by Rose ("Some Historical Facts," 132): "Soon after the birth of their only child, John M. Heffernan of Cuero, both he and his wife died." A birth date of 1848 for the son is consistent with three U.S. censuses: John M. Heffernan is listed as age 12 in the 1860 census (Victoria Co.), age 22 in the 1870 census (Victoria Co.), and age 32 in the 1880 census (DeWitt Co.).

63. Henry Wolff Jr., "Up the Trail, but Not Forgotten." Wolff says that Louisa was born in Virginia; Milton Hardy brought her as a slave to Victoria in 1846. She is buried in the "colored" section of Evergreen Cemetery in Victoria. Her gravestone, with an alternate spelling of her name, bears this inscription:

Louise Hardy Johnson
Died October 28, 1910 Age 102
Mammy: by children of Margaret Borland

The gravestone information indicates that Louisa was born in 1808. During probate of Milton Hardy's estate in 1852, an inventory of his property lists the slave Louisa (Luisa) as 32 years old, with children ages 9 and 7; see Victoria County probate minutes, vol. 2, 178–89. This would place her birth around 1820. Such a time frame is more consistent with her being a nanny to the Borland children, who were born between 1857 and 1864 (see note 1).

64. Marriage records, Victoria Co., Texas, vol. 1, 1838–1870.

65. I am indebted for this suggestion to Charles Spurlin of Victoria. Borland may well have been Protestant. Moreover, Margaret's grave is found not in the Catholic cemetery of Victoria but rather in Evergreen Cemetery. However, Margaret's daughter Nellie Borland Wood-Kreisle *is* buried in the Catholic cemetery, possibly as a result of her Catholic boarding-school experience after Margaret's death. See *Victoria Advocate,* Mar. 31, 1929, obituary titled "Mrs. Kreisle Passed Away Last Night."

66. Rose, "Some Historical Facts," 35.

67. King, "Margaret Borland," 323, citing various documents in Borland Papers, Center for American History, University of Texas–Austin.

68. Ibid., 322, citing *Victoria Advocate,* May 12, 1968; Grimes, ed., *300 Years in Victoria County,* 246.

69. U.S. Bureau of the Census, 1860, Victoria Co., Tex., lists these people as part of the

Borland household: James Heffernan, twenty-six, stock raiser, born in Texas; John Heffernan, twelve, born in Texas; and H___ V___ (illegible), laborer, born in Germany.

70. Rose ("Some Historical Facts," 19) describes the livestock exhibition. As one of the prominent stockmen of the region, Alexander Borland certainly would have been expected to participate. In 1859 he made two payments to the Gulf Coast Fair Association: receipts for $20 and $3 are in Borland Papers, Center for American History, Austin, Tex.

71. For Alex's, Jesse's, and Nellie's birth dates, see note 1. Willie was six years old when he died in 1867, according to Rose ("Some Historical Facts," 131).

72. "Schedule of Household and Kitchen Furniture, Estate of Margaret A. Borland," July 13, 1873, Borland Papers, Center for American History, Austin, Tex. (see note 93).

73. Rose, "Some Historical Facts," 131.

74. Flanagan, *Trailing the Longhorns,* 14.

75. Ibid., 16.

76. Rose, "Some Historical Facts," 19, 118.

77. Residents of Victoria were enthusiastic secessionists, according to Kate Stoner O'Connor, introduction to Rose, "Some Historical Facts," viii. Enlistment fever and long-horn development are described in Flanagan, *Trailing the Longhorns,* 14–16.

78. For the numbers of cattle see Flanagan, *Trailing the Longhorns,* 15; *New Handbook of Texas Online,* s.v. "Cattle Trailing," 1.

79. Julia Hardy and Victor Rose married on Mar. 5, 1866, from marriage records, Victoria Co., vol. 1, 1838–1870. Rose's experiences in the Civil War are told by Kate Stoner O'Connor, introduction to Rose, "Some Historical Facts," ix–xii. O'Connor also says that Rose was "quite a ladies' man and wrote love poems to the girls for himself and his friends" (vii). O'Connor cites Rose's sister, who reports that Rose courted several girls when he returned from the war but chose to marry Julia (xiii).

80. Mary Dunbar and A. B. Peticolas married May 3, 1866, marriage records, Victoria Co., vol. 1, 1838–1870. Details of Peticolas's life are from Henry Wolff Jr., "Some Movers and Shak-ers of Early Victoria: Evergreen Cemetery Tour—A. B. Peticolas," part 2, 4.

81. Julia's daughter was six months old when yellow fever struck in autumn 1867; Mary's son was an infant; see Rose, "Some Historical Facts," 131.

82. King, "Margaret Borland," 322; Borland Papers, Center for American History. It is probable, but unproven, that the Borlands opened the market while Alexander was still alive. Surviving paperwork shows payments to butchers for work in May 1867 and afterward. Margaret paid the 1867 butcher tax assessment on Feb. 15, 1868.

83. Hide and tallow factories are described in Flanagan, *Trailing the Longhorns,* 73.

84. Rose, "Some Historical Facts," 131.

85. Ibid.

86. King, "Margaret Borland," 322, referencing receipts in the Borland Papers.

87. On the extraordinary heat of summer 1867, see Murphy Givens, "Year of the Yellow Fever," 1; Diary of Capt. Ned Mercer, July 31, 1867, quoted in Dee Woods, "Yellow Fever Killed Many Early Settlers: John Dunn Recalls When He Took Down with Dread Disease," 1. Reports of fever are also found in D. W. C. Baker, "The Yellow Fever in Texas in 1867," *A Texas Scrap-book, Made Up of the History, Biography, and Miscellany of Texas and Its People,* 487.

88. Texas State Library and Archives Commission, introduction to "Livingston Lindsay to

Pease, October 9, 1867," 1; "Yellow Fever," Encyclopedia.com, http://www.encyclopedia.com/printable.asp?url=/ssi/y1/yellowf.html (accessed Sept. 18, 2003).

89. Heather Green Campbell, "The Yellow Pestilence: A Comparative Study of the 1853 Yellow Fever Epidemic in New Orleans and the Galveston, Texas, Scourge of 1867," 23; Givens, "The Yellow Hand of Death," 1.

90. Tar burning is discussed in Campbell, "The Yellow Pestilence," 25, and in Givens, "The Yellow Hand of Death," 1. Quarantines are discussed in Givens, "The Yellow Hand of Death," 2, and in the *New Handbook of Texas Online,* s.v. "Epidemic Diseases," 1–2. The precaution of smoking the mail is reported in Givens, "The Yellow Hand of Death," 2. Pouring lime in the sewers is given in Campbell, "The Yellow Pestilence," 24. Mule-drawn collection carts are mentioned in Campbell, "The Yellow Pestilence," 25.

91. Rose, "Some Historical Facts," 131.

92. On standards of yellow fever care, see Campbell, "The Yellow Pestilence," 26.

93. "Rec'd of Mrs. Borland, ten dollars in specie for one mattress, pillow & pillow slip," Sept. 15, 1868, Borland Papers, Center for American History.

94. Rose, "Some Historical Facts," 131. That Rosa was the first to die can be determined from a settlement of property that Rosa had inherited from her father. At the time of her death, Rosa's surviving heirs included her mother, Margaret; her sisters Mary, Julia, and Nellie; and her brothers Alex, Jesse, and Willie. Victoria County probate minutes, vol. 4, 109.

95. Rose, "Some Historical Facts," 131. Malcolm's name is chiseled on his grave beside his mother in Victoria, Texas; Charles Spurlin, e-mail correspondence to Phyllis McKenzie, May 20, 2003.

96. Ibid. For Julia's age, see note 53. We know that Rosa died first and that Malcolm died shortly after his mother. The sequence of the other yellow fever deaths is unknown.

97. On Victor Rose's recovery from yellow fever, see Wolff Jr., "Some Movers and Shakers of Early Victoria: Evergreen Cemetery Tour—Victor Marion Rose," http://www.viptx.net/vcgs/evergreencem.html (accessed Oct. 18, 2005), part 1, 5. Grimes (*300 Years in Victoria County,* 377–78) says that Margaret took charge of little Julia until the time of her own death. Margaret's raising of Julia is confirmed by the U.S. Bureau of the Census, 1870, Victoria Co., Tex., which lists Julia Rose as a member of the Borland household. Rose ("Some Historical Facts," 131) mentions that Margaret brought a grandchild with her when she went up the trail in 1873. Julia was that grandchild, for Margaret had no other.

98. Rose, "Some Historical Facts," 131. Rose is the only source for Willie's age. Willie did not live long enough to be recorded in a U.S. census.

99. "Margaret Borland to J. D. Sneigr for digging grave for son," Sept. 29, 1867, Borland Papers, Center for American History.

100. The U.S. Bureau of the Census, 1870, Victoria Co., Tex., lists John Heffernan as a twenty-two-year-old stockkeeper residing in the Borland household.

101. Rose, "Some Historical Facts," 131. Semiramis was a legendary queen of Babylon. Philippa of Hainault (1311–1369) was queen of England and consort of Edward III.

102. Borland Papers, Center for American History, various bills and receipts issued Mar. to Sept., 1868; King, "Margaret Borland," 323.

103. King, "Margaret Borland," 323.

104. "Receipt to M. Borland for $230 for seven horses purchased," Borland Papers, Center for American History, Apr. 15, 1868.

105. Rose, "Some Historical Facts," 132.

106. U.S. Bureau of the Census, 1880, Victoria Co., Tex.

107. "Sworn statements signed by John Heffernan, A. B. Peticolas, and Alex Borland," Borland Papers, Nov. 17, 1873. The question of ownership came up during probate of Margaret Borland's estate; both John and Alex declared that the colts belonged to Alex.

108. King, "Margaret Borland," 324; "Bill of sale for cattle conveyed by Christian Zirjack and wife to Mrs. M. Borland," July 22, 1872, and "Bill of sale for steers conveyed by S. A. Frederick and wife to M. Borland," Sept. 11, 1872, Borland Papers.

109. Flanagan, *Trailing the Longhorns,* 83; "Some Movers and Shakers of Early Victoria: Victoria Cemetery Tour—Margaret Heffernan Borland," http://www.viptx.net/vcgs/evergreencem.html (accessed Oct. 18, 2005), part 2, 5.

110. For Chisholm Trail development and statistics, see Flanagan, *Trailing the Longhorns,* 36, 55, 70.

111. Ibid., 77, for discussion of Wichita's rise.

112. Ibid., 80, for information about the 1871 trailing season and the wintering cattle; also see Joseph G. McCoy, *Historical Sketches of the Cattle Trade of the West and Southwest,* chap. 12, 1–2.

113. *New Orleans Picayune,* quoted in the *Rocky Mountain News,* Apr. 5, 1872, cited in Flanagan, *Trailing the Longhorns,* 80.

114. Flanagan, *Trailing the Longhorns,* 85.

115. For the roles and age range of waddies and ramrods, see the *New Handbook of Texas Online,* s.v. "Cattle Trailing," 3. For the ages of Alex and Jesse, see note 1. Many writers, beginning with Flanagan (*Trailing the Longhorns,* 83), have claimed that Alex and Jesse were both under fifteen at the time of the trail drive. Flanagan's source for determining their ages was probably Rose, who erroneously states that their parents married "about the year 1858"; see Rose ("Some Historical Facts," 131). In fact, Margaret and Alexander Borland married in 1856; see marriage records, Victoria Co., vol. 1, 1838–1870. Alex was born the next year. For the size of the Borland trail drive, see the *Wichita Beacon,* June 4, 1873, announcing Margaret's arrival in the city with "about one thousand head of cattle." Flanagan (*Trailing the Longhorns,* 83) states that the Borland group drove 2,500 animals, but the period newspaper is a more reliable primary source. The number of hired hands is extrapolated from "Chisholm Trail," Oklahoma Historical Society Encyclopedia, 1, which states that ten to fourteen cowboys would be needed for an average herd of 2,500–3,000 cattle. Margaret's herd was less than half that size, so, presumably, fewer cowboys were needed.

116. Presence of the black cook is from Flanagan (*Trailing the Longhorns,* 83). For the girls' ages, see note 1. Rose says that Nellie was seven and Julia four, but he believed the trail drive took place in 1872; see Rose ("Some Historical Facts," 131). Margaret went up the trail in 1873, as attested by Wichita newspapers and by the date of death on her gravestone.

117. The wet year of 1873 is reported in Flanagan (*Trailing the Longhorns,* 85); the Waco suspension bridge is also described there (63, 68).

118. Ibid., 63, 68.

119. Trail drives typically traveled ten to twelve miles per day, according to "Texas

Chisholm Trail," 6; ten miles per day, according to "Chisholm Trail," Oklahoma Historical Society Encyclopedia Online, 1; and ten to fifteen miles daily according to the *New Handbook of Texas Online,* s.v. "Cattle Trailing," 3.

120. The estimated travel time was 2–2¼ months, which was determined by taking the modern highway distance between Victoria and Wichita (approximately 650 miles), adding 20 percent for indirectness and deviations along the Chisholm Trail (130 miles), and dividing by the average distance covered per day, which is a conservative 10–12 miles.

121. On the numbers of cattle and the conditions in Wichita, see King, "Margaret Borland," 325; Flanagan, *Trailing the Longhorns,* 77.

122. *Wichita Beacon,* June 4, 1873. Copy provided to the author by Charles Spurlin.

123. Ibid., July 9, 1873. Copy provided to the author by Charles Spurlin.

124. For a description of Karatofsky's store, see King, "Margaret Borland," 325; "Bill to Mrs. Borland for goods bought of J. Karatofsky," Borland Papers, July 6, 1873.

125. For the losses of the 1873 cattle market, see McCoy, *Historical Sketches of the Cattle Trade,* chap. 13, 1–3.

126. Receipt, J. L. Cunningham to A. B. Peticolas and Thos. Sterne, Borland Papers, June 25, 1873.

127. For Nellie's date of birth, see note 1.

128. "Congestion of the Brain" from *Wichita City Eagle,* July 10, 1873; "trail driving fever" from Flanagan, *Trailing the Longhorns,* 83. Flanagan says her source was a "family member," probably Corinne Wood, who was one of the daughters of the Wood family that raised Margaret's daughter Nellie and whom Flanagan had interviewed.

129. This diagnosis was suggested by Mary Ann Wright, of Victoria, e-mail correspondence to Charles Spurlin, Apr. 10, 2003.

130. *Wichita Beacon,* July 9, 1873.

131. Rose, "Some Historical Facts," 131.

132. *Wichita Beacon,* July 9, 1873.

133. "Bill and receipt from New York Store, Wichita, to Mrs. Martin," July 5, 1873, penciled in parentheses "shroud"; bill, Charles W. Hill to Mrs. Borland, Wichita, July 5, 1873; receipt, Henry Bolt to J. M. Heffernan for coffin and box, Wichita, July 7, 1873; receipt, Charles W. Hill to J. H. Heffernan for payment in full of medicines furnished to Mrs. Borland, Wichita, July 8, 1873, Borland Papers, Center for American History.

134. The *Wichita Beacon* of July 9, 1873, says, "Her remains were sent to Victoria, Texas, her former home on Tuesday evening." Margaret Borland died on Saturday, July 5, so the following Tuesday would have been July 8.

135. Flanagan, *Trailing the Longhorns,* 83. Photo of marker at Wolff Jr., "Some Movers and Shakers of Early Victoria: Evergreen Cemetery Tour," s.v. "Margaret Heffernan Borland," part 2, 5.

136. Rose, "Some Historical Facts," 131.

137. Margaret Borland, estate, Victoria County probate minutes, vol. A-3, 396.

138. Ibid., 430.

139. Ibid., vol. 4, 118.

140. Cattle market conditions in 1873 are from McCoy, *Historical Sketches of the Cattle Trade,* chap. 13, 2–3; Flanagan, *Trailing the Longhorns,* 85.

141. Flanagan discusses barbed wire and fencing (*Trailing the Longhorns,* 85, 88) and railroads (viii, 90); also see the *New Handbook of Texas Online,* s.v. "Cattle Trailing," 2. Information about the advancing quarantine line is found in Flanagan (*Trailing the Longhorns,* 93) and in the *New Handbook of Texas Online,* s.v. "Cattle Trailing," 3.

142. Information about the Western Trail and the Texas trail extension comes from Flanagan (*Trailing the Longhorns,* 95, 118, 122, 124, 126).

143. Rose says that Alex and Jesse were livestock dealers ("Some Historical Facts," 79, 131). Information about Alex's later life comes from Leopold Morris, *Pictorial History of Victoria and Victoria County: Where the History of Texas Begins,* 32; and from Nellie Borland's obituary, *Victoria Advocate,* Mar. 31, 1929, 1, 3.

144. Information about Jesse, including date and place of death, is found in Nellie Borland's obituary, *Victoria Advocate,* Mar. 31, 1929, 1, 3. Information about the friendship of Jesse and John Kendrick comes from Morris, *Pictorial History of Victoria,* 32; Flanagan, *Trailing the Longhorns,* 124, 27n, 180–81; and Grimes, ed., *300 Years in Victoria County,* 374–75.

145. Rose reports that James Heffernan "died a few years hence, leaving several small children" ("Some Historical Facts," 132). Because James's name does not appear in the 1880 Texas census, it is likely that he died before the census was taken.

146. U.S. Bureau of the Census, 1880, Cuero, DeWitt Co., Tex. Quotation from Rose, "Some Historical Facts," 132.

147. The U.S. Bureau of the Census, 1880, Victoria Co., Tex., lists the following people living in the household:

> William Jones, head of household, 30, born South Carolina, farmer
> M. J. Jones, wife, 28, born South Carolina, keeping house
> Julia Rosa Rose, niece, 13, born Texas
> Clarence Jones, daughter, 9, born South Carolina
> Lela Jones, daughter, 6, born South Carolina
> Fannie Jones, daughter, 3, born Texas
> Ellen Jones, daughter, 3, born Texas
> Virginia Jones, daughter, 1, born Texas

The census record suggests that the Jones family moved from South Carolina to Texas sometime after the birth of Lela in 1874 and before the births of Fannie and Ellen (twins?) in 1877.

148. Quotation and details of Nellie Borland's life are from her obituary, "Mrs. Kreisle Passed Away Friday Night," in the *Victoria Advocate,* Mar. 31, 1929, 1, 3. That Nazareth Academy was a boarding school is indicated by the 1880 census of Victoria Co., Tex., where Nellie Borland is listed as "at school," with head of household given as Mother Superior Mary St. Clair.

149. The names of Margaret's children from her three marriages appear in various records: (1) Mary Dunbar; (2) Eliza, Julia, William, and Rosa Hardy; and (3) Alex, Jesse, Willie, and Nellie Borland. Rose ("Some Historical Facts," 131) indicates that several Hardy children died in infancy, but my research has yielded the names of only two that died, Eliza and William.

Araminta ("Minta) Corum Holmsley

MRS. JAMES MONROE HOLMSLEY

Jean A. Stuntz

IN HER LATER YEARS, MINTA HOLMSLEY LIKED to tell tales about her early days in Comanche, Texas, and the times she traveled the cattle drives with her husband.[1] She made her life's experiences sound interesting and even fun. A good storyteller, she chose to emphasize the exciting times and omit those less pleasant. Occasionally she embellished the bare facts with juicy additions in order to make a better story. "Aunt Minta" died at age eighty-five, respected by all who knew her and beloved by her community. It was said that "Mrs. James M. Homsley [*sic*] of Comanche—undaunted by hardship and superstition—was one of the few women to 'go up the trail.'"[2]

Araminta Corum was born on August 9, 1847, in Clifton, Missouri.[3] Her parents moved the family to San Antonio, Texas, in 1864, probably to escape the bitter fighting that was prevalent in Missouri during the Civil War. Minta was in her early teens at that time and was not pressured to marry a soldier during the conflict, as were so many other Southern women. San Antonio was also far from any battle scene, and Texas did not suffer the devastation experienced by so much of the Confederacy.

In Texas to avoid the worst ravages of the war, Minta did, however, find that life was difficult because of the shortages the blockade created. Needles and pins, so necessary to the women's major work of sewing, were impossible to get. Thorns, especially mesquite thorns, became the main substitute. Salt became very scarce, and there was no substitute for that. Instead, women dug up the floors of their smokehouses and boiled the dirt to extract the salt that had dripped from above. Coffee vanished, and, although recipes for "Confederate coffee" were devised, nothing tasted as good as the real thing. When paper became scarce, people wrote letters on the back of old wallpaper. Women became experts at concocting medicines from available materials. That particular experience would later aid Minta on one of her trail drives.[4]

When the Civil War ended, Minta's family moved to Bosque County, Texas, where she lived in the new town of Clifton, about forty miles northwest of Waco.

Figure 18.   Minta Holmsley with Robert T. Hill.
Dallas Morning News (August 28, 1932).

Little information is available about this portion of her life, but it was probably similar to that of other young women on the Texas frontier. Post–Civil War Texas was a rough and lawless place, full of outlaws and hostile Indians. Former soldiers roamed the state, stealing whatever they could find, so towns formed vigilante groups to stop them. These battles often evolved into violent feuds in which many innocent civilians suffered. Mexican outlaws rode into Central Texas on raids and then returned to Mexico with their loot. Indians, especially Comanches, Kiowas, Apaches, Cheyennes, and Arapahos, saw West Texas as their land, where whites were interlopers to be killed or captured. In the first two years following the Civil War, more than two hundred Texans were killed, wounded, or captured by Indians, mostly along the Central Texas frontier, where Minta lived.[5] Race relations also caused problems in Bosque County. According to the Austin *Daily State Journal,* an average of two race-related killings occurred every week in the county. White Democrats, of course, blamed Republicans for inciting the freedmen.[6]

It was in Clifton that Minta met and married Capt. James Monroe Holmsley of Comanche, located between Waco and Abilene in Central Texas. There are no extant records of the courtship, but the marriage seems to have been one of love and companionship. James was one of nine children born to Burrell J. (1807–91) and Lucinda Wagnon Holmsley (1814–1866), original settlers of Comanche County, Texas.[7] James was born April 4, 1838, in Madison County, Arkansas, and his family migrated to Texas in 1852, when he was fourteen. The family first farmed in Williamson County, then moved on to Coryell County, and in 1854 finally settled in Comanche County, six miles east of the village of Comanche, where they decided to go into the cattle business.[8] Within two years, James had begun ranching with W. H. Kingsberry (sometimes spelled Kingsbery or Kingsbury), forming the Kingsberry and Holmsley partnership. They registered their brand in June 1856.[9]

As a young man, James was frequently one of the scouts who pursued marauding Indians and wrought vengeance upon them. In 1857 he joined Capt. T. C. Frost's company of rangers to protect his adopted home from threats. When Texas seceded from the Union in 1861, James joined the Confederate forces and served with Col. Henry E. McCullough's (McCulloch) Company G, 1st Regiment, Texas Mounted Riflemen, which was garrisoned at Camp Colorado to fight the Indians on the frontier. He was quickly promoted from lieutenant to captain and served as commandant from the fall of 1861 until at least April 1862. According to his records, as officer in charge he oversaw the dispensing of rations and forage for the animals, disability discharges, and roll call and carried out orders to detail troops to other forts.[10] He retained the title of captain for the rest of his life.[11]

After the war Minta and James Holmsley married and set up housekeeping in Comanche, Texas. Comanche County in 1874 was home to about one thousand people, and the small town of Comanche was a typical cattleman's town with seven saloons. With more than enough taverns in town, James opened a general

Figure 19.   Daguerreotype of Thomas Jefferson Holmsley (1834–1903),
James's brother (left); James Monroe Holmsley (1838–81), Minta's husband
(middle); and W. H. Kingsberry, a business partner of James. James Holmsley
Papers. Courtesy of Mintah Holmsley Harris (Minta's daughter), Lubbock,
Texas; Center for American History, University of Texas–Austin.

Figure 20.   Minta Holmsley in the doorway of her native stone home built in 1869–70. Photograph by granddaughter Mintah Harris Chappelle. James Holmsley Papers, Center for American History, University of Texas–Austin.

merchandise store while also dealing in cattle. He hired workers to build a large two-story house of native stone, and in October 1873 he and Minta moved into their new home. Within five years of their marriage, James had acquired more than five hundred acres of land near Comanche, as well as three whole city blocks and fourteen other lots in downtown Comanche. In 1874 his total personal worth was $8,076, quite a large sum in those days. In the same year he contracted with the Texas Rangers to supply rations for a company of the Frontier Battalion stationed in Eastland County, adding to the family's income. James was an astute business-man and frequently sold cattle on credit with a 10 percent rate of interest.[12]

James Holmsley continued his partnership with Kingsberry for more than twenty years and made numerous trail drives, which were quite profitable. After Holms-ley's untimely death in 1881, Kingsberry went on to become one of the greatest cattle dealers in Kansas.[13] It was this affiliation with the cattle industry that led to Minta's trips northward on at least two (and possibly four) cattle drives.[14]

One trip that Minta loved to recall was the one on which she went up the Chisholm Trail to Abilene, probably in 1874, when she was twenty-seven. During this journey, she used her medical experience to concoct a new remedy that was to make the news. When one of the five cooks on the drive came down with a bad case of poison oak, Minta put together a mixture of cream of tartar, sulfur, and salts. She reasoned that the cream of tartar would cool the inflamed area, the sul-fur would purify the blood, and the salts would draw out the poisons. She recalled that the cook quickly got better, but she did not specify whether this mixture was used as a poultice or taken internally. Either procedure might have been used in the 1870s. When Minta arrived in Kansas City at the end of the drive, she visited a doctor and his wife; during their conversation she gave him the prescription. In her telling of this story, the prescription soon appeared in a medical journal (unspecified and undocumented), giving her credit for its invention.[15]

Just two years before Minta took to the trail in 1877, the town of Ellis on the Kansas Pacific Railroad became a shipping point for Texas cattle. Minta's husband, James, and his partner, Kingsberry, had driven a mixed herd of seventeen hundred head over the new Western Trail in 1876. The herd started from Comanche on a feeder trail that connected with the Chisholm Trail, proceeded north to Red River Station, and crossed into Indian Territory. As they went farther into the Indian lands, they took the cutoff at Salt Fork or Bluff Creek to connect with the Western Trail, which was not yet clearly established, and then went north into Dodge City or Ellis.[16] The next year Minta made the trail drive with James, heading for Ellis. At times Minta worked with him scouting for watering holes and places to bed the herd at night, but most of the time she followed the herd in a $1,700 carriage that her husband had bought for the trip.[17] Even then the trek was dusty and very slow going, but Minta did occasionally ride a horse. She rode sidesaddle, she said, "because we didn't have better sense."

Minta liked to tell stories that poked fun at herself. In one such tale she was riding out to watch her husband and the other men shoot buffalo from a passing herd when she was thrown from her horse. No one saw her mishap, and she did not want any of the men to worry about her, so she remounted and returned to her buggy. She was quite badly bruised but did not tell James. When he remarked on her quietness and asked whether she felt unwell, she told him it was just a headache and hid the bruises.

On another occasion when she rode out to see the buffalo, instead of taking the time to put a sidesaddle on her own horse, the cowboys just threw one of their saddle blankets over their saddle for her to ride. It was not long before she found out that the saddle blanket had small insects as occupants. When she discovered two of these on her neck, she immediately jumped off the horse and threw the blanket onto the ground, where she tried to stomp the inhabitants to death, all the while using most unlady-like language. The cowboys witnessing this behavior were amazed because Minta was normally quite genteel. Upon learning the circumstances, however, they forgave her.[18]

On the 1877 drive, when they reached the stock pens at the railhead in Ellis, Kansas, James and his partner went on to St. Louis to transact other business. While they were gone, a telegram for Holmsley and Kingsberry arrived from a Chicago cattle company that wanted to buy some of their herd. Minta knew that the prices would drop as soon as all the other herds arrived in Kansas, so she completed the sale without taking the time to get her husband's approval. This event took place while she was at a fancy-dress ball, supposedly while there was snow on the ground. Most of the cattle drives left Texas in early spring and arrived at the railheads in early summer, so if there was snow, they must have left very early, which is likely, and encountered a freakish late Kansas snowfall.

Nevertheless, Minta reported that she left the ball, went to the rail station to arrange with the agent for rail cars to transport the cattle to Chicago, and hired a carriage from a livery stable to make the twenty-mile drive out of town—by herself at night—to tell the herd boss to prepare the cattle for shipment. On returning to town, Minta spent the rest of the night arranging the cattle cars for the trip. She did all of this, she said, while dressed in her finest clothing. When Holmsley and Kingsberry returned a few days later, the cattle market had indeed dropped severely, and they initially thought that Minta's act had been ruinous for them. Later at the hotel, Minta received a telegram congratulating her on having made "one of the biggest and best sales that had been made in Chicago."[19] The sale was negotiated two days before the prices dropped, so they made a tidy profit, all because of her initiative, good sense, and hard work that night.[20]

On the 1877 trail drive, Minta added to her tales and told of meeting the notorious outlaw John Wesley Hardin. Hardin's family members were respectable people who lived in Comanche, and almost everyone in the area had a story to tell about the infamous gunslinger. Minta said that, on the cattle drive, while she and James were scouting out in front of the herd for a good trail, they saw a number of Indians. Captain Holmsley waved his hat as a signal to the trailing cowboys to come quickly. Before the raiders fled, Minta recognized one of the group as John Hardin, who was dressed in an Indian disguise.

The true story of John Wesley Hardin is a matter of some debate to this day. He was born in 1853 in Bonham, just south of the Red River between Sherman and Paris in North Texas. His father was a preacher and circuit rider who also taught school and practiced law. When Hardin was only fourteen, he chalked up his first victim when he shot a schoolmate after an argument. The next year he shot an African American man, also during a dispute. He claimed to have shot three soldiers who tried to arrest him and then shot another soldier less than a year later. At eighteen, he went up the Chisholm Trail as a cowboy, but he spent more time killing than herding. He supposedly shot seven people along the way and three more after arriving in Abilene. In 1878 he stood trial in Comanche and was found guilty of murder. During his prison term he studied law and theology and repeatedly tried to escape. In 1895 he received a pardon but soon went back to his murderous ways. In total, he killed more than thirty people, but the gentlemanly Hardin always claimed either that they needed killing or that he was acting in self-defense.[21] Such was the man Minta said she saw masquerading as an Indian the year before his trial.

Later on the same trip, Minta recalled meeting with real Indians—several hundred Sioux who had fought at the Battle of Little Bighorn. These Indians were unarmed and did not bother them, but this story might be another of Minta's embellishments.[22] One unpleasant event that Minta left out when recalling this trip was the death of her son, John. John Claiborn Holmsley was born on February 12, 1876, and, when less than a year old, accompanied his parents on their trip up the trail in 1877. He died in Wyandotte, Kansas, on August 28 of that year. The cause of his death is not recorded.[23]

Daily life on the cattle drives was fairly tedious. The Holmsleys separated their cattle into herds of 2,000–3,000 head each. Every herd had a crew of ten to fifteen cowboys, a trail boss, and a cook. The cattle slowly grazed their way northward, making ten to twelve miles a day. The most common early route for the Holmsley herds was to go straight north from Comanche and then to trail west to a pass near Vernon before crossing the Red River into western Oklahoma. Another option was to go a little east before heading north and then cross the Red River near Wichita Falls. All of the trails from Texas to Kansas had to go through present-day Oklahoma, then known as Indian Territory. Because of encounters with Indians, that part of the trip was the most dangerous.

The various tribal groups that were forcibly settled on the reservations were promised rations from the U.S. government, but the food was either bad, insufficient, or both. The Indians sought to supplement their provisions with beef from the herds that trailed through their allotted lands. Some of the trail bosses shot a steer or two when they saw the Indians approach, justifying the loss of beef as sort of a toll charged to pass through the land. Other trail bosses refused to do so, and then the Indians tried to steal cattle from the herds. This tactic could be fatal for both the cowboys and the Indians, although usually it was not. The encounters did make for some good stories on the cowboys' return, however.[24]

Many pioneers told of their brushes with the Indians, and Minta was no exception. Her story was about saving her favorite pony from the raiding braves. The incident occurred on a night with a full moon, when the Comanches often raided. Suspecting that they would invade her house one night, Minta crept out after dark to stake her pony closer to the house, where it would be safe. As she bent down to pull up the pony's stake, she bumped heads with an Indian who was about to do the same thing. She screamed and the Indian ran away.[25] The plot of that tale is often repeated in pioneer stories, and this may be another one of Minta's flourishes. It seems unlikely that, on a night with a full moon, neither she nor the Comanche saw each other before bumping heads.

Another common topic for old-timers to tell the younger generation about was the dreadful era known as Reconstruction. In Texas mythology, Reconstruction was a terrible time to be white and Democratic, and Gov. Edmund J. Davis (1870–1874) was the most horrible of the Radical Republicans. One thing Davis did that earned him so much hatred was to establish a state police force to control the law-lessness and the Klan activities of post-war Texas.[26] Minta always enjoyed relating her efforts to face down the despised police. When charges were filed against sev-eral men of the Comanche area, the state police came to town to arrest them and stopped at the Holmsley house to get directions. Minta told them it was in their own best interest not to arrest those men if they wanted to get out of town alive. She told them just to throw the warrants into her fireplace and leave, and so they did.[27] No evidence could be found to corroborate this story.

Perhaps the most remarkable facets of Minta Holmsley's life were not those she chose to tell. Snippets can be gleaned from reminisces of other early residents of Comanche. For example, school was held in the Holmsley house during the 1870s, with Mr. and Mrs. A. C. Hilton and Mack Burks as teachers. In the spring of 1871 the Masonic Order of Comanche Lodge 316 (with James as a member) finally got a school built; it opened in the fall of 1872.[28] Census records provide additional fac-tual details. In 1880, when the census was taken, Minta and James had four sons: Frank Marion, age ten; Thomas Howe, age eight; James Sutton, age six; and William, age five months. The Holmsleys also had a daughter, Araminta (sometimes spelled Mintah), age two.[29]

In 1881, tragedy struck the Holmsley household. Minta's husband, James, died unexpectedly on April 28, when he was not quite forty-three. Their youngest son, William ("Billie"), died eight weeks later, in early June, at seventeen months; he was buried in his father's grave. Pregnant when her husband died, Minta gave birth on September 1 to their last child, Monroe, who lived only three days. Neither the causes nor the circumstances of these deaths were recorded. The deaths of spouses and children were common occurrences on the frontier, but this did not diminish their profound impact on the survivors.[30]

Of Minta's seven children, only two survived her. Frank married Lillian Lee Paine in 1876, and they had eight children. He died in 1943 in Pittsburg, Texas. Thomas was killed in an automobile accident in 1915, James died in San Angelo in 1889, and John died in Kansas in 1877. Daughter Mintah married George Harris in 1897, and they had two children. Minta's two youngest, Billie and Monroe, both died in 1881.[31] It was not uncommon for pioneer women to experience the deaths of their children. What was unusual was for widows to remain unmarried after a husband's death, as Minta did. Most widows were forced by financial necessity to remarry, but James left Minta with enough property to enable her not to have to make that choice. Still, as the years passed, she did experience financial difficulty.

Capt. James Holmsley was a well-respected businessman, so it is not surprising to frequently find his name in the deed records of Comanche County. However, it is startling to learn that Minta bought and sold property in her own name dur-ing her marriage. As a republic and later a state, Texas had adopted the commu-nity property system from the Spanish legal practice, so a married woman could legally own land in her own name.[32] However, most of the married women in Texas did not buy or sell land; instead, they normally let their husbands transact all such business. Minta appears in the deed records of Comanche County twelve times during her marriage. She even claimed a patent, which indicates that she was given 76.5 acres of previously unclaimed land free from the state of Texas in 1880, which she then sold for $250. Sometimes purchases and sales of land parcels were by James and Minta together, but each also bought and sold land individually.[33]

Minta was first listed as a property owner separate from her husband on the 1879 tax rolls. In that year, he owned twenty-one parcels of land, two carriages, two horses, six cows, and $200 worth of personal property, while she owned six pieces of land, seven horses, and $200 worth of personal property. James's total worth in 1879 was $16,470, and Minta's was $5,130. The next year James's land was worth $8,231, and Minta's was worth $4,705. They were quite a wealthy family. James remained in ranching and the dry goods business until his death. In 1881, of course, James died. His estate was valued at $6,740, while Minta's total worth was $3,450. It took a few years to settle the estate, but in 1883 it was valued at $4,740, while Minta's was worth $3,475. Minta then vanished from the tax rolls for several years but reappeared in 1890, owning $1,500 of unspecified land in Comanche County.[34] She was listed sporadically on the tax rolls until 1902, when she sold her house and moved away for a few years.[35]

Minta's land purchases and her personal worth indicate that she had a good understanding of business matters. Minta evidently continued in the cattle business as, a year following her husband's death, she is noted as having bought a mare and two colts from W. B. Wagnon. However, as time passed, she apparently faced financial difficulties, so her son Thomas was giving her advice. Writing from Parral, Chihuahua, in 1892, Thomas said, "I am sorry you had to let the piano go back but don't see how you could have done otherwise . . . with proper management you would do quite well until you get the stock paid for."[36]

The U.S. Census of 1900 showed that Araminta was then fifty-one and living alone. She owned her own home free and clear and was also listed in the farm schedule. The 1910 census listed Mrs. Minta Holmsley as living in Crockett County, Texas, with her sister, Mrs. Ella Schairer. Minta's age was given as fifty-five years and reported her occupation as seamstress. The 1920 census had Minta, at age seventy-one, back in Comanche as head of her household, with another family boarding in her home. Mintie Chandler, probably a relative, was a widow with a son, a daughter, and a son-in-law. They all lived in the two-story stone house that James had built for Minta.[37]

Minta saw many changes in the town of Comanche during her life there. Anglo settlement began in 1855 with James's father, Burrell Holmsley, as one of the original settlers. Enough other people moved in and settled so that, by 1856, Comanche County was formed from the surrounding counties. The town of Comanche became the county seat in 1859, and James's brother, Thomas Jefferson Holmsley, served as the county's first sheriff, as well as becoming a bank owner and cattleman with a large operation. Slightly more than seven hundred people lived in Comanche in 1860, including sixty-one slaves. In contrast, there were 14,700 head of cattle in the area, which Minta's husband was to increase a few years later. Most of the farmers grew wheat and corn. Many people left during the Civil War because of Indian depredations, but after the war the population began to increase again. In 1870, shortly after Minta moved there, Comanche had 1,001 residents, 126 farms, and the only newspaper—the *Comanche Chief*—in that part of the state.[38]

The *Comanche Chief* was owned for a year or so by Joe and Robert Hill (1858–1941). When Joe and Robert were orphaned during the Civil War, Joe ran away and became a printer in Comanche. He wrote to Robert in Tennessee and encouraged him to come to Texas. Robert arrived in Comanche in 1874 at the age of sixteen. In 1877 Robert made the trip up the trail with James and Minta Holmsley, probably the most memorable event of his youth in Comanche. Robert developed an interest in geology and today is known as the father of Texas geology. He left Comanche in 1882 but remained Minta's lifelong friend.[39] He described her as "entirely self-educated. She read and talked good literature and had the carriage and manners of one native and to the manor born."[40]

By 1880, the area had grown considerably. James was not alone in thinking that investing in Comanche County land was a good idea. The county's population was 8,608, with 1,985 farms and ranches and more than 21,000 head of cattle. The railroad came to Comanche in 1881, ending the need to drive livestock up the arduous trail to market. That was also the year that James died. The 1890s were bad for many people in the country, with financial panics (now referred to as depressions), droughts, and severe winters, but Comanche prospered. Ranching continued to be important; the county was home to 43,000 head of cattle and 15,000 sheep in 1890, and the population continued to grow substantially, from 15,679 in 1890 to 23,009 in 1900.[41]

Minta's last years were spent comfortably, and even though she was in poor health her final year, she was surrounded by her extended family and loyal friends. She had enough money to remain a lady in the eyes of her community. She was a member of the local Presbyterian church and a favorite of the town's children. Although she had never attended a formal school, she was self-taught and read extensively. She loved to discuss literature with her friends, and her husband had made even a few literary efforts.[42] Minta stayed involved in community activities, especially those concerning children. When she died on March 2, 1933, at the age of eighty-five, former Comanche Boy Scouts served as pallbearers at her funeral. Her life was full of the normal joys and sorrows of a pioneer woman, even if it lacked the more exciting flourishes of her stories about going up the Texas cattle trails during the boom years, when cattle were king.[43]

NOTES

1. The author wishes to thank both Margaret T. Waring, director of the Comanche Public Library, for her assistance and personal insights, and Betty Bustos, archivist at the Panhandle-Plains Historical Museum Research Center, for her help.

2. Heritage Division of Comanche County Texas, *Patchwork of Memories: Historical Sketches of Comanche County, Texas,* 6.

3. *Comanche Chief,* March 10, 1933, 5.

4. Ralph A. Wooster, *Civil War Texas,* 31–33.

5. Jo Ella Powell Exley, ed., *Texas Tears and Texas Sunshine: Voices of Frontier Women,* 179.

6. *The New Handbook of Texas Online,* s.v. "Bosque County."

7. U.S. Bureau of the Census, 1860, 1870, Comanche Co., Tex., 257, 182; Margaret Waring and Samuel J. C. Waring, *Comanche County Gravestone Inscriptions,* vol. 1, 6. In the 1860 census, the family name is incorrectly spelled as "Burrel Homsley." Burrell was age fifty-three and born in Kentucky, with real estate valued at $3,372 and personal property valued at $13,874. Lucinda was age forty-six and born in Indiana, with all of the children except the last one born in Arkansas. In the 1870 census Burrell ("Burrel") is listed as a stock raiser and a widower living with his oldest daughter, Amanda, and her eleven-year-old son, Burrell (also listed as "Burrel" by the census).

8. *The New Handbook of Texas Online,* s.v. "Holmsley, James Monroe."

9. Dick King, "The Businesswoman of Comanche County," 48, 54–56; Mark and Brand Records, book A, Comanche Co. Courthouse, Comanche, Tex.

10. James Holmsley, military records, c. Aug. 1861–Apr. 1862.

11. *Comanche Chief,* May 28, 1881; Eulalia Nabors Wells, comp., *Blazing the Way: Tales of Comanche County Pioneers,* 159; *The New Handbook of Texas Online,* s.v. "Camp Colorado."

12. James Holmsley, promissory notes, 1871–1872.

13. Comanche County, tax rolls, 1867–1904.

14. D. K. Doyle, "Mrs. Holmsley Went up the Chisholm Trail," 28; "Woman Who Pioneered in West Texas Dies," 478; "Mrs. Araminta Holmsley," obituary, 27.

15. Doyle, "Mrs. Holmsley Went up the Chisholm Trail," 28. Thomas Uvan Taylor states that this incident occurred on an 1877 drive that went up the Western Trail to Dodge City ("Honeymoon on the Old Cattle Trail," 4).

16. "Cattle and Cowley County Cattle Drives 1876–1880." Between May 8 and May 24, 1876, the following herds passed Red Fork Agency in Indian Territory: May 16, Captain King, four mixed herds of 7,400; May 20, Kingsberry and Holmsley, mixed herd of 1,577; May 20, Quinlan and Shepard, mixed herd of 1,200; May 20, Hughes and Hood, four mixed herds of 7,000; May 21, J. L. Driskill, two mixed herds of 4,200; and May 22, J. W. L. Slavens, mixed herd of 2,100. Three sightings were made of the Kingsberry and Holmsley herd. They were obviously undecided about their destination on this drive, given the newness of the Western Trail. On May 22 their destination was unknown; on May 24 they were headed for Dodge City, and on June 16 they were headed for Bluff Creek.

17. King, "Businesswoman," 54.

18. Ibid., 29; Robert T. Hill, "No Cowboy Was Ever Caught Wearing a Nightie."

19. King, "Businesswoman," 56.

20. Doyle, "Mrs. Holmsley," 28.

21. Ibid., 28–29; *The New Handbook of Texas Online*, s.v. "Hardin, John Wesley."

22. Doyle, "Mrs. Holmsley," 28–29; Margaret T. Waring, director of the Comanche Public Library, believes that Minta most likely made up both of these encounters.

23. Carrie Holmsley Cunningham, "Historical Record of the Holmsley Family," 33.

24. Wells, *Blazing the Way*, 134–36.

25. "Woman Who Pioneered," 478–79.

26. Carl Moneyhon, *Republicanism in Reconstruction Texas*, 162–67.

27. "Woman Who Pioneered," 479.

28. Wells, *Blazing the Way*, 45; Heritage Division, *Patchwork of Memories*, 154.

29. U.S. Bureau of the Census, 1880, Comanche Co., Tex.

30. Waring and Waring, *Comanche County Gravestone Inscriptions;* Cunningham, *Historical Record*, 33–34.

31. Cunningham, *Historical Record*, 31–35.

32. This is quite different from the English common law system, in which married women were not allowed to own anything because they did not legally exist apart from their husbands.

33. Jean A. Stuntz, "Spanish Laws for Texas Women," 543–59; Comanche County, Tex., deed records.

34. It is possible that, at this time, Minta went to live with her married daughter, Mintah Harris, in Fort Worth in view of the fact that a church pastor in Comanche wrote her a letter transferring her church membership; see Pastor in Comanche, Texas, letter to Mrs. Holmsley and Mrs. Harris in Fort Worth, May 6, 1898.

35. Comanche County, Tex., tax rolls.

36. T. H. Holmsley in Parral, Chihuahua, Mexico, letter to Mrs. M. Holmsley, Comanche, Tex., March 23, 1892; King, "Businesswoman," 5; Heritage Division, *Patchwork of Memories*, 241–42.

37. U.S. Bureau of the Census, 1900, 1920, Comanche Co., Tex.; 1910, Crockett Co., Tex. At times Minta was also called Mintie, as noted on a receipt to her from W. B. Wagnon; see James Holmsley, Papers, miscellaneous records, Aug. 8, 1882.

38. *The New Handbook of Texas Online*, s.v. "Comanche County."

39. Margaret Waring, "Comanche, Texas: Robert Thomas Hill, Dean of Texas Geology," http://www.texasescapes.com (accessed Nov. 30, 2005).

40. King, "Businesswoman," 56.

41. Ibid.

42. See James Holmsley Papers, "Essay on Juan Nepomuceno Almonte."

43. "Mrs. Minta Holmsley Buried at Oakwood," 5; "Woman Who Pioneered," 478–79.

PART 2

The Boom Years of the Cattle Drives, 1877–86

Mary Ann ("Molly") Dyer Goodnight

MRS. CHARLES A. GOODNIGHT

Michaele Thurgood Haynes

FONDLY KNOWN AS THE "MOTHER OF THE PLAINS," Mary Ann ("Molly") Dyer Goodnight is often included in published works on women in frontier Texas.[1] Her fame has long rested on the fact that, in the 1870s, she was the only white woman within a seventy-five-mile radius on the Texas High Plains. She is also renowned for the motherly care she gave the cowboys who worked for her husband, Charles Goodnight.[2] She also joins the list of women who went up the cattle trails, an ever-growing number as continuing research reveals the women who helped their husbands and followed herds of cattle to market or to new grazing lands.

Mary Ann Dyer was born on September 12, 1830, into a prominent Tennessee family. Her father, Joel Henry Dyer, was attorney general of west Tennessee and had been a hero in the Battle of New Orleans. Molly's mother, Susan Lynch Miller, came from an equally accomplished family that included Susan's grandfather, the first governor of Tennessee. If the Dyer family had stayed in Tennessee, young Molly would probably have led a fairly comfortable life. However, in 1854, when Molly was fourteen, the Dyer family left the state for Texas. They traveled in wagons and by boat to a small settlement that was being established in North Texas at Fort Belknap, a U.S. Army post that was part of a chain of garrisons set up to protect the Texas frontier from raiding bands of Indians.

The Dyer family that arrived in Texas was a large one. The 1860 census lists the children as Robert H., thirty-four; Albert M., twenty-nine; John P., twenty-four; Mary Ann (Molly), eighteen; J. B. (Joel), sixteen; Grainger, fourteen; Leigh R., eleven; Samuel (Sam) M., eight; and Walter W., four.[3]

Molly and her three youngest brothers remained close throughout their lives. The strong relationship was undoubtedly due to the early death of the children's mother, Susan Miller Dyer, in 1864, when her youngest child, Walter, was only eight years old. Two years later, their father also died. After the deaths of her parents, Molly assumed responsibility for her three younger brothers—Leigh, Samuel, and Walter. Leigh went to work for Charles Goodnight as a drover in 1867, but twelve-year-old Walter and sixteen-year-old Samuel remained with Molly, even-

Figure 21.   Molly Goodnight. Courtesy of the Panhandle-Plains
Historical Museum, Canyon, Texas.

tually moving with her to Colorado after her marriage to Charles Goodnight in 1870. At various times, all of Molly's brothers were involved in ranching in the Texas Panhandle and worked for Molly's future husband.[4]

According to the 1860 Texas census, Molly was a teacher in Young County before she took on the responsibility of caring for her brothers. She had little formal education and later remarked, "I don't know what it is about me that makes people ask me where I went to college. Why, I never went to college at all or to any other school. There were no colleges in Texas nor public schools either when I was a girl.

My only teachers were my father and mother, both of whom were well educated for their times. Then too, I learned a lot from Nature."[5]

Charles Goodnight was born March 5, 1836, on the family farm in Macoupin County, Illinois, and moved eight hundred miles with his family to Milam County, Texas, as a child. He had little chance to go to school and spent most of his childhood working on the family farm. He began his first venture in the cattle business when he was nineteen years old and also worked for some time as a freighter. During the Civil War, he did not become a Confederate soldier as had Molly's brothers but instead joined the Texas Rangers and helped protect the settlers against Indians.

After the war, Goodnight searched for a route to take his cattle to market in New Mexico and Colorado instead of driving them to the railheads in Missouri and Kansas as cattlemen in Central and South Texas did. Potential routes to New Mexico were dangerous because they crossed the traditional Comanche country. Goodnight joined up with experienced cowman Oliver Loving and started out on the trail with a herd of two thousand head. The drive was successful. The trail they followed eventually became known as the Goodnight-Loving Trail; it ran from the Concho River to Horsehead Crossing on the Pecos River and then up the Pecos to Fort Sumner, New Mexico.[6] Goodnight and Loving made three drives together over this route; the one they made in 1867 was the last one for Loving, who was wounded by Indians and died at Fort Sumner.[7]

The details of the first meeting between Mary Ann Dyer and Charles Goodnight are unclear, but she may have been introduced to him by her brothers. Molly's brother Leigh was a drover for Goodnight, and there is some conjecture that one or more of the Dyer brothers met Goodnight when he was a Texas Ranger during the Civil War. On the other hand, authors Crawford and Ragsdale report that, "When Charles Goodnight first glimpsed the woman who was to become his wife, she was riding horseback accompanied by a small boy and a retinue of soldiers. The soldiers were an escort for the schoolteacher, Molly, who arrived at Goodnight's mother's inn one fine summer day in 1864 on her way with her young brother Walter to the school at Black Springs on Keechie Creek."[8] However the two actually met, they courted for at least five years until Charles's cattle business was successful enough for him to take a wife.

In 1870 Molly took her two youngest brothers, Walter and Samuel, back to Tennessee and Kentucky to visit relatives. Charles came from Pueblo, Colorado, where he and Molly's brother Leigh had started a new ranch. Charles and Molly married in the parlor of her uncle's home in Hickman, Kentucky, on July 26, 1870. After the wedding, the couple, with Samuel and Walter, traveled by boat to St. Louis and by rail to Abilene. After a night at the Drovers' Hotel in Abilene, they left by stage for Pueblo—a long, grueling ride across the sun-baked plains. Arriving in Pueblo, they stayed at another Drovers' Hotel, where friends met them.[9]

The newlyweds' arrival in Pueblo coincided with the hanging of two men from a telegraph pole. Charles was anxious that his bride not learn of this, but she soon did and demanded to know whether it were true: "Having been married such a short while, and not accustomed to making excuses," Goodnight recalled, "I hardly knew how to reply, but finally stammered out in a very abashed manner, 'Well, I don't think it hurt the telegraph pole.' This seemed to irritate her very much, and she said: 'I used to think I knew you in Texas, but you have been out here among the Yankees and ruffians until I don't know whether I know you or not, and I want you to take me back to Texas. I won't live in such a country.' I agreed to this, but insisted that she must first have a rest, and during the next few days made it a point to acquaint her with all the good ladies of Pueblo, whom she found quite as human as herself, and the trip back to Texas was soon forgotten."[10]

A more welcome surprise was the sidesaddle Charles presented to his wife, an accomplished horsewoman. Women's sidesaddles were dangerous and hard on both the rider and the horse. Charles's friend S. C. Gallup of Pueblo, Colorado, made the saddle in June 1870 to have ready when the bride arrived. The sidesaddle was based on a man's regular saddletree with an adjustable side horn that curved downward instead of upward. In combination with the traditional adjustable stirrups, the individual rider could be better fitted, creating a more solid seat for safer riding. Molly used this saddle for years on both the ranch in Pueblo and later in Palo Duro Canyon.[11]

The Goodnights spent the first six years of their marriage in Pueblo. The success of the cattle ranch soon encouraged Charles to expand into banking, real estate, and mining. Molly founded the town's first Southern Methodist Church (ME [Methodist Episcopal] Church), and Charles, with his business associates, financed the town's first building. In the early 1870s, however, stock speculation, the too-rapid expansion of the agricultural West, and a worldwide drop in prices brought on the panic of 1873 and a three-year depression. Colorado ranchers were not immune to the effects of the national economy. Charles's investments in a Pueblo bank and the opera house, combined with a year of drought, led to Goodnight's financial collapse. Molly then went to California to stay with relatives, while Charles drove cattle back to Texas.

In 1876 Charles and his hands, including Leigh, Samuel, and Walter Dyer, drove sixteen hundred head of cattle from Pueblo, Colorado, to Palo Duro Canyon in the Texas Panhandle, where he staked a claim to establish his "home ranch" near the Prairie Dog Town Fork of the Red River. Goodnight built a dugout topped with cottonwood and cedar logs as his first temporary quarters while building a four-room log house for himself and Molly.

In 1877 Goodnight, on his return to Colorado, was introduced by friends to John George Adair to discuss the possibility of a financial partnership that would allow him to expand the Palo Duro acreage. Adair was an Irish financier who was in the West to set up a brokerage firm and to get in on the profits to be had in the cattle business. Charles also made arrangements for Molly, who was still in California, to return and join him. Molly had sent him a letter with an ultimatum to leave the Panhandle and return to civilization; otherwise, she would join him on the ranch. Charles replied, "By this time I had contracted to enter partnership with the Adairs, and could not honorably leave Panhandle if I had wished to do so."[12] After Molly arrived from California, plans got under way to move to Palo Duro. Adair wanted to see the ranch before finalizing an agreement, so, in 1877, he and his wife, Cornelia, joined the Goodnights and Molly's brother Al, along with several other cowhands, on a cattle drive to Texas.

In preparation for the four-hundred-mile drive, the two couples went by rail to Trinidad, Colorado, where they were outfitted for the journey. In addition to purchasing four wagons and enough supplies to last six months, Charles bought one hundred Durham bulls, as well as the necessary horses, to upgrade his herd in Texas. On July 18, 1877, the cattle, cowboys (including Molly's brother Albert), and entourage headed for Texas.[13] Expert horsewoman Cornelia Adair rode a large white horse the whole trip, and Molly alternated between driving a team of horses pulling a wagon full of supplies and riding her fine saddle horse, Paddy. The party had several difficult experiences on the trail, including one in which they almost lost the cattle from lack of water when Molly mistook a patch of bear grass for a band of Indians in the distance and failed to ramrod the group toward the much-needed water. Nonetheless, the group arrived at Palo Duro without serious loss of cattle or mishap.

Molly's first sight of Palo Duro, named for the cedar trees, was breathtaking: a solitary canyon fifteen hundred feet deep, ten miles wide, and almost one hundred miles long, with steep red cliffs on both sides. Since fencing was unnecessary, the canyon was ideal for raising cattle. Moreover, water was plentiful, and the thick buffalo grass made a velvety green sea.[14] Cedar, chinaberry, and cottonwood trees provided shade in the summertime. It was a beautiful sight, but getting the entourage down the old Indian trail took significant effort: "The descent was so abrupt and steep that we were compelled to take our wagons to pieces, first unloading them, and let them down into the valley below with ropes. We had to do the same thing with their contents. We had heavy loaded teams of provisions and many other necessary things for establishing a permanent camp or quarters."[15]

Transporting everything to the bottom of the canyon took eight days; then they still had to move the supplies the final ten miles through the canyon. Once safely at the small log cabin Charles had built the previous year, the cowhands went to work building shelters and making a corral for the horses. Game—turkeys, deer, and bear—abounded, but the weather quickly turned foul as one winter storm followed another; fortunately, the canyon walls offered some protection. Despite the weather and the hardships, Molly always declared these to be the happiest days of her life, according to Charles.[16]

After two weeks, Adair and Goodnight signed a partnership, which was heavily loaded in Adair's favor. Running five years, the contract provided that "Adair should finance the enterprise while Goodnight should furnish the foundation herd and direct the ranch for an annual salary of $2,500, which was to be paid from the operating budget. Goodnight was to repay Adair's investment in full, with 10% interest. At the end of five years, all assets were to be divided, one third going to Goodnight and two thirds to Adair."[17] It was Goodnight's suggestion to name the ranch with Adair's initials.

After Cornelia Adair left the ranch, Molly was said to be the only white woman within two hundred miles. "Mary Goodnight was Queen of the canyon with no other woman from the Red to the Rio Grande River on the South, Ft. Dodge, Kansas, on the north, Henrietta, Texas, on the East, and Pueblo, Colorado, on the West to contest her sovereign rights."[18] Since other women lived in the Panhandle, this is certainly an exaggeration, but it is true that in the beginning Molly was totally isolated from other women. Seventy-five miles away, Molly Bugbee lived with her husband at the Quarter Circle T Ranch.[19] Visits were infrequent, but the women were grateful to see each other once or twice a year.

Molly Goodnight enjoyed the natural world around her and often rode with her husband across their vast property. She was interested in the cattle business as well. She owned herds under her separate PATM brand and others jointly with her brother Walter under the Flying T brand. They shared the Dyer-Coleman range and had a one-third interest in Coleman and Company. However, loneliness was a frequent problem. A cowboy once gave her three chickens as pets. "No one can ever know how much pleasure and company they were to me. They were someone I could talk to. They would run to me when I called them and follow me everywhere I went. They knew me and tried to talk to me in their language."[20]

Charles Goodnight was known as a strict but fair employer. He enforced three rules for his cowhands: no gambling, no drinking, and no fighting.[21] The JA Ranch attracted good workers, and Molly's care and concern for the young men were widely known and appreciated. Although she never had children, she provided a motherly figure for the young cowhands and their families. She repaired britches, darned socks, and hosted holiday dinners and parties for the men and their families. She set up a Sunday school on the ranch and gave reading lessons to those who needed them. She rode many miles to take berry cobblers or cakes to the workers at the distant line camps. Some of the cowhands called her "Aunt Molly," and others referred to her as the "darling of the Plains." On one occasion, the cowboys pooled their money and ordered a silver tea service from New York to present to Molly as a token of their affection and gratitude.

Charles Goodnight was known as a somewhat taciturn man with strict standards of behavior for those who worked for him. In contrast was the affection he demonstrated when he presented his wife with a grandfather clock with the following inscription: "For many months in 1877–78, she saw few men and no women, her nearest neighbor being seventy-five miles distant, and the nearest settlement two hundred miles. She met isolation and hardships with a cheerful heart and danger with undaunted courage. With unfailing optimism, she took life's varied gifts and made her home a house of joy."[22]

In the fall of 1878, Molly found herself with unexpected Indian guests at the Old Home Ranch. Bands of Kiowas and Comanches had entered the canyon to search for buffalo. When they were unsuccessful, they began killing the Goodnights' cattle. Charles learned of this and rode out to confront them. He arranged a meeting at the ranch's headquarters with the leader, Comanche Chief Quanah Parker. Molly's experience as a single woman on the frontier, even with responsibility for her brothers, had not prepared her for hosting Indians in her yard, so she was somewhat uneasy when Quanah Parker rode up with ten or twelve of his braves. After a good bit of discussion, Parker and Goodnight came to an agreement: The Indians could take two beeves every other day until they were able to find buffalo, as long as they did not interfere with the workings of the ranch.

Although Goodnight believed that Parker would keep his word, the townspeople in Clarendon, the closest town (about sixty miles away), were upset by the Indians' presence in the canyon and demanded that the buffalo soldiers from Fort Elliott return them to Fort Sill in Indian Territory. However, the Indians stayed in the canyon until the following spring, when they finally agreed to leave peacefully with the soldiers. Molly, busy with her work on the ranch, eventually overcame her fear of the Indians, and in later years Charles invited his friend Quanah Parker and his followers to visit the ranch.[23]

During the months the Indians camped in the canyon, the ranch continued to grow and prosper. In 1879 Goodnight decided to move the headquarters about twenty-five miles east, closer to the railroad and supplies. A new two-story log house was built, and water was brought to it down the canyon wall through iron pipes. As the months passed, Molly also got help with the housekeeping chores. Dennis Murphy trailed a herd to the JA Ranch, bringing his wife and Martha, an African American woman, with her three children. Mrs. Murphy became Molly's housekeeper, and Martha the cook. The children played in the canyon hunting rabbits and birds' nests, but on Sundays they put on nice clothes and sat while Molly read aloud stories from the Bible.[24]

Freed from household chores, Molly handled the business transactions of the ranch, reviewing the numerous accounts and contracts for cattle sales.[25] In addition, she visited the line camps, taking with her a small black bag that served as her medical kit. In the Texas of the 1880s, doctors were few and far between, and the people living in the Panhandle relied upon home remedies or folk medicine. The different ethnic groups that settled in Texas in these years brought their own medical beliefs and practices and sometimes combined them with their religious convictions. Anglo Americans tended toward a practical approach, using whatever ingredients were available. Common household items such as soda, coal oil, kerosene, sugar, whiskey, vinegar, turpentine, and soot were used. Medicinal plants such as pennyroyal, anise, oregano, horehound, senna, sassafras, and other native roots, barks, and leaves also found their way into various potions. Paregoric, sulfur, alum, Epsom salts, and camphor were among the medicines used by doctors and home practitioners alike.[26] Among Molly's cures were "coal-oil for lice, prickly pear for wounds, salt and buffalo tallow for piles, mud for inflammation and fevers, and buffalo meat broth for a general tonic."[27] In 1885, at Molly's suggestion, Charles worked with the citizens of Clarendon to convince a doctor to set up a medical practice. Charles himself provided a large part of the $1,000 donation that the community raised as incentive pay for the new physician.[28]

In the 1870s, the great herds of Southern Plains buffalo, numbering in the millions just two decades earlier, were on the verge of extinction. For thousands of years, Plains tribes had hunted them with bows and arrows, at first on foot and later on horseback. For almost two centuries, Mexican *ciboleros* (buffalo hunters) on horseback hunted the shaggy animals with lances for meat, hides, and sport, taking as many as twelve thousand in the early 1830s. At the beginning of the nineteenth century, the ciboleros were not only providing food for their own families but also supplying meat to the New Mexico settlements and hides for the Santa Fe–Chihuahua trade. As Euro-Americans moved onto the western frontier, they too hunted the great animals, primarily for their skins. However, it was the completion of the transcontinental railroad in 1869 that sealed the buffaloes' fate. Now the hides were profitably shipped to the northeast for use as industrial belts. The greater demand and the efficiency of the long-range Sharps rifles led to the final slaughter in 1874. By late 1878, three and a half million animals had been killed on the Texas plains.[29] The U.S. government supported this action because extinction of the buffalo would end the nomadic way of life of the Plains Indians and make them more amenable to sedentary life on the reservations.

Although not a buffalo hunter himself, Charles Goodnight believed that their removal was necessary before cattle ranching could be successful. When he established the JA Ranch in Palo Duro Canyon, he drove the buffalo deep into the canyon to make way for his livestock. Molly Goodnight was aware of the large numbers of buffalo that were being killed and was concerned about their future. Additionally, she pitied the orphaned calves that were left to die because their hides were not large enough for commercial use. She asked her husband to bring her some of the calves to bottle-feed. In June 1879 Charles roped two buffalo calves and gave them to his wife. Two years later a neighboring ranchman captured two full-grown buffalo and presented them to her. Another three calves were added to her little group as a present from her brother.[30] Her success in hand-raising the calves established the beginning of the Goodnight domesticated buffalo herd. Molly

Figure 22. Molly Goodnight's home. Courtesy of the
Panhandle-Plains Historical Museum, Canyon, Texas.

was responsible for saving a small herd of Southern Plains buffalo before they became extinct. In later years, the herd was known as the Charles Goodnight Herd,
rather than the Molly Goodnight Herd, even though Charles always gave full credit
to his wife for saving the animals.

From 1878 to 1888, cattle on the JA Ranch were driven north to market. Molly
accompanied her husband on two cattle drives over the two hundred fifty miles
from the Palo Duro Canyon to Dodge City, Kansas, where they bought all of their
ranch supplies.[31] With more than one hundred thousand head of cattle at one
time, the JA Ranch prospered. The business employed an "army" of cowboys under Goodnight's leadership and Adair's financial investment. In 1882 the partnership was renewed, and Goodnight's salary was increased to $7,500. By the time of
Adair's death in 1885, the JA Ranch covered 1,325,000 acres, had nearly fifty houses,
hundreds of miles of roads, twenty or thirty large water tanks, many corrals, and
two thousand bulls. It also had its own hay farm, a dairy house, a poultry facility,
a tin house, and a blacksmith's shop. Goodnight reportedly was one of the first
Panhandle ranchers to use barbed-wire fences. The Goodnights established a community school and a church for the workers and neighboring ranchers.[32] In the late
1880s the Goodnights, at Molly's instigation, hired artist J. C. Cowles, a student
and friend of Albert Bierstadt of Taos, New Mexico, to come to Palo Duro to paint
scenes around the ranch, including their home and Palo Duro Canyon.

Drought, falling beef prices, and the depression of the mid-1880s, as well as a troubling stomach ailment, convinced Charles to curtail his ranching activities at the end of the second contract with Adair. In 1887, with sixty-three thousand cattle on the ranch, he sold out his interest in the JA and moved sixteen miles north to a smaller ranch near the site of the future town of Goodnight. A many-gabled modern ranch house was built according to Molly's tastes, with Charles adding a den with a fireplace and an upstairs sleeping porch that offered views across the plains. Formally organized as the Goodnight–Thayer Cattle Company, the new venture retained Molly's herd of two hundred fifty buffalo. During the years on the JA Ranch, Goodnight developed the "cattalo" by crossing buffalo with polled Angus cattle.

Soon a station on the Fort Worth and Denver Railroad line was established, and in 1888 a post office was opened in the growing town of Goodnight.[33] At almost fifty, Molly was happy to be living nearer to town. With its doors open to people of every age and persuasion, her spacious two-story home became a center of social life. In 1898 Charles and Molly founded Goodnight College with the help of Marshall McIlhaney, who became its first president. Goodnight gave the school 340 acres so that the school could run cattle and raise crops in order to provide both food and jobs for the students in exchange for tuition. Molly nurtured the students as she had the young cowboys. In 1905 the Goodnights transferred that property to the Baptist church, under which the school continued to prosper. A new administration building was constructed, and the faculty was expanded. However, the opening of the nearby West Texas State Normal College (now West Texas A&M University) and Clarendon College led to the closing of Goodnight College in 1917.[34]

In 1900 further reductions were made in the ranching activities, but the buffalo, as well as the elk, antelope, and various other animals, were kept, and the Goodnight Ranch became a tourist attraction. Buffalo from their herd were sent to a New York zoo, to Yellowstone National Park, and even to Europe. Buffalo hides, mounted heads, and meats were desired by the wealthy as novel luxuries. From their meeting in 1878, Charles became a long-time friend of Comanche leader Quanah Parker and other Indians and occasionally invited them to partake in "staged" buffalo hunts.[35] The herd survived long after the deaths of the Goodnights, and in 1997 the buffalo were transported to Caprock Canyons State Park in Quitaque, Texas.

Molly's death in early April 1926 ended a life that crossed from one century into another. Her role as caregiver and nurturer of young people, whether cowboys on the ranch or students at Goodnight College, reflects her nineteenth-century birth and the traditional role assigned to Victorian women. Her active role in the cattle business and in going up the Palo Duro–Dodge City Trail with her husband marked her ability to act outside of nineteenth-century restrictions. Then, when Molly Goodnight insisted on saving the lives of orphaned calves and began the

Figure 23.　Molly Goodnight in her later years, c. 1925. Courtesy
of the Panhandle-Plains Historical Museum, Canyon, Texas.

Goodnight herd of Southern Plains buffalo, she also secured a place in the twentieth-century conservation movement.[36]

NOTES

1. Information regarding the life of Mary Ann (Molly) Dyer Goodnight has been synthesized from Ann Fears Crawford and Crystal Sasse Ragsdale, *Women in Texas: Their Lives, Their Experiences, Their Accomplishments;* Joyce Gibson Roach, *The Cowgirls;* and "Goodnight, Mary Ann Dyer," in Ron Tyler, *The New Handbook of Texas,* vol. 3, 243–44; Mary Beth Rogers, Sherry A. Smith, and Janelle D. Scott, *We Can Fly: Stories of Katherine Stinson and Other Gutsy Texas Women;* and Phebe Kerrick Warner (niece of Mary Ann Goodnight), "Mary Ann Goodnight."

2. The basic facts of the life and career of Charles Goodnight are from H. Allen Anderson, "Goodnight, Charles," in Tyler, *The New Handbook of Texas,* vol. 3, 240–43; Pauline Durret Robertson and R. L. Robertson, *Cowman's Country: Fifty Frontier Ranches in the Texas Panhandle, 1876–1887,* 17–34; and J. Evetts Haley, *Charles Goodnight: Cowman and Plainsman.* Other sources state that, since Molly Bugbee and her husband arrived two years earlier, as did Ellen O'Loughlin, Molly Goodnight was not the first white woman in the area.

3. U.S. Bureau of the Census, 1850, Madison County, Tenn.; U.S. Bureau of the Census, 1860, Young County, Tex.

4. Leigh Dyer worked as a trail driver for several ranchers, including brothers George and Jim Baker on the Quitaque Ranch in 1878. After the Quitaque Ranch was sold, Walter Dyer became the range foreman. After starting up the Shoe Bar Ranch in 1879, Leigh became prominent in civic affairs and was one of Donley County's first commissioners. He is buried in the cemetery in the town of Goodnight. H. Allen Anderson, "Dyer, Leigh Richmond," "Quitaque Ranch," and "Shoe Bar Ranch," in Tyler, *The New Handbook of Texas,* vol. 2, 747; vol. 5, 395; vol. 5, 1032; and Millie Jones Porter, *Memory Cups of Panhandle Pioneers,* 82–83.

5. Warner, "Mary Ann Goodnight," 4.

6. The trail that became the Goodnight-Loving Trail was used before the trail drive of Goodnight and Loving by drover James Patterson in 1864. Thus the route has undoubtedly been misnamed. See Charles Kenner, "The Origins of the 'Goodnight' Trail Reconsidered," 390–94.

7. George Reynolds, husband of Bettie Reynolds (another woman who went on trail drives), worked with Goodnight in 1867.

8. Crawford and Ragsdale, *Women in Texas,* 111.

9. Haley, *Charles Goodnight,* 262.

10. Ibid., 262–63.

11. J. Marvin Hunter, "Mrs. Goodnight's Saddle," 8.

12. Haley, *Charles Goodnight,* 296.

13. Phebe Kerrick Warner, "The Wife of a Pioneer Ranchman," 65–71.

14. Dee Brown and Martin F. Schmitt, *Trail Driving Days,* 125.

15. Emanuel Dubbs, "Charles Goodnight," in *Pioneer Days in the Southwest from 1850 to 1879: Thrilling Descriptions of Buffalo Hunting, Indian Fighting and Massacres, Cowboy Life and Home Building,* 22. Dubbs, a former buffalo hunter, served as county judge of Wheeler

County in the 1870s and knew Goodnight. The chapter in his book is by Charles Goodnight, who tells his own story.

16. J. Evetts Haley, "Historic Saddle Is Saved," 30; Annie Dyer Nunn, "She Saved the Buffaloes," 2, 8.

17. Robertson, *Cowman's Country,* 24.

18. Warner, "Mary Ann Goodnight," 6. However, H. Allen Anderson suggests that the Goodnights spent their first night in the Panhandle with Thomas and Ellen O'Loughlin at their boarding house in Mobeetie, approximately fifty miles from Palo Duro Canyon; see "O'Loughlin, Thomas," in Tyler, *The New Handbook of Texas,* vol. 4, 1131.

19. Ellen O'Loughlin, another white woman, lived fifty miles away (see note 18).

20. Crawford and Ragsdale, *Women in Texas,* 117.

21. Robertson, *Cowman's Country,* 27.

22. Haley, *Charles Goodnight,* 459.

23. Harley True Bunton, "A History of the JA Ranch."

24. Willie Newbury Lewis, *Between Sun and Sod: An Informal History of the Texas Panhandle,* 93–95.

25. Rogers, Smith, and Scott, *We Can Fly,* 134.

26. Joe Graham, "Folk Medicine," in Tyler, *New Handbook of Texas,* vol. 2, 1061–62.

27. Crawford and Ragsdale, *Women in Texas,* 115.

28. Lewis, *Between Sun and Sod,* 117–18.

29. H. Allen Anderson, "Ciboleros," in Tyler, *The New Handbook of Texas,* vol. 2, 108; David M. Vigness, "Buffalo Hunting," in Tyler, *The New Handbook of Texas,* vol. 1, 814.

30. Elmo Scott Watson, "To Save Famous Goodnight Herd of Buffalo."

31. This third trail that Goodnight blazed was known as the Palo Duro–Dodge City Trail. Watson, "To Save Famous Goodnight Herd"; Haley, "Historic Saddle," 30; Hunter, "Mrs. Goodnight's Saddle," 8. Critics of Emerson Hough's novel *North of 36* have claimed that there were no women on the cattle trail, yet, to refute these critics, Hunter makes statements about Mrs. Goodnight traveling on the trails. See chapter on Amanda Burks in this volume for more discussion of this novel and the making of the movie.

32. Anderson, "JA Ranch," in Tyler, *The New Handbook of Texas,* vol. 3, 885–86.

33. Anderson, "Goodnight, Texas," in Tyler, *The New Handbook of Texas,* vol. 3, 244.

34. J. P. Reynolds, "Goodnight College," in Tyler, *The New Handbook of Texas,* vol. 3, 244.

35. Robertson, *Cowman's Country,* 31–32.

36. Glenda Riley, *Women and Nature,* 87–98, 112–13.

CORNELIA WADSWORTH RITCHIE ADAIR

MRS. JOHN GEORGE ADAIR

Frances B. Vick

How did this genteel new york woman of means and property, a Union general's daughter, a Union general's wife, and later wife of Irish landed gentry, come to be called the Queen of the Cattle Country in the Texas Panhandle— a far cry from the place she had started? The story is one of the best tales of the West and includes buffalo hunts, a legendary Texas cattleman, a cattle drive from Colorado to the Palo Duro Canyon, and the birth of the oldest privately owned cattle company in West Texas—owned by a woman and today in the hands of the descendant who bears the name of the original Queen of the Cattle Country.

This Panhandle story begins in the Genesee Valley of New York with the birth of Cornelia Wadsworth on April 6, 1837, into a world of wealth and privilege. Cornelia was named for her Aunt Cornelia, who died in 1831, probably in the cholera epidemic. She had an older brother, Charles Frederick, who was born in 1835, and her younger siblings were Craig Wharton (1841), Nancy (1843), James Wolcott (1846), and Elizabeth (1848).[1]

At the time of Cornelia's birth, the census indicated that her family owned more than fifty thousand acres in the Genesee Valley of New York State. Cornelia spent her early days at Hartford House, her father's country estate near Geneseo, New York. It was in the Genesee Valley that she became an accomplished horsewoman, a skill that further encouraged her adventuresome spirit in her wish to gallop across the western prairies. With its lush grasslands and English-style woods, the Genesee Valley was excellent for riding and fox hunting. The Genesee Valley Hunt, founded by Cornelia's cousin, Col. William P. Wadsworth, is the second oldest hunt in the United States, but the Wadsworths had hunted on horseback for many years before the hunt was initiated.[2]

During Cornelia's girlhood, the Wadsworth family owned more than twenty farms, some of them with riding stables. Cornelia also rode on the Wadsworths' Long Island estates, under the tutelage of Irish grooms. In addition to riding, the Wadsworth girls, unlike typical Victorian young ladies, worked in the family's farm

Figure 24. Portrait of Cornelia Adair. Courtesy of the
Panhandle-Plains Historical Museum, Canyon, Texas.

fields alongside the boys, with little concern for their complexions.[3] They were usually well sunburned in spite of their upper-class position in the forefront of fashion.[4]

As early as 1839, *Godey's Lady's Book* included articles on riding, embroidery, popular music, and drawings of Philadelphia fashions. Riding was a popular activity.[5] While the girls may have been sunburned in the Wadsworth fields of the Genesee Valley, they also wintered at their New York City townhouse on Sixteenth Street between Fifth Avenue and Broadway, where they were exposed to the social life of the city.[6] Both areas offered them opportunities for riding and hunts as part of the glamorous social scene.

Theodore Roosevelt, who rode and hunted with the Wadsworths of Genesee Valley, wrote that the hard-riding farmers from the countryside around Geneseo were beginning to find the breeding and selling of good hunters a valuable part of their stock raising, particularly since the horses were known to be good jumpers: "Only high-jumping horses can live with Mr. Wadsworth's hounds" because of the countryside and the many fences.[7] This emphasis on cross-country riding helped Cornelia develop into the superior horsewoman she was, as no other kind of riding, with the exception of steeplechasing, required such hard galloping and high jumping. The Wadsworth women participated as well, and riding sidesaddle made the course considerably more difficult.

In describing one of the hunts, Theodore Roosevelt wrote that they ran about ten miles "at a rattling pace," crossing more than sixty fences, most of them post-and-rail barriers, many of which were four to five feet high.[8] Mrs. Herbert Wadsworth stayed in the saddle for an unbelievable fourteen hours before hosting a party at her Ashantee home in the evening, thus proving that she could outride Theodore Roosevelt.[9]

At Geneseo, Cornelia also learned to love the idea of the West. As a child, she read the stories of Indians, the prairies, wild animals, and frontier adventures.[10] She dreamed of riding over the boundless plains, tenting under the stars, and meeting Indian braves. Later Cornelia wrote in her diary about the way these Indian stories affected her: "I remember all the traditions of Indians that used to be told us children at Geneseo, of the battles that were fought there by the first settlers, of the great tree where they used to hold councils: how we used to scan the floor of the old 'Homestead' for the marks of the Indian moccasins which were made when they came in with wet feet to hold councils with my grandfather, how imagination used to run riot in dwelling on these strange wild creatures."[11] The West remained deeply interesting to her before she finally got a chance to see those "strange wild creatures" for herself.

The home the Wadsworths built in the Genesee Valley was copied from a villa in England and called Hartford House, named for the Marquis of Hartford, who had shared his house plans with them. It was built not far from The Homestead, the home of her grandfather, James Wadsworth, who was still smarting over the War of 1812.[12] Unlike his father, who distrusted the English, James Samuel Wadsworth set about to create a bit of England at Hartford House in the Genesee Valley. In 1855 the family spent two years abroad, and during this sojourn Cornelia became well versed in English and French society.[13]

When the family returned to the United States in 1857, Cornelia, then twenty years old, met, fell in love with, and married Montgomery Ritchie of Boston in a wedding said to be the greatest fete her father ever gave. Cornelia and her new husband divided the winter social season between New York and Boston. Their 54 West Sixteenth Street townhouse in New York was only four blocks from Teddy Roosevelt's brownstone at 28 East Twentieth Street.[14] One can assume the riding and hunting continued, along with the rest of their social calendar.

That Cornelia was already interested in the horse business beyond riding is shown by her reported sadness in 1858, when the great Wadsworth stallion, Henry Clay, was sold for $550. Earlier, in 1854, Cornelia's father had gotten into the cattle business by buying a herd of shorthorns, and her brother Charles was to become a respected cattle raiser at his Westerly, New York, property. This early family interest in horses and cattle also became important to Cornelia in later years.[15]

Two sons were born of her marriage to Montgomery Ritchie, James ("Jack") W. and Arthur Montgomery.[16] In 1864 Cornelia's husband died from an illness brought on by his years of service in the Civil War.[17] In May 1864 Cornelia's father also lost his life during the Battle of the Wilderness. The widowed Cornelia took her two small sons to Paris, where the older child, Arthur Montgomery Ritchie, died a few years later.[18] In 1869 Cornelia, described at thirty-two as a "remarkably attractive widow," married a wealthy Englishman/Irishman, John G. Adair.[19] They met at a ball in the New York home of Congressman J. C. Hughes, a friend of the Wadsworth family.[20] Adair was educated and trained for the English diplomatic service, but the work did not appeal to him. As a matter of fact, others described him as being very undiplomatic. Certainly this proved true in his later dealings with the JA cowboys.

Adair had a brokerage business in New York, where he spent much time tending to his affairs.[21] This would later play a part in his dealings out West. Adair had established a prosperous firm by negotiating large loans in England and Ireland at a low interest rate and lending to creditors in the United States at a higher rate.[22] It is reported in the history of Geneseo, however, that this brokerage firm was unsuccessful, so, after a honeymoon at Adair's Irish estate, the couple moved to Geneseo with the idea of Adair's assisting in the management of the Wadsworth property. That idea did not work, however, as Adair never fit in at Geneseo.[23] Perhaps some of the Wadsworths still did not trust the English. With many of the Wadsworth farms sold and Adair's Irish estates in the hands of capable managers, the couple decided to set off on a buffalo hunt in Nebraska.[24] Well traveled, Cornelia had al-

ready toured Europe, enjoyed English castles, and sipped tea in Boston high society, but she had never been to the American prairie of her dreams, which still beckoned to her from her childhood readings.[25]

In 1874 Cornelia easily talked Adair into taking part in the buffalo hunt since,
at that time, hunting for buffalo and other game on the western prairies was a popular activity among well-to-do people in the United States and Europe.[26] This was
only two years before General Custer's "last stand" at Little Big Horn in 1876, so
the prairies were not benign. Cornelia's younger brother, Craig, had been Gen.
Philip Sheridan's aide during the Civil War,[27] and Sheridan was instrumental in
helping Cornelia plan a buffalo hunt and also in providing a military escort for the
expedition. This tradition and courtesy would last for years. Charles Goodnight
said later that the War Department sent an escort for Cornelia for each trip she
made to the Palo Duro Canyon until the railroads reached the Panhandle in 1887.[28]

After meeting with General Sheridan, the Adairs left Chicago and sailed to
Michigan City on Lake Superior. From there they made their way to Duluth and
St. Paul, then down the Mississippi to Clinton, Iowa, where they took the train west
to Omaha. Cornelia was both entranced by the beauty of the area—she reported
that the sky suddenly darkened with sandhill cranes, each six feet in length—and
repelled by the crude manner and uncouth spitting of the American men they met
on the trip.[29]

The Adairs arrived at Sydney Barracks in Nebraska, where Sioux Chief Two-
Lance greeted Cornelia as the "daughter of a great chief," referring to General
Wadsworth. As she had dreamed as a girl, she slept out on the prairie under the
stars—refusing the honor of sleeping in the ambulance wagon—beside fires fueled
with buffalo chips. Cornelia was one of only five or six women in the whole Nebraska Territory at that time.[30]

Cornelia related the adventures of this hunt in her diary, and they give us insight into her feelings about the West and horses. She wrote that the horse she rode
was "a charming little chestnut. . . . I am delighted with him. He has a good
mouth, a nice canter, and he ambles, which is a delightful pace for long journeys;
one can ride all day without feeling tired. What a piece of luck finding such a good
horse. We enjoyed our ride on the prairie and had several gallops after jack rabbits."[31] Cornelia's flair for judging horseflesh crops up again and again in her story.

Cornelia was surprised to find that very few of the women at the army posts
rode and said they considered her as a lunatic for looking forward to camping out
and living in tents. For them, that sort of activity was hardly pleasurable. Since
Cornelia enjoyed the sport of hunting, she found it a mystery that no one at the
forts participated in this amusement.[32] She was outfitted with an English saddle
and saddle girth, which seemed very simple things, "but it was half-an-hour before we could get ours properly put on, and, twice after I mounted, my chestnut
pirouetting a little, the saddle turned with me before I got away from the door,

which was great 'divarshun' [*sic*] for the command, who had all come out to see us start."[33] After finally getting under way, Cornelia went cantering off across the prairie, looking for buffalo, antelope, or any other animal that would prove sporting. She was almost giddy with excitement at the prospect of such an adventure.

Cornelia was ecstatic about the American West and described it throughout the diary: "The sun is setting in a blaze of light and colour, as, I believe, only an American sun can set. Not a tree or a bush have we in sight, only the vast stretch of rolling plain with its short yellow buffalo grass."[34] "The morning was most beautiful, and the clear delicious air put us all in the highest spirits; and then the intense, delightful excitement of starting out on such a novel expedition, not knowing what adventures we may have; our spirited little horses bounding under us, enjoying it as much as we did; the great prairies all before us rolling away in wave after wave, the most perfect ground for riding. . . . We cantered quickly on . . . we descried five or six faint shadowy specks on the skyline: we galloped towards them,"[35] but it all came to naught as no game was shot.

When buffalo were finally sighted on October 12, 1874, the party tried to infiltrate the herd; shots were fired, and an animal went down. Unfortunately, it was not a buffalo but John Adair's horse, shot in the head by Adair, who, trying to force his mount ahead, discharged his pistol, killing the animal instantly. Once Cornelia was assured that her husband had suffered only a shoulder injury, she returned to the hunt. She later teased Adair about the incident, saying, "he gained a new military rank every week—untitled in New York, a captain on the Mississippi, a major in Omaha, and a colonel after the prairie wounding."[36]

Cornelia also observed the Indian women and their method of riding: "Mrs. Two-Lance came over to call upon me. She rode up to our tent sitting on a man's saddle, but quite at her ease, as a Queen should be; all the squaws ride in this way. She is a young, very pleasant-looking woman, with the filthiest old short calico petticoat on, a very smart modern striped shawl, and leather leggings and moccasins most beautifully and richly embroidered with beads. I never saw such beautiful bead-work, very pretty shades of blue predominated. . . . It is all like a dream, it seems too strange to be true, that I should see these uncivilized Indians now really for the first time in my life, when I return to America almost as a foreigner. . . . And here we were surrounded by them in all their paint and feathers and leather and beadwork, their wicked faces glaring at us from all directions."[37]

With all of that, it was the land that drew Cornelia. "Even when we rode, as we sometimes did for hours almost quite silently, there was something exhilarating in the air, in the wonderful sense of freedom, with the vast open expanse in every direction," she wrote.[38] The pleasure that she had discovered while riding and hunting in New York was doubled on the Western plains.[39]

The Nebraska adventure whetted the couple's appetite for permanent Western investment. Historians early took note of evidence that the American West owed its cattle development to British investors, and Adair was to become one of them. Making their way back east, they went from Cheyenne to Denver, to Central City, and on to Colorado Springs, where Cornelia admired the beauty of Pike's Peak and the Garden of the Gods. The couple eventually returned to New York.[40]

In 1877 the Adairs returned to Denver and made a tentative agreement with legendary Texas cattleman Charles Goodnight that changed the Texas Panhandle forever and gave Cornelia her own piece of the West. The buffalo trip that caused the Adairs to want large tracts of land in the West inspired John Adair to move his brokerage business from New York to Denver the following year.[41]

Meanwhile, Charles Goodnight, who had made a fortune in the cattle business, had lost most of his holdings in Trinidad and Pueblo, Colorado, in the panic of 1873. All he had left was sixteen hundred head of cattle, which he decided to gather up and take to the Palo Duro Canyon, where he would start over again. When he got men and cattle settled in the canyon, corrals built, and a small house erected beside a creek, he returned to Colorado to get his wife, Molly, and make arrangements to move her to the Palo Duro.[42]

On his return to Colorado he met John Adair. Goodnight says of that meeting that "He [Adair] had been running all over the country trying to get somebody to go into the cattle business with him in the West. He stood in with men that made Colorado. . . . They were men of high standing and were also friends of mine. [George Clayton, agent for Adair Brokerage, had loaned Goodnight money.] They told Adair that they knew of only one man to get, and they brought us together."[43]

John and Cornelia had a sporting impulse to learn the cattle business. Cornelia was and always would be fascinated with life in the West and its promises, so it was not hard for Goodnight to induce them to go to the Palo Duro to see his spread, the one for which he needed a financial partner.

That journey has inspired many tales. In one of them, Goodnight is said to have carried the Adairs to the Palo Duro in high style, with John Adair, "a debonair Irishman who had inherited a fortune," galloping ahead. Next, "graceful on sidesaddle, came his wife Cornelia, the daughter of a New York banking tycoon and the sister of a senator." At the reins of a wagon behind them was Molly Goodnight, with Charles in the rear driving one hundred shorthorn bulls. After arriving at the ranch, the Adairs "reveled in the grandeur of the West, the bracing air, the buffalo hunting." They also talked business.[44]

Another account of the trail drive has it that, a year from the time Goodnight took his first herd to the Palo Duro in 1876, the second trip was ready to start— in the spring of 1877. This time he was accompanied by John and Cornelia Adair riding horseback, with Molly Goodnight driving one of the four mule-drawn wagons. Cornelia rode the entire four hundred miles on horseback from Trinidad, Colorado, to Palo Duro Canyon.[45]

The twelve-day trip turned out to be quite an adventure for Cornelia and the rest of the group. After they were outfitted for the trip with one hundred head of high-grade Durham bulls, the Goodnights and the Adairs left Trinidad. The wagons were loaded with six months' worth of provisions and equipment since Trinidad was the closest supply depot to Palo Duro Canyon. They had a light ambulance, horses, and hands. The group included six people, in addition to two cowboys, who joked along the way about the difficulty of starting a ranch with a herd of bulls.[46]

They crossed the Raton Range, came down by Cimarron Plaza, and from there launched into the wilderness. They went south to the Canadian River, crossing at the newly founded settlement of Tascosa, and passed south and east along the divide between a stream and the Palo Duro, aiming to enter the canyon from the northeast, opposite the home ranch that Goodnight had established the previous year. On the divide, the water was inaccessible because of the steep canyon walls, so the stock had nothing to drink for three days and nights. The weather was extremely hot, and Goodnight told Molly that, if they did not find water that night, they would likely lose much of the stock. According to Goodnight biographer J. Evetts Haley, the conversation went thus: "Mary, we've got to reach water tonight. The cattle and mules are famishing. I am sure we are within ten miles of a pool of water, but we cannot afford to miss it a foot. We must reach it before dark, so I'll ride on ahead and locate it exactly, then come back and meet you. I want you to take charge of this outfit and keep everything moving. Watch me as far as you can see me and aim toward that point on the horizon where I disappear."[47]

As Molly was following instructions, one of the cowboys came galloping up to tell her that there were Indians in the distance. Molly looked through her field glasses and, thinking she saw them, too, circled the wagons, formed a corral for the cattle, and waited for the Indians to attack. The story goes on that Goodnight returned to find they had not moved more than a mile. He asked, "What in Hell's the matter, Mary? What had you been doing here?" Molly responded, "Oh! Charlie! Charlie! The Indians! They are nearly out of sight now, but we were afraid to go any nearer." Goodnight took the field glasses and, looking through them, said, "For God's sake, Mary, that army of Indians is nothing but a patch of bear grass in a mirage."[48]

It was nearly dark when they set out once again on the nine-mile trip to the water Goodnight had located. Only one of the wagons reached the pool that night. The other teams refused to pull the wagons and had to be led to the water. The group remained there for three days to let the teams and stock rest and recuperate. When they got to the Caprock, they learned that the cavalry escort from Fort Dodge, which was supposed to accompany the Adairs, had missed them on the trail down from Colorado.[49] Goodnight said he was glad to have the cavalry because a band of outlaws was nearby, and he was afraid they would try to capture the Adairs and hold them for ransom. The following story is told by Frederick R. Bechdolt about the incident:

> Over near the head of the Red River the JA outfit had fallen into the hands of the Adairs, who were Irish Gentry. One day when the news went around that Mr. and Mrs. Adair were coming out to visit the ranch, the punchers held a big medicine talk among themselves and decided to make their fortunes by kidnapping the pair. The names of the bold spirits who conceived the plan have not come down, but it was perfected to the point where the conspirators built a dugout in a secluded spot, stocked it up with the best food they could procure, and hung the earthen walls with the finest Indian blankets. All that was lacking was the victims themselves; but before they arrived, Charles Goodnight heard rumors of what was going on, and when they appeared a troop of cavalry accompanied them, which put an end to some high hopes.[50]

When the group finally stood on the rim of the Palo Duro Canyon, the sight must have taken Cornelia's breath away. The deep gorge held a thousand buffalo grazing on the edge of the river. It was everything she had hoped to find in the West. Even the terrible storm that came up that night could not dampen her enthusiasm. The Adairs stayed in the two-room cabin Goodnight had built on his earlier trip and spent the next two weeks exploring the wonders of the valley.[51] They saw the country and the cattle and frequently hunted for buffaloes on the plains above the ranch. On one such occasion, Adair went to the corral and told one of the men, in his imperial manner, to saddle him a horse. The cowboy chose Old Idaho, an outlaw horse that always pitched when he was saddled. He was roped and outfitted with Adair's saddle, Adair's gun was tied under the stirrup leather, and Idaho was then hitched to the fence. When Adair returned, dressed in his "buffalo hunting" attire, Old Idaho eyed him suspiciously. The horse "shied to one side, and snorted like a mustang stud," and then mildly allowed Adair to mount and "walked off like the gentlest horse in the world," much to the cowboys' disgust. Their disdain for Adair and his European ways is well recorded.[52]

In a later reminiscence Goodnight said that Adair "was an overbearing old son-of-a-gun, and would have been beat up several times if it hadn't been for me. I don't see why I took it. I ought to have challenged him to fight, and if he wouldn't I should have pulled him off his horse and beaten him."[53]

While riding the vast lands of the Palo Duro, Cornelia looked for a spot for a permanent headquarters. She found it in a wide valley that had more room for the cattle than around the old home ranch. The new spot had a high bank to keep off the winter winds but was still accessible from three sides. Goodnight had located one of the line camps there, calling it Grande Vista Camp. Agreeing that it would be a good site for the permanent center of operations, he began to make plans for the house he would someday build.[54]

The result of this partnership was that Adair furnished the money and Goodnight bought, managed, and developed the ranch.[55] Adair was businessman enough to know that the success of the ranch depended upon the man who managed it. One suspects that Cornelia's fine hand was behind much of this. Using Adair's investment, Goodnight began acquiring land. He purchased twenty-four thousand acres of public lands at seventy-five cents an acre, but the lands were selected in what became known as a "crazy quilt pattern," that is, checkered across the areas that had water and hay fields so that he soon had control of the whole Palo Duro Canyon.[56]

Using 2,000 blooded bulls at a cost of $150,000, Goodnight built up the herds until they numbered 100,000. By 1882, John and Cornelia Adair had made a profit of $512,000 on their initial investment.[57] At one time the JA controlled 1,350,000 acres in Randall, Armstrong, Donley, Hall, Briscoe, and Swisher counties, much of it in the Palo Duro Canyon, and had more than 100,000 head of cattle, along with a large number of horses and mules.[58]

Over the years, the Adairs divided their time between the United States and Europe, living on one of Adair's vast estates in England or Ireland while overseas. Cornelia said that one of the estates had twenty-seven thousand acres of grazing land, which was large by European standards but certainly not in comparison with the JA Ranch.[59] Adair also owned a beautiful home, Rathdaire, near the town of Ballybrittas in Ireland, where they spent much of their time.[60]

In 1882 Adair had Goodnight buy the Quitaque Ranch, or F Ranch, as it was also known, for Cornelia. Now she was a ranch owner in her own right. Goodnight paid 22 cents an acre and then stocked it with three thousand head of cattle. The ranch was located in Briscoe, Floyd, and Hall counties. When Cornelia traded the ranch to Charles Goodnight in 1887, one hundred forty thousand acres were written into the contract.[61]

Cornelia seemed to be very popular with the cowboys on the JA. When Adair died in St. Louis in 1885 while returning from his third trip to the ranch, the cowboys felt no sense of personal loss, for they could not stand him, but they were learning to admire Cornelia more and more.[62] Adair's will left all of his range properties to Cornelia as sole owner of the JA Ranch. Goodnight continued the partnership with her until 1887.[63]

In 1886, with the expiration of the contract coming up in 1887, Goodnight and Cornelia divided the properties, with Cornelia designating an alleged illegitimate son of John Adair, William Henry Plunkett Maquay, banker, of Florence, Italy, as her agent in the division. By the terms of Adair's will, he was beneficiary to $100,000 and, in Goodnight's opinion, was interested in nothing but the money. Goodnight agreed to take the Quitaque Ranch, 140,000 acres of land, and twenty thousand cattle in exchange for his one-third interest in the Palo Duro. This arrangement left Cornelia the sole owner of the JA Ranch. During the ten

Figure 25.   Cornelia Adair with Charles Goodnight. Courtesy
of the Panhandle-Plains Historical Museum, Canyon, Texas.

years of his management, Goodnight made an annual profit of 72 percent on the capital first advanced by Adair.[64]

Cornelia arranged to conduct the ranching business, which was 100 miles from the nearest neighborhood and 250 miles from the nearest railroad, through a series of ranch managers. With the division of the business from Charles Goodnight, Cornelia became one of the few women in the world to preside over such a huge enterprise and financial empire. She took a strong interest in the management of the ranch and became even more active in the cattle business than John Adair had been.[65] She apparently surprised some people by becoming an excellent manager of her affairs. She visited the JA each fall, riding the range with the cowboys and sharing in their chuck wagon meals. She presided over the business—hiring and firing managers and authorizing purchases and sales.[66]

After the dissolution of the Adair-Goodnight partnership, Goodnight stayed on for a time, and Cornelia's son, Jack Ritchie, arrived to learn the cattle business. Jack worked as a cowhand and was promoted to foreman of the Tule Division of the ranch, but, in 1888, his gambling, which Goodnight forbade, led to his demotion. Jack became a sportsman and worldwide adventurer. He bought JA horses for the New York City police and visited ranches in Australia. His greatest adventure, however, was enlisting in the British army during the Boer War, where his knowledge of living on the Texas prairie enabled him to organize the movements

Figure 26.   Cornelia Adair sidesaddle on horse with others on
the JA Ranch, c. 1891. Courtesy of Mrs. W. H. Hess, Claude,
Texas; Panhandle-Plains Historical Museum, Canyon, Texas.

of men and horses across the South African veldt. When Cornelia died in 1921 in England, Jack was living there, too, but his health was so poor that he could not take charge of the JA.[67]

The JA had been managed by a number of men—J. C. Farrington (1888–1890), Arthur Tisdale (1891), and Richard Walsh (1891–1910). Walsh, an Irish immigrant who first came to the ranch in 1885 with visitor Jack Ritchie, soon built up one of the finest herds in the country and helped consolidate the land into 450,000 acres before resigning to take charge of a large British-owned outfit in Southern Rhodesia. Cornelia, however, kept a strict eye on affairs at the ranch. According to one story, when she discovered that a foreman had stocked part of the ranch with spotted San Simone cattle, she promptly fired him. She had strict preferences for the cattle and horses at the JA. The horses were to be bays, brown with a black mane and tail, and preferably with black stockings.[68] Cornelia kept a tight rein on the workings of the JA and continued her yearly visits to ensure that her wishes were followed.

The Stayer newspaper of Canyon City, Texas, carried the following account of Cornelia's movements in 1901:

> October 17, 1901: Mrs. C. Adair, the English cattle queen, sailed the 2nd for America. She is expected to be at the JA ranch the 15th of this month. She will bring a cabinet [group] of 12 or 14 with her. The cowboys are expecting a grand time when she arrives.
>
> November 7, 1901: Mrs. C. Adair and her cabinet arrived at the JA ranch last Monday, the 28th.
>
> November 14, 1901: Mrs. C. Adair is expected to be at the Tule ranch next

Figure 27.   Cornelia Adair (left, next to chuck wagon) eating with cowboys on JA Ranch. Courtesy of Panhandle-Plains Historical Museum, Canyon, Texas.

week. She will be with the cowboys during this week. She is an expert rider and has her horses and saddle and will do a great deal of riding at the round-up.

November 28, 1901: Mrs. C. Adair arrived at the Tule ranch this evening, also the JA cowboys. They will commence work in the morning. They will have big roundups this time as they are going to gather everything. They will soon be through with their work on this side of the canyon.[69]

The newspaper account attests to Cornelia's participation in the roundups when she arrived at the JA and confirms that the cowboys looked forward to her visits and enjoyed her company. She also traveled with a large entourage, in keeping with her social position.

Cornelia's grandsons, Montie (1910–1999) and Dick Ritchie, also came to the ranch. Dick unfortunately died of carbon monoxide poisoning while sleeping too close to a boat motor, but Montie stayed on to run the ranch. His decision to remain there may have been influenced by his father, who had often told him that the times he spent in the Palo Duro were perhaps the happiest days of his life.[70]

Having grown up as an English aristocrat, Montie had graduated from Cambridge in 1931, where he studied history and languages. However, he and his brother, Dick, returned to their American roots in the early 1930s, and the handsome pair moved in New York society with ease and grace.[71] In 1935 Montie assumed the management of the JA. He got the ranch out of debt, bought out the other heirs, and cared for the land. He sold off part of the original ranch and purchased a Colorado farm and a spectacular art collection.[72] Montie managed to keep his feet firmly in two worlds—one at the JA and the other in Cambridge and art.[73]

Montie bragged of "a fourth generation who loves the ranch and knows most of its secret places and will likely carry on the family tradition, my daughter Cornelia." Andrew Bivins, son of Montie's daughter Cornelia, provides a fifth-generation connection.[74] The ranch has now come full circle. It is once again in the hands of a Cornelia—Cornelia ("Ninia") Ritchie, Montie's only child and Cornelia Adair's great-granddaughter.[75] Ninia is even more involved in the running of the JA than was her great-grandmother. Following the pattern of the earlier Cornelia, Ninia formed a partnership with Jay O'Brien to manage the ranch. The JA remains the oldest privately owned cattle company in West Texas. Cornelia Adair would most certainly approve of the arrangement, including the fact that JA horseflesh is one of the best bloodlines of any of the great western ranches.[76]

The success of the JA helped develop the Texas Panhandle, including the settlement of Amarillo, which became one of the largest cattle-shipping points in the world. Cornelia Adair maintained a house in Clarendon and built a hospital and the town's first YMCA there. She was also a great supporter of the Episcopal church.[77]

Cornelia, who died on September 22, 1921, at eighty-four, is buried at Rathdaire, Ballybrittas, Ireland. She was a part of the founding of the legendary JA Ranch even though her prior experience was completely foreign to the cattle country of the Texas Panhandle. "Her spirit and broad vision were as truly Western as if she had lived here her entire life. She was an all round good scout and a real Queen of the Cattle Country."[78]

NOTES

1. David W. Parish, "Cornelia's Worlds: A History of Geneseo, 1850–1900," 3.

2. David W. Parish, town historian of Geneseo, New York, e-mail to author, Apr. 21, 2003.

3. Ibid.

4. Parish, "Cornelia's Worlds," 13.

5. Ibid., 8.

6. Ibid., 13.

7. Theodore Roosevelt, "Cross-country Riding in America," 335.

8. Ibid., 338.

9. Parish, "Cornelia's Worlds," 47.

10. Mary Beth Rogers, Sherry A. Smith, and Janelle D. Scott, *We Can Fly: Stories of Katherine Stinson and Other Gutsy Texas Women,* 130.

11. Cornelia Adair, *My Diary: August 30th to November 5, 1874,* 87.

12. Ibid., xiv.

13. Parish, "Cornelia's Worlds," 8–9.

14. Ibid., 15.

15. Ibid., 10.

16. "Adair, Cornelia Wadsworth," *The Handbook of Texas Online.*

17. Adair, *My Diary,* xvii.

18. Ninia Ritchie, telephone conversation with author, Sept. 9, 2003; "Adair, Cornelia Wadsworth," *The New Handbook of Texas Online.*

19. J. Evetts Haley, *Charles Goodnight: Cowman and Plainsman,* 295.

20. Adair, *My Diary,* xvii.

21. Harley True Burton, *History of the JA Ranch,* 20.

22. Haley, *Charles Goodnight,* 295.

23. Parish, "Cornelia's Worlds," 27, 33.

24. Ibid., 34–35.

25. Ibid., 35.

26. Rogers, Smith, and Scott, *We Can Fly,* 130.

27. Burton, *History of the JA Ranch,* 21.

28. Ibid.

29. Parish, "Cornelia's Worlds," 35.

30. Ibid.

31. Adair, *My Diary,* 72.

32. Ibid., 73.

33. Ibid., 75.

34. Ibid., 79.

35. Ibid., 76.

36. Parish, "Cornelia's Worlds," 36.

37. Adair, *My Diary,* 87.

38. Rogers, Smith, and Scott, *We Can Fly,* 131.

39. Joyce Gibson Roach, *The Cowgirls,* xxi.

40. Parish, "Cornelia's World," 36.

41. Burton, *History of the JA Ranch,* 23.

42. William H. Forbis, *The Cowboys,* 56; Lawrence Clayton, *Contemporary Ranches of Texas,* 83.

43. Burton, *History of the JA Ranch,* 26; Haley, *Charles Goodnight,* 295–96.

44. Forbis, *The Cowboys,* 56–57.

45. Burton, *History of the JA Ranch,* 30; Haley, *Charles Goodnight,* 296.

46. Haley, *Charles Goodnight,* 296.

47. Ibid., 297–98.

48. Ibid., 298.

49. The Caprock is an escarpment that forms a natural boundary between the High Plains and the lower rolling plains of West Texas; "Caprock," *The New Handbook of Texas Online.*

50. Burton, *History of the JA Ranch,* 32.

51. Rogers, Smith, and Scott, *We Can Fly,* 129–30.

52. Haley, *Charles Goodnight,* 300.

53. Ibid., 301.

54. Laura V. Hamner, *No-gun Man of Texas: A Century of Achievement, 1835–1929,* 129.

55. Burton, *History of the JA Ranch,* 26–27.

56. Forbis, *The Cowboys,* 57.

57. Ibid.

58. Clayton, *Contemporary Ranches of Texas,* 83; Rogers, Smith, and Scott, *We Can Fly,* 126.

59. Adair, *My Diary,* xvii.

60. Ninia Ritchie, telephone conversation with author, Sept. 9, 2004.

61. Burton, *History of the JA Ranch,* 46.

62. Hamner, *No-gun Man of Texas,* 194.

63. Haley, *Charles Goodnight,* 326.

64. Pauline Durrett Robertson and R. L. Robertson, *Cowman's Country: Fifty Frontier Ranches in the Texas Panhandle, 1876–1887,* 104.

65. Rogers, Smith, and Scott, *We Can Fly,* 134.

66. Ibid., 136–37.

67. "History of the JA, the Ritchie Family, and the JA Family."

68. Clayton, *Contemporary Ranches of Texas,* 87.

69. William Elton Green, curator of history, Panhandle-Plains Historical Museum, Canyon, Texas, e-mail to author, Sept. 4, 2003.

70. "History of the JA, the Ritchie family, and the JA Family."

71. "Montgomery Harrison Wadsworth Ritchie, 1910–1999; Remarks by Stuart Symington Jr. at Interment Ceremony, Temple Hill Cemetery, Geneseo, New York," http://www.ranches.org/montgomery_harrison_wadsworth_ri.htm (accessed Oct. 20, 2005).

72. "History of the JA, the Ritchie family, and the JA Family."

73. Ibid.

74. Ibid.

75. Ibid.; JA Cattle Company Records, 1813–1994 and undated.

76. "History of the JA, the Ritchie family, and the JA Family."

77. "Adair, Cornelia Wadsworth," *The New Handbook of Texas Online.*

78. Adair, *My Diary,* xv.

ANNA McADAMS SLAUGHTER

MRS. WILLIAM BAXTER SLAUGHTER

James M. Smallwood

Anna McAdams was a woman destined to go up the trail in style, using a state-of-the-art Hines buggy on her trips. She was the daughter of cattleman William Carroll and Ann Alexander McAdams, both from Tennessee. They were well settled in Palo Pinto County at their ranch near Sand Valley Peak when Anna came along in the late 1850s. The family was distantly related by blood to Mary, Queen of Scots, and William's father, Douglas McAdams, made his mark in U.S. history by constructing the first "macadamized" hard-surfaced road in the United States.

Anna and her older sister Molly attended one-room schools in Palo Pinto County, and both joined the Eastern Star when they became teenagers. Anna's other siblings included William, Mary, Corrina, and Elizabeth.[1] Everyone in the family became staunch Methodists and attended services regularly. William and Ann also loved camp meetings, and they usually arranged for a Methodist minister to hold one on their ranch at least once every summer. These were good times for the growing children. They had a chance to meet all of their "far away" neighbors and socialize with others their age, besides learning more about their religion. Anna and her siblings became lifelong practicing Christians.[2]

Anna came from sturdy stock. Her father, William McAdams, arrived in Texas in 1842. He served the Republic of Texas as an army scout and was stationed primarily near the Rio Grande. In the 1840s he helped turn back Mexican armies that twice crossed the Rio Grande to invade the republic. After annexation in 1845, he continued for a time as a border scout with the U.S. Army. Known as "Mustang Bill" because he was an expert at capturing and taming wild horses, William fought under Gen. Zachary Taylor and later under Gen. Winfield Scott during the Mexican War.

Promoted to captain, William saw action in various battles, including Palo Alto, Resaca de la Palma, and Buena Vista. At one point, he led a small group of men on an exceptionally dangerous mission. The party he headed moved for several miles past Mexican lines until they located a prisoner-of-war compound. Cap-

Figure 28.   Anna Slaughter. From *The Trail Drivers of Texas* (1985).

tain McAdams and his squad liberated several prisoners of war who were under a death sentence from Santa Anna. The Mexican general had little use for prisoners, a fact he had demonstrated earlier at the Alamo and Goliad, in the latter case ordering a subordinate to kill all of the captured men. Because of his exceptional service, McAdams emerged from the war as a genuine military hero.[3]

During the Civil War, William and Ann settled in Palo Pinto County near the upper Brazos River, and William made his first trail drive. By 1863 the resources of families in Texas were exhausted, and the state of Texas appropriated $600,000 for direct relief. William got busy and drove a small herd to Mexico, where he bartered the beeves for sundry items, including staples such as sugar, coffee, beans, and corn-meal.[4] Two years later, as the Civil War was ending, he drove a herd to Shreveport, Louisiana, where he sold the cattle for a good profit before buying various goods and hauling them back to Palo Pinto for resale. Later he made drives to Baxter Springs, Kansas, and to Fort Gibson in Indian Territory. After 1870, William continued raising cattle but made only a few more drives. He also served as a Palo Pinto minuteman during the Indian wars to carry warnings and news near and far. Observers said that he could ride farther with less food and sleep than any of his contemporaries. Nonetheless, that did not protect him from being wounded in a skirmish with a band of Comanche and Kiowa warriors. When the Red River War ended in 1875, he settled back into a peaceful life as a well-known rancher, and all of his children, including Anna, learned the ranching business from the ground up.

Anna was a cowgirl at a very young age. When she was only six, her parents gave her a small pony, which she learned to ride. By ten, she virtually shadowed her father, learning all she could about the family's cattle operations.[5] As a young cowgirl, Anna was much like her mother. Whenever William was gone, Ann dressed as a man and kept a belted, holstered six-gun around her waist in plain sight. She also carried a rifle holstered on the saddle of her horse. She worked like a man and made displays of her weapons to ward off anyone who might think of trifling with the McAdams cattle or other property. Anna grew up helping her parents but was especially valuable to her mother when her father was away. Practicing target shooting frequently, she became a good markswoman with handguns and rifles, as well as with shotguns.[6]

At fourteen, Anna handled a man's job as well as her mother did, and both of them continued to openly display their arms when necessary to protect all that belonged to the family. Like her father, "Mustang Bill," Anna proved to be good with both cattle and horses. Equally important, she helped her mother early on, by learning to cook for her family and the workers her father employed. Anna learned to sew and helped make clothes for family members. Additionally, she became well versed in folk remedies and patent medicines and served as a nurse for anyone on the ranch who became ill. She learned first aid and dealt with both minor and serious accidents—everything from broken bones to headaches.[7]

Over time, the McAdamses formed a close relationship with another family of cattle barons, one destined to become famous: the Slaughter clan. Minister George Webb Slaughter and his wife, Sarah Jane, moved from Alabama to Texas in 1830, when the future Lone Star State was still a province of Mexico. After fighting in the Texas Revolution under the command of the redoubtable Sam Houston, George received a land bounty, whereupon he and Sarah moved to Freestone County. There William Baxter ("Bill") Slaughter, who was destined to become Anna McAdams's husband, was born in 1852. His ten siblings included older brothers George Webb Jr., John B., C. C., and Peter E. Slaughter.[8]

In 1857 George Sr. loaded up his entire brood, moved to Palo Pinto County, established a ranch, and went into the cattle business. Upon their arrival, the Slaughters met the McAdams clan. The children of both families became close friends, and all of them attended the annual camp meetings, which gave them an opportunity to socialize with each other. George Sr. would later become a minister, preaching the gospel and practicing medicine. At first a Methodist, he later joined the Baptist church to spread the "good news." Over the years the families visited each other on one or another of the two ranches. Soon, however, the Civil War caused strains as everyone had to do whatever they could to help Texas and the Confederacy. Because of the disruption caused by the Civil War, Captain McAdams helped the Slaughters and other settlers of Palo Pinto by pushing a herd to Mexico, in addition to trailing a herd to Shreveport.[9]

During the war, the McAdamses and the Slaughters proved resilient enough to withstand the attacks by the Comanches and Kiowas; despite the danger, these were exciting times for Anna and the other youngsters of both clans. Indeed, many ranchers could not hold out. The population of Palo Pinto, like those of Parker, Denton, Wise, and San Saba counties, declined drastically. By 1866 only one in five of the prewar ranches in the area was still occupied. Even worse perhaps, in 1865 and 1866, when both state and federal authorities withdrew their troops from the frontier, the Indians had gotten busy, running off thousands of cattle and horses and driving them westward to trade with the Comancheros of the New Mexico Territory.[10]

During these hard times, the men of several nearby ranches sent their families to safety while they, along with the hired hands, stayed and protected their cattle. However, the Slaughter women never left, and neither did Anna or her mother. Instead, they remained at home, continued to do the housework, and went armed to hold the Indians at bay. Holding out benefited both the Slaughters and the McAdamses since the families increased their operations by buying the cattle and horses of other spreads when their owners loaded up their families and headed for safer country to the east.[11]

Meanwhile, the men fervently continued to help the new confederacy from its birth to its collapse. In particular, George Slaughter Sr. did all he could to help the Texas military. After moving part of his herd to Young County, beginning in 1861, George Sr. secured a contract with the Confederate government to supply the Tonkawa Indians with beef, a contract that necessitated short cattle drives. Like his older brothers, young Bill grew up in the saddle, riding his own pony when he was old enough to straddle the steed. Then, during the Civil War, with the older Slaughter men off helping the Confederacy (some became soldiers), the management of the ranches sometimes fell on the youngster, Billy. He made his first drive in 1865 with his father, George, and older brother C. C. They gathered a herd of nine hundred steers and, with the help of three hands, drove them to Shreveport to sell to the Confederate authorities. Excitement came when the group reached the swollen Trinity River at Scyene, just south of Dallas. The horses and cattle had to swim across while some of the men helped float their chuck wagon to the opposite bank.

Young Billy made his second drive when he was only fourteen.[12] In 1866 he helped his father take a herd to Emporia, Kansas, to sell. The trip was an adventure for Bill, to say the least. Crossing through Indian Territory, the men were attacked by a group of thirteen Indians, probably Comanches and/or Kiowas. Although the warriors wounded his father, Bill and the other cowboys dealt lead in doses sufficient to drive the raiders away.

Bill made his third drive in 1867. He joined his father, an older brother, and three cowhands in moving about nine hundred steers from Palo Pinto to Jefferson, Texas. This was an especially hard drive because the cowhands had to herd the live-stock through great stands of timber once they reached East Texas. Nevertheless, the trip was worth the effort. Upon delivery to Jefferson, George Sr. received $24,300 in gold for the sale. In both 1869 and 1870 Bill also participated in other early drives that went from Palo Pinto to Abilene, Kansas, over one or another of the branches of the Chisholm Trail. On the latter trip, the teenaged Billy was the trail boss. Thus, the youngster had become an experienced cowhand who was learning the cattle business the hard way—by working the herds. He was destined to make a total of at least fifteen trips up the trail, every one of them profitable as the Cattle Kingdom of Texas expanded.[13]

In 1871 the Slaughters and the McAdamses had a joint drive, with both Bill and Captain McAdams acting as trail bosses. However, the situation was laden with problems for both families. Most of the women remained behind, going about the day-to-day business of managing the sprawling ranches in the absence of their men. For Anna and the rest, the times were particularly perilous, for the braves in the Comanche and Kiowa tribes frequently bolted from their reservations in Indian Territory and raided deep into Western and Central Texas. Not until after the U.S. Army's victory at the battle of Palo Duro Canyon in 1875 did women like Anna feel safe enough to relax and continue helping their fathers and husbands build the Cattle Kingdom.[14]

Meanwhile, the men—who also feared Indian attacks—drove their combined herd northeastward, intending to reach Red River Station and the start of the Chisholm Trail. However, one night an electrical storm developed, and the herd stampeded. The cowhands spent the night hunting about two hundred steers and driving them back to the main herd. Two of the cowboys never made it back to the camp. Indians attacked and killed them, taking their scalps and then mutilating their bodies, cutting out the heart of one of the dead men and laying it on his stomach. Bill led the party that found and buried the two dead cowhands. The horrible sight sickened everyone in the burial detail, but they did their jobs. Henceforward, as a precaution against any more surprise attacks, all of the cowboys kept close watch for Indians and did not venture too far from their cohorts. At night, extra guards were posted. The extra vigilance worked; there was strength in numbers. Indians preferred not to take on settlers and drovers unless they had the advantage of surprise and superior numbers.[15]

Bill Slaughter continued his annual cattle drives up the trails into the mid-

1870s, with 1877 proving to be a significant year: He courted and married young Anna McAdams, whom he had known since childhood; indeed, they had watched each other grow up. The same year, he also formed a partnership with his older brother John B. The two men pooled their capital and came up with a total of about $6,000. With their combined resources, they bought steers and moved them up the trail to the railroad in Kansas, where they sold the herd for a good profit. In 1877 the brothers also became founders and charter members in the North-West Texas Cattle Raisers Association, which eventually evolved into the Texas and Southwestern Cattle Raisers Association. Meanwhile, Anna and Bill settled into married life, worked their ranch, and welcomed their son, Coney, who made his appearance in 1878.[16]

In 1879 Anna made her first cattle drive. She helped her husband move the live-stock to a new range in Crosby County, close to Scallowag Creek and McDonald Creek, a tributary of the Brazos. Although the drive was a short one, Anna got her first taste of life on the trail. Working as a cook, wrangler, and scout, she labored alongside Bill's hired hands. She also experienced what it was like to sleep in a bedroll and drift off while gazing at stars overhead.

Soon Bill's brother John trailed his cattle to Crosby County, and the brothers' partnership continued. Together they staked out a ranch on the open range that was a twenty-mile square. At first, Anna and John's wife had to live in a rough camp with little protection from the elements, something that Anna was now getting accustomed to. She spent time living in tents, in covered wagons, and out in the middle of Mother Nature. She worked over an open fire to prepare meals. She bathed in creeks and springs. She did without many of the accouterments that many a "proper" lady expected. Moreover, soon Anna was helping the brothers and the family's cowhands build a sturdy frame home.[17]

When Anna had completed her move, bringing little Coney along, she busied herself for a time getting things in order. Afterward, Anna and Bill hosted a real shindig for all of the area's ranchers and other settlers. The party lasted three days and two nights, resulting in a bunch of tired but happy people. In the process, they ate huge amounts of beef and beans and drank pots of coffee, and many of the men also partook of various "spirits," a nice word for whiskey and other liquors. They talked, they laughed, and they danced their nights away and generally enjoyed a time of relaxation with one another. Importantly, the Slaughters got to know most of their new neighbors, something that was essential on the frontier in times of emergency. The women needed each other to help with illness or accidents and as midwives during the numerous births. Further, women like Anna did not feel so isolated once they made friends. Meanwhile, the women continued to help their husbands develop the families' herds. The use of brands was important in helping to establish ownership. On the Slaughter place, cowhands used "Anna-A" as the brand for the heifers that belonged to Anna and Bill.[18]

For about four years, Bill, Anna, and other members of the Slaughter clan continued their ranching operation in Crosby County and made at least one long drive each year. In 1881 Bill made two drives to Caldwell, Kansas, a terminal that had greatly improved its stockyards. However, despite these successful trips, civilization caught up with Bill and Anna in 1883. The Texas government demanded payment from ranchers who were using state land as pastures. The Espuela Cattle Company, usually called "The Spurs," acquired title to the range where the Slaughters had been grazing their cattle. After that development, brothers Bill and John moved their herds farther west into New Mexico. Jack Alley, the trail boss for Bill and Anna's cattle drive, later recalled how hard the trip was. For one thing, there were no trails to follow. The herd had to survive desertlike conditions and cross a mountain range before reaching their destination. While some ranchers lost hundreds of cattle when trying to make that drive, Alley saved almost all of Bill and Anna's livestock by camping at Spring Lake until the rains came.[19]

Anna eventually joined the drive and helped with cooking, as well as scouting out in front of the herd for water. The trek was not at all safe, for bands of Apaches frequently made forays from their reservation and complicated life for the pioneers; luckily, the drive was without serious incident as Bill, Anna, and trail boss Alley moved their herd into the American Valley in Sierra County, while John staked out a range near the head of the Tularosa River. Bill and Anna, along with their small son, Coney, became exceptionally successful on their new ranch. They turned a $4,200 investment into a fortune of $260,000.[20]

John and Bill continued their partnership until 1886, when John sold his holdings to an English company and went to Utah, where for a time he ran herds near the Green River, about thirty miles east of Salt Lake City. Meanwhile, Bill and Anna continued working their ranch in American Valley. In a bizarre incident in 1887, rustlers almost killed Bill. Rustling cattle was a serious crime. Since each stolen cow was lost money to ranchers, justice was harsh. Earlier, Bill had served on a grand jury that indicted several known rustlers who had brought chaos to the local ranchers. For a time, so many cattle thieves bedeviled the area that the ranchers began referring to their travail as the "Rustlers' War." Anna once again strapped on weapons, fearing she might be attacked when Bill was out working the cattle.

One day Bill was out on the range and, inexplicably, had not carried his weapons. His oversight led to disaster. Desperadoes known only as Youngblood and Adkins accosted him with the intention of punishing him for his votes on the grand jury that had indicted them. When he realized that he was under attack, Bill tried to turn his horse for a getaway but was not fast enough. The villains made it rain lead, and one bullet hit Bill in the back. Although he slipped virtually into unconsciousness, he hung onto the saddle horn, and his horse carried him home, where the alarmed Anna cared for him until cowhands could find and bring a physician to remove the bullet. After several months of slowed activity, coupled with much care from Anna, Bill was able to get back to his business. Authorities soon captured the villains and brought them to justice.[21]

Subsequently, Bill continued to make the long drives each year, sometimes push-ing the herds all the way to Nebraska or Wyoming. In 1896 Anna made the trail drive with him. With their herd of fifteen hundred head, they left Fort Sumner, New Mexico, on May 25, traveling northeastward toward Liberal, Kansas. There they were able to strike the Western Trail, which, after 1885, was used to reach both Nebraska and Wyoming. As she had in the past, Anna worked several jobs on this drive. She rode well out in front of the herd, searching for watering holes and places to bed down the cattle at night. With the trail boss, she scouted ahead for the easiest paths for the herd to follow. She also helped young cowhand George Longan, a future newspaperman, in the remuda, catching the change of horses for the morning, afternoon, and night shifts. Another of her jobs was to gather wood for the wagon cook and help him get the meals ready.[22]

Doing her work as scout, Anna rode horseback as she had done since child-hood; on other days, when the lay of the land made riding easy, she opted for her large, comfortable, state-of-the-art Hines buggy. Meanwhile, at night, after a hard day's work, it was early to bed after the cowhands followed the usual practice of aligning the wagon tongues to point toward the North Star. A new workday began at first light, and Anna was up even earlier to help the cook get the coffee brewing for the men.[23]

Excitement mounted when the drive reached the banks of the Canadian River near old Fort Bascom, New Mexico. Everyone, cattle included, had to swim the river, which was near flood level. This was a dangerous situation for the men be-cause the cattle could not be trusted in the water; they were too big and too wild. There was a real risk that Anna or some of the men might be injured; however, the cowgirl, the men, and the beasts negotiated the river with no serious injuries. How Anna got her buggy across is not known, but her husband's experience as a youth in getting his wagon across the swollen Trinity in '65 undoubtedly helped. Stop-ping the drive near Clayton, New Mexico, Anna traveled with her husband and trail hand Longan to Springer, where they picked up another two hundred fifty head and trailed them back to join the main herd. Anna rode on horseback and worked as a wrangler on this short part of the drive. About the only job she ever refused was riding drag; ownership and gender had its privileges, after all.[24]

Although Anna had helped her father and later her husband on short drives, this was her first long trip. After leaving Clayton, Bill, Anna, and the hands pushed the cattle along the north line of Texas but could not cross because the Capitol Freehold Land and Cattle Company had the border fenced for a distance of about fifty miles. Near present-day Guyman, Oklahoma, the drive finally crossed into Indian Territory. The rest of the journey was uneventful, with the drovers and their herd reaching the Rock Island Railroad terminal at Liberal, Kansas, on July 25. The entire trip consumed about sixty days, most of them hard and tiring. As Bill knew she would, Anna had done the work of a cowhand on the trail and contributed greatly to the success of the drive. She and Bill made a healthy profit, and, with delight, she boarded a train to Kansas City for a few days of shopping and recreation. Later she related that the trip had been an easy one. She averred that the weather had been fine all the way and that everything had gone smoothly. Perhaps she had forgotten about the hazardous crossing of the Canadian River at flood tide.[25]

Anna and her husband soon readied themselves for a move back to Texas because, in New Mexico, the era of the open range was disappearing there as well. As early as 1889, they had begun buying up tracts of land in Sherman County, Texas, along Coldwater Creek. The land was located in the northern Panhandle bordering the new Oklahoma Territory. By 1895, Bill and Anna had also acquired an interest in the Snyder Brothers' Coldwater Cattle Company. After the drive of 1896, they moved to the new ranch near the small town of Stratford. Bill and his hands built Anna a large, roomy house from which she helped run Bill's new empire. They soon had 150,000 fenced acres on which they ran about ten thousand cattle.[26]

Once settled, they entertained their neighbors often and sponsored a big religious revival every summer. During these evangelistic meetings, which lasted a week or ten days, visitors would come from near and far, usually camping out near the house in their wagons or tents. They came to hear thundering preachers like George W. Truett, minister of the First Baptist Church of Dallas, and the noted James B. Grambrell, editor of the *Baptist Standard,* which was published in Waco. Each day Bill and Anna had two of their hands, John Lanners and Tom Moy—the latter a black cowboy in charge of the ranch's north camp—butcher a steer and cook it for the guests. Anna supervised the preparation of other dishes to accompany the barbecue. For such occasions, Bill usually had his men catch a maverick and then endured the ribbing of the local cattlemen as to who had supplied the beef. Still, everyone had good times, and Anna loved having company. Such celebrations helped break the regular routine of ranch life and provided a welcome change of pace.[27]

Bill was often gone on drives that lasted for extended periods of time, leaving Anna behind to run the ranch. In 1889 he moved two herds from New Mexico and the Panhandle to Malta Valley, Montana. He made his last cattle drive in 1901, a time when most long drives were a thing of the past. Again Anna rode the trail with him as they moved a herd from Clifton, Arizona, to the railhead at Liberal, Kansas. Although nearing fifty years of age, Anna performed much as she had five years earlier, riding ahead, finding watering holes, and looking for camping grounds. She helped with the meals and nursed men who became sick or injured. Anna just plain did whatever needed to be done. This last trip was another moneymaker, and afterward Anna again enjoyed a trip to Kansas City, where she took in the delights of city life.[28]

Later in the year, Bill moved a herd of 104 domesticated buffalo from Dalhart, Texas, to Fort Garland, Colorado. With the buffalo in danger of extinction, the army was attempting to save the few that remained and use them to rebuild a larger herd. Bill told Anna that he had almost no trouble with the animals, something he could not say about cattle. He fed the herd cottonseed cake at dusk each day. The buffalo ate and then slept until about midnight, when they roused and fed on the prairie grass before sleeping again until daybreak. Bill said the trip was the easiest drive he ever made.[29]

Shortly after that trip, Bill became the Sherman County judge when he was appointed to finish the term of an official who had resigned. With Anna's help, he also operated a dry goods store in Stratford. Anna did most of the clerking since Bill was busy organizing and running a new bank in town, a task that occupied him for a time. Their son, Coney, helped in both the store and the bank. The Slaughters remained in Sherman County until 1905, when they moved to Dalhart, Dallam County, where Bill opened another bank. The next stop was Texline, where Bill once again opened a bank. Then, in a major change, the Slaughters moved to Pueblo, Colorado, where Bill became president of the Mercantile National Bank, and Coney worked as a cashier. In 1914 Bill organized the Bankers Trust Company, which claimed to have five million dollars in capital. The company was meant to handle the financial interests of the entire Slaughter clan, which included his brothers and sisters and their offspring.[30]

Bill and Anna lived well, and Anna continued to help her husband in his financial dealings. Nonetheless, tragedy struck—and changed their lives completely. In March of 1915, Coney suddenly resigned, and Bill's bank in Colorado closed amid charges of embezzlement. After disappearing for a time, Coney was later found in Chicago. By then, Bill had been tried in both state and federal courts for his alleged part in the bank's financial misfortunes. However, juries acquitted him when it was demonstrated that he had played no role in the calamity and did not know about Coney's illegal act of embezzling $112,987. Nevertheless, Bill and Anna lost most of their wealth and their wayward son as well. Having been raised in wealth and privilege and owning the first automobile in Dalhart, Coney apparently believed that, since his salary did not cover his expensive lifestyle, he could squeeze cash from the bank without being apprehended. But he did get caught.[31]

After the scandal, Bill and Anna lived in Dallas for a time, and Bill helped his brother C. C. manage his business dealings. Later they moved to San Antonio, where Anna watched her husband's health fail as he grieved for his errant son and lamented the loss of much of his share of the family fortune. However, both he and Anna joined the Trail Drivers Association and enjoyed participating in its activities. At the annual reunion of trail drivers in 1922, both Bill and Anna proudly watched while their granddaughter, Elizabeth, entertained the guests. The teenager came on stage dressed as a cowgirl and recited, complete with cowboy slang, a poem called "The Chisholm Trail."[32]

However, nothing could completely take Bill's mind off the son who had disappointed him and caused so much money to be lost. Having gradually wasted away, Bill died on March 28, 1929. Funeral services for him were held at the First Baptist Church in San Antonio. Afterward, Slaughter's last wish was granted. His survivors took his body back to his old place in Palo Pinto County for burial in the family cemetery.[33]

After losing her husband, Anna continued to reside in San Antonio, where she spent much of her time worrying about Coney. Once found in Chicago, he fled before the authorities could arrest him. After evading the law for eight years, Coney was finally captured in Phoenixville, Pennsylvania. Tried and convicted for embezzlement, he served two years of a six-year sentence in a federal lockup before escaping. Later caught in Englewood, Colorado, he was forced to finish his term. Once released, he moved to San Antonio to be near his mother, who was torn between love and pain. Her only child had essentially thrown his life away. Coney suffered further financial losses because of faulty decisions and the impact of the Great Depression. He must have had much the same thoughts as his mother—because on March 18, 1932, he ended his life by shooting himself in the head. Anna buried him while still mourning the loss of her husband. In this final tragedy, which darkened an otherwise extraordinary life, Anna also died of her grief.[34]

Anna McAdams Slaughter, who was a part of two ranching families, one headed by her father, the other by her husband, enjoyed a life as a wife and mother and had a profitable career as a rancher and trail rider. As Joyce Gibson Roach has noted in *The Cowgirls*, Anna and other ranching women like her were a rare breed. They were the precursors of the modern women's liberation movement just as much as Susan B. Anthony, Kate Stanton, and other women of the nineteenth and early twentieth centuries.

While leaders like Anthony were demanding their rights, Anna and other cow women simply *took* their freedom, much to the relief of their men, who always needed help. Those women like Anna who worked on the ranches or went up the trails often did the work of men and were much appreciated by their ranching fathers and husbands. There were those, also like Anna, who could handle almost any job, be it spotter, trail boss, wrangler, or cook. Not only did they make ranching life easier for the men in their families, but they also learned to deal with hard work and harsh weather, which ranged from droughts to floods. To cope with feelings of isolation in the early years, they set about making connections with the other ranching women, bringing civilization to the West. They learned to ride as equals with the men. Because firearms were a necessary part of everyday life, they used them when they had to. They dealt with hostile Indians and cutthroat rustlers. On the trails they endured and often enjoyed the rustic conditions. Like Anna, through it all they persevered.[35]

NOTES

1. U.S. Bureau of the Census, 1860, Palo Pinto County, microfilm copy 653, roll 1302, 343.

2. J. Marvin Hunter, comp. and ed., *The Trail Drivers of Texas* (1985), 797, 799–800.

3. Ibid., 798–99.

4. David Dary, *Cowboy Culture: A Saga of Five Centuries,* 132.

5. Wayne Gard, *The Chisholm Trail,* 43; Hunter, *The Trail Drivers of Texas,* 799–800; J. Evetts Haley, *Charles Goodnight: Cowman and Plainsman,* 27.

6. Hunter, *The Trail Drivers of Texas,* 799. For more on the ranching life of women, see Mamie Sypert Burns, *This I Can Leave You: A Woman's Days on the Pitchfork Ranch;* Agnes Moreley, *No Life for a Lady.*

7. Hunter, *The Trail Drivers of Texas,* 799; Burns, *A Woman's Days on the Pitchfork Ranch;* Moreley, *No Life for a Lady.*

8. For more on the entire Slaughter clan, see David J. Murrah, *C. C. Slaughter: Rancher, Banker, Baptist;* Mary Whatley Clarke, *The Slaughter Ranches and Their Makers,* 30–43; "Recollections of William Baxter Slaughter," in Hunter, *The Trail Drivers of Texas,* 863–64; Cora Melton Cross, "Early Texas Cattle Industry," 476–77; Claudia Hazlewood, "George Webb Slaughter," in Ron Tyler, ed., *The New Handbook of Texas,* vol. 5, 1075; H. Allen Anderson, "William Baxter Slaughter," in *The New Handbook of Texas,* vol. 5, 1077–78; Sam Acheson, "C. C. Slaughter Helped Create City"; "C. C. Slaughter," 13–14.

9. "Recollections of W. B. Slaughter," in Hunter, *The Trail Drivers of Texas,* 864–70; Hazlewood, "G. W. Slaughter," in *The New Handbook of Texas,* vol. 5, 1075; Anderson, "W. B. Slaughter," in *The New Handbook of Texas,* vol. 5, 1077–78; Gard, *Chisholm Trail,* 37–40, 43.

10. Comancheros were Mexicans who traded with the Comanche Indians in the early days of the Southwest.

11. Rupert N. Richardson, *The Frontier of Northwest Texas, 1846 to 1876: Advance and Defense by the Pioneer Settlers of the Cross Timbers and Prairies,* 253; Don Worcester, *The Chisholm Trail: High Road of the Cattle Kingdom,* 6, 24–25.

12. "Recollections of W. B. Slaughter," in Hunter, *The Trail Drivers of Texas,* 864–70; Cora Melton Cross, "William B. Slaughter, Trail Driver of 1866," 465–69; Cross, "Early Texas Cattle Industry," 477–78; Hazlewood, "G. W. Slaughter," in *The New Handbook of Texas,* vol. 5, 1075; Anderson, "W. B. Slaughter," in *The New Handbook of Texas,* vol. 5, 1077–78; Clarke, *The Slaughter Ranches and Their Makers,* 180–81.

13. "Recollections of W. B. Slaughter," in Hunter, *The Trail Drivers of Texas,* 864–70; Cross, "William B. Slaughter, Trail Driver of 1866," 465–69; Cross, "Early Texas Cattle Industry," 477–78; Hazlewood, "G. W. Slaughter," in *The New Handbook of Texas,* vol. 5, 1075; Anderson, "W. B. Slaughter," in *The New Handbook of Texas,* vol. 5, 1077–78; Clarke, *The Slaughter Ranches and Their Makers,* 180–81.

14. See C. L. Douglas, *Cattle Kings of Texas;* Edward Charles ("Teddy Blue") Abbott and

Helena Huntington Smith, *We Pointed Them North: Recollections of a Cowpuncher;* and Edward Everett Dale, *The Range Cattle Industry: Ranching on the Great Plains from 1865 to 1925.*

15. Gard, *Chisholm Trail,* 153; Clarke, *The Slaughter Ranches and Their Makers,* 168–69. Clarke mistakenly identified McAdams as one of the dead men. Also see "Recollections of W. B. Slaughter," in Hunter, *The Trail Drivers of Texas,* 870.

16. "Recollections of John B. Slaughter," in Hunter, *The Trail Drivers of Texas,* 920; *Graham Leader,* Feb. 16, 1877; Mary Whatley Clarke, *A Century of Cow Business: The History of the Texas and Southwestern Cattle Raisers Association,* 12–13, 77; Anderson, "W. B. Slaughter," in *The New Handbook of Texas,* vol. 5, 1077–78; Cora M. Cross, "W. B. Slaughter, of Post, Travels Last Long Trail," 194–97.

17. Clarke, *The Slaughter Ranches and Their Makers,* 170–71, 186; Clarke, *A Century of Cow Business,* 77; Jack Alley, "Fifty-four Years of Pioneering on the Plains of Texas."

18. Alley, "Fifty-four Years of Pioneering on the Plains of Texas"; Clarke, *The Slaughter Ranches and Their Makers,* 170–71, 186; Clarke, *A Century of Cow Business,* 77.

19. Alley, "Fifty-four Years of Pioneering on the Plains of Texas"; *Santa Fe Daily New Mexican,* Apr. 14, 1884; Gard, *Chisholm Trail,* 253; Clarke, *The Slaughter Ranches and Their Makers,* 172–74; Anderson, "W. B. Slaughter," in *The New Handbook of Texas,* vol. 5, 1077–78; Clarke, *A Century of Cow Business,* 77; for more on the Spur ranch, see W. C. Holden, *Espuela Land and Cattle Company.*

20. *Santa Fe Daily New Mexican,* Apr. 14, 1884; Alley, "Fifty-four Years of Pioneering on the Plains of Texas"; Gard, *Chisholm Trail,* 253; Clarke, *The Slaughter Ranches and Their Makers,* 172–74; Anderson, "W. B. Slaughter," in *The New Handbook of Texas,* vol. 5, 1077–78; Clarke, *A Century of Cow Business,* 77.

21. "Recollections of J. B. Slaughter," in Hunter, *The Trail Drivers of Texas,* 920; *Tombstone Daily Prospector,* May 16, 1887; Philip J. Rasch, "Murder in American Valley"; Clarke, *The Slaughter Ranches and Their Makers,* 187.

22. "Recollections of Anna Slaughter," in Hunter, *The Trail Drivers of Texas,* 885; Anderson, "W. B. Slaughter," in *The New Handbook of Texas,* vol. 5, 1077–78; Steve Wilhelm, *Cavalcade of Hooves and Horns,* 69–70; Joyce Gibson Roach, *The Cowgirls,* 5. A remuda is a herd of horses from which those to be used the next day are chosen.

23. "Recollections of Anna Slaughter," in Hunter, *The Trail Drivers of Texas,* 885; Anderson, "W. B. Slaughter," in *The New Handbook of Texas,* vol. 5, 1077–78; Wilhelm, *Hooves and Horns,* 69–70; Roach, *The Cowgirls,* 5.

24. "Riding drag" refers to the cowboys who followed behind the herd, in the dust or mud, pushing the stragglers and bringing up the rear. "Recollections of Anna Slaughter," in Hunter, *The Trail Drivers of Texas,* 885; Anderson, "W. B. Slaughter," in *The New Handbook of Texas,* vol. 5, 1077–78; Wilhelm, *Hooves and Horns,* 69–70; Roach, *The Cowgirls,* 5; for more on life along the trail see Roach, *The Cowgirls,* and Worcester, *Chisholm Trail.*

25. "Recollections of A. Slaughter," in Hunter, *The Trail Drivers of Texas,* 885–86; Clarke, *The Slaughter Ranches and Their Makers,* 181.

26. Anderson, "W. B. Slaughter," in *The New Handbook of Texas,* vol. 5, 1077–78; Clarke, *The Slaughter Ranches and Their Makers,* 188.

27. Marylou McDaniel, comp. and ed., *God, Grass, and Grit: History of the Sherman*

County Trade Area, vol. 1 (1975), 7; Anderson, "W. B. Slaughter," in *The New Handbook of Texas,* vol. 5, 1077–78; Clarke, *The Slaughter Ranches and Their Makers,* 188–89.

28. "Recollections of W. B. Slaughter," in Hunter, *The Trail Drivers of Texas,* 873–74; Gard, *Chisholm Trail,* 259; Anderson, "W. B. Slaughter," in *The New Handbook of Texas,* vol. 5, 1077–78; Clarke, *The Slaughter Ranches and Their Makers,* 181–82.

29. "Recollections of W. B. Slaughter," in Hunter, *The Trail Drivers of Texas,* 873–74; Gard, *Chisholm Trail,* 259; Anderson, "W. B. Slaughter," in *The New Handbook of Texas,* vol. 5, 1077–78; Clarke, *The Slaughter Ranches and Their Makers,* 181–82.

30. Murrah, *C. C. Slaughter,* 130; Anderson, "W. B. Slaughter," in *The New Handbook of Texas,* vol. 5, 1077–78.

31. See Lillie Mae Hunter, *The Book of Years: A History of Dallas and Hartley Counties; Pueblo Chieftain,* Mar. 24, 1915; Murrah, *C. C. Slaughter,* 130–31; Anderson, "W. B. Slaughter," in *The New Handbook of Texas,* vol. 5, 1077–78; Clarke, *The Slaughter Ranches and Their Makers,* 190–91.

32. "Character Impersonation," in Hunter, *The Trail Drivers of Texas,* 930–33.

33. *Pueblo Chieftain,* Mar. 24, 1915; Murrah, *C. C. Slaughter,* 130–31; Cross, "William B. Slaughter, Trail Driver of 1866," 468; Anderson, "W. B. Slaughter," in *The New Handbook of Texas,* vol. 5, 1077–78; Clarke, *The Slaughter Ranches and Their Makers,* 190–91; McDaniel, *God, Grass, and Grit,* vol. 1, 8–10; *Dallas Times Herald,* Dec. 9, 1921; "W. B. Slaughter's Obituary," *San Antonio Express,* Mar. 29, 1929.

34. *San Antonio Express,* Mar. 19, 1932; Clarke, *The Slaughter Ranches and Their Makers,* 190–91.

35. Roach, *The Cowgirls,* xvii–xix.

ELIZABETH (LIZZIE) JOHNSON WILLIAMS

MRS. HEZEKIAH GEORGE WILLIAMS

Sara R. Massey

LIZZIE, AS SHE WAS CALLED, HAS BEEN DESCRIBED as a teacher, book-keeper, writer, cattle broker, rancher, financier, real estate baron, and cattle queen. In her eighty-four years of life between 1840 and 1924, Lizzie did amazing things, which included building a fortune from the sale of cattle. Others saw her as stern and miserly, a woman who disclosed little to her family, but no one can deny Lizzie had a grand life. Hers was not the normal existence of a passive, obedient pioneer wife who cooked, sewed, and reared children. Instead, she was an educated, independent woman who was very good with numbers and enjoyed the thrill of making a deal.[1]

Not marrying until she was thirty-nine, Lizzie enjoyed a raucous competition with her husband for thirty-five years, and, together, each drove their own cattle up the trail several times. Her niece, who cared for Lizzie in the final year of her life, said, "Lizzie was one of the few women ever to go up the Chisholm Trail . . . the only [woman] to ever go up it who owned her own cattle and ran them under her own brand. She went up the trail two or three times after 1879 when she married Hezekiah Williams. She went up the trail with her husband who also was in the cattle business. He had entered the business on Lizzie's urgings, as she had been in the business several years before they were married."[2]

Although Margaret Borland also took her own cattle up the trail, Lizzie is undoubtedly the only woman who was intimately involved in all aspects of the cattle business for most of her lifetime. She bought cattle, had cowboys brand them with her brand, went up the trail with her own herd, kept meticulous tallies of the cattle, negotiated their sale with the cattle brokers at the stock pens, and, most important, kept the profit. The friendly rivalry with her husband continued throughout their lives together until his death in 1914. With his demise, much of the joy in her life clearly departed as she settled into widowhood. She began dressing in black and lived a solitary life in a darkened room on the second floor of Austin's Brueggerhoff Building, which she owned.

In her final years others saw her as eccentric and overly frugal, but she was not

Figure 29.   Lizzie Johnson. Courtesy of Emmett Shelton, Austin, Texas;
Institute of Texan Cultures at the University of Texas–San Antonio.

that way out of necessity. She continued to engage the cattle barons, who now owned the banks, she still delighted in getting the best of a bargain, even if it was only the price of her soup for dinner, and her fortune was intact. This woman with a Midas touch found her pleasure in the financial world of men. Dying without a will, she left an estate for others to settle. She had had her fun, doing life her way.

AN EDUCATED LADY

Lizzie began life on May 9, 1840, in Jefferson City, Missouri, the second of six sur-viving children born to Catharine Hyde (1810–83) and Thomas Jefferson Johnson (1805–68).[3] Her father, Thomas, had arrived in Jefferson City as a young man and worked as a teacher. In Missouri, this tall, imposing man met Catharine Hyde, and they were married on May 7, 1837. The young couple lived in Jefferson City for about five years and began their family while Thomas was busy teaching.[4] During this time both Lizzie and her elder brother John were born.[5]

Lizzie's parents were devoutly religious. Theirs was a Presbyterian family that held daily Bible readings, recitations, and prayers in the home. In the early 1840s, Pres-byterians in Texas valued education and took an active role in starting schools.[6] Many pioneer school teachers migrated to Texas to meet the new state's educa-tional needs, and Lizzie's Presbyterian father was among this group.

In 1846 Lizzie was a little girl when her family left Missouri and headed for the new state of Texas.[7] They settled in Huntsville, a place that had good schools and an established Presbyterian church. Thomas once again made a living by teaching, but what he really wanted was to run his own school. To do so, he moved the fam-ily to Webber's Prairie (present-day Webberville) in Travis County, downriver from Austin, where he hoped to start a school. He soon had students and began teach-ing, but the school was too close to "the town's notorious Hell's Half acre and race-track."[8] As devout Presbyterians, the Johnson family was very temperance minded, and they did not condone strong liquor. Naïve, impressionable youth had to be kept from such evils, they believed. Thomas thus moved the family once again, this time to Lockhart.

In the latter part of 1851, after rejecting land that eventually became home to the University of Texas, he ventured into the mountainous section of Hays County. At that time the county had 387 settlers, including those in San Marcos.[9] Liking what he saw, Thomas bought three hundred acres of land situated seventeen miles south of Austin and thirty miles northwest of San Marcos. At forty-seven years of age and with a family that now included six children, Thomas broke ground and began the Johnson Institute.[10]

The Johnson Institute stood at the foot of Friday Mountain, which had been named by a Mr. Hudson, who surveyed the area on a Friday. The school was built between the branches of Bear Creek, facing the mountain. The Johnsons' first home and school began as a log cabin with two doors and no windows, and the desks were made of puncheon logs. Tallow candles provided light.[11] The structure was later expanded to include one large room a story and a half high, with a shed room on each side. The open upper part, which served as a sleeping loft, was accessible by a ladder set up outside.[12] The earliest school buildings began as sixteen-square-foot cabins built from native logs; they had puncheon floors and used local stone for the chimneys. In 1853, when the old slave bell Thomas had hauled from Virginia to Missouri and on to Texas was hung from an oak tree, the school officially opened. At first it had forty students, including Lizzie and her five siblings.[13] The school census for 1855 shows that Lizzie, Catharine, and William were receiving instruction there.[14]

A school term lasted three to four months, and the cost for board, tuition, and laundry was $12 per month for students under fourteen years of age and $15 for ages fourteen and over. Half of the payment was due in advance or at the close of each month.[15] The students, who were expected to help with all of the daily chores at the school, came from the nearby communities of Austin, Blanco, San Marcos, and Mountain City. Although most of the pupils were from Texas, a surprising number came from Georgia, the Carolinas, Virginia, and Mississippi. Many of them boarded at surrounding farms until the Johnsons constructed a large, two-story, L-shaped stone building that included a dormitory for the girls.

Thomas planned his school as one for boys because, back East, he had seen many young boys dismissed when they were mischievous, and he felt that they deserved an education.[16] He therefore began his school for young male students, but so many girls also applied for admission that the Johnson Institute opened as a co-educational establishment. Eventually the boys slept in the cabins, and the girls on the second floor of the stone building under the tutelage of Mrs. Johnson.[17] Catharine Johnson was responsible not only for supervising the girls but also for doing all of the cooking in the large open fireplaces, for laundering the clothes of all of the students, and for ministering to everyone's physical ailments. The nearest doctor was in Austin, a day's journey away, so Mrs. Johnson was often called upon to care for the sick adolescents.

When the bell rang at 6 A.M., Lizzie and her classmates tumbled out of bed, poured water into a basin and splashed it on their faces, and headed for the kitchen on the lower floor, where her mother, known to students as Aunt Katy, baked bread and fixed breakfast for everyone. After eating, it was off to classes in arithmetic, spelling, grammar, and, later on, music. Thomas sent an inquiry to New York about purchasing a piano and learned that he could order what he wanted. When the first piano in Hays County arrived at the school sometime after 1860, music became part of the curriculum. With the piano installed on the second floor, Lizzie's mother now also functioned as the music teacher, banging a stick on the ceiling to mark the rhythm as students practiced above her while she cooked.

At age eighteen, Lizzie, along with her elder brother, John Hyde, left Johnson

Institute for additional education. Both attended schools in Chappell Hill, located in Washington County, with John matriculating at Soule University and Lizzie at Chappell Hill Female Institute. Their father wanted "John to become a literary gentleman and qualified for usefulness."[18] John completed his studies and received a Bachelor of Arts degree on January 11, 1862.[19] After finishing her studies, Lizzie returned home to teach at her father's prospering school. Since 1850, the population in the county had increased from 387 to 2,126, and many families welcomed the education that was available at the Johnson Institute.[20] Not only Lizzie but also her sisters, Emma and Annie, and her brother Ben taught classes for their father at various times over the ensuing years. Lizzie's teaching responsibilities included arithmetic, bookkeeping, French, grammar, spelling, and eventually music, which left her mother free for other chores. Her father taught the classes in Latin and higher mathematics, such as algebra.[21] At the Johnson Institute, students could complete the equivalent of today's bachelor's degree.

One day during the Civil War, Thomas noticed a black figure lingering on the side of the hill in front of the school. "Supposing it to be a runaway slave, he took his rifle and climbed to where he had seen the object. But the slave turned out to be a large black bear. The Professor shot it and had it carried back to the school to the delight of the students."[22]

Lizzie's childhood and adolescence were filled with education and religion. Ministers came to the institute to preach on Sundays, and, in their absence, her father assumed the role.[23] There were daily Bible recitations and readings, along with morning prayers, and, afterward, homework and lessons had to be done. Home for Lizzie was a strict boarding school perpetually filled with children, books, learning, and daily religious devotions. Few women in Texas in the 1850s and 1860s had Lizzie's opportunities for education, but her ability with numbers became clear as she progressed to teaching bookkeeping.

Lizzie's students recalled her as a stern teacher and harsh disciplinarian who drilled them in their multiplication tables. At one point while teaching at the school in the town of Pleasant Hill, she punished a German boy. As a result of this, the board of trustees assembled to hear a complaint made against her. Residents of the town felt Lizzie had "made an example of the [German] youth."[24] Still, she continued to teach at Pleasant Hill and refine the math skills that were to serve her well in the years ahead.

ENTERING THE CATTLE BUSINESS

Cattle were always a part of Lizzie's young life at home. Within six years of settling in Hays County, on January 26, 1858, Thomas registered his own brand, as well as brands in the names of his children.[25] Cattle provided a way for Professor Johnson to supplement his income, but Lizzie had yet to show any interest in them. In 1860, at age twenty, Lizzie and her brother John left home. A majority of the Hays

County citizens favored secession, and the 4th Texas Regiment was mobilized at Camp Clark, south of San Marcos. The men of Hays County, including John, promptly joined up.

After a major battle in Arkansas, John's Confederate division surrendered, and he was taken prisoner on January 11, 1863. Along with the rest of his division, he was placed on a boat headed north. He spent the next eight months in various prisoner-of-war camps in Illinois, Indiana, Ohio, Pennsylvania, New York, Maryland, and Virginia. During the summer he returned to the Confederate forces as part of a prisoner exchange. Once more he saw action and was wounded in the throat, causing the loss of his voice. As an invalid, he was relieved from field duty on August 16, 1863.[26]

John returned home and by the fall of 1866 was working as a clerk with the Texas Senate, as well as actively purchasing land for himself and his sister Lizzie: "I went out and purchased 640 acres of land . . . a part of which our pasture covers. I gave him One Thousand Dollars for the tract and paid him 680 Dollars down the Balance in specie next March. I let him have five mules and my riding horse at $550 and the balance in money. So you see I have the land at last in spite of opposition from a great many who attend to my business more than their own. . . . I have paid up and got both our notes at Hancock's and also P. Johnston's so you see we are about even with this world at last. . . . I got a letter from Wm D. [William Day] a few days since he asked me if you are at Lockhart. I thought he was better posted."[27]

Large families of the time gave freely offered advice, and small communities such as Mountain City were rampant with local gossip. Talk (or, more politely, conversation) was a primary form of entertainment. In order to avoid the gossip network, some people decided to keep their actions private and not to share personal business with others, a practice that Lizzie followed, along with her brother John, who was clearly not following the wishes of others in his land acquisitions.

In March 1867 John received a letter from William H. Day, a friend and cattle rancher back in Hays County, offering to employ him as a bookkeeper at $75 per month. John accepted and moved that summer to the Days' Mills cattle headquarters in Montgomery County, Texas. John worked hard to save money, envisioning his own cattle operation some day.[28] In the employ of Will Day, John learned the cattle business. Day's letter from the Drovers' Cottage in Abilene, Kansas, dated October 14, 1869, explains the situation: "We have closed all our cattle but 30 head and 4 ponies which we will dispose of I think today—and then we will be off for Texas. I can't tell exactly what we have made but we have done well—am satisfied. . . . Cattle have declined very fast for the [last] 20 days beevs [*sic*] are selling now at 20 to 27½ per head and all markets East are down. . . . I think we will strike the cattle trade this winter."[29]

From 1865 to 1868 Lizzie taught school in Lockhart, where there were numerous bellowing longhorn cattle as the town was a gathering place for livestock coming up from South Texas. With her math and bookkeeping abilities, Lizzie began to earn extra income by keeping the records and books of local cattlemen. While working for them, she learned the practice of selling cattle by "book count," which increased the profit to the seller.[30] Lizzie quickly realized that lots of money could be made in cattle.

After the Civil War, the cattle drives started in Hays County, and George Neill took the first herd up the trail to Abilene in 1867.[31] The loud bawling of the livestock was a common sound as the herds crossed at Montopolis and Shoal Creek, passing through Austin.[32] Lizzie changed teaching jobs several times following her stints in Lockhart. She taught at Pleasant Hill, south of Austin, and then moved on to teach at Parson's Female Seminary in Manor from 1870 to 1871, increasing her income with each successive assignment.[33] Meanwhile, enrollment at the Johnson Institute had reached two hundred pupils by September 1868, when Lizzie's father died. Her brother Ben took over the running of the Johnson Institute, where he had taught for sixteen years.[34] To help out, Lizzie returned home briefly to teach for one term.

In 1870 the state of Texas passed a provision for public education, and public schools were started in the counties along with requirements for the state's first teacher certification. Lizzie passed an examination in "Reading, Orthography, English, Grammar, Higher Arithmetic, Penmanship, Geography, Constitution of the United States, Algebra, Geometry, Ancient & Modern History, Natural Philosophy, Elocution, Composition, Anatomy, Physiology, and the rudiments of Latin as well as in the arts of imparting Instruction and managing a school." On August 4, 1871, she was granted her "Teacher's Certificate of the First Class."[35] Lizzie returned home again to help out and teach but left the next year, in 1872, to teach at Austin's Oak Grove Academy. With fewer students enrolling at the Johnson Institute, Ben, who was now married, closed the school in 1872, after twenty years of successful operation, and left home to attend medical school.[36]

These were busy years that buzzed with teaching, social visits, bookkeeping, and journeys home, but Lizzie was also bored: "I can not think of one word of news, in fact, I don't believe I know any. I have heard nothing but one monotonous round of lessons for so many weeks. And we have had rain here almost every day for the last ten. And there is no such thing as escape from the black mud."[37]

Fighting the boredom in the small communities, Lizzie turned her active imagination to writing pulp fiction using a nom de plume and sold her stories to the nation's largest weekly magazine, *Frank Leslie's Illustrated Newspaper.* Writing from home, her brother John mentioned, "Your magazine is here but if you are coming home in a few days it is useless to send it to you."[38] As a published author in the popular newsweekly, Lizzie was certainly in good company. The newspaper was serializing Anthony Trollope's *The Last Chronicle of Barset*. Trollope's chapters arrived each week by steamer, and Lizzie's articles undoubtedly also had a long, difficult journey getting to New York City. Frank Leslie's magazine accepted several stories and paid sufficient money to finance her start as a cattle investor. Thus Lizzie passed these years teaching school and writing fiction.[39]

Although it is not possible to prove which stories Lizzie wrote for Frank Leslie's magazine, a story authored by a Lizzie Campbell contains references to Shakespeare's *Taming of the Shrew* and describes a temperamental girl and a situation that could easily have been a fictionalized Lizzie: "Katherine De Lorme was a haughty, handsome girl, heiress to a fortune of thirty thousand dollars, and to a temper, which might of itself have cured her namesake of Padua without the assistance of Petruchio. Many bitter tears fair Katherine had shed in consequence of that dire temper of hers; for, by the means of it she had lost many dear friends; and said and done many things on one day which she would have given much to unsay and undo on the next."[40] Lizzie was simply a very talented lady who was much ahead of the societal norms of the time.

Not only was Lizzie busy working but she also faced an emotional time. The rebuilding of the Johnson Institute from native rock quarried on their land was barely completed in 1868, when her father died, and Lizzie's brother Ben took over the operation of the school. A few short years later, in 1871, her brother John died. When he had gone to Arkansas for treatment, he became ill again from his old throat injury and died there. Lizzie's sister Emma married William Greer of Navasota, a former student at the institute, and her younger sister Annie married Melvin Lockett and settled in Georgetown, where the couple reared their five daughters.[41] Her brother Ben was also now married.

Lizzie, now the oldest sibling in the family, was still unmarried, but she had her own pleasures and at least three sources of income: teaching in area schools, selling her stories for publication, and bookkeeping for the cattlemen. In 1872 Lizzie bought a home in Austin at 1105 East Live Oak (later renamed Second Street). At thirty-two, Lizzie was a single, educated, professional woman living on her own and earning very good money. She was most unusual.

From her bookkeeping for the cattlemen, her friendship with the Day brothers, and her brother John's work with William Day, which she assumed after her brother's death, Lizzie learned that there was even more money to be made as a cattle broker, so she began investing her savings. Following the Civil War, Lizzie became a shrewd cattle investor. "At one time she bought $2,500 worth of stock in the Evans, Snider, Bewell Cattle Company of Chicago; this paid her 100 percent dividends for three years straight, and she sold it at the crucial time for $20,000."[42]

Lizzie was not only investing but also learning all of the aspects of the cattle business. Using her initial profits, she reinvested in both cattle and land. Even though her father had branded cattle under a mark he had registered in her name when she was younger, she officially entered the cattle business using the CY brand, which she bought along with a herd of cattle. On June 1, 1871, she registered the brand in Travis County.[43] Although Lizzie did not quit teaching, she had learned that there was definitely more money in cattle than in instructing students and that the work was probably less boring.

During the Civil War, maverick or unbranded longhorn cattle went untended and multiplied at the rate of 25 percent annually. Cattle were free for the taking. After the war ended, the animals did well on the long drives. J. Evetts Haley has described the characteristics of the cattle that made them so good on the trail:

> During the decade and a half following the Civil War, Longhorn cattle were the economic salvation of Texas. They were gaunt and wiry, independent and perverse. As a product of the wilderness they did well where blooded cattle would have perished of drought, travel, and thirst. They were more easily handled than blooded stock, both in the roundup and upon the trail. Because of breadth of horn they spaced themselves better under herd—keeping plenty of room—thus traveling with greater ease, less heat, and less loss of flesh. Their hoofs were tougher, their legs longer, and their endurance greater than high-grade "stuff." They ranged a much wider scope of country, went longer without water, suffered more hardships, and took better care of themselves upon the range or in stampedes than any other breed. Old age did not find them toothless as it often finds improved cattle, and in breeding usefulness they lived nearly double the span of their successors.[44]

The Texas cattle boom was under way, and Lizzie was there at the beginning. Quietly keeping her own counsel, she bought land and hired cowboys to round up wild cattle and brand them. She did not tell her family members about these "extracurricular" activities. Lizzie kept tally at the roundups and had the cattle branded with her CY brand, which she registered in Hays County on November 13, 1873. By 1879 she was sending cattle up the trail to increase her earnings. She had become an independent woman who attended to her own business.

Prior to the Civil War, the principal markets for Texas beef were New Orleans, Alexandria, and Shreveport, Louisiana, although a few herds were driven to St. Louis and Chicago. The first cattle drive to Chicago occurred in 1856, and profits were very good.[45] During the Civil War, a little farther north (in Bell County), a small number of men served on a special detail called Davidson's Beef Squad to purchase beeves for the Confederate Army. An observant and intelligent Lizzie set out to make money in the enterprise. She had all the connections she needed to succeed in this new business, even as a woman. She knew the local cattlemen because she kept their tally books, she knew the bankers from her land purchases, and she knew the cattle brokers from her investments. Lizzie was on her way to acquiring wealth.

CATTLE QUEEN

Lizzie was an attractive young woman. A student from Pleasant Hill recalled many years later that Miss Lizzie, in her store-bought clothes, was the most beautifully dressed person she had ever seen.[46] Lizzie married late in life—at thirty-nine—which was most unusual for that era. Young women were considered spinsters if not married by their early twenties, but Lizzie was following her own path, and, like her heroine, Shakespeare's Katherine, she also had a sharp tongue and temper, but it was certainly not for lack of suitors that she did not marry.

> Miss Lizzie Johnson
> At Home
> Mountain City, Tex.
> Oct. 4th, 1864
> Miss Lizzie
>
> I have no apology to make for addressing you this note. I do it, to disclose a passion that I have long indulged for you[;] one which I flatter myself has not been wholly unperceived or disapproved of by you. Your company has ever been pleasant and agreeable to me, and this has caused me to cast aside all misgiving, and perhaps with too much presumption, but with a confident belief that the cincerity [*sic*] of my *love* renders me not wholly undeserving of your regard.
>
> Owing to our national difficulties and other circumstances with which I have been surrounded, has caused me for sometime to feel a delicacy in making known to you the fact that I ever *loved* or respected you more than a friend;
>
> But such has been the case for several years, and I see no good reason why I should withhold the fact any longer; for if my Love is reciprocated, let me cherish it, and if not let me learn to forget.
>
> Miss Lizzie you may think that I am writing from the impulse of the moment, or that I am governed by the blind impulses of *love* regardless of consequences. Such I know is too often the case, and choosing a companion is made a matter of feeling; and not enough of reflection, reason, and judgment.
>
> You are the object of my first from the fact that I love you, and regard you a young lady of amiable and affectionate disposition, with a high standard of virtue and morality, correct principles, good intilectual [*sic*] powers, a well trained and balanced mind, with the age, knowledge, and experience necessary to make a happy companion.

You are well acquainted with my character. Wealth I have it not to offer. But a true hand, and *loving heart* is yours, if you but think me worthy of your affections, if not worthy let me as ever remain

Your most Affectionate Friend
Wm H. Day
P.S. My address will be Austin City. Will.[47]

William H. Day, who later hired Lizzie's brother John as the bookkeeper on his ranch in Montgomery County, definitely wanted Lizzie to be his wife. The seven Day brothers were well known around Austin as the "Weeks boys"; there were seven of them, along with three sisters, and Lizzie knew them well as neighbors on a nearby farm at Mountain City. The boys were pioneer cowmen, and each one served in the Confederacy. As a suitor, William (or Bill or Will, as he was variously known) definitely had much to offer Lizzie. He had graduated as a civil engineer from Cumberland University at Lebanon, Tennessee, in 1858, before returning home, where he gathered a herd of horses and mules and set out for Louisiana.

Later that year William, along with his brother, Doc, who was to visit Lizzie in Lockhart just prior to Doc's marriage, set out for Kansas City. After the death of their father on the trail, they were met by armed settlers in southeast Kansas, where they turned the herd around into the Indian Nation and then went northeast through Missouri. Eventually they sold the herd in St. Louis.[48] With the profits they bought horses and herded them back to Louisiana to sell. Returning home in January 1861, William headed for Matamoros to buy more horses. During the war, he served as a teamster out of Camp Colorado with Henry McCulloch's Texas Cavalry. For all his labors, he returned home from the war broke, having all of his assets in worthless Confederate currency. To recoup his losses, he got busy using letters of credit and made numerous cattle drives.[49] Lizzie listened to their stories of the various trail drives as a friend but was not interested in Bill's proposal for whatever reason. Other suitors soon followed.

From September 1869 until at least March 1871, Lizzie was courted by C. W. Whitis of Austin.

Miss Lizzie E. Johnson
Wheelers Store
Parsons Seminary, Texas
Feby 14th 1870
My Darling "Lillie,"

Some weeks since I wrote you a long letter, but not a word have I heard from you. What is the matter.[*sic*] Is my darling sick or is she mad[?]

Oh that I could see her. What would she say: I guess I would steal a sweet kiss, but I shall not tell her how much I love her until she answers my letter. So you see I am a little mad myself—

From your "Charlie"[50]

A year later Charlie was still an active suitor, as well as a bank manager on some of Lizzie's land purchases:

Mar. 3rd 1871
Dear Lillie

Disappointment has followed from time immemorial—Tomorrow morning I start for Galveston on important business. Will write you on my return home when I will send after you—your deeds will all be complete and this [means] you need not doubt [the] amount—and I have [illegible] will more than be satisfactory to you—I hope to be home in time to send after you but if I am not do not be disappointed—I think I will be in time—miss your *precious heart I wish* you were with me.

Yours,
Charlie[51]

Charlie used imprinted bank stationery from the Banking and Exchange Office of Raymond and Whitis, which listed Jas. H. Raymond and C. W. Whitis of Austin as proprietors. Charlie was C. W. Whitis, an owner of the bank, so it seems that Lizzie selected her suitors wisely. In 1876 a physician who had returned home to Louisiana to renew his practice also wrote Lizzie, stating his interest in marriage, but nothing came of that offer, either. Lizzie may have passed the normal age for marriage, but she certainly was not without desirable proposals.

Still, in her teaching jobs, Lizzie was frequently bored. Charlie wrote again "to hear from you and know you were satisfied with your new field of labors, but I see you are not happy, although willing to toil. You must not get gloomy and discouraged. You are made of better materials than this and I have not the slightest doubt of your ultimate success."[52]

Lizzie met her future husband, Hezekiah George Williams, a retired Baptist preacher, on a visit to her brother Ben at Jergenton.[53] A stock driver from Seguin, Hezekiah was a tall, bearded, handsome widower with several children.[54] He also was a gambler and drinker, but whether Lizzie was aware of his bad habits at the time they married is not known. However, prior to their marriage in 1879, she had him sign a contract stating that her property, along with all future financial gains she might make, belonged to her.[55] This rare arrangement with Hezekiah proved to be to her benefit during their thirty-five years as husband and wife.

The boom years of the cattle industry in Texas lasted until the mid-1880s. During the boom years, Lizzie kept meticulous cattle records, just as she had while teaching school. With her diverse involvement in the cattle industry, she accrued the fortune that formed the foundation for her life with her new husband. On the evening of June 8, 1879, Lizzie and Hezekiah were married at the Presbyterian church (probably in Austin) by Pastor Smoot. Lizzie thus ended her life as a spinster—but definitely not her independence: "She was dressed in a beautiful silk [dress] made to order and bridal hat. Gen. Shelly and Mr. Noble and his wife walked up the aisle in front of them and stood beside them at the altar[.] Mr. Williams hired two city carriages to take us up and bring us back. We had nice cake and coffee passed round everything went off very nice. They are gone now to get their photographs taken."[56]

Lizzie's wedding photograph presents another dimension of her personality. As a published author in *Frank Leslie's Illustrated Newspaper,* she assembled a wedding ensemble that demonstrated that she kept up with the latest fashions and paid attention to her appearance. She showed off her tiny eighteen-inch waist in a tight-fitting jacket over a bell-shaped skirt with a lengthy train. She wore long earrings and pinned a broach in the lace ruffles at her neck. Her hair, which was covered with a feathered hat, was groomed with a few curls carefully arranged across her forehead. Lizzie was a fashionable bride who was reveling in her marriage to a handsome man.

By 1880 Austin was a bustling, progressive city with a population of 11,013. Workers were leveling the gravel streets and erecting more bridges. Congress Street had sidewalks, and one hundred new lamps lit the city streets at night. Lizzie had purchased a home on Austin's Second Street in 1872, and Hezekiah simply moved into the two-story residence with her. She continued taking students and teaching in the downstairs room, while she and Hezekiah occupied the four rooms upstairs. Meanwhile, Lizzie also continued to keep records for cattlemen, write for several magazines, and invest her money in cattle. The couple also jointly owned a ranch consisting of several thousand acres near Driftwood in Hays County and extending into Blanco County. They spent time there overseeing their separate cattle operations.[57] Bill Bob, foreman on the Williams ranch, worked for both Lizzie and Hezekiah separately. He told tales of the conflicting instructions from the competing couple as he tried to do his work: "Lizzie would instruct [me] to steal Hezekiah's unbranded calves and burn her brand on them. . . . Hezekiah gave [me] the same instructions regarding Lizzie's calves. So [I] was kept busy branding Hezekiah's calves with Lizzie's brand and Lizzie's calves with Hezekiah's road brand."[58]

Even though the couple arrived in their buggy at the cattle pens together, they bought the animals separately. After all, Lizzie was no novice at assessing them. She was an experienced cattle buyer and trusted her own judgment, while Hezekiah's expertise was as yet unproven: "She might stand all day long, pointing out the steers she wanted and displaying excellent judgment. . . . Often Hezekiah and Lizzie would buy from the same herd at the same time but handle their cattle separately.

Figure 30. Wedding portrait of Lizzie and Hezekiah Williams,
June 8, 1879. Courtesy of Mrs. Polk Shelton, Austin, Texas; Institute
of Texan Cultures at the University of Texas–San Antonio.

Lizzie would buy and sell again almost in one motion and make a good profit. Hezekiah, who was a gambler, would hold on to his for a better future price and lose money."[59]

Hezekiah's involvement in the cattle business before his marriage to Lizzie is curious, as he is listed as a stock driver in the 1870 census. In the 1880 census, a year after his marriage to Lizzie, he is listed as a stock dealer, but he did not register a cattle brand until August 13, 1881.[60] The 1880 census reports Lizzie's occupation as "keeping house," which, given her personality, seems most unlikely, but the record is in keeping with the accepted norm for wives and census takers of the time.

By the mid-1880s, after the North had recovered from the war and cattle were regularly reaching the markets, the lucrative boom years of the Texas cattle industry began to decline. In Kansas, farmers erected fences to protect their crops from the free-ranging cattle. "Fever" in Midwestern cattle that had been exposed to Texas herds created a demand for an increased imposition of quarantines. Even though the Texas longhorns did not get the fever, apparently something in their saliva (or so they thought at the time) remained on the vegetation after the Texas cattle passed by. When non-Texas cattle ate the grass, many of them got the fever and died.[61] The afflicted cattle were not a pleasant sight: "The most reliable symptoms of Texas fever are arched, or roached back, head carried low; ears drooping; eyes staring, with a dull, glassy appearance; gait tremulous and staggering in the hindquarter. . . . As the disease advances, the urine is dark-colored or bloody . . . the breath has a fetid odor, and there is evidence of great nervous prostration, the animal staggering on being made to move."[62]

Registering his brand in 1881, Hezekiah actively worked in the cattle business during the 1880s, and the happy couple went up the trail several times together.[63] However, by 1884 Hezekiah was having difficulty with the quarantine, so he wrote to Lizzie from Pueblo for the necessary inspection papers:

> Mrs. H. G. Williams
> Austin
> Texas
> Pueblo, Colorado
> Sept. 23, 1884
> My darling wife Lizzie
>
> Life has found me and intends to run an attachment on my cattle and I want you to look among my papers and find an inspecktion [sic] list of the cattle shipped By M. E. Williams or By Miles Williams from Kyle for 5 or 6 hundred cattle and that will clear them and then I will sell them and let him go to thunder[.] I have offered ever[y]thing that I could to compromise and if he still claims I owe Damage and wont [sic] sell any other way I will make the best fit I can with him and then get what money I can out of the cattle and

come home and sell out. . . . Dear I think I will come out all right but if I loose [*sic*] the cattle I will haf [*sic*] to sell all I have down there or give it to you so they can't take it out of me. I am going to sell every one I can get a dollar for, put the money in my pocket and bring it home to my pet[.] Don't fail to bring those papers to the office as quick as you can find them and mail them[.] Has it rained there yet[?] Your Darling H. G. Williams[64]

Even with the quarantines in force, Lizzie and Hezekiah were still going up the trails and hoping to make a profit. After the fencing of their ranch with the new barbed wire, Lizzie and Hezekiah made at least three trips up the Chisholm Trail together, taking their separate herds at the same time.[65] The trail was a long dusty route that ran northward through Texas and Indian Territory and into Kansas.

The railroads were reaching farther and farther west, creating new terminal points to avoid the quarantine areas for cattle coming out of Texas. Over the years, as the railroads ran their lines westward, the Chisholm Trail ended at various times in Ellsworth, Abilene, and Dodge City, Kansas. Between 1879 and 1889, the Williamses took cattle up the trail and then returned several more times, driving "community herds" along with their own. Community herds were made up of livestock from local owners who road-marked their cattle for identification and entrusted them to the Williamses. Lizzie and Hezekiah then took them up the trail, sold them, returned, and handed over the profit.[66]

Although Lizzie and Hezekiah traveled together with their own herds, their cattle were branded and carried a road brand as well. Thus, when they reached the end of the trail and made deals with the cattle brokers, the brands ensured a proper accounting: "A brand is simply a mark burned on livestock with a hot iron. In Texas, brands must be recorded by a county clerk to be legal, and the law states that no brand can be duplicated in the same county. In the open-range era, a brand was of great value even as it is today. It proved claim of ownership, and identified cattle, not only on their home range but on distant ranges to which they might stray."[67]

On the trail, Lizzie and Hezekiah followed the herd and the chuck wagon in their buggy, which was drawn by a team of strong horses all the way to Abilene, Kansas.[68] Although Lizzie loved and wore silks and satins, for the cattle drive she wore calicos and cottons with voluminous gathered skirts, many petticoats, a bonnet, and a gray shawl. Of course, she received lots of attention when the cowhands came to the chuck wagon for evening chow. Family members recall that Lizzie often told about the cowhands stringing a rope around the bedroll she and Hezekiah slept in to ward off rattlesnakes—a common, but ineffective, practice of the time.

Lizzie's methods on the trail were similar to those used by other cattle drivers. Each morning before the herd was moved, Lizzie, armed with her tally book, counted and recounted her cattle to be sure that none had gone astray during the night. Each steer clearly meant more money at the end of the trail.[69] She also kept a time book in which she recorded each cowboy's hours. Pay for the cowhands was withheld until the end of the drive, when Lizzie always subtracted the cost of their food and anything else they had needed on the trip.

At the end of the trail, Lizzie's tallies revealed their individual costs and profits. Lizzie was a real cattle woman. She bought and built her own herds, hired the hands, and now organized the drives. Then, along with Hezekiah, she followed her herd up the Chisholm Trail to market, where she brokered and sold the cattle, paid off the hands, and calculated the profits in her ledgers. Moreover, while busy with her herds, she earned even more money: Throughout her life various cattlemen trusted her to keep accurate records of their cattle.

Once the business transactions were over, it was time for fun, and there is little doubt that Lizzie and Hezekiah seized the opportunity. They stayed in the best hotels, and Lizzie shopped for elegant clothes. Her purchases, however, often remained packed in boxes and often were never worn or made into gowns. Lizzie's niece found all kinds of luxury goods and dresses packed away. "You never saw dresses any more beautiful than the fancy silks Lizzie bought in New York and Kansas City. Such brocades! Why, after she died we filled three trucks with boxes of clothes. Many of those old silks had never been unpacked, but they were so old they crumbled in our fingers when we tried to lift them from the store boxes."[70]

After her death, a few of the items found in the nine trunks were the following: "2 yds. black grain silk, 9 yds bright Challis, 10 yds blue and black strip [*sic*] silk, 11 yds brocade satin, 9 yds changeable silk, a white embroidered lawn dress, a brown satin dress with waist, black China silk dress and a pistol."[71] Even though a pistol was among Lizzie's belongings, there is no record of her ability to use it. Nevertheless, given her arrival in 1852 and the frontier conditions in Texas at the time, we must assume that she could at least fire it properly. After Lizzie's shopping forays, the couple frequently dined and enjoyed the company of other cattlemen and their wives.

Lizzie and Hezekiah did not have children, although Hezekiah had four sons by his previous marriage.[72] The sons, now grown, led their own lives, leaving the Williamses to their cattle business and travels. Lizzie retired from teaching since she and Hezekiah were spending more time at their ranch in Hays County, putting together herds to take north for shipment east.[73] Every fall and winter, even when not taking cattle up the trail, they went to St. Louis to stay for the season. There she continued to reconcile cattle books for various cattlemen, write stories for magazines, and shop. In the 1870s, St. Louis was the fourth largest city in the United States and a very cosmopolitan trading center. Goods from miles around came to St. Louis for transport down the Mississippi River. The swanky stores allowed Lizzie to keep up with the latest fashions and replenish her always stylish wardrobe.

Beyond the expensive velvet and brocade dresses, the beribboned hats, and high-buttoned shoes, it was the jewelry that Lizzie bought on a trip to New York City that family members remembered most vividly. On one trip she purchased $10,000 worth of jewelry, which included the following items:

· a pair of two-carat diamond earrings
· a tiara with a center diamond of three carats, surrounded by nine half-carat stones
· a sunburst pin of eighty-four diamonds in a gold setting
· a diamond and emerald dinner ring in an antique-gold mounting[74]

Lizzie had lots of other jewelry as well, including the useful American gold watch she wore in a pocket at her waist.[75] When traveling, Hezekiah and Lizzie made quite a fashionable couple. Heads turned when Lizzie, dressed in her lace, velvets, and jewelry, entered a room. This woman, whom others knew as a miser, spent lavishly on clothes and luxuries for herself. She clearly liked and enjoyed beautiful accouterments. She made her deals, pinched her pennies, and then spent her earnings as she chose.

Around that time, Cuba was another market for Texas cattle: "In 1878 the Morgan Steamship Company contracted to supply the government of Cuba with cattle averaging 900 pounds live weight, for which they were to receive $45 in gold per head. By later terms of their contract they were to receive about $45 in gold per bullock. . . . Besides the companies trading in cattle from Texas to Cuba, there were private individuals participating."[76]

Cattle were shipped from Indianola on Matagorda Bay and Galveston. The journey to Havana took about four days, during which time the cattle consumed 60–80 pounds of hay per head and were kept well watered to maintain good weight—to increase the profits. The average head lost only 100–125 pounds on the journey, and deaths rarely exceeded 1 percent.[77] As prices dropped in the northern market, the Williamses looked toward the lucrative market in Cuba. During the 1890s, with Hezekiah off enjoying the camaraderie of men about town, Lizzie worked quietly behind the scenes at home, keeping track of debts, loans, and profits. The decision was made to increase their fortune in Cuba.

The Williamses' cattle sales in Cuba compelled them to move there for several years. On September 16, 1904, Lizzie, identified as employed in domestic duties, and Hezekiah, identified as a raiser of cattle, bought—for $3,675—a rural farm appraised at $4,175 in U.S. gold. The farm, which they acquired through Manuel Padilla y Padilla, was near the city of Camagüey, on the Camujiro Road bordering the Tatihonico River.[78] While residing in Cuba, they lost a shipment of cattle worth $40,000. Legend has it that, also while there, Hezekiah was captured by bandits, who held him for a $50,000 ransom, which Lizzie quickly paid. After coughing up the payoff, she made Hezekiah sign his property over to her.[79] In Cuba Lizzie acquired a talking parrot, which returned to Texas with them aboard the ship *Titlis,* which docked at Galveston harbor on Christmas eve of 1905.[80]

Although Hezekiah continued to be a drinker throughout his life, he never drank in Lizzie's presence. Liquor and religion just did not mix, as far as Lizzie was concerned. Nevertheless, there was a mutual respect and competitive camaraderie between husband and wife, who came late into each other's life. They were always trying to make the best deal, whether against each other or against some other financier. Theirs was a rare marriage, in which there was pleasure as they each amassed and spent fortunes they had earned from cattle and investments.

REAL ESTATE INVESTOR

After her marriage in 1879, Lizzie began investing in real estate in an organized manner, buying lots and buildings in Austin and several surrounding counties. One of her first purchases was the Brueggerhoff Building, on the southeast corner of East Tenth Street and Congress Avenue, where she lived in a room after Hezekiah's death in 1914. Jacob L. Larmour, the architect for the building, came to Austin in 1871 and found work designing buildings for the State of Texas. The structure that Lizzie purchased began as a store, with a wax museum on the second floor.[81] As landlord, she leased the Brueggerhoff Building in 1886 to Nat Henderson, who operated it as a print shop, where he published the *Georgetown Record.* Lizzie made numerous other land purchases and acquired 65,000 acres plus several buildings in her name, including the following:

- east half of lot nine, block 57, at 215 East Sixth Street, or the "old Warren Store" in Austin
- a lot fronting 108 feet on West Twenty-sixth Street in Austin
- land holdings in Llano and Hays counties
- a 4,257-acre ranch in Trinity County, which was probably the Eagle Springs Ranch
- a 10,184-acre ranch that crossed the line from Culbertson into Jeff Davis County
- acreage in East Texas near Conroe and Livingston[82]

In 1896 the couple purchased a ranch between present-day Kyle and Driftwood, where they spent a great deal of time. Hezekiah, who had dreams of becoming a colonizer, wanted to build a town on their new ranch holdings in Hays County. At one time, the Williams ranch there was the site of his short-lived Hays City. Some of the residents proposed moving the county seat from San Marcos, and that idea held much appeal for Hezekiah; however, he failed in his petition to bring about the change. Six years before his death, Hezekiah set out to build what he hoped would be the new county seat and thus became a land developer.

In 1908 Hezekiah laid out Hays City with two streets: Williams Street and

Johnson Street. He plotted the lots for sale and installed the biggest windmill in the state. He also published a newspaper, the *Hays City Journal,* from about 1908 to 1910 and hired a Mr. Waller as editor. He employed Herbert Bell of Buda as a foreman to promote and sell his lots. Soon a large stone hotel with porches on three sides upstairs and down graced the town. Serving as a stage stop, the hotel included a stable and blacksmith shop, as well as a general store. Lizzie and Hezekiah built a church for the town that also functioned as a school. Rooms at the hotel cost fifty cents a night, while a meal could be had for two bits (twenty-five cents).

In the middle of August 1908, Hezekiah put on the biggest celebration the county had ever seen: a three-day free barbecue and dance, with the featured attraction "a fight to the finish between a savage lobo wolf and a brutal English Pit Bulldog." Hess, as Hezekiah was sometimes called, brought in a high-powered auctioneer to sell the town lots, and anyone who purchased two or more was allowed to name the streets bordering them.[83] "There was a big breeder of Jackasses who lived just down the road from Hays City. When he heard about the street-naming deal, he bought a bunch of lots and named the streets after his Jacks."[84]

A thousand celebrators milled the town the first day, and as many as 2,500–3,000 people arrived from across the county for the main event. Doc Duty of Kyle owned the white pit bull, named Bluger, and Henry Whisenant of Driftwood had spent months trapping the vicious wolf that had killed his sheep and goats. With Joe Cruze taking all bets, the bell rang at 3 P.M. "The lobo wolf was in her 'Oestrous [estrous] cycle' and when Bluger realized this upon entering the field of combat, he simply obeyed the rutting instinct right there before twenty-five hundred shocked sets of eyeballs."[85] Scandalized, the throng quickly departed, and only a few onlookers were willing to admit that they had witnessed the infamous event.

In 1916, after Hezekiah's death, the hotel was the site for the filming of a silent motion picture starring Lillian Russell and William S. Hart, *Down by the Rio Grande.* The Baptist church building the Williamses had constructed was eventually sold and moved to Wimberley, where it was rebuilt and used as the First Christian Church.[86] Lizzie's profit-making instincts and attempts to recoup their financial losses were undoubtedly motives behind these deals. In 1920 Lizzie sold the Williams ranch to Joe Stewart; the hotel was dismantled, and the lumber used to build new structures.[87]

From 1890 on, Hezekiah's physical condition declined. His lifetime of drinking was taking its toll. Also expressed in their feisty marriage and camaraderie was a mutual compassion. The couple traveled during these years and went to several pleasant spas, such as the one at Hot Springs, Arkansas, for Hezekiah's health. They also went to El Paso, seeking sunshine and a warmer climate. In 1896, as Hezekiah's strength failed, he ensured an easy transfer of his assets after his death by selling Lizzie all of his stock, land, and cattle.

Llano, Texas
July 30, 1896

Know all men by thee present: That I, H. G. Williams, have granted, bargained and sold to L. E. Williams my lawful wife, the following articles and property, to wit: all stock I own in the Iron City National Bank of Llano, and all interest I own and hold in the Llano County Bank, also all my entire interest in all cattle in Llano County and San Saba Counties, and all notes and other property not herein described, belonging to me in anywise. All my land and cattle in Hays County, Texas, or any place whatever, for the sum of Twenty Thousand dollars to me in hand paid by Mrs. L. E. Williams of her separate money to have and to hold forever, for the above consideration, given under my hand this day July 30, 1896.

H. G. Williams[88]

Even with this transfer of assets by her husband eight years before his death, Lizzie held the agreement and did not file the transaction until after Hezekiah died.[89] Nonetheless, he passed away owing Lizzie money. As executor of her husband's estate, Lizzie waited to collect on Hezekiah's note of May 7, 1912, for $500 with 6 percent interest and the May 11, 1914, note for $300 with 8 percent interest.[90]

On July 26, 1914, Hezekiah died of apoplexy while staying in El Paso.[91] Lizzie bought his casket for $600 and brought his body back to Austin. Across the undertaker's bill she wrote, "I loved this old buzzard this much."[92] Lizzie bought a cemetery plot for Hezekiah inside the main gate of Oakwood Cemetery in Austin and erected a large, double, gray granite tombstone complemented by an initialized footstone.[93]

There was a delightful joy in Lizzie's love for Hezekiah. "She was all wrapped up in Hess. Where he went, she went."[94] Regardless of his bills and bad debts, Lizzie paid them. Hezekiah was the public figure, enjoying others, whereas Lizzie stayed behind the scenes keeping the books. She knew where the money was and nurtured it well throughout their life together. Hezekiah and the money were her life. She had little time for his or her family members and certainly did not confide to them tidbits of her financial life or the deals she made. Lizzie had made a good marriage in her handsome widower.

THE YEARS ALONE AGAIN

Lizzie was in her seventies when Hezekiah died. Her niece said that, "after Hezekiah's death Lizzie didn't care much about herself or anything anymore, but she was still good in business."[95] She moved into a second-story room in the Brueggerhoff Building and leased out other parts of the building. She continued to manage her investments and made frequent trips to the bank and daily trips to the post office, "wearing a full black skirt which reached to the floor and a grey shawl she'd had for forty years. She wore a little black hood or bonnet on her head."[96]

Lizzie was always shrewd in her dealings with others, and even in her later years she retained the ability to remember amazing details of events and recall names and places. Throughout her adult life influential people courted her, hoping she would donate money to their cause. She kept churches, schools, and even the University of Texas hoping for donations, which they thought she was considering.[97] This was a shrewd practice that Lizzie was well acquainted with. When she and Hezekiah returned from Cuba, a Galveston banker who had reserved rooms for them at a local hotel met them at the wharf and showered them with flowers. The banker hoped to get their business, but in this instance, as in many others, they graciously accepted the complimentary gifts but never transacted any business with him.[98]

Family members tell many stories of Lizzie's final years, which she spent alone in a cold, unlit room. She hoarded firewood, refusing to burn more than one piece at a time regardless of the chill. She stored the wood in a room and issued it to her tenants one stick at a time. Her facility with numbers continued, however, and her brother Ben was convinced she knew exactly how many pieces of wood were stored in the room at any one time.[99] Another family member related how Lizzie lived frugally on a bowl of vegetable soup supplied by the terms of an annual contract with the nearby Maverick Café. For Lizzie, getting the best on a deal was now an obsession: "A bowl of vegetable soup with bread or crackers was priced at ten cents during the summer. During the winter the price of vegetable soup advanced because of the scarcity of the vegetables, but shrewd Aunt Lizzie made a contract with the proprietor that her bowl of soup the year around was to be only ten cents."[100]

David Lamme Sr. used to deliver Lizzie's orange juice every morning from his family's soda fountain across from the Brueggerhoff Building. He remembered his fierce encounter with Lizzie the day they raised the price of the juice from a nickel to seven cents. As senility and loneliness took hold of Lizzie, her reputation as a miser grew, and it seemed to some that she was even starving herself.[101] The fortune she had amassed as a cattlewoman during the era of the trail drives makes her unique, but of more importance were the cattle and investment deals she made as a woman in the financial world of men, often getting the best of the bargain.

On January 5, 1924, after the holidays, Lizzie moved out of the solitary room where she had spent so many years. Her increasing senility made it necessary for her to have constant care, and her niece Willie (Mrs. John E. Shelton) took on that task. Lizzie proved a difficult guest in her final eighteen months as she wandered about her new living quarters. Many people thought she had lost her mind. None of the family really knew of her fortune until after her death, when Willie began the process of settling her estate.

Lizzie died around 5:55 P.M. on Thursday, October 9, 1924, at 211 West Live Oak, Willie's home.[102] Lizzie became a legend within the family, in part because she had amassed a fortune and kept it a secret from them all. But from Lizzie's perspective, if the family had known she had money, they would probably have come wanting handouts for various things, and Lizzie was not about to give anything away: "After Lizzie's death I went through her belongings as I was administratix [*sic*]. In the Breugerhoff [*sic*] Building behind a boarded up pane in an old book case I found hundreds of dollars in five dollar bills. Scattered around the room in various crevices were one hundred dollar bills. The total of the cash I found there was $2,800. She had $65,000.00 in the bank when she died."[103]

In the probate document of Travis County, Lizzie's estate was valued at $245,701.89, which included two $25,000 certificates of deposit, as well as $2,000–3,000 in cash found in numerous places throughout her room. Family members wondered about the jewelry, which was last seen at a grandnephew's wedding in 1916. After an extensive search, it was found in the basement of the Sixth Street building, wrapped in a scorched cloth inside a small, unlocked box.[104] Lizzie's other jewelry included a breast pin containing nine diamonds, a ring with nine diamonds, a hair ornament with ten diamonds, eleven gold shirt buttons, two pairs of cameo earrings, a breast pin, a gold necklace, and a gold thimble. Four other boxes contained French gold coins, crosses, earbobs, stickpins, a silver card case, a coral necklace, and much more. In another locked box, family members found parrot feathers from the parrot she had brought back from Cuba and dried flowers from the wreaths at Hezekiah's funeral.[105] She really did love "that old buzzard."

Lizzie is buried next to Hezekiah at Oakwood Cemetery in Austin. In 1947 her niece wrote that "There can be no denying that she was not only a gallant frontier Texas woman in the cattle trade but also a pioneer among women in the field of finance—a character so colorful and varied that she has become almost a legend less than thirty years after her death."[106]

Without a doubt, Lizzie is a legend. A woman far in advance of her time, she knew how to wheel, deal, and broker in the financial world of men. In addition, she built a fortune from cattle and real estate deals while delighting in and overseeing the antics of her rather worthless, yet handsome, husband. Her talents were many. As she reflected on her memories, Lizzie penned these words:

God, keep my memory green.
Let me not forget the sunny spots in the past.
Moments that have the perfume of the violet and the rose.[107]

NOTES

1. I was fortunate to work with Lizzie's great-great-niece Cyndie Shelton Schmitt (granddaughter of Emmett Shelton, nephew of Lizzie), who is a pugnacious researcher of her legendary ancestor. She graciously shared her research files and was an able collaborator in verifying extensive information for this chapter.

2. Mrs. John F. Shelton (the daughter of Lizzie's younger sister Emma, with whom Lizzie lived during the final year of her life), "Statement concerning Elizabeth E. Johnson Williams," 1.

3. Numerous published sources have listed Lizzie's birth year as 1842 or 1843. In the 1850 U.S. Census taken in August, she is listed as ten years old, making her birth year 1840; see U.S. Bureau of the Census, 1850, Travis County, microfilm 432, roll 915, 134. Ten years later, in 1860, she is listed as eighteen years old, making 1842 her birth year; see U.S. Bureau of the Census, 1860, Hays County, Dripping Springs, microfilm 653, roll 1297. However, her death certificate gives May 9, 1840, as her official birth date; see Lizzie E. Johnson Williams, death certificate. Other siblings listed in the 1860 census include John, age twenty-one, born in Missouri; Emily (Emma), age fifteen, born in Texas; William, age twelve, born in Texas; Benjamin, age ten, born in Texas; and Missouria (Annie), age eight, born in Texas. This information conflicts with other sources.

The August 1870 census lists only the mother, Catharine, age sixty, with W. A. (William), age twenty-two, as head of the household, which also includes Emily (Emma), age twenty-four; Benjamin, age twenty-one; and Annaelle (Annie), age sixteen. The ages of the siblings conflict with those taken ten years earlier; see U.S. Bureau of the Census, 1870, Hays County, 10.

In the June 1880 census, Travis County, Elisebeth (Lizzie) is listed with her husband as being age thirty-four, making her birth year 1846; see U.S. Bureau of the Census, 1880, Travis County, microfilm T9, roll 1329, 287. Lizzie's tombstone lists 1840, which agrees with the birth date on her death certificate, which was probably provided by the niece, Willie Shelton.

4. Thomas Jefferson Johnson was born October 8, 1805, in Norfolk, Virginia; see Dudley Richard Dobie, "The History of Hays County, Texas," 54; Thomas Ulvan Taylor, "Johnson Institute," 224–25. Thomas is listed as age fifty-four in U.S. Bureau of the Census, July 1860, Dripping Springs, Hays County, microfilm 653, roll 1297, 16. A leather pocket wallet belonging to Thomas Johnson has written into the leather that "Thos Johnson was living in St. Louis County July 2, 1829, and born Oct. 8, 1805"; see Johnson Institute, Special Collections.

5. The U.S. Census of Hays County for both 1850 and 1860 indicates that John was born in 1839.

6. Taylor, "Johnson Institute," 224.

7. "Prof. Johnson Removed Youth from Temptation," *Austin Daily Tribune,* June 14, 1941; Tula Townsend Wyatt, *Historical Markers in Hays County 1907–1976,* 66.

8. Ann Fears Crawford and Crystal Sasse Ragsdale, *Women in Texas: Their Lives, Their Experiences, Their Accomplishments,* 125.

9. John H. Jenkins, *Cracker Barrel Chronicles: A Bibliography of Texas Town and County Histories,* 420.

10. Crawford and Ragsdale, *Women in Texas,* 125.

11. Frances Stovall et. al, *Cedar Springs and Limestone Ledges: A History of San Marcos and Hays County,* 467.

12. Dobie, "History of Hays County," 55.

13. In 1970 the slave bell was still hanging, and a historical marker marked the site; see Mary Starr Barkley, *History of Travis County and Austin, 1839–1899,* 125, 158. Another article states that the bell was in the church that Lizzie and Hezekiah built in their short-lived town of Hays City. When the church was sold and moved to Wimberly, the bell went as well and

was still there in 1969; see Spencer Guimarin, "The Rise and Fall of a Town," in "Hays City—Fact or Fiasco," part 3, "The Day of Infamy," 8.

14. Wyatt, *Historical Markers in Hays County,* 66.

15. E. Garrett, "Two Years after Death: School Teacher Amassed Fortune," 14.

16. Robert T. Hill, "Prof. Johnson Removed Youth from Temptation."

17. The census for 1860 and 1870 agree that Catharine (age fifty and sixty respectively) was born in 1810, with the 1860 census noting birth in North Carolina, while the 1870 census indicates she was born in Missouri; see U.S. Bureau of the Census, 1860, Hays County, Dripping Springs, microfilm 653, roll 1297, and U.S. Bureau of the Census, 1870, Johnson Institute, Hays County, microfilm 593, roll 1590.

18. Thomas Johnson (father), letter to Lizzie Johnson (daughter), Feb. 9, 1860, Johnson Institute; Crawford and Ragsdale, *Women in Texas,* 126.

19. John H. Johnson, letter of certification for Bachelor of Arts diploma, Jan. 11, 1862.

20. Jenkins, *Cracker Barrel Chronicles,* 420.

21. Emmett Shelton, "Statement concerning Elizabeth E. Johnson Williams," Mar. 30, 1946.

22. Hill, "Prof. Johnson Removed Youth from Temptation."

23. In the 1860 U.S. Census, taken eight years after the Johnson Institute opened, "Thos. Johnson" is listed as a farmer with real estate valued at $1,500 and personal property valued at $2,050; see U.S. Bureau of the Census, 1860, Hays County, Dripping Springs, microfilm 653, roll 1297.

24. Dick King, "Two Austin Women and the Chisholm Trail," 568.

25. Mark and Brand Records, Hays County, book 1, Jan. 26, 1858.

26. J. H. (John Hyde) Johnson, letter to his sister Lizzie Johnson, from Chattanooga, Tenn., Aug. 16, 1863.

27. J. H. J. (John Hyde Johnson), letter to Dear Sister (Lizzie Johnson), from Austin, Tex., Oct. 4, 1866.

28. J. H. J. (John Hyde Johnson), letter to his sister Em (Emma Johnson), from Days' Mills, Montgomery County, Tex., July 6, 1867.

29. W. H. Day, letter to Jno H. Johnson, from Drovers' Cottage, Abilene, Kans., Oct. 14, 1869.

30. Crawford and Ragsdale, *Women in Texas,* 127.

31. Dobie, "History of Hays County," 84.

32. Barkley, *History of Travis County and Austin, 1839–1899,* 259.

33. Ibid., 126, and Emily Jones Shelton, "Lizzie E. Johnson: A Cattle Queen of Texas," 352.

34. Dudley Richard Dobie, "The History of Hays County, Texas," 54; Taylor, "Johnson Institute," 28. Theresa Bennett states that Lizzie assumed ownership of the Johnson Institute at her father's death but later sold it ("Lizzie E. Johnson Williams: Cattle Queen and Financial Wizard," 8). This may well be true since her sister Emma states in a letter that Bennie, her brother, had given up the school to his sister Lizzie and that they had eighteen boarders; see Johnson Institute, letter from Emma (Johnson) to My Dearest Friend, from Mountain Home, Jan. 24, 1871.

35. Miss Lizzie Johnson, teacher certificate.

36. The site of the Johnson Institute later became a camp named for noted Texas historian Walter Prescott Webb.

37. Johnson Institute, Lizzie E. J. (Lizzie Johnson), letter to Dear Brother (John H. Johnson), from Parson's Seminary, June 26, 1870.

38. Johnson Institute, J. H. J. (John Hyde Johnson), letter to Lizzie Johnson, Mar. 5, 1867.

39. Crawford and Ragsdale, *Women in Texas*, 127, cite the titles of several articles from *Frank Leslie's Illustrated Newspaper* that are examples of the types of articles it published. Most of them list the authors, whereas a few of the stories mention none. There was no author listed for the stories titled "Lady Inez" or "The Passion Flower, An American Romance," but the latter story involved Indians, which makes it possible that the author was Lizzie Johnson.

40. Lizzie Campbell, "Katherine De Lorme." The references to Padua and Petruchio refer to Shakespeare's *Taming of the Shrew*, which is about a young man named Petruchio who arrives in the town of Padua desirous of a rich wife. He hears about Kate (Katherine) and sets out to win her, despite her reputation as a shrew. When Kate meets Petruchio, she lashes out at him with her sharp tongue, but he insists that they will marry, and he sets out to tame her; see "Taming of the Shrew," http://www.arkangelshakespeare.com/tamingshrew-1.html (accessed Oct. 22, 2005).

41. Emma and William Greer also settled in Hayes County and raised one daughter; see Taylor, "Johnson Institute," 227–28.

42. Shelton, "Lizzie E. Johnson," 353.

43. Crawford and Ragsdale, *Women in Texas*, 127; Shelton, "Lizzie E. Johnson," 353; Travis County, Mark and Brand Records, 61, no. 45.

44. J. Evetts Haley, *The XIT Ranch of Texas and the Early Days of the Llano Estacado*, 182–83.

45. Daniel Evander McArthur, "The Cattle Industry of Texas, 1685–1918," 138.

46. King, "Two Austin Women and the Chisholm Trail," 68.

47. Johnson Institute, William H. Day, letter to Lizzie Johnson, from Mountain City, Tex., Oct. 4, 1864.

48. David Dary, *Cowboy Culture: A Saga of Five Centuries*, 122.

49. James T. Padgitt, "Colonel William H. Day: Texas Ranchman," 347–53.

50. Johnson Institute, Charlie (C. W. Whitis), letter to Lizzie E. Johnson at Parson's Seminary, Tex., Feb. 14, 1870.

51. Johnson Institute, Charlie (C. W. Whitis), from Austin, Tex., letter to Lizzie E. Johnson at Parson's Seminary, Mar. 3, 1871.

52. Johnson Institute, Charlie (C. W. Whitis), letter to Lizzie Johnson, Sept. 15, 1869.

53. Bennett, "Lizzie E. Johnson Williams," 5; also comments by Mrs. John E. Shelton to reporter in Marj Wightman, "Stones of Memory Fall, but Legend of Lizzie Lives." Given Lizzie's religious upbringing, it is reasonable to think that she would have been attracted to a preacher, although there is no evidence he ever preached after their marriage.

54. The July 1870 U.S. Census lists H. G. Williams, age thirty-seven, as a stock driver born in Mississippi, who was married to Mary, age thirty-two, who was keeping house and also born in Mississippi; see U.S. Bureau of the Census, 1870, Guadalupe County, microfilm 593, roll 1589, 369. At the time of his marriage to Lizzie, Hezekiah would have been forty-six years old and, since he was born in 1833, seven years older than Lizzie.

55. Anne Seagraves, *Daughters of the West*, 27.

56. Johnson Institute, Catharine Johnson (Lizzie's mother), letter from Austin, to Emma (Lizzie's sister), June 23, 1879.

57. Shelton, "Lizzie E. Johnson," 355–56, 360.

58. Ibid., 359.

59. Ibid., 358.

60. U.S. Bureau of the Census, 1870, Guadalupe County, 369, and U.S. Bureau of the Census, 1880, Travis County, microfilm T9, roll 1329, 287.

61. The cattle fever is at various times called Spanish fever, Texas fever, and tick fever.

62. James Cox, ed., "A Few Facts concerning Texas Fever, Actual and Alleged," *Historical Biographical Record of the Cattle Industry and the Cattlemen of Texas and Adjacent Territory,* vol. 1, 72.

63. Mrs. John E. Shelton is the source of the information that Lizzie went up the trail; see Wightman, "Stones of Memory Fall, but Legend of Lizzie Lives."

64. Johnson Institute, H. G. Williams, letter from Pueblo, Colorado, to Mrs. H. G. Williams, Sept. 23, 1884.

65. Emmett Shelton, "Statement concerning Elizabeth E. Johnson Williams," 1–2; Sue Flanagan, *Trailing the Longhorns: A Century Later,* 83.

66. Flanagan, *Trailing the Longhorns: A Century Later,* 357.

67. Dulcie Sullivan, *The LS Brand: The Story of a Texas Panhandle Ranch,* 43.

68. Emmett Shelton, "Statement concerning Elizabeth E. Johnson Williams," 1.

69. Crawford and Ragsdale, *Women in Texas,* 129.

70. Wightman, "Stones of Memory Fall, but Legend of Lizzie Lives."

71. Lizzie E. Johnson Williams, estate, Travis County Court probate file 5915, Oct. 1924.

72. U.S. Bureau of the Census, 1870, Guadalupe County, microfilm T9, roll 1329. In the 1870 census, nine years before his marriage to Lizzie, H. G. and Mary Williams, both of Mississippi, had four sons: William, age fourteen; Miles, age eleven; Daniel, age nine; and James, age four, all born in Texas.

73. In 1884 T. T. Hawkins was a cowboy who trailed a horse herd for Hezekiah to Abilene, and in 1885 and 1886 he drove cattle herds for him from Kyle, Texas, to Arkansas City, Kansas. T. T. Hawkins, "When George Saunders Made a Bluff Stick," in J. Marvin Hunter, *Trail Drivers of Texas,* 1985, 390–96.

74. Crawford and Ragsdale, *Women in Texas,* 130; Shelton, "Lizzie E. Johnson: A Cattle Queen of Texas," 360.

75. Crawford and Ragsdale, *Women in Texas,* 130.

76. McArthur, "The Cattle Industry of Texas, 1685–1918," 211, 213.

77. Clarence W. Gordon, "Report on Cattle, Sheep, and Swine, Supplementary to Enumeration of Live Stock on Farms in 1880," vol. 3, 976–77, in David Dary, *Cowboy Culture: A Saga of Five Centuries,* 169.

78. Deed of sale, executed Sept. 16, 1904, by José J. Martínez Días, trans. by Ricardo Trayas Bazán y Olazábal. This document states that Lizzie was fifty-two (born in 1852) and Hezekiah was sixty-four (born in 1840), which makes Hezekiah twelve years older than Lizzie. These ages and birth years, however, do not conform to those given by other sources. It seems possible that age (and birth dates) must have been an issue for Lizzie since apparently she frequently gave false information.

79. Emmett Shelton, "Statement concerning Elizabeth E. Johnson Williams," 3.

80. Galveston immigration data online, National Archives Record Group 85, microcopy 1359, roll 3, http://tsm.pearland.com/tsmviewfamily:tsm?family=22268 (accessed Oct. 24, 2003).

81. The building was named for William Brueggerhoff, who was a partner in the Austin and Northwestern Railroad, which ran from Austin to Burnet and was completed in 1882; see "Cedar Park, TX" *The Handbook of Texas Online,* http://www.tsha.utexas.edu/handbook/online (accessed Oct. 27, 2005); Barkley, *History of Travis County and Austin.*

82. Shelton, "Lizzie E. Johnson," 359.

83. Stovall, *Cedar Springs and Limestone Ledges,* 220.

84. Spencer Guimarin, "The Rise and Fall of a Town" (Feb. 1969): 2.

85. Ibid. (Mar. 1969): 1.

86. Mary Starr Barkley, *A History of Central Texas,* 131–32.

87. Stovall, *Cedar Springs and Limestone Ledges,* 220.

88. Hays County, deed records, book 66, 258.

89. Ibid.

90. H. G. Williams, estate, "Deceased Exhibit with Application to Sell."

91. A transit permit for the corpse of H. G. Williams on the El Paso and Southwestern Railroad details his death on July 26, 1914, at the age of seventy-four years, five months, and twelve days, which would make his birth date Mar. 14, 1840.

92. Crawford and Ragsdale, *Women in Texas,* 131; Shelton, "Lizzie E. Johnson," 361.

93. Cyndie Shelton Schmitt (granddaughter of Emmett Shelton, who was the nephew of Lizzie E. Johnson Williams), e-mail to author, Oct. 20, 2003. The birth dates for both Lizzie and Hezekiah change throughout the numerous records. While all evidence indicates that Hezekiah was eight to twelve years older than Lizzie, their tombstone records *both* their birth dates as 1840.

94. Emmett Shelton, "Statement concerning Elizabeth E. Johnson Williams," 2.

95. Ibid., 4.

96. Ibid.

97. Shelton, "Lizzie E. Johnson," 362.

98. Ibid., 361.

99. Emmett Shelton, "Statement concerning Elizabeth E. Johnson Williams," 2.

100. Taylor, "Johnson Institute," 229.

101. Wightman, "Stones of Memory Fall, but Legend of Lizzie Lives."

102. "Local Deaths: Mrs. Lizzie E. Williams," 2. Her obituary states that she died at the age of eighty-four, making her birth year 1840, which is also the date on her tombstone. The same person responsible for putting the date on Lizzie's tombstone probably provided the reporter with information for the obituary and the date to the doctor for her certificate of death.

103. Mrs. John F. Shelton, "Statement concerning Elizabeth E. Johnson Williams," 5.

104. The Brueggerhoff Building was demolished on Mar. 21, 1960; see Wightman, "Stones of Memory Fall, but Legend of Lizzie Lives."

105. Lizzie E. Williams Johnson, estate, "Inventory and Appraisement," 7–9.

106. Shelton, "Lizzie E. Johnson," 366.

107. Lizzie E. Johnson Williams, "Memory," excerpt from unpublished poem.

ELLEN VIOLA PERRY WILSON ANDERSON

MRS. NELS LOUIS ANDERSON

Harriet L. Bishop and Laurie Gudzikowski

IN THE LATE 1800S YOUNG MEN WERE ENCOURAGED to "Go West!" This advice was also taken by some young women, such as Ellen Viola Perry Wilson Anderson. Throughout her long life, Viola, who was always known by her second name, constantly moved west in search of a healthy climate and opportunities for work and education. During her adventurous lifetime she drove a chuck wagon on a cattle drive, cooked for twenty-four men in a lumber camp near Pikes Peak, and did fancy sewing in Spearfish, South Dakota.[1]

In the summer of 1932, Viola spent a month with her daughter-in-law, Grace Bunce Wilson, who remembered that "[Viola's] life had been so unusual that we planned to make a magazine article of what she would tell us—dictated to me—who used a typewriter after a fashion. . . . She talked easily and freely. . . . This was taken down absolutely in her own words."[2] Excerpts from Viola's story give a first-hand account of life on the Western frontier and Viola's trip from Kansas to Texas to purchase cattle and drive them back to the Kansas livestock markets.

Ellen Viola Perry was born December 2, 1864, in the town of Coal Run, near Marietta, Ohio. Her mother, Rachel Starlin Perry Hanson, was of Danish descent and "died Aug. 15, 1900, at the age of 65 years, 5 months and 14 days, wife of B. F. Hanson."[3] Viola's father, Capt. James B. Perry, was with an Ohio regiment in the Union Army.[4] He died May 24, 1864, just a few months before Viola's birth. He was coming home from duty in the Civil War to visit his pregnant wife, Rachel, and their two sons, Dan Irvin and George Ira. One night the boat that he was traveling on collided with another boat, and he was washed overboard and crushed between the two vessels. His body was so badly mangled that only half of it was recovered and taken for burial near his home on the Ohio River. After Viola's birth and with the death of her husband, Rachel found it necessary to send her two sons to live with an uncle near the Ohio River.

When Viola was three years old, Rachel remarried—to B. F. Hanson, a skilled cooper (a craftsman who made wooden buckets and barrels). Together they had a

Figure 31.   Ellen Viola Perry, age twenty-four. Courtesy
of Beverly Caruso, Sherwood, Oregon; Institute of Texan
Cultures at the University of Texas–San Antonio.

son, Frank I. Hanson, who was Viola's younger half-brother. B. F. Hanson was the
only father Viola ever knew. The family farmed in Ohio—growing, gathering, and
making almost everything they needed. Viola said of those times:

> My father was a cooper by trade and very handy with tools. He made big
> barrels and kegs and casks and wooden buckets of every description. . . . My
> mother's washtubs were all of wood and so were all the buckets that had to be
> used for every purpose about the farm and house. Her churn was of cedar. So

were the milk buckets, with brass ears, bails, and hoops. We kept these hoops
as bright as gold by a weekly scouring with salt and vinegar.

I never saw store sugar as long as we lived in Ohio. We had our own maple
trees, and my mother's pantry often was piled high to the ceiling with the
sugar she had made.

My mother used to make genuine corn pone. . . . You make regular corn
meal mush, then add yeast and let it rise. It gets more moist as it rises, and then
you add a good deal of sugar and more corn meal, to make a dough. When
that dough has risen you bake it three or four hours and it is so sweet, and as
different from ordinary corn bread as light bread is from baking powder biscuits. You would think the corn meal would fall, but it stands up beautifully.

There was no cotton in Ohio. . . . For our linsey clothing she [Mother]
used her own wool and bought the cotton thread. We washed the sheep in the
creek with soft soap before we sheared them. . . . The men took out all the
burrs and sticks in this washing, and the sheep were turned into a pasture that
had not been used that spring so as to keep them clean. When the wool had
been cut it had to be tub washed through several waters. We rubbed it on a
washboard, but when it was dry, it was as fluffy as you please.

Almost every year mother changed the color of our clothes. She made our
own dyes from barks that we gathered in the woods. Gathering the bark was a
picnic for us all. Every child had a basket and tools for cutting and scraping
the tree trunks. Hickory, butternut, and sassafras are some of the trees that I
remember. . . . When we got home we dumped our baskets into the big dye
kettle.

She nearly always dyed the wool before it was carded. If she waited until it
was carded, it would tangle and make a rough yarn. . . . One trouble with all
this was that each year my new dress and underclothing, the boys' shirts, and
anything else that she made were all the same color.

Every stitch of our clothing had to be made by hand. Mother did not
double seam things, but they were all sewed in a fine back stitch. I can't remember when I could not sew my own clothing. It seemed as if the seams on
the boys' pants were endless.

I can remember going to school only one winter. In the summer we had a six
week term and I went to that, but we would forget it all by the next summer.
The teachers were dreadful and so were most of the children. I remember one
hot summer day when I went to sleep, and to punish me the teacher made me
stand on the big drum stove. I stepped off backwards and knocked myself sense-
less. . . . There was a great to do. I never saw him punish anyone that way again.[5]

A constant natural gas fire on their Ohio property made Viola's stepfather B. F. ill,
so he went west in search of cleaner air. Finding what he wanted at Kiowa, in Barber County, Kansas, he sent for Rachel, Viola, and Frank. In 1878 Rachel sold most

of the family's belongings and livestock before heading west on the train with their cow, barrels of dried fruit, and other goods to see them through their first year. The family had their goods and the cow in a baggage car, and of course, the cow had to be milked regularly during the trip. At the end of the line—in Abilene, Kansas— Rachel bought a covered wagon and a team of oxen to pull it and drove the family south to their new homestead of 640 acres that bordered on Indian Territory.

Barber County was lush grassland that comprised 10 percent bottomland and 90 percent upland. Timber occupied but 1 percent of the surface; the remainder was prairie, which was good for grazing cattle. The eastern half of the county was very level. There were numerous streams and springs, and water was obtained from wells that were 10–50 feet deep. It was a perfect place for farming, and, with free land from the Homestead Act of 1862, a population boom was under way. In 1875, the county had 366 inhabitants, but by 1885, 7,868 people lived there.

> From the sale [of the Ohio property] we realized enough money to get a good start. We took our blue Jersey cow with us, and father bought more cattle right away. He bought short horn thoroughbreds. They were good for both milk and beef.
>
> We came to Kansas in the summer of 1878. Father had tuberculosis and went six months before we did. Mother and Frank and I reached Abilene by train and went the rest of the 300 miles by covered wagon. We followed the old Santa Fe trail as far as it went, and then had to feel our way by trails that we could hardly see. The government had surveyed all this new country and we counted the distance traveled by the section corners, one at the corner of each mile square. That year the only way of marking the corners was a hole, square, twice the width and depth of a spade, with a strip of sod the width of a spade laid out on its back to each of the four main points of the compass. These "corner stones" were hard to find in the monotony of the prairie, so we measured our mileage by a "speedometer." So many turns of the wagon wheel made a mile, and someone had to count the passing of a red rag tied to the wheel to estimate how far we had gone.[6]

Because wood was scarce in the area, the family lived in a dugout. The requirements for "proving up" the land required homesteaders to fence an area, so wood for fence posts was a higher priority than wood for a house. Later on, lumber was purchased to build a frame house, but the family kept the dugout for storage and shelter from the frequent storms and tornados.

> We went over into Oklahoma, which was still Indian land, and cut those fine cedar timbers, as I have told you. Father would cut the trees and trim them, and Frank and I would snake them down the mountainside to the wagon with a mule.

Our house was built of buffalo grass sod, or some of it had bunch grass in it. The buffalo grass has such long roots that it holds together for years. The bunch grass is so stiff and long that we made pretty good brooms of it. The thick buffalo grass is wonderful for grazing the cattle. Those sods were so strong and thick that we would cut a sod, perhaps fifty feet long, and hitch a mule to it to draw it where we were building. It would not rattle to pieces at all.

The floor of our sod house was dirt, but we kept it hard and clean by sprinkling and tramping. A year or two later we went to the cedar hills in Oklahoma for gypsum, which we burned and made into plaster for the inside of our sod house. Among careless people sod houses were pretty bad, for vermin would hide in the walls, but not in our house.

There is no natural fuel in Kansas, and by the time we went there the buffalo chips were gone. But that is one thing that we got from the cattlemen. We children worked by the day in dry weather gathering the cow chips. They were not so bad to handle when they were dry. They had the most heat in them when they were about six months old. We had a stove made especially for burning them. No, I did not mind gathering them. They were hard and dry and there was no odor.[7]

Education was always important to Viola. In Ohio, her schooling had been sporadic, and "the teachers were dreadful." In Kansas, she and Frank wanted schooling so badly they took matters into their own hands. They planted a crop together to earn money to pay the schoolmaster:

Frank and I wanted to go to school, but our father did not see how he could spare the money. A tomato cannery was to be started nearby, and finally father agreed that Frank and I could have any money that we could make from tomatoes. So we spent all our combined capital, eighty cents, on tomato seeds, and we raised four thousand fine plants. Finally we got them all set out in the open ground when they were about four inches high, and they looked fine. We spent the evening planning how we would spend the money. When we went to bed the wind was rising, and in the morning our whole tomato farm was under four feet of Medicine River sand. It sounds impossible, but there it was, and our eighty cents, and all our work, and all our hopes.

Then we got another idea. That coarse sand is very fertile. It will grow anything. It was in waves and ridges, so Frank loaded a stone boat with weights and leveled it down. That was awful hard work. Then we planted it to peanuts, and how they grew! In the fall we pulled the vines, dried and stripped them, and we had two wagons full of peanuts. We had to haul them to Wichita, 140 miles away, to market them, but with that we cleared 80 dollars.

Frank and I used our peanut money for a winter's schooling in Kiowa and I learned more there than I did in all the rest of my attempts to go to school. . . .

We had the "Three R's" and the older ones even had some algebra. Frank and I rode our pony to school, from our farm and across the Medicine River. We had a stable for him on the edge of town, for the main part of the town was on a high bluff and it was so hard for wagons to get up there that we couldn't afford to buy hay for him in town.[8]

In later years Rachel, Viola's mother, became a teacher. Hired as the first super-intendent of the Kiowa schools, she deeded some of the Kansas family homestead to the state for a public school. Her elegant handwriting is evident in the old fam-ily Bible.

Before the arrival of the homesteaders and the fencing of the range, the land was used primarily for grazing. Farms, of course, ruined the open range for this purpose. For farm families such as Viola's, it was a major heartbreak to have cattle break through their fences and destroy the crops. The conflicts between farmers and cowmen in the West are legendary:

> You know how the cattlemen fought the homesteaders. They cut their fences and let the cattle in on the growing crops, etc. The cattle men poisoned our dogs or shot them so we could not know of their coming till [*sic*] morning, when our fields would be ruined. If we succeeded in getting hay for the winter for ourselves, they would destroy it. If it were fenced till [*sic*] they could not get their cattle to destroy it, they would fire it.
>
> Did you know that one castor bean is poison to a cow? Let her get into a castor bean patch and there is no saving her. So we planted castor beans, acres and acres of them. They were green so that any accidentally started prairie fire could not burn them. And the cattlemen could not destroy them by grazing the cattle on them. So the cattlemen moved on to the west and south.
>
> Hauling the castor beans to Wichita, that same old 140 miles, we made more on them than we made later on any more common field crop. I forgot to say that the castor oil factory there started any farmer free of charge in raising the beans. They are pretty plants and I grow them now for their beauty, not for poisoning cattle.[9]

As a teenager in a homesteading family, Viola did the unthinkable: She fell in love with a cowboy. Neither family agreed to a marriage between the farm girl and the cattleman. So, to marry her cowboy, John Charles Fremont Wilson, Viola, not yet sixteen, eloped to Anthony, Kansas, where they wed on August 9, 1880: "It was here [at school] that I met the man who afterward became my husband. His people were cattlemen and my parents objected to our marriage, so we just rode out to Anthony in the next county east and were married. . . . The first time I ever went with Mr. Wilson, we went to a Fourth of July celebration at Sharon, Kansas. Some boy threw a firecracker into the back of the buggy. When it went off, we thought that was all there was to it. My dress was made of a very light material with ruffles all the way from the bottom of the skirt to the waist. All of a sudden, it blazed up. It had caught fire from the firecracker. We smothered it out with a robe, but the whole side of my dress was gone. I had to stay in the buggy all day. If I hadn't had on heavy underclothing, I would have been naked!"[10]

The traditional tale of the cattle drive is one of Texas cattlemen driving their herds north to the railhead in Kansas. Charles and Viola Wilson did it the other way. They mounted their horses, loaded a wagon, rode from Kansas to Texas, and herded the cattle back to their Kansas ranch to fatten for market. Cartersville, Texas, their destination, was located thirty miles west of present-day Fort Worth, in north central Parker County. Later called Carter, Texas, its population declined in the early twentieth century and by the 1920s had disappeared.[11] The distance from Kiowa, Kansas, to Fort Worth is about 350 miles on today's highways, a mere one-day trip. In the 1880s, however, Viola and Charles spent much longer riding on horseback "down" the Chisholm Trail.

A cattle drive moves very slowly, traveling only ten to twelve miles a day. The drive from Parker County, Texas, to Barber County, Kansas, probably took a month and then an additional month to reach the shipping pens in Abilene: "Shortly after we were married, Mr. Wilson [and I] went to Cartersville, almost in the middle of Texas, after a bunch of cattle. The Texas ranges were dry that year, and too crowded, too. Kansas had good grass, so that we could get them ready [fattened] for market. There were six or seven men, and a girl named Lora Thomas went along for company. We girls wore overalls and chaps when we were riding, but of course we had dresses along too. While we were on the way, Lora married one of the hands and they stayed to work for a Texan. That left us short one hand, and on the way back I had to drive a four-horse wagon."[12]

Viola was needed to drive the team that pulled the chuck wagon, which carried all of the supplies. The cook, who normally drives the chuck wagon, was the heart of the cattle drive. Not only did the cook supply hot food, or "chuck," as it was called, to begin and end each day, that person also doctored injuries and carried bedrolls, drinking water, and other supplies. The chuck wagon was home to the cowboys on the cattle trail.

Chuck wagons started out as farm or army (Civil War) surplus wagons. Famed Texas rancher Charles Goodnight is credited with the innovation of adding a compartmentalized box on the rear of the wagon to store supplies. Food provisions typically included flour, Arbuckle's coffee, salt, soda, a sourdough barrel, salt pork, and, of course, beans. The box was fitted with a hinged lid that opened and closed flat to serve as a work surface. The wagon hauled a barrel filled with water and had a cowhide called a "possum belly" slung as a hammock underneath to store fuel—dried cow manure—that the cook gathered on the trail.[13] Traveling alone ahead of the herd, the cook started the fire and prepared the meals, which were ready when the cowboys had bedded down the cattle for the night. Viola tells of one long, harrowing night she spent alone when no one showed up for chuck, and she had to keep the wolves away from the team:

> The cattle, of course, had to go very slowly, and the horses fretted. One evening the horses were so restless that Mr. Wilson told me to go on ahead. He said to go to a little stream that lay across the trail, take the first trail to the right, go about a mile, and there prepare supper for the men. I had no trouble finding the trail, went what I thought was a mile, and soon had a big boiler of coffee and hot biscuits ready. I waited and waited, and no one came. Darkness came, and I was alone. As the night went by, coyotes attacked the horses on the picket ropes, so I had to fire a shotgun several times to scare them away, and then I had to tie the horses to the wagon wheels. The little wolves would take turns chasing the poor horses around in circles until they were tired out, and then there would have been a sad feast.
>
> When morning came, I hitched up and started back to the main trail. Before I got there, Mr. Wilson came along on horseback. The trail that I had taken after crossing the stream had been opened since we had gone south. I had followed instructions to the letter, but had lost the party. The poor men had not had a drop to drink or a bite to eat since the day before. The water was so bad that they had emptied their canteens, for they were depending on my coffee.
>
> We baked biscuits and beans in a Dutch oven. That is a cylinder of heavy steel, with a wide upstanding rim around the lid. We would make a fire, set the oven on the coals, put in our bread or beans, replace the lid, and heap hot coals on it. No bread baked in a gas oven is ever as good as Dutch oven bread.
>
> Didn't you ever eat sour dough bread? It is good but I doubt if many people now know how to make it. You start with yeast, like making sponge for bread now. You let it get sour, and then stir up a biscuit dough with soda and flour. You save out a little of the soured sponge, add some more flour and water, and before long it is sour enough to use again, We did not use baking powder because there wasn't any. Dr. Price's [baking powder] could be had in some towns, but a tiny can cost 60 cents. When we were on the drive with the cattle, I carried the dough in a wide-mouthed stone jar with a flour sack tied over the mouth.[14]

Both the cattle and their herders encountered many hazards on the trail. The danger of lightning and the peril of crossing rivers and streams are well documented, but Viola tells of another danger: the threat posed by tumbleweeds:

> What pests tumbleweeds are. You know how they burn. Each plant seems to explode, and when they have not already pulled loose, the force of the explosion and the draft made by the fire send them up with a jerk.

Once we were driving along the Kaw River between Manhattan and Junction City, where the bluffs right next to the river must be three hundred feet high. There was a prairie fire along the edge of the bluffs above, and every time that a tumble weed took fire the wind would carry it above our heads and across the river. I was dreadfully afraid the blazing things would fall into our wagon. They missed us, but they started a dreadful fire across the river.

I have seen tumbleweeds drift until they filled good-sized gullies up level with the prairie. If anything happened to stampede the cattle, they would think that the tumbleweed was solid ground and plunge right into it. Of course, they fell to the bottom with broken bones and died.[15]

By the time they reached the end of the trail at the Kansas homestead, Viola had added a bonus to the family's cattle herd: "When calves are born on a cattle drive, the men always killed them right away, because, of course, the little things could not keep up with the herd. It made me sick to see the men kill the little things, and when we were within forty miles of home, I insisted that they should save the rest of them. So when we got home I had four little calves in my wagon. And then their mothers did not know them and would not let them nurse. So the men roped four fresh cows and made them let the babies have their dinner. After that the cows were all right, and their owner was the richer by four calves."[16]

Like many pioneer women, Viola spent a great deal of time by herself since Mr. Wilson was often away on business. She had to deal not only with days and weeks of solitude but also with unexpected dangers. Though she faced many hazards on the trail, perhaps her most harrowing moments came at home when she was alone. Disease was a constant threat on the frontier. Rabies, a painful, incurable, and fatal disease was passed to humans through contact with infected animals. Not only dogs but also sheep, cattle, and many wild animals are carriers of rabies. Until the development of a vaccine by Louis Pasteur in 1885, rabies was always fatal, and rabid animals were greatly feared. In cattle, rabies affects the ability to swallow. Infected cattle have a characteristic bellow, sometimes stagger, and exhibit unusual behavior:[17]

It was in the spring of 1882, my husband was away on business to be gone three or four days, leaving me to myself. I was out in the garden at work. The garden was a few rods from the house, in a low place surrounded by bluffs. I heard the most mournful sound. At first I could not think what it was, but as it came closer I realized it was from the cows, but so different from anything I had heard. I had steps up over a 10-strand barbwire fence. I went on the top of them and saw a lone cow with long horns frothing at the mouth and coming in my direction. I knew in an instant if I was there when she came, nothing could save me but a bullet in her brain. I had no defense but a hoe and two feet, so I ran as only fear could make me. She was after me only a few feet away. I ran into the house. As I shut the door, I heard her feet on the steps. I ran upstairs. When I was a few steps up, the cow came through the door with her front feet, which went through the floor, leaving her half through the door, her head on the floor. I could not get downstairs to get anything. There I was, with only some stale water in the pitcher. The heat was awful. It was four miles to a neighbor. I thought I was doomed.

Towards evening I managed to get courage to get out the window on [to] the kitchen roof and was planning my way down when I saw on the trail over a mile away a man on horseback. I took my bonnet off and waved. He waved his hat. I kept waving till [sic] he came to my rescue. He looked at the cow and said that it was one of Circle Campbell's old cows locoed to kill. He shot her on my floor, helped me down from the kitchen roof. Together we pulled that cow by the horns of our saddles far enough for the coyotes to save me the trouble of anyone asking questions about the brand.[18]

And then there were the snakes. After his little niece died from a rattlesnake bite, Charles Wilson vowed to kill every rattler that he saw: "Another time he [Charles] showed me three antelope coming down a draw. He told me to get the kettle boiling and we would have some fresh meat. He went away with his rifle and in a few minutes I heard him shoot. I was looking out of the window, and saw the three antelope run away. When he came in, I began to tease him for shooting too soon and missing his mark. Then he said that he had the meat with him, and showed me a rattlesnake's head hanging to the fringe of his chaps. The creature had struck there, and he had blown its body from its head with his big rifle."[19]

Throughout their marriage Viola and Charles Wilson lived on the Hanson homestead, contributing their labor to the farming, dairying, and ranching operations. Viola had many memories of milking the cows, drinking buttermilk, and selling the cream and butter. By 1887 the couple had two sons, Wade Angus and Ira Benjamin, both born in Garden City, Kansas. Once again Viola's desire for education would change her life. She was adamant that her sons be allowed to go to school, but Charles would have none of it, so Viola left him and moved farther west—to Spearfish, South Dakota—where gold mining promised a future for her and her sons.

Mining around Deadwood was in full swing, and Viola settled down with her two children. She started out making a living as a fancy seamstress, sewing the elaborate tucked and ruffled dresses that were the fashion of the era. But, because all of the miners needed meals, Viola decided to draw on her experience as a chuck cook on the trail and her years as a Kansas farmer's wife. She opened a café kitty-corner across the street from the shop of the richest man in town—the harness maker, Nels Louis Anderson, who was a Norwegian bachelor from Mankato, Min-

Figure 32.   Viola and Nels Anderson with children and
daughter-in-law, Graphia, taken on the wedding day of Viola's
son Ira, November 30, 1912. Courtesy of Harriet Bishop, Canyon Lake,
Texas; Institute of Texan Cultures at the University of Texas–San Antonio.

nesota. Around the time of the battle of Wounded Knee, Nels first settled in Fort
Pierre, where he ran a leather business, making bridles, saddles, and harnesses.
However, the Sioux raided his store and carried off all of the stock. So, with the
railroad now going into Spearfish, he decided to open a store there. Nels had
a room off the back of his store where he did his cooking, but he liked eating at
Viola's café across the street better; he loved to eat her pies.[20] Viola's recipe for
cream pie has been a family treasure for generations.

Viola and Nels married in 1896. She had four more children with her second
husband, three of whom lived to adulthood—Florence, Mabel, and Gladys. Her
son Wade Wilson received the education that meant so much to Viola. He graduated from Spearfish State Normal College and then studied law at the University
of Nebraska in Lincoln. Afterward he practiced law in Kearney, Nebraska, for
many years.[21] Ira Wilson had little education and ran away from home when he
was twelve years old. As an adult he settled near Gillette, Wyoming, where he acquired acreage that he used for grazing. Huge coal deposits were found on the land
after his death, making his son a very wealthy man.[22]

When automobiles came into vogue and the need for harness makers died out, Viola and Nels moved their family to Eureka Springs, Arkansas, where they earned a living keeping bees. Their honey, which was much in demand, was of superior quality because Nels imported his queen bees from Italy. Later the family moved farther west to College View, Nebraska. In April 1925 Nels died there from diabetes and was buried in the Pioneer Cemetery in Lincoln, Nebraska.

After Nels's death, Viola lived with her daughter and son-in-law, Gladys and Charles Harvey, in Greenwood, Nebraska. Her daughters Gladys and Mabel were the town's telephone operators. In the late 1930s both Mabel and Gladys moved to California, and Viola, still heading west, went with them. During World War II Gladys and Mabel worked in aircraft factories, building fuel pumps for B-29 bombers. Viola died on January 4, 1949, at eighty-five, in Burbank, California, and is buried in Forest Lawn Cemetery in Glendale, California.

Viola lived an adventurous life. From her youthful enterprise of growing peanuts to pay for her schooling to her move as a single mother to South Dakota, where she parlayed her chuck wagon cooking to start her own café, she manifested unusual gumption and independent spirit. Never one to wallow in self-pity, Viola turned her hard times into the wonderful stories of a lifetime, which have served as an inspiration to her family—the legacy of a woman on a Texas cattle drive.

NOTES

1. Harriet L. Bishop, granddaughter of Viola Anderson, provided the family history for this chapter.

2. Grace Bunce Wilson, letter to Harriet L. Bishop, July 2, 1957.

3. Rachael Starlin Perry Hanson, cemetery marker, Valley View Cemetery, Garden City, Kans.

4. James B. Perry was born December 20, 1836, as noted in the Perry family Bible.

5. Viola Anderson, interview with Grace Bunce Wilson, Kearney, Nebr., summer, 1932, 1–6.

6. Ibid., 6.

7. Ibid., 10.

8. Ibid., 11.

9. Ibid., 12–13.

10. Ibid., 11–13.

11. "Carter, Texas," *The New Handbook of Texas Online*.

12. Anderson, interview manuscript, 15.

13. "Lonehand Western: Journal of the Old West," http://www.lonehand.com/chuckwagon_central.htm (accessed Nov. 15, 2005); William Foster Harris, *The Look of the Old West*, 233.

14. Anderson, interview manuscript, 15–16.

15. Ibid., 14–15.

16. Ibid., 15.

17. Agricultural Bulletin, North Dakota State University website, http://www.ext.nodak.edu/extnews/newsrelease/back-issues/000433.txt (accessed Dec. 1, 2005).

18. Anderson interview manuscript, 17.

19. Ibid., 14.

20. Harriet Bishop, e-mail communication to Sara R. Massey, Dec. 16, 2003.

21. Jesse Harris Wilson (daughter of Viola's son Ira Wilson), telephone conversation with Harriet Bishop, Oct. 9, 2003.

22. Ibid.

MARY ("MOLLIE) O. TAYLOR BUNTON

MRS. JAMES HOWELL BUNTON

Ana Carolina Castillo Crimm

IN 1885 MARY TAYLOR BUNTON, KNOWN AS MOLLIE to her friends and a young lady used to having her own way, married James Howell Bunton and joined him in taking three herds of cattle to Kansas. The men who had traveled the cattle trails from Texas to Kansas, even as late as 1886, knew that danger existed for everyone, male and female. They rightly feared death from angry, bitter Indians, blinding lightning storms, terrifying cattle stampedes, and treacherous quicksand and flooded rivers. Mary, warned against the perils of such an adventure by men who knew those risks from personal experience, still chose to set out on her daring adventure.[1]

As a youngster, Mary O. Taylor learned courage from her father, Matthew Taylor, who in 1854 had arrived penniless from Ohio. He brought with him an invalid wife and a medical degree. Matthew had no money to open a practice, and the small town of Austin, with a population of only fifteen hundred inhabitants, had few jobs available. Nonetheless, Taylor settled there with his family and spent only one year doing odd jobs before he earned enough to buy a small home and to open his own medical practice.[2]

Comfortably settled in Austin, the Taylor family looked forward to a pleasurable life in a bustling town. The need for doctors expanded as the town grew, and Dr. Taylor benefited from a growing and profitable practice. In 1857, however, his wife gave birth to a daughter, Harriett Ann, and, within a year, in spite of all of Dr. Taylor's medical skills, his wife, weakened by the demands of childbirth, died of pneumonia, leaving the struggling doctor to care for his small daughter. A hired nurse could not replace the care of a mother, so, as was common with widowers of the day, Matthew realized he needed to find another wife.

Some time shortly before 1859, Mary Helen Millican, a young, attractive, single woman looking for a husband, arrived in Texas with her father, Capt. O. H. Millican, a Mississippi planter who moved to Texas, bringing along his family and slaves to start a new life growing cotton on the fertile lands around Austin.[3] Although several years Mary Helen's senior and with the added burden of a small

Figure 33. Mary and James Howell Bunton on their wedding day, October 14, 1885. Courtesy of the Austin History Center, Austin Public Library, Austin, Texas.

daughter to care for, Dr. Taylor had an established practice and was one of the best marriage prospects in the new town. Miss Millican did not hesitate long after he proposed, and in Austin on April 27, 1859, the couple married. The new Mrs. Taylor took over the care of Harriett Ann, and the following year, the couple's first son, Edward H., was born. Two years later, on August 24, 1862, Mary Helen gave birth to her first daughter, whom the couple named Mary O., although the baby soon acquired the nickname Mollie.[4]

With the beginning of the Civil War in 1861, Taylor, by saving carefully and investing wisely, had already acquired a considerable fortune. He was said to be worth more than $100,000, which placed him among the town's very wealthy elite. When the Civil War ended in 1865, it also destroyed the affluence of those who had their capital in Southern currency. Dr. Taylor suffered the same financial losses as other Texans, but the money he had invested in lands retained its value, and he emerged from the war with more than most.

Matthew and Mary Helen also endured their own private calamity in 1865. A child named Addison, born in 1864, died eighteen months later. The couple had another daughter, Elizabeth, in 1868 but lost their next child, Laura, who died in infancy in 1871. Mary Helen had only one other child, a girl named Daisee Belle, born in 1878. The doctor's family, now consisting of the four girls and a son—Harriett, Edward, Mary, Elizabeth and Daisee Belle—survived the years of Reconstruction in relative ease as their father slowly rebuilt his practice and his wealth.[5]

By the time Harriett, Edward, and Mary were ready for an education, Dr. Taylor could afford to send his children to the very best schools. Mary was sent to Elmira Female College in Elmira, New York, a ladies' finishing school. There she shopped with her female friends and, thanks to her father's generosity, became well acquainted with the growing number of department stores in New York City and Chicago. At college, she studied music, with an emphasis on the harp, and acquired all of the ladylike graces necessary to a young woman of quality. She graduated from Elmira and returned to Austin sometime in the early 1880s to begin her life as one of Austin's Southern belles.[6]

Like everyone else in Austin, Mary "traveled on horseback. . . . [She] rode on a two-horned sidesaddle; rarely did a lady ride astride. She wore a riding skirt designed to cover everything below the waistline. The garment was an over-top skirt that fitted nowhere, with six inches of it trailing on the ground when standing and was in color sad-brown or black. These sidesaddles were not easy to mount, and [at] almost every hitch rack was a stile or mountain block—some called upping block—from which women could get into their saddles."[7]

Austin's elite young men courted the young socialite Mary, and she had numerous opportunities to marry the well-to-do sons of Texas entrepreneurs. The rebellious Mary, however, who was used to having her own way, chose instead a cowboy from West Texas, James Howell Bunton.[8] Her cowboy was, as Mary's shocked friends described him, "coarse and common," although, unlike many of the western cowhands, Bunton had already invested in his own small ranch, the Bar S, outside Sweetwater, Texas.[9] While courting Mary, Bunton had the temerity to defy convention and lease a road wagon and horse in which he drove her down Congress Avenue with his feet propped up on the dashboard. Mary's half-sister Harriett had married well, to a St. Louis lawyer, William A. Dixon, and her sister Elizabeth had also wedded a lawyer, John W. Phillips of Austin. When Mary and J. Howell married on October 14, 1885, in Austin, Mary was elegantly outfitted in a wedding dress from Marshall Field's in Chicago.[10] Her father's gift to the couple was a two-month honeymoon trip to Chicago and the East Coast.[11]

After their honeymoon, Mary and Howell returned to Austin. In late January and early February of 1886, a series of winter storms swept down out of Canada and across the western part of the United States. Pushed by the howling winds, the cattle on the ranches piled up against the newly strung barbed wire. As other cattle pushed against them, the growing mounds of livestock stumbled, fell, and froze. The wily longhorns, even if they reached sheltered valleys, were trampled to death in the arroyos and gullies, where they were crushed by the sheer number of cattle.[12]

By the time the blizzards had passed, the Western ranchers looked out across thousands of acres of dead cattle. When word arrived from his Bar S ranch in Sweetwater, Howell Bunton learned that he had lost almost his entire herd and thus his potential fortune. He was not alone. Most of the western cattle barons, as Mary said, "had their princely fortunes swept away in a single night."[13] Even Jesse Driskell, Austin's only millionaire and owner of the Driskell Hotel, was wiped out by the blizzards, which ruined his Dakota ranches. The storms spared no one, and the drought that beset them the following summer destroyed and drove out the foreign investors, who closed down their ranches and sold them. Local cattlemen like J. Howell Bunton, however, had nowhere else to go. He had no choice but to rebuild his herds.[14]

Bunton, in Austin with his young wife early that spring, knew there were still plenty of cattle in South Texas. He and a number of other cattlemen realized that driving herds north to restock the now-barren plains or transporting them on the railroad in Kansas could bring a quick profit. Bunton, without funding, therefore decided to invest in a herd that could be driven north to Kansas. With the financial help of James H. Raymond and Frank Hamilton (of the Raymond Bank) and Eugene Bremond (of the Bremond Bank in Austin) and perhaps with the backing of his father-in-law, Bunton gathered enough capital to buy up a herd of five thousand head. With experienced buyers to assist him, he joined them in a sweep across South Texas to buy and collect herds of cattle, including some from Richard King of the King Ranch, southwest of Corpus Christi. Once gathered, the herds would be trailed to Sweetwater, where Bunton's few remaining cattle would join the new herd and move north to the railheads in Kansas.[15]

By early April, Howell and Mary moved to the Bar S ranch near Sweetwater, in Nolan County. Mary had never been on a ranch, much less the ramshackle, hard-scrabble ones of West Texas. Her father's home in Austin was a mansion in the center of town, and she had grown up surrounded by the most elegant of luxuries. The homes on the treeless plains of West Texas were anything but elegant, and Mary was amazed to find that most homes consisted of a large, square dirt room cut into the south side of a rolling hill. At the back of the earthen room, a fireplace provided a semblance of a kitchen. Mary learned that a chimney was dug through to the top of the hill, where smoke could sometimes make its escape. The rooms had no windows, and only the opening to the south gave light and ventilation. Mary learned that, when the bitter cold northern storms blew across the plains or the choking dust storms of late summer descended on the hills, the only protection came from a wagon sheet or tarpaulin fastened over the entrance opening. To her surprise, an earthen shelter, as these modern cave dwellers knew, maintained an almost constant 75 degrees throughout the 100-degree heat of summer and the subzero winters.[16]

Howell Bunton, however, insisted on more modern amenities for his young bride. While they were on their honeymoon back East, he had sent milled lumber from Abilene and had his ranch hands laboriously construct a small room for Mary beside the dugout. Unlike the earthen structure, this room was uncomfortably hot in the summer and freezing cold in the winter, but at least it had walls, windows, a proper door, and a wood floor. As he proudly explained to her, it was the first lumber "house" built on Sweetwater Creek.[17]

During the lovely days of early spring on the ranges of West Texas, Mary, already an accomplished horsewoman, enjoyed riding among the Sweetwater hills with her husband. They were waiting for the herds that had been gathered in South Texas to arrive in Sweetwater, to which Howell's own cattle would be added and moved to Kansas. While waiting, Mary befriended the cowboys, and, as they sat around the campfires, she learned about riding, roping, branding, and life on the open range in general. They plaited ropes for her from the hair in the manes and tails of the horses and assured her that the prickly ropes, when spread on the ground around a sleeping bag, would keep rattlesnakes away. One cowboy braided narrow rawhide strips into a particularly lovely quirt and bridle for her. As she said, "They were things of beauty and a joy forever."[18] She made good use of her rawhide gifts during the ten years that she lived on ranches, and, when she moved back to Austin, she brought along these prized possessions as mementos of her life in the West.[19]

Like all proper young women of the day, Mary rode sidesaddle. Her mother, however, must have been among the avant-garde since she sent Mary a pair of riding breeches and boots so that she could ride astride. One morning, while her husband and his cowboys were gathering the herd, Mary donned her new outfit and galloped out to visit the men. Shouts of laughter greeted her arrival, and one old white-haired man bellowed, "My God! I knew she'd do it! Here she comes wearin' them britches!"[20] The commotion stampeded the cattle, and Mary's husband had no time to comment on her attire as he galloped off to round them up. Mary returned home and replaced the offending pants with her long riding skirt.[21]

During the pleasant spring days, Mary learned to hunt. Because the bison had been killed off, the deer, quail, and antelope had spread rapidly on the grassy prairies, and meat for supper from one of these wild animals meant that one more cow could be saved for the market. One of the cowboys, an expert marksman, taught Mary to shoot a small-caliber rifle. On her rides in the rolling hills, she thus had a purpose, and before long she proudly contributed to her keep by bringing home quail and sometimes a deer. She had a hard time killing antelopes, though not from lack of skill but rather, as she said, she was "too chicken-hearted to shoot at the antelope with their great big human eyes."[22]

Prairie dogs were another matter entirely. A colony of the furry, squirrel-like animals had established burrows near the ranch house and popped out periodically to check on the cowboys' comings and goings. Sitting up on their haunches, much like curious squirrels, their front paws folded in front, they watched in silence, undisturbed as the men walked to and fro, laughing and talking, their spurs jingling and their saddles flapping. But let Mary Bunton appear, and the entire colony broke into a raucous, cackling bark as if warning each other of her existence. Mary could not go anywhere without the rude prairie dogs' bark erupting around her. The cowboys suggested that the rustling of her silk petticoats must have been irritating the small animals.[23]

Mary Bunton decided to improve her marksmanship by shooting at the noisy prairie dogs. She sat on the steps of the porch for hours, taking aim as they popped up out of their burrows and carefully squeezing off her shots. The creatures, hearing the crack of her rifle, dropped back down into their burrows to avoid the bullets. As Mary reported, "just as I was flattering myself that at last I had a scalp for my belt the little varmint would pop out again like a 'jack-in-the-box,' sit up on its hind legs and bark at me more furiously than ever."[24]

Mary took to ranch life as if she were born to it. She asked endless questions of her husband and the cowboys and listened eagerly to their long stories, the amusing anecdotes, and the songs with which they settled the herds at night. Mary loved leisurely riding with her husband across the grassy, flower-covered prairie in the delightful spring weather and felt that life could get no better. For her, ranch life held no fears, and she enjoyed the lovely landscapes and the soft gentle breezes. She had not, however, experienced the terrible, killing heat of a West Texas summer or the blasting cold of the blizzards that had destroyed her husband's cattle the previous winter.

Just as Mary had grown accustomed to the quiet ranch life, a cowboy rode in with word that the herds had arrived from the south. She remained alone at the ranch as her husband and the cowboys rode down to inspect the vast herds. It was the first time she had been left by herself at the ranch, and there was little to do but wait. By evening her husband had still not returned, and she began to worry about the dangers that might have befallen him. Suddenly all those anecdotes and stories seemed far too real.[25]

Bunton returned long after dark, anxious and concerned. After apologizing for the long delay, he explained that the man who was to take the herds to Kansas was almost blind. He had started from South Texas with eyes already sore and inflamed, and the heat and dust of the trail had aggravated the condition. By the time the herd reached Sweetwater, he was in agony and could take the cattle no farther. In desperation, Bunton had ridden from ranch to ranch, trying to find another herd boss who knew the trail and could lead the cattle through to the railheads. Nevertheless, he had not found anyone who could or would help.[26]

Bunton had invested everything in this gamble. He had put his own reputation and that of his father-in-law on the line with the bankers in Austin. If this herd did not make it to market, he would be ruined. Something had to be done. The cattle were in Sweetwater, and somehow they had to be moved to Kansas. Bunton told Mary that "trail bosses are born, not made," and he had not been able to find a single one to help him. "I fully realize that with my little experience," he admitted, "I am undertaking a Herculean task but I can find no other solution to my problem except to take charge of the herds and have the cattle driven through to market myself."[27]

With only a single day's experience of loneliness, Mary dreaded the thought of being left behind. Although she had seen little of life on the range, what she had seen she had enjoyed and so decided that she would accompany her husband on the trail drive. It did not occur to her that she would be adding more fears to her husband's already overwhelming burden, and she felt naively confident that she could take care of herself. After all, she could ride and shoot, and she was certain that she could even help with the herd. When she told him of her decision, Bunton was horrified. After days of pleading, her tears won the day, as so often happens between men and women. "If your heart is set on going, I guess it is up to me to find the way," he said.[28] His solution, he decided, would be to let her start the trip and, when she became worn out, he would leave the herds long enough to get her to the closest rail line, where he could put her on a train for home. Both satisfied that each had won the day, they began preparing for the trip.

Mary realized she had nothing to wear that would be appropriate for weeks on the trail. The wife of her husband's cousin, however, loaned her several washable dresses and a green woolen riding habit. During the coming weeks, mesquite and tumbleweeds shredded the hem and tore at the edges of the cloth. The cowboys claimed they could trail the herd by looking for the green scraps from her skirt that had snagged on the bushes. Undaunted, Mary packed her things into a small suitcase. So certain was she of reaching the end of the trail that she even included an evening dress so she would be properly attired for the "social affairs of civilization when we reached the end of our trip."[29]

While Mary was preparing, so was her husband. Bunton called on Sam, the elderly black cook who would drive the chuck wagon with the lead herd. Bunton knew that he himself would be unable to take care of Mary during the day, what with attending to the cattle and the cowboys and scouting ahead for watering holes. He asked Sam to promise that he would watch over Mary and never let her out of sight of the chuck wagon. If he did, Bunton promised to give Sam a reward, but, if he failed and anything happened, Bunton swore that Sam would never see another sunrise. The old cook thought long and hard and finally said, "It sho is a big order youse trustin' me with, Big Chief, but as youse have always been kind to me in [e]very way, I'se going to promise youse and cross my heart to take as good care of the Young Missus as I can, with God's help."[30] The two men shook hands, and Old Sam was as good as his word.

The news of Mary's determination to go on the cattle drive spread like wildfire throughout the surrounding countryside. A group of Bunton's friends and relatives arrived to dissuade him from taking her along. Since Bunton himself had never been on one of the long drives, they told him he had no idea how dangerous it would be. They explained in gory detail the many perils they would encounter. They assured him that, even if Mary just went part of the way, the trip would surely end in tragedy. Bunton sent them to talk to Mary. The members of the Sweetwater delegation reminded her of the responsibilities she was adding to her husband's already great burdens. She thanked them sweetly and said her husband had promised to take her on the trip and so she would go.[31] The group left, shaking their heads and mumbling ominously.

Bunton knew that, even though the journey would be long and hard, he wanted it to be as pleasant for Mary as it could be. He bought a sturdy Concord buggy, the finest and most comfortable of its kind, and chose a team of two spirited bay horses for her to drive. Mary had never driven a team before and was terrified of the feisty beasts. However, realizing that, if she showed any fear, she might be left behind, she hid her quaking and declared to both her husband and the cowboys that she would be fine. In part to compensate for her terror, she named one of the horses Darling and the other Beauty, and, after several days on the trail, she and the horses had settled into an amicable acceptance of one another.[32]

Mary also needed a riding horse since she planned to spend some of her time on horseback. She found a suitable animal among the remuda, or herd of horses, purchased by her husband for the drive. It was a small, Spanish palomino, cream colored with a long, flowing white mane and tail. The cowboys had found the horse "mean as the devil" and impossible to ride since every one of them had tried and been painfully bucked off. The horse would not let a man ride him or even catch him if he were loose. Bunton learned that the horse had belonged to the wife of the man from whom he had bought the remuda. She had spoiled the animal from the time it was a colt, and she herself had been the only one to ride it. It was gentle, the owner assured Bunton, but only for a woman rider. The pony was perfect for Mary. Although it fought and kicked when the men tried to saddle it, the beautiful palomino settled down immediately when Mary arrived, ate sugar from her hand, and neighed when it heard her voice. Calling it "the best gaited saddle pony she ever rode," she rode 10–15 miles a day on the horse without tiring either herself or the animal.[33] She also "laid down the law" to the cowboys and forbade them to attempt to ride her pony ever again.[34]

After a busy four days, they were ready to ride out. Mary had packed her satchel into Old Sam's already full chuck wagon, along with blankets rolled in a tarpaulin for herself and her husband and a small tent that someone had loaned to them. Mary would ride ahead of the first herd in order to stay out of the dust as much as possible. Except for a passing cowboy moving forward or back along the edge of the herd and Old Sam in his chuck wagon, she spent much of the trip alone. Her husband, always up at dawn, rode ahead to find grass and water for the next night's camp, then circled back to find the freight wagons and supplies that were to join the herd at designated points. He checked the remuda, tallied the cattle, and at nightfall saw to the needs of his small army of cowboys and tried to keep peace in the camps. It was an exhausting and grueling pace, but he and his bride found time for each other in the evenings as they slept on their tarpaulin and blankets under the stars.[35]

The five thousand head of cattle were divided into three groups. The lead herd consisted of heifer yearlings, all red Durhams of the same size, age, and color, which Howell had bought from the King Ranch in South Texas. The second herd consisted of steers, and the third of cows and stock cattle. Each herd had its own crew of cowboys and its own chuck wagon and cook. The large herd stretched for miles along the trail. Bunton checked with each group several times a day, making sure they had everything they needed and attempting to prevent problems from erupting.[36]

In the evenings, Bunton and Mary or one of the cowboys laid out their bedding. Since it never rained, they soon quit setting up the small tent and simply spread out the tarpaulin and laid down their quilts and blankets to make their pallets. At first Mary had difficulty sleeping. The ground was hard, even with the thin pallet of quilts underneath them. Worse were the many stories she had heard of snakes, scorpions, spiders, and various insects that abounded along the trail. Equally unnerving were the nighttime sounds of barking, snarling wolf packs that were prowling closer and closer to the camp. Mary huddled near to her sleeping husband, afraid to wake him from his exhausted slumber. She would often lie awake and trace the constellations she had learned as a girl in her astronomy class in far-off New York. Most of all she enjoyed the Pleiades, a small cluster of seven stars named for seven Greek sisters. Describing the stars that "glistened like millions of fireflies tangled in a silver braid," she found courage in their company.[37]

Mary reveled in the first few weeks of the trip. She rode her palomino around the herds, enjoying the mild breezes, the sunny blue skies, and the multicolored carpets of spring flowers along the trail. Riding ahead of the herd, she could look back at the sea of heads and horns, which looked to her "as if a dark-red velvet carpet with its wide border of green grass was stretched just as far as the eye could see."[38] At times she hitched her horse to the back of the chuck wagon or turned him loose among the remuda and climbed up to talk to Old Sam and listen to his hair-raising stories of other cattle drives. When in her buggy behind Darling and Beauty, she often stopped to admire the wild berries ripening in clumps of vines and later recalled that, "early in the morning, wet with dew they would sparkle in the sunshine as if the fairies had sprinkled them with diamond dust."[39] As the day brightened, the many varieties of wildflowers opened to the sun, nodding and blowing in the gentle breeze, covering the land in brilliant orange, yellows, pinks, and blues. Sometimes she pulled up big armfuls of the delicate flowers and decorated the buggy and the horses' bridles and harnesses. Occasionally she also wove a wreath for her hair and a cape of the beautiful blossoms for her shoulders. Pretending she was part of a grand flower parade, she laughed gaily, waving as the cowboys doffed their hats, bowed over their saddles, and exclaimed, "Hail to the cowboys' beautiful queen of the flowers!"[40]

With nature all about her, Mary also became acquainted with the wild animals along the trail. Taking a side trip one day, she heard a soft mewling noise coming from an old stump. Inside she found three of the "darlingest little kittens I had ever seen. . . . They were all black and as soft as down and had a white stripe running down their backs from their heads to their tails. I wondered what kind of kittens they were."[41] After playing with them for a while, she wrapped them in her skirt and carried them back to camp. When he saw them, Old Sam rapidly backed away and told her to get rid of them immediately. They were polecats, he said, and added, "It sho is fortunate you didn't meet the old mammy cat on your way . . . for she would have showered you with her perfume, and we'd of had to bury you in the ground to get rid of the turrible smell!"[42] Mary quickly returned the furry "kittens" to their stump.

Mary particularly enjoyed the cooling shade of the trees beside the infrequent streams. She often took her fishing pole to try her luck at catching some tasty fish for dinner. One day she noticed a small partridge nest under a bush and hunkered down to watch happily as the tiny baby birds chipped their way out of their shells. Suddenly she realized that she was not the only observer at the birth. A large rattlesnake lay curled nearby, awaiting a particularly tasty breakfast. Mary stumbled to her feet, startling the snake into a warning buzz, and ran for the buggy. Some distance from the snake, she halted and, realizing the danger to the baby partridges, determined to overcome her fear. By using her fishing pole, she reasoned, she could beat the snake to death from a safe distance. Just in case, she also armed herself with rocks and then approached the annoyed rattler. As she hit the snake again and again, it writhed and thrashed, lashing about for its enemy. When it finally lay still, Mary, shaking with fear and gasping from the exertion, bashed in its head with the rocks for good measure. She also took out her small knife and, still squeamish at having to touch the dry, dead scales, she cut off the rattles. When she returned to camp, still pale from her encounter, she proudly displayed her trophy to the cowboys, who cheered her courage. Assuring her that she was no longer a tenderfoot, they "dubbed her a seasoned veteran."[43]

This was not to be her last run-in with rattlesnakes. Because they are cold blooded, snakes spend most of the winter hibernating in rocky dens or caves. Early in the spring, they emerge to lie in the sun but are still sluggish from their winter nap. One evening, while Mary and Bunton were eating a late supper, a young cowboy offered to lay out their tarpaulin and bedrolls for the night. Inadvertently, he laid the tarp over a snake den. During the night, a snake emerged but could not get out from under the tarp because of Mary's and Bunton's bodies lying on either side of the hole. The snake stretched its length between them, and in the morning Mary noticed the ridge under the tarp. When she called it to her husband's attention, he dismissed her fears and assured her it was probably just a branch. When the cowboys rolled up the bedding, however, Mary had been right. They discovered a five-foot diamondback rattler still lying sluggishly beside the hole. Thankful that it had not bitten them, Mary insisted that the men let the snake return to its home.[44]

The cattle trail was no clearly marked road. Bunton, using information gleaned from cowboys who had been up the trail before, followed a generally northwestly direction. On the flat plains of North Texas, there was no need to worry about where they were, but he needed to be far enough west to avoid the farms that had cropped up along the Red River. The Old Chisholm Trail, established originally by Jesse Chisholm, identified only that portion of the trail that crossed into Oklahoma (then still considered Indian Territory) and then on into Kansas. The name had stuck, however, and came to be used for all of the feeder trails coming out of South Texas that converged at the Red River before entering Indian Territory, just north of Fort Worth.

By 1886, farmers, always the bane of cattlemen, had fenced their lands along the Red River. Two years earlier, the northern reaches of the Old Chisholm Trail were closed, forcing cattlemen to take their herds farther and farther West to avoid the growing number of settlements along Texas' northern border. Unaware of any name change, Bunton was actually following what came to be called the Western Trail. It still, however, led through the Oklahoma Indian Territory.[45]

The Indian tribes in Oklahoma constituted a motley collection of the remaining members of dozens of tribes. As the whites moved west, the U.S. government systematically removed first the vast herds of buffalo, which had once provided food and sustenance for the Plains Indians, and then removed the Indian tribes themselves, whether by cajolery, forced treaties, or outright warfare. Each tribe was sent to what was called the Indian Territory—land the government was certain no white person would ever want because of its aridity. The Indians, once considered among the best cavalry forces the world had ever seen, were forced onto allocations of useless land called reservations, often side by side with their mortal tribal enemies. They were reduced to chasing scrawny, underfed cows that the Indian agents released for them to pretend to hunt. Frequently sullen over their treatment at the hands of white officials and anxious to keep their families from starving, the Indians saw no harm in stealing a few cows from the vast herds that crossed their lands. Driven to desperation by the ineptitude or outright chicanery of government agents, they sometimes erupted into violence, killing the invading whites in a vicious fury. The cattlemen, such as Bunton, however, gave little thought to the injustices perpetrated on the tribes and saw only the danger to themselves and their cattle.

As Mary, Bunton, and the herd neared Indian Territory, local cattlemen stopped to chat and to make sure none of their cattle had inadvertently joined the herd. They told Mary and Bunton stories of Indian "cruelties and atrocities . . . and warned us of their treachery."[46] Mary had already seen the danger for herself. While out riding, she had come across a group of men standing at a small cabin beside the road. They warned her away, telling her that, early that morning, a band of marauding Indians had murdered and scalped a man, his wife, and their child. The blood was still fresh. From then on, Mary had no trouble believing the stories she heard about the Indians.

By June, the summer heat had settled in. Plodding along behind the chuck wagon, Mary found the combination of dust, high temperatures, and noise almost insufferable. Beyond a bluff far off to one side, she saw the tops of trees marking a creek or stream, so she decided to get a drink for her horses and enjoy a peaceful rest in the cool, quiet shade. Without Old Sam noticing her leave in the buggy, she loosened the horses' reins, having heard that horses could find water on their own. Moving at a good clip, they soon reached the bluff and went over the side and down into a clear stream at the bottom. Even before taking a drink, however, they snorted, sensing danger, then turned and bolted back up the bluff. As the buggy turned, Mary glimpsed five or six Indians bathing in the creek, as startled at the sight of her as she was of them. The horses, now at a dead run, reached the top of the rise and raced for the herd, with Mary hanging on to the sides of the buggy. In the distance, she could see Old Sam and the chuck wagon in a cloud of dust with the mules galloping hard toward her. "The wagon sheet was flapping, the tin pans and plates were rattling and at every turn of the wheels the jolting was scattering everything loose out of the wagon all along the trail."[47] As Mary reached Old Sam, he wheeled the chuck wagon around, and she managed to bring the buggy to a stop. Gasping out her explanation, she anxiously looked back toward the creek, expecting to see the Indians coming up over the rise. When they did not, both Mary and Old Sam gratefully returned to the herd. Vowing not to take off alone again, Mary was very thankful that the horses had had sense enough to get her out of danger. Only later did the two share their story with Bunton and laugh over her narrow escape.

As the herd moved deeper into Indian Territory, the contacts with Indians became more frequent. One afternoon, after Old Sam had unhooked the mules and gone for water, Mary sat down to write a letter to her mother, describing the beautiful scenery and the peaceful camp. Hearing the mules stamping and blowing, she looked up to find an entire group of Indians clambering into the chuck wagon and pulling back the tarp to see what they could steal. Old Sam, coming back up from the creek with a keg of water, took in the situation and grabbed his long, black muleskinner's whip. As he swung the leather, it cracked like pistol shots, and he advanced on the Indians. The older Indian women among them began crying, "Mush away! Mush away!" asking for bread. Old Sam threatened them but then pulled out a fifty-pound can "filled with cooked beans, potatoes, onions, dried beef and stale bread, things he had been salvaging all the way up for just such an occasion." He gave them the can and then drove them away from the camp, the Indians already hungrily eating the contents of the can.[48]

A far more dangerous altercation occurred at the Red River. A large group of mounted Indians, riding one behind the other (hence the term Indian file) and led by a chief in a feathered headdress, approached the herd just as the cattle reached the rough country along the river. His people were hungry, the chief said, and demanded one of the big red Durham steers. Bunton refused but then agreed to give the meat to the chief if the Indians would help all of the cattle, wagons, and men get across the tricky—and dangerous—Red River. The chief agreed, and the Indians quickly moved the herd across the treacherous river, avoiding the quicksand and bogs in the river bottom.

Once on the far side, the chief requested the big red steer he had been promised. Bunton ordered his herd boss to cut out a crippled cow that had joined the herd the day before and offered it to the Indians. In a fury, the chief refused the animal, maintaining that it would be degrading to the Indian men to eat a cow. Fearing just such an altercation, Bunton had already sent one of his men for the cowboys with the other two herds, which were not yet across the river. The chief led his people to a small bluff and sat smoking his pipe while the Indian men gathered stones and sticks, lit a fire on top the rocks, and began a slow war dance around the flames. Old Sam told Bunton that the Indians were trying to frighten the whites into giving up the promised steer. Suddenly the remaining cowboys came racing across the river, yelling and shooting their pistols into the air. The chief, certain that the U.S. Cavalry had arrived (since the troops were rumored to be patrolling the trail), tied an old rag on a stick and rode at a lope toward Bunton. His people did not want to fight, he said, and they would take the cow. Bunton turned over the animal, and the Indians butchered it on the spot, ate their fill, and left the women to cut up the last scraps of meat, which they tied into bundles and carried off.[49]

Once the herd reached Kansas, more dangers cropped up, this time not from Indians but from the summer storms that raged periodically. One afternoon, Mary saw giant black clouds boiling up in the northwest, and by nightfall the storm was upon them. Bunton put her in the chuck wagon, whose big, arching, wooden ribs had been removed to keep it from blowing away, and covered her with a tarp that she could lift to peer out at the sky. He and all of the available men mounted up to patrol the herd and keep them calm throughout the night.

Mary wrote, "When the storm began, the air was so charged with electricity, the boys had taken off their pistols and spurs and had me take the steel hairpins out of my hair and the rings from my fingers."[50] Alone in the chuck wagon and with nothing but the tarp to protect her, Mary watched as the storm got worse, the rain falling in torrents and beating at the thin canvas while lightning crashed overhead. "Sometimes," she said, "the lightning would fall from the sky in fiery darts of flame; again there would be a flash and it would look as if millions of fairies in glittering robes of fire were dancing in mad glee over the backs of the cattle and jumping from the horns of one steer to another."[51] Amazingly, the sound of the men's singing, in between the bolts of thunder, kept the cattle from stampeding. When morning dawned at last, Mary, who had slept as little as the men, crawled from her damp haven and breathed a sigh of relief upon finding that everyone was safe, including her husband, the cowboys, and the cattle.[52]

Moving on across Kansas, the long, exhausting trip was nearly over. Several days later, Bunton and Mary drove their buggy to Coolidge, where he hoped to sell the cattle. Mary had heard stories that the town was infested with murderers and thieves, but she also knew it had a hotel where she could take a good hot bath and sleep in a comfortable bed. When they arrived, Mary recognized other men from Sweetwater, who had also come up the trail. John R. Blocker, Ike Pryor, Bill Jennings, and Bill Pumphrey had to take back their dire predictions. Laughing and shouting in surprise, they surrounded the buggy and then lifted Mary from the seat and carried her into the hotel. That night, after a luxurious bath, Mary was able to wear her evening dress, which she had brought all the way from Sweetwater, to a feast and a ball in her honor at the hotel. She was crowned "Queen of the Old Chisholm Trail."[53]

With the cattle sold and the men paid, Mary and Howell drove the buggy on to Kansas City. Old Sam took some of the remuda, including her little palomino, back to Sweetwater with the chuck wagons for the winter. After their fun time in

Figure 34.   Mary Bunton, bride on the old Chisholm Trail in 1886.

Kansas City, Bunton sold the buggy and its team, much to Mary's regret as she kissed Darling and Beauty good-bye, and the couple boarded the train to make the trip back to their dugout home in Sweetwater.[54]

Back in Sweetwater, Bunton paid off his debts. He and Mary remained on the Bar S ranch, where Mary learned both the good and the bad of ranching life. Her experiences on the trail stood her in good stead, and she became an accomplished rancher in her own right, helping her husband with the cattle roundups, although she never went on another cattle drive. Some time later, the couple sold the Bar S ranch in Sweetwater and moved south to ranchland belonging to Mary's father in Kinney County, west of Cotulla (150 miles south of Austin). There, for the next ten years, Bunton managed the fifty-thousand-acre ranch for his father-in-law. It appears that Howell may have suffered from an incapacitating illness during this time, which required Mary to run the ranch while also helping her husband to recuperate. By the turn of the century, cattle thieves and rustlers had mounted well-planned attacks on the South Texas ranch, but Mary, along with her cowboys, fought back against the marauders. The ranchers had called for help from Austin, but when the Texas adjutant general tried to get Mary to return to the safety of Austin, she refused. When he threatened to take her by force, she wired her father, who interceded with Governor Hogg. Hogg provided Mary with three rangers to stop the rustlers. She and her husband stayed on the ranch for several more years.[55]

With the advent of the automobile and then roads that spread across the country, modern times arrived in Texas. In the early years of the twentieth century, Mary and her husband at last returned to Austin, now a thriving metropolis. Back in the state capital, she rejoined many of her girlhood friends and made new acquaintances among the wives of ranchers, bankers, and politicians. Having inherited her father's wealth, Mary became an important part of Austin society, and she joined clubs, gave parties, and, according to one society editor, hosted the largest bridge party of the times at the Driskell Hotel. Among her friends Mary included Lizzie Breedlove Hay, Maggie Glasscock, Fannie Manlove, Brewye Bunton, and Emma Carpenter Everitt. Her friends bragged about her fame as the "Queen of the Cattle Trail," and she was often called on to give speeches and recount her thrilling experiences.

Living the life of a retiree, Bunton died of pneumonia on February 14, 1923, at sixty-nine years of age. Mary had him buried in Austin's Oakwood Cemetery. After her husband's death, Mary leased the 50,000-acre ranch to her nephew David Holding, who kept it stocked with cattle while she continued to manage her business and social affairs in Austin. In 1927, much to her delight, she was inducted as an honorary member into the Old Trail Drivers' Association, an organization she and Howell had joined when it was formed in 1915. In 1939, as part of the Texas centennial celebration, Mary's friends persuaded her to publish her memoirs, which she titled *A Bride on the Old Chisholm Trail in 1886,* the only description of the cattle trail ever told from a woman's point of view. Her small, beautifully written book, with its entertaining and lyrical descriptions of her adventures on the trail, remains delightful reading today. Its publication led a few years later to her being honored at the Dallas motion picture premier of *Red River,* since it was believed that she "alone among women was found to have made the whole long journey (up the trail.)"[56]

Fifty years after Mary went up the trail, Thomas Ulvan Taylor commented, when interviewing her, that she looked like a young matron. When he asked what cosmetics she used, Mary replied that, on the ranch, she used nothing but red Vaseline for her face and ordinary mutton suet for her hands.[57] Such was Mary's ingenuity when it came to taking care of herself. She continued to live comfortably in Austin after her beloved Howell passed on, watching the town grow and change. Although she had no children of her own, she enjoyed telling her nieces and nephews the stories of her life on the ranges of West Texas. Mary remained hale and hearty long into her eighties and died at Seton Hospital in Austin of a cerebral hemorrhage on January 4, 1952, at the age of eighty-nine.[58]

In an era when women were supposed to faint in the face of danger, Mary proved that women could be as brave and bold as any man. Her pluck and sense of humor turned potentially frightening experiences into engaging and entertaining adventures. Cheerfully confident Mary Taylor Bunton has left a powerful legacy of strength and self-assurance for modern women to follow. "At the time the trip was a very hazardous one . . . an adventure that tested the courage and endurance of sturdy men, and was considered entirely too dangerous to be undertaken by a woman."[59]

NOTES

1. Mary Taylor Bunton, *A Bride on the Old Chisholm Trail in 1886,* 75–76.

2. John Henry Brown, *Indian Wars and Pioneers of Texas,* 276; Dick King, "Two Austin Women and the Chisholm Trail," 62.

3. Mary Millican was born in Virginia; see Mary Taylor Bunton, Death Certificate.

4. Brown, *Indian Wars and Pioneers of Texas,* 276; Mary Taylor Bunton, death certificate.

5. Brown, *Indian Wars and Pioneers of Texas,* 276.

6. Dudley Early, "Austin Woman Recalls Chisholm Trail," 83.

7. Clarence Allen Bridges, *History of Denton Texas, from Its Beginning to 1960.*

8. James H. Bunton, death certificate. James was born June 1854 in Texas and died Feb. 13, 1923, in Austin.

9. King, "Two Austin Women and the Chisholm Trail," 62.

10. In her book, *A Bride on the Old Chisholm Trail in 1886* (10–11), Mary Bunton maintains she married on Oct. 14, 1885, whereas Dick King writes that they married on Oct. 10, 1885. King, "Two Austin Women and the Chisholm Trail," 62.

11. King, "Two Austin Women and the Chisholm Trail," 62.

12. It appears likely that Mary Bunton and her husband were not at the Sweetwater ranch during the blizzards. Mary described her experiences in great detail, but her only comment about this catastrophe was that her husband lost his fortune; see Bunton, *A Bride on the Old Chisholm Trail in 1886,* 11–12.

13. Ibid.

14. Ana Carolina Castillo Crimm, "Mathew 'Bones' Hooks: A Pioneer of Honor," in *Black Cowboys of Texas,* edited by Sara R. Massey, 232.

15. Bunton, *A Bride on the Old Chisholm Trail in 1886,* 13; Thomas Ulvan Taylor, "Honeymoon on the Old Cattle Trail," 1.

16. Bunton, *A Bride on the Old Chisholm Trail in 1886,* 14–15.

17. Ibid., 14.

18. Ibid., 18.

19. Crimm, "Mathew 'Bones' Hooks," 233; Jane Clements Monday and Betty Bailey Colley, *Voices from the Wild Horse Desert: The Vaquero Families of the King and Kenedy Ranches,* xxvii.

20. Bunton, *A Bride on the Old Chisholm Trail in 1886,* 19; King, "Two Austin Women and the Chisholm Trail," 64.

21. Taylor, "Honeymoon on the Old Cattle Trail," 1.

22. Bunton, *A Bride on the Old Chisholm Trail in 1886,* 20.

23. Ibid., 20–21.

24. Ibid., 21.

25. Ibid., 22.

26. Ibid., 22–23; Taylor, "Honeymoon on the Old Cattle Trail," 1.

27. Bunton, *A Bride on the Old Chisholm Trail in 1886,* 23; Taylor, "Honeymoon on the Old Cattle Trail," 1.

28. Bunton, *A Bride on the Old Chisholm Trail in 1886,* 28; Early, "Austin Woman Recalls Chisholm Trail," 83.

29. Bunton, *A Bride on the Old Chisholm Trail in 1886,* 31.

30. Ibid., 54–55.

31. Ibid., 30.

32. Ibid., 33; Taylor, "Honeymoon on the Old Cattle Trail," 1.

33. Bunton, *A Bride on the Old Chisholm Trail in 1886,* 35.

34. Ibid.

35. Ibid., 36.

36. Ibid., 36–38. Taylor, in his article "Honeymoon on the Old Cattle Trail" (1), maintains that the first herd consisted of steers, the second of cows and stock cattle, and the third of long yearlings. Mary Bunton, however, specifically describes the red Durham yearlings from the King Ranch as constituting the lead herd; see *A Bride on the Old Chisholm Trail in 1886,* 38.

37. Bunton, *A Bride on the Old Chisholm Trail in 1886,* 38.

38. Ibid., 38–39.

39. Ibid., 44.

40. Ibid., 39–40.

41. Ibid., 42.

42. Ibid.

43. Ibid., 40–41.

44. Ibid., 65; Elizabeth Maret, *Women of the Range: Women's Roles in the Texas Beef Cattle Industry,* 24–25.

45. Wayne Gard, *The Chisholm Trail,* vi.

46. Bunton, *A Bride on the Old Chisholm Trail in 1886,* 45.

47. Ibid., 49.

48. Ibid., 52–53.

49. Ibid., 56–61.

50. Ibid., 67.

51. Ibid., 67–68.

52. Ibid.

53. Ibid., 69–70, 76–77.

54. Ibid., 70; Taylor, "Honeymoon on the Old Cattle Trail," 3.

55. Taylor, "Honeymoon on the Old Cattle Trail," 3; Early, "Austin Woman Recalls Chisholm Trail," 83.

56. Bunton, *A Bride on the Old Chisholm Trail in 1886,* 75.

57. Ibid., 305, 75–76.

58. King, "Two Austin Women and the Chisholm Trail," 64; Mary Taylor Bunton, death certificate.

59. Bunton, *A Bride on the Old Chisholm Trail in 1886,* 4–5.

PART 3

The End of the Cattle Drives, 1887–89

ALMA ELIZA BAILEY MILES

MRS. JACK WOLLARD MILES

Lou Halsell Rodenberger

WITH THE COMING OF THE RAILROADS TO TEXAS TOWNS, the days of the long cattle drives wound down, but there were still cattle on ranches that needed to be moved to distant pastures or to the railroad in nearby towns. Alma Miles, as a cowgirl during the early years of her marriage to Tom Green County rancher Jack Miles, made an indispensable hand working and trailing cattle. She also participated in annual roundups on the three ranches that Jonathan Miles, Jack's father, had acquired in Tom Green County near Fort McKavett. Alma demonstrated the skills needed for driving cattle when she and Jack, along with the ranch cowboys, moved the Miles herds on the long treks from one ranch to another. A savvy horsewoman, Alma Miles earned an early reputation as a competent cowhand. In her oral history she said, "Jack liked nothing better than to have me at every round-up and often said he wondered how he had ever made long drives without me."[1]

When Alma Eliza Bailey moved with her family to Tom Green County in 1885, the fourteen-year-old's chief passions were her love for her horses and her active role in ranch life. She was also in love with a Tom Green cowboy whom she had never met. Although she was born in Sulphur Springs in East Texas, Alma grew up on a Uvalde County ranch, where her family settled soon after her birth on September 2, 1871.[2] When her favorite uncle, a rancher from the Concho River country, came to visit her family before they moved to Tom Green County, he brought with him a photo of his friend, Jack Miles, who was becoming famous for his abilities as a championship roper and rider in the San Angelo area competitions. Fate soon handed Alma the chance to meet the celebrated roper when her family settled on a ranch in Jack Miles's native region.

As soon as the Bailey family moved to the T. F. Ranch on the North Concho River, the lively Alma realized she had found "her own element." She recalled that "I could stay in the saddle from morning until night, eat out of the chuck wagon and attend all the square dances for miles around. I hunted and fished and ran races with the dashing vaqueros." Soon Alma's energetic and obvious enjoyment of both work and play, so long as those activities involved riding Ball Stockings, her favorite mount at the time, attracted the attention of the local cowboys. Alma says that she "did not lack for suitors." That this vibrant young woman enjoyed their efforts to impress her is clear in her description of her life before she met Jack. She remembered that she "rode like an Indian and at the age of 16 did not lack for suitors. I led them all a wild race from one end of the Concho country to the other."

One cowboy, however, lost his place in Alma's affections when he mistreated Ball Stockings. A present from this would-be suitor and the "most treasured gift that love could buy" a girl, Ball Stockings earned his donor a special place in Alma's young heart for a time. Then another smitten cowhand gave her a horse more handsome than Ball Stockings, and the former owner of Ball Stockings requested that she return his gift to him. When Alma refused, a wild ride ensued, during which she rode with yet another admirer; on that ride, the jealous cowboy laid a whip across Ball Stockings' rear. She remembered that her "adorable Ball Stockings broke into a startled and furious run and I had a race as wildly exciting as my heart could crave, while my anxious comrade flew after me. This settled my interest in the jealous suitor."

Predictably, on one of her daily rides, Alma finally met the "dashing Young Lockinvar" [*sic*], just as she imagined he might appear—driving a herd of horses. She and Jack went riding out, often thirty or forty miles, to attend frontier socials,

Figure 35.   Jack Miles, husband of Alma. Courtesy of the West
Texas Collection, Angelo State University, San Angelo, Texas.

picnics, fish fries, races, and "glorious old time square dances." They danced to tunes well known in frontier Texas, including "Sally Gooden," "Turkey in the Straw," and "Pop Goes the Weasel," with the music provided by a fiddler, a banjo player, and a guitar picker. Alma's account of these events suggests that her sense of humor as much as her love of a good time colors her memories of these long, lively evenings. She recalls nights "of hilarious break downs," fueled with black coffee and cake, and she says that "the old time dance was a test of endurance as well as skill."

Soon Alma was engaged to her cowboy, Jack Wollard Miles, son of Jonathan Miles, a prominent early settler in Tom Green County. Jack could match Alma's energetic pursuit of outdoor life in the Concho River country with his own "deviling," as old-time cowboy Ben Mayes remembers Jack as a boy. The young cowpoke worked for the Iowa and Texas Cattle Company VP Ranch in Water Valley at the time. In "The Tom Green County Cowboy," old-timer Ben Mayes has transcribed a firsthand account in his imaginative colloquial phrasing. Mayes states that Jack, as a very young cowboy, worked for rancher Wayne Harris "when he could get away from his dad." This suggests that Jonathan Miles, for whom the town of Miles in Runnels County is named, kept Jack busy on his own spread most of the time. Mayes reveals much about Jack's personality in one anecdote: He says that Jack's teasing of Cithro [sic], a Mexican horse herder, irritated Jack's boss. Finally, the rancher ordered the hands to throw Jack into the river until he gave up this pastime. The cowhands gave Jack six soakings before he capitulated, and the horse herder suffered no more of his teasing.[3]

Jack's energy soon was expended through other outlets, however. Mayes describes Jack's superior ability as a horseman, although rancher Wayne Harris mounted Jack on mules for some time before he let him ride his horses. Mayes continues, "He made a cowhand and taken first money here at San Angelo Fair." In the roping events at the fair, Jack went after the cows and got them with his "brother loop," as Mayes phrases this skill.[4] It may be that Jack's confident handling of his horses impressed horse-lover Alma as much as his good looks. Whatever the attraction between the two young cow people, they were soon engaged. On January 1, 1887, a *San Angelo Times* story describes a dance and oyster supper hosted by young Jack Miles for his friends. At the time, Jack was constructing a house on a town lot he owned in San Angelo, but he denied to his inquisitive friends on the gala evening that he planned to be married.[5] As they suspected, however, he and the "intelligent, beautiful young lady," as their wedding story describes Alma, were married on March 20, 1887, on the T. F. Ranch at the Grape Creek home of Alma's parents, Joseph Martin and Martha Elizabeth Bailey. The bride was sixteen; the groom twenty-one.[6]

According to Alma's description of the festivities after the wedding, guests first enjoyed dinner and then a square dance. As the guests left, Alma gave each of her friends a piece of the wedding veil as a souvenir. Alma and Jack left the T. F. Ranch the next day "in grand style," riding in an elegant four-wheeled carriage, which Alma called a barouche, with a seat up front for the driver. A black servant drove the couple to San Angelo, probably to their new home, although Alma did not say.

One of Jack's first presents to his bride was a thoroughbred dun horse imported from England. Baby Dun became the "darling of my heart," Alma said, and she lived on him from the first days of her marriage. Jack traded two lots in the business area of the fast-developing San Angelo for Baby Dun, who occupied part of Alma's time for several months. She described the results of her devoted schooling, as well as Jack's contribution to the training of this "magnificent creature" that could pace a mile in three minutes and was obviously a prize entry in local horse shows: "I spent months in gently training him, the result of which would have given him entry into a circus. Jack taught him to kneel for me to mount him, bow to the judge, tell his age by pawing with his left foot and we would have to teach him to paw one more time each year. When I would go out to bridle him he would stand on his hind feet, shake his head at me, then come meekly up and take the bits in his mouth. His tricks always delighted his many admirers."

Alma's life as her husband's ranch hand partner began almost immediately after their wedding. "Again the wide open spaces claimed me, I lived in the saddle from then on." However, in 1887, when Alma began working cattle with Jack, trail-driving activity out of San Angelo ranch country had almost ceased for individual outfits. Contract drovers bargained to take cattle up the trail to Kansas or Nebraska for $1.00–1.50 a head, while the ranchers and their cowboys stayed in Texas and tended their remaining herds. Although in the 1870s the Goodnight-Loving trail provided passage for large herds through Tom Green County, early in the 1880s, ranchers learned of barbed wire and began to enclose their land. Texas's famous fence-cutting war in 1883 ended when fence cutting was declared a felony, and drovers had to learn ways to circumvent the enclosed ranches.[7]

On the trail, the Texas cattle often spread the highly contagious Texas fever in some Texas counties and into Kansas. As quarantines to prevent the spread of the fever were extended, ranchers began to see their profits decrease. Moreover, the cowboys were threatened by hostile Kiowas and Comanches until they were confined to reservations in the early 1870s; then, however, the tribes began demanding grazing fees where trails crossed their reservations. The history of Tom Green County boasts the largest roundup in West Texas, when fifteen ranch outfits brought together twenty-five thousand head of cattle at Knickerbocker, a then-thriving town south of San Angelo. Nonetheless, local historians have failed to reveal how the huge herd was driven north, if indeed that was the purpose of the roundup. This event occurred in 1886, the year before Alma married Jack, so it is doubtful that she was involved in this record-breaking roundup. It is certain, however, that she proved to be a competent hand in the roundups on the Miles ranch by the summer of 1887.[8]

Alma's equipment for ranch work included a saddle, bridle, blanket, spurs, quirt, and rope, all of excellent quality if their cost is an indication of their worth. Alma valued her riding equipment at $100, expensive for the time. Her bridle was trimmed with silver, and her hat was a John B. Stetson. Completing this cowgirl's fashionable rig was a riding habit of waterproof flannel trimmed with brass buttons and buckskin gauntlet gloves. As was the custom with many of the early cowgirls, her footwear was laced-up boots that reached almost to her knees. One implement that movie cowboys would later consider indispensable, a pistol, was not part of Alma's outfit, but she stated that, despite not wearing a firearm, she nevertheless was a good shot when she did fire a gun.

Proof that Alma knew how to ride well is evident in her description of the annual San Angelo fair, the "greatest event of our Concho country." Events that tested the entrants' skills included riding, roping, and branding, with horse racing as the major contest. An eager adversary against local cowboys, Alma raced on a sidesaddle "with big black hair saddle pockets," and she won many of those races. The saddle pockets provided a handy place to stash the candy Alma collected from her cowpoke competitors in these races, which she usually won riding Pumpkin, a small brown pony.

Much of Alma's personal account describes her adventures as a cow puncher. She slept in her own special tent, which the cook set up for her every evening, but she enjoyed the companionship of the cowboys when they gathered for meals. Supper included chili beans spiced with garlic, fried calf meat or broiled calf ribs, and biscuits baked in a dutch oven. Black coffee was their beverage, and stewed dried apples and molasses served as dessert. Alma adds that the cook sometimes prepared "sun-of-a-gun" stew. It may be that Alma never actually heard the true name of the stew—sonofabitch stew—since the cowboys never referred to it by that name when women were present, but she says the cowboys considered the concoction a treat: "I must say it was good."

For the knowledgeable, the question becomes, "Did Alma know what she was eating?" Almost everything but the tail of a calf usually went into the stew pot. Ramon F. Adams lists the ingredients in his account of the old-time cowboy camp cooks. After cutting up the fat into little pieces and putting them in the pot, the cook added the heart, liver, skinned and cubed tongue, narrow gut, pieces of tenderloin, sweetbreads, and the brains after they had been cooked separately. Sometimes the cook added a chopped onion, or "skunk egg," as some cowboys called it. No vegetables were required. Adams says that, after several hours of slow cooking, "you had something sweet and delicious, and after eating it you would no longer be a skeptic." Alma's enjoyment of the dish supports his assessment.[9]

While out on the range, Alma was never bored. One adrenalin-producing activity involved chasing and capturing the wild mustangs that plagued the ranchers since they ate their share of forage on the ranches and often led the ranch mounts astray. Alma recalls one unique method that she and Jack employed to let these wild horses know that they were unwelcome visitors. One day they managed to round up a herd of the mustangs, rope them, and tie old dry cowhides to their tails. Alma says the "last we saw of them, they were going over the hill with the cowhides standing straight out in the air" as the horses tried to rid themselves of the cowhides. They had banished the horses permanently and "had a good laugh" besides.

Not all of their efforts to rid the region of wild horses proved as easy as the cowhide solution. The most difficult ride she ever experienced occurred one afternoon when she and Jack set out to capture a big mustang. Alma was riding Baby Dun the day they spotted this "beautiful creature with long silken mane and tail." "Jack and I had captured several [mustangs]. This one got with an old outlaw horse that had on a big bell. We knew we would have to run him down to catch him, so we started toward the ranch. We ran them about fifteen miles and the clang of the big bell got louder and louder. I can hear it yet, when I think of that ride. We captured the old rascal about sundown. I didn't have a dry thread on me."

Alma did not let such rides intimidate her. She enjoyed the challenge of riding hard across the rough ranch land, covered with algerita (a plant in the thorny barberry family), cat's claw, prickly pear, yucca, and cacti. One particularly hard day concluded with a surprised and bruised Alma after an encounter with a stubborn cow. Her detailed narrative of this adventure, which took place while their outfit was gathering eleven hundred cattle from the Fort McKavett pastures, proves her courage: "We threw them together on the side of a rocky hill. Jack cut out all the strays and it fell my lot to be placed between the cut and the herd, which is a very hard place. One old wild cow was thrown with the cut-backs. She tried to run over me and get back to into the herd. I was riding a little grey pacing pony named Grand Pap. He was as quick as lightning. I ran that old heifer for thirty minutes. All at once she made a break, simply sniffing the air. I slapped my spurs into Grand Pap and wheeled around to head her off when my saddle turned under his belly and I fell to the ground among the rocks and mesquite bushes. My horse planted his foot on the skirt of my riding habit and stopped dead still. Bless his heart! Jack and the boys came running to me but I only had a few bruises and scratches. They fixed my saddle back on and I went on duty again." Alma's determination to finish the job is evident in her final words about this arduous ride: "This time I took after that old cow and ran her so far she never came back."

Cutting stubborn old cows out of the herd proved difficult, but one evening's work reveals that, if Alma had ever joined a trail crew to take their cattle to northern markets, she would have made a capable drover. After supper one stormy evening, she and her husband drew first guard. The storm came up by surprise as they rode around the herd, singing to keep the cattle quiet. Alma describes the thunder as "terrific," followed by heavy rainfall. Darkness was so intense that even her white horse became invisible except when lightning illuminated the livestock. As expected, the cattle started milling, and even though all of the cowboys saddled up and rode out to calm them, the agitated herd finally stampeded. Fearing that the cattle might run through the barbed wire fence near their camp, the outfit boss ordered the cowboys to let the herd run. According to Alma, "We all went to the wagon, got in and sat there the rest of the night. We ate breakfast before daylight next morning and overtook the lead cattle about seven miles from camp." Only about fifty head were missing, and Alma says they recovered those cows during the spring roundup.

As Alma soon learned, riding as a cowpoke on the roundup of the Miles family cattle involved more than savvy as a horsewoman. Working the huge herds that Jonathan Miles owned at the time required months in the saddle. After long drives to round up the herds for the annual branding and to cut out stray cows, Alma learned that keeping the herd together required great skill. That she was accepted as an equal of the experienced hands is reflected in the assignment of "seven dandy horses" from the remuda as her mounts: "[T]hey were all No. 1 cow horses."

She soon learned, however, that experienced cowboys had little patience with inexperienced tenderfeet in the outfit. Alma's skill as a horsewoman, her knowledge of cattle, and her relationship with the boss guaranteed that she was accepted without initiation when she first arrived in the Miles family's cow camp, but greenhorns could expect practical jokes and even more drastic action if they demonstrated their ignorance. Alma describes the ultimate punishment—"putting on the leggings." Her presence did not temper the flogging with leather leggings that an ignorant beginner suffered, and this was often followed by a toss into the river, where the perpetrators would order him to "sink or swim." One of the cowboys' favorite practical jokes involved the dreaded rattlesnake, which frequently sought warmth in a cowboy's blankets. Alma says one of the cowboys had perfected the art of hissing like a rattlesnake. One victim could not be persuaded to return to his bed and spent the rest of the night leaning on a tree with a big stick in his hand.

Life in the saddle with Jack Miles by her side clearly suited Alma. Even a dangerous collision of horses, which briefly stunned her, is narrated with zest. On this occasion, the cowboys pushed the Miles family's herd toward the Colorado River to pasture on their Colorado Ranch. Tired and dirty, Jack suggested a bath in the river after the herd had settled for the night. Since Alma had been keeping tally that day as the hands branded the cattle, she felt an equal need to get cleaned up. Then she saw that the Colorado, on a rise that day, lived up to its name. The dirty water was red and uninviting. Rather than saddle another horse, Jack climbed up behind Alma, and off they rode the short distance to the river. On their way back to camp, still riding double, Alma suddenly found herself involved in the worst accident of her cowgirl career: "Old Dun was single footing and Jack [riding behind Alma] slapped him on the hips, he [Old Dun] got faster and pretty soon down he went and I went on over his head about five feet and landed right on my head. Jack,

Old Dun and I were all piled up together. My horse scrambled to his feet and Jack jumped up and picked me up. I was only stunned and came out of it in a minute with no bad effects except a big knot on my head. Jack was not hurt but my darling horse was standing there shaking all over and covered with dirt. His mouth was bleeding as the bit had broken and cut it. The sight of him in that condition hurt me worse than the fall I got." Apparently Baby Dun, who was usually as "light footed as an elk," had stepped into a hole. Later that evening Alma and Jack saddled fresh mounts and, led by a pack of ranch hounds, set out to hunt coyotes. Evidently, for Alma, her "worst" accident was not all that bad.

Alma does not tell us how long she rode as a ranch hand. Since Jack's father, Jonathan, had established an early reputation as one of San Angelo's city founders and the family had remained influential in city life, Alma became one of the respected hostesses in the social life of the city. Jonathan Miles was known for his generosity to the poor as early as 1885, when he killed two beeves daily to feed the hungry. When the town of Ben Ficklin was destroyed in the infamous 1882 flood, Miles gave lots in San Angelo to many of the homeless families and helped them build new homes. Bad investments finally led to the loss of most of his land.[10]

By 1900, Jack's reputation as a cattleman led to a commission by Cecil Rhodes, who established the Rhodes scholarships, to oversee a shipment of cows and horses and take a cowboy outfit to South Africa. While there, Jack managed the herd and rode with the guests of ranch overseer A. L. Lawley. The guests included a Portuguese governor and several British lords and ladies. Jack's friend W. A. Dellagana reported to Alma on Jack's passage over: "Somehow or other I do not think that Jack was born to be a sailor. I do not know whether you have seen him seasick or not, but if you have I doubt whether you have ever seen anything more miserable. Had I a camera with me, I could have sent you a lovely picture of Jack coiled up in a corner, seasick, not caring a hang whether it snowed, rained or thundered. But he has got over that now—and well the men know it."[11] Clearly, Alma's handsome "Lockinvar" [*sic*] was meant to ride a horse, not a rocking ship.

Even though circumstances prevented Alma from going up the trail or becoming a lifelong cow woman, she always remembered the years she rode as the best ones of her life: "I certainly enjoyed ranch life and wish I could live it all over again, but time had brought changes that ranching is not what it used to be. I want to say that the old fashioned cowboys were the finest fellows I ever knew, loyal and true in every respect and had the greatest respect for women. They would lay down their lives if necessary for a woman. They were congenial among themselves and would give their boss the best they had in them. I will always say, luck to the cowboys wherever they may be found and sing to myself, I'm a jolly cowgirl, I hunt cows all the time. I always catch the Son-of-a-Gun who steals a cow of mine. I can ride a bronco and ride him with all ease. I can rope a streak of lightning and ride it where I please."

In 1944 Jack Wollard Miles died at the age of seventy-eight. His long and lauda-tory obituary underscores Alma's reasons for the high regard she had for the man with whom she rode at the Concho County rodeos so many times. Jack's history included several legendary events that added to his early reputation for "deviling." Before he met Alma, he attended Texas A&M College and was involved in firing a Civil War cannon into one of the campus buildings. In San Angelo in 1883, he threw a rope around the first schoolhouse built in the region and pulled it down. He was best known, however, as a world champion steer roper, a title he held for six years. By the 1920s Miles had been elected constable and established a reputa-tion as a "nemesis of scores of bootleggers" in Tom Green County.[12]

Alma and her fun-loving Jack never had children, and she outlived him by four-teen years. During the last years of her life, she lived with her cousin, Mrs. D. D. Schilling, in Henrietta, Texas, where she died on July 28, 1958. She is buried beside her Lochinvar in the San Angelo Fairmount Cemetery.[13] Her own words sum up her life as a cow woman and one of the "wilder, stronger breed" of West Texas pi-oneer women: "Few women in the entire history of the cow country ever threw their sugins [*sic*] [bedding] in the wagon and rode the range with their husband like a man as I did."[14]

NOTES

1. Alma's history was recorded and transcribed by the Federal Writers' Project as part of the American Life Histories collection of the late 1930s; see Mrs. Jack Miles, "Folkstuff and Range Lore" http://memory.loc.gov/ammem, s.v. "Mrs. Jack Miles"; also in Jim Lanning and Judy Lanning, eds., *Texas Cowboys: Memories of the Early Days,* 210–17. Alma Miles's oral history provides the resource for all of the information and quotations referring to her life as a cow-girl. All other information is available in the West Texas Collection, Angelo State University Library, San Angelo, Tex.

2. "Mrs. Jack Miles Rites Set," *San Angelo Standard Times,* July 30, 1958.

3. Ben C. Mayes (1863–1941), "Jack Miles Takes a Bath," in "The Tom Green County Cowboy," 17.

4. Ibid.

5. "Party in San Angelo," (San Angelo) *Standard,* Jan. 22, 1887, microfilm, West Texas Col-lection, Angelo State University Library, San Angelo, Tex.

6. (San Angelo) *Standard,* Mar. 26, 1887, microfilm, West Texas Collection, Angelo State University Library, San Angelo, Tex.

7. Jimmy M. Skaggs, "Cattle Trailing," in Ron Tyler, *The New Handbook of Texas,* vol. 1, 1041–43.

8. "Tom Green County," *The New Handbook of Texas Online.*

9. Ramon F. Adams, *Come and Get It: The Story of the Old Cowboy Cook,* 95–97.

10. "Services Today for Jack Miles, Pioneer Cowboy, Peace Officer," *San Angelo Standard Times,* Dec. 14, 1944.

11. W. A. Dellagana, letter to Alma Miles, Apr. 11, 1900.

12. "Services Today for Jack Miles, Pioneer Cowboy, Peace Officer."

13. "Mrs. Jack Miles Rites Set."

14. Shirley Abbott, *Womenfolks: Growing Up Down South,* 185. Abbott says in her memoir that the West Texas women she met while attending college in Texas were a "wilder, stronger breed." See also Lou Rodenberger, "West Texas Pioneer Women: 'The Wilder, Stronger Breed,'" 38–53, and in the *Haley Library Newsletter,* 1, 8–10.

ᵂ̓ILLIE ᵂ̓MATTHEWS

Allan O. Kownslar

Born in 1858, Samuel Dunn Houston was a native Texan who grew up in Gonzales. He went on cattle drives between 1876 and 1886 and was a trail boss from 1888 to 1893. His destinations on these drives included Kansas, New Mexico, Colorado, Wyoming, North Dakota, and Montana. He had cattle ranches in the Pecos, Pandora, and Sanderson areas. When the cattle boom ended in the late 1880s, he, his wife, Lelia, and their three daughters settled in San Antonio, where Samuel hand-carved wooden longhorns that were advertised for sale at the Frontier Times Museum in Bandera at one dollar each. While raising his daughters, he said he kept "my gun at the head of my bed to keep the young, up-to-date cowboys away."[1]

In an article for *Trail Drivers of Texas,* Houston wrote of a drive that had a most unusual happening. It began on a cattle drive he managed for the Holt Live Stock Company of New Mexico in the spring of 1888 along the Colorado Trail to Wyoming. For the large drive with twenty-five hundred cattle, he employed four extra men at Seven Rivers, New Mexico. Little did he realize the trouble those cowhands would cause him, even though they were desperately needed.

Near Roswell, Houston made the mistake of bedding the herd in an area full of gopher holes. At nine o'clock that evening the cattle spooked and stampeded, and most of them could not be stopped until seven hours later. Houston, with every available hand, managed to recover much of the herd but was still missing 635 steers. He and some of the hands found them later that day six miles down the Pecos River. Fortunately, in total he lost only five head.

Gus Votaw was one of the cowboys working the herd on that drive with Houston. Votaw, who was about twenty years of age, was from San Antonio and, according to Houston, an excellent worker. However, the four new men Houston had hired at Seven Rivers disliked Votaw. They repeatedly harassed him and finally exhausted Houston's patience. He had gone to Fort Sumner to write and mail some letters, and, on his return to the herd, "I finished my job at the post office, mounted my horse and pulled out for camp. When I got up within two hundred

Figure 36.   Texas longhorns. Courtesy of the Institute of
Texan Cultures at the University of Texas–San Antonio.

yards of camp I looked up and saw what I thought, every man in camp and only one man with the herd. When I rode up every man had a gun in his hand but Gus Votaw. I got off my horse and, of course, knew the cause. The cook said, 'Boss, there is going to be hell here. I am glad you came.'

I went to the front of the wagon, got my gun off of the water barrel and told the men that I would play my trump card that I had to have every gun in camp. I didn't expect to live to get the last one, but I did. I got six of them, knocked the loads out, threw them in the wagon, got out my time and check books and gave the four men [hired at Seven Rivers] their time. I told the cook and horse rustler to hitch up the mules and we would move camp. I left the four bad men sitting on their saddles under a cottonwood tree and felt that I had done the right thing. I went up the river about two miles and camped."[2]

Shorthanded and facing a ninety-mile wasteland without water, Houston put his extra horses with the herd and moved the animals as quickly as possible across that harsh section of the Staked Plains between the Pecos and the Canadian rivers. Fifty-two hours later, the group reached the Canadian River. There he stopped for three days to give his men, cattle, and horses a much-needed rest. Still undermanned and fearing a stampede or other problems, he left camp and went to nearby Clayton, New Mexico, hoping to hire two or three more men:

I met an old friend of mine and he told me that there was a kid of a boy around town that wanted to get with a herd and go up the trail, but he had not seen him for an hour or so. I put out to hunt that kid and found him over at the livery stable. I hired him and took him to camp, and put him with the horses and put my [horse] rustler [a wrangler who cared for the extra horses in the remuda] with the cattle. I got along fine for three or four months. The kid would get up the darkest stormy nights and stay with the cattle until the storm was over. He was good-natured, very modest, didn't use any cuss words

Figure 37.   Samuel Dunn Houston, the trail boss who hired Willie Matthews. Courtesy of Pioneer Memorial Hall, San Antonio, Texas.

or tobacco, and always pleasant. His name was Willie Matthews, was nineteen years old and weighed one hundred and twenty-five pounds. His home was in Caldwell, Kansas, and I was so pleased with him that I wished many times I could find two or three more like him.

Everything went fine until I got to Hugo, Colorado, a little town on the old K. P. [Kansas Pacific] Railroad, near the Colorado and Wyoming line. There was good grass and water close to town, so I pulled up about a half a mile that noon and struck camp. After dinner the kid came to where I was sitting and asked me if he could quit. He insisted, said he was homesick, and I had to let him go.

About sundown we were all sitting around camp and the old herd was coming in on the bed ground. I looked up towards town and saw a lady, all dressed up, coming toward camp, walking. I told the boys we were going to have company. I couldn't imagine why a woman would be coming on foot to a cow camp, but she kept right on coming, and when within fifty feet of camp I got up to be ready to receive my guest. Our eyes were all set on her, and every man holding his breath. When she got up within about twenty feet of me, she began to laugh, and said, "Mr. Houston, you don't know me, do you?"

Well, for one minute I couldn't speak. She reached her hand out to me, to shake hands, and I said, "Kid, is it possible that you are a lady?" That was one time that I could not think of anything to say, for everything that had been said on the old cow trail in the last three or four days entered my mind at that moment. In a little while we all crowded around the girl and shook her hand, but we were so dumbfounded we couldn't hardly think of anything to say. I told the cook to get one of the tomato boxes for a chair. The kid sat down and I said, "Now I want you to explain yourself."

"Well," she said, "I will tell you all about it, Mr. Houston. My papa is an old-time trail driver from Southern Texas. He drove from Texas to Caldwell, Kansas, in the '70s. He liked the country around Caldwell very much, so the last trip he made he went to work on a ranch up there and never returned to Texas any more. In two or three years he and my mother were married. After I was ten or twelve years old, I used to hear papa talk so much about the old cow trail and I made up my mind that when I was grown I was going up the trail if I had to run off. I had a pony of my own and read in the paper of the big herds passing Clayton, New Mexico, so I said, now is my chance to get on the trail. Not being far over to Clayton, I saddled my pony and told brother I was going out in the country, and I might be gone for a week, but for him to tell papa not to worry about me, I would be back. I had on a suit of brother's clothes and a pair of his boots. In three or four days I was in Clayton looking for a job and I found one. Now, Mr. Houston, I am glad I found you to make the trip with, for I have enjoyed it. I am going just as straight home as I can and that old train can't run too fast for me, when I get on it."

The train left Hugo at 11:20 o'clock in the evening. I left one man with the herd and took the kid and every man in town to see the little girl off. I supposed she was the only girl that ever made such a trip as that. She was a perfect lady.

The next morning I went to Hugo and secured three more men and hit the trail for Pole Creek, Wyoming, about fifty miles from the Montana and Wyoming line, where I turned over the big herd to the Russell Brothers Ranch, and that was the end of this drive.[3] After I got through and returned to the ranch on the Pecos River, I had many letters from the little girl and her father also, thanking me for the kindness towards Willie and begging me to visit them.

The skills Willie Matthews exhibited on the trail drive with Samuel Dunn Houston were not unusual for girls at the time. In rural areas and especially on the frontier, there was little gender distinction in the chores assigned to farm or ranch children because there was so much to do in getting a new homestead or ranch started. As soon as the children were physically able, girls and boys plowed and worked the fields, hauled water, milked cows, herded livestock, hunted for food, did housework, took care of younger siblings, and managed teams of horses or mules to transport crops or pick up supplies. Examples abound of girls with such skills and especially of those who were expert horsewomen. In *Frontier Children,* Linda Peavy and Ursula Smith state that although much of agricultural work was tiresome and boring, sometimes

> children on horseback found it easy to bridge the worlds of work and play. While tending cows or sheep, they raced their ponies, practiced stunts, and chased coyotes and antelope. "It has been a novel sight," noted an observer newly arrived in northern Nebraska in the early 1880s, "to watch a little girl about ten years old herding sheep . . . handling her pony with a masterly hand, galloping around the herd if they begin to scatter out, and driving them into a corral."
>
> Ursula Camastral, a ten-year-old immigrant from Switzerland, learned to ride a horse soon after arriving at the family's new homestead on the Judith River in central Montana. Because her mother thought it "very bad . . . for a girl or woman to ride straddle," Ursula was constrained to ride sidesaddle anytime she was near her home. However, her father allowed her to ride astride when she helped him round up wild horses, and she quickly gained a reputation as a skilled horsewoman.[4]

What was unusual in the case of Willie Matthews was that her riding and herding skills were equal to those of men and that her male disguise kept her secret safe. In this respect she was similar to Little Jo or Joe Monaghan of Idaho. According to folklorist Joyce Gibson Roach, Jo, for some reason still unknown today, felt she had been wronged and decided "she might as well go west. She left her small son in the care of her sister and tried mining and sheepherding before she began trailing cows. Jo had problems from the beginning. When you are barely five feet tall in a pair of high-heeled boots, when you shun saloons and will not spend money on dance halls or gambling or liquor, and when your appearance is delicate and your voice high-pitched, folks notice. The fact that Jo was a superb horseman and bronc buster, a dependable drover, and an expert with the lariat was not peculiar. Nevertheless, Jo kept to herself, raised cattle, horses and chickens on a ranch and generally lived the life of a recluse. When she died and the secret was discovered, it gave folks around Rockville, Idaho, something to talk about for a long time afterward."[5]

While scholars have managed to unearth some information about Jo Monaghan, that has not been the case for Houston's mysterious Willie Matthews. The letters Willie and her father wrote to Samuel Dunn Houston cannot be found, if they still exist, and my efforts to contact (by telephone and letter) Houston's great-granddaughter living in San Antonio have elicited no response. The archives at the Frontier Times Museum in Bandera, Texas, did not contain any of Houston's papers, nor were there any at the Texas Trail Drivers Memorial Hall and Museum in San Antonio; the latter had only his photograph with one of his carved wooden longhorns.

However, there is little reason to doubt what Houston wrote about Willie Matthews. As a trail boss, he carefully documented in his diaries the activities of each cattle drive. He said it was from those diaries that he wrote the full accounts of his cattle drive experiences.[6]

Houston told us that, when he met Willie Matthews, she was from the Caldwell, Sumner County, Kansas, area. At the time, Caldwell was one of the first cow towns in Kansas. Located on the Chisholm Trail, Caldwell was a major shipping point for Texas longhorn cattle from 1872 to 1884. In 1872, some 292 herds totaling nearly 350,000 head arrived at Caldwell. One year later the total was nearly 500,000 head, and in 1874, 175,000 cattle entered the town. After that, the number of cattle arriving at Caldwell slowly declined, and "loadings continued to diminish rapidly through the remaining eighties. Barbed wire was blocking the drovers [from Texas]. Too, railroads were piercing deeper into the Texas ranges and were offering better facilities and favorable rates for stock shipment."[7]

In the mid-1880s more and more farmers settled the Caldwell area to grow Russian hard winter wheat, and the cattle drives no longer passed through that area. These factors explain why, in 1888, Willie Matthews had to ride alone from Caldwell, Kansas, to Clayton, New Mexico, in order to join a cattle drive moving northward, especially along the Texas–New Mexico–Colorado–Wyoming–Montana trails.

To learn the identity of Willie Matthews was a challenge worthy of research. An examination of the records for the three main Sumner County cemeteries revealed no burials of a Matthews or anyone with a similar surname in either the

Milam, Goodell, or Corzine cemeteries between 1877 and 2000.[8] However, any of the Matthews family members could have been buried in another cemetery of that county. Moreover, considering the rural culture of Kansas in the late nineteenth and early twentieth centuries, it is possible that Willie or her family members, if they died in the area, were interred at home on ranch or farm land.

Data from the U.S. Census should have proved helpful in identifying Willie, but the most important census for her case, that of 1890, was destroyed by fire. The 1880 census provided the following data regarding Matthews families and other families with somewhat similar surname spellings in Sumner County, Kansas:

Jackson Township, Sumner County, Kansas
Simpson B. Mathews, grandfather, age 59, railroad worker, born Ohio
Sarah E. Mathews, grandmother, age 58, born Ohio
Their grandchildren
Warren, grandson, age 9, born Kansas
Emma, granddaughter, age 7, born Kansas

Caldwell, Sumner County, Kansas
A. Mayhew, husband, age 28, born England
L. T. Mayhew, wife, age 23, born Virginia
Five sons, ages 3–10
One daughter, Gyeie, age 1, born Kansas

Sumner County, Kansas
John Matherley, husband, age 38, farmer, no birth information
Elizabeth Matherley, wife, age 31, no birth information
Josephine, daughter, age 13, no birth information
Clara, daughter, age 6, no birth information

Jackson Township, Sumner County, Kansas
James Mathews, husband, age 29, laborer and hay loader, born Indiana
Hanna, wife, age 30, born Ohio
Claud, son, age 10, born Indiana
Luz, daughter, age 4, born Kansas
Maud, daughter, age 2, born Kansas
Glenwood, son, age 1, born Kansas[9]

From the census data, several possibilities exist, if Willie was truthful about her age. If she was nineteen years old in 1888, she would have been born around 1869 or 1870. Yet, according to what Houston recalled her saying, her father did not arrive and settle in Caldwell or Sumner County until the 1870s and did not marry Willie's mother until two or three years later. Assuming that Willie was born about nine months or so after her parent's marriage, that would at best place Willie's birth year in the mid-1870s and perhaps have made her anywhere from twelve to fifteen years old in 1888. The same would generally apply if she had been born out of wed-lock. Samuel Dunn Houston also estimated her weight at about one hundred and twenty pounds, which would have been characteristic of some young but physi-cally mature females twelve years old or older.

One scholar has noted that, other than the trail driver and foremen, of the reg-ular cowboys who made the late-nineteenth-century cattle drives, "about three out of four . . . appear to have first taken the trail between the ages of sixteen and twenty-two. Another twenty percent embarked on their first drive at an older age, while about six percent started younger."[10] Willie Matthews was thus well within the age range of young people making a trail drive for the first time. Even if she ex-aggerated her age in order to appear older than she was, it is possible that she is one of several females listed in the 1880 federal census.

One female in the census was Emma Mathews of the Simpson B. Mathews fam-ily from Jackson Township. In 1888 she was fifteen years old and had a seventeen-year-old brother. In 1880 she was under the care of her grandfather, a railroad worker, and her grandmother. Such an arrangement was not unusual during this time. If Willie's father was the first of his family to settle in Sumner County, perhaps her fraternal grandparents moved there after her father so the grandfather could ob-tain work on the railroad. Still, the 1880 absence of Emma Mathews's parents in the federal census data remains a mystery.

Gyeie Mayhew of the A. Mayhew family from Caldwell is another possibility but a very questionable one. In 1888 Gyeie was only eight or nine years old. Her father, who was born in England, was thirty-six and had no occupation listed. As a young man, Gyeie's father could have been, in Willie's words, "an old trail driver from Southern Texas" and made a cattle drive from South Texas to Caldwell. How-ever, it seems unlikely that an eight- or nine-year-old girl disguised as a boy and without an accompanying family member or close friend could have had the skills that Willie did with responsibilities for the remuda. Moreover, it seems unlikely that the census taker could have mangled the spelling of "Matthews" so badly to list Mayhew instead.

A third choice for identifying Willie comes from Clara Matherley of the John Matherley family of Sumner County. In 1888 Clara was fourteen years old. An-other daughter, Josephine, was twenty-one years old in 1888. In 1880 their father, whose birthplace was not given in the census data, was a farmer who, at a younger age, could have gone on a cattle drive from South Texas and later become a ranch hand in the Caldwell area. Either Clara or Josephine could also have been the elu-sive Willie, but Willie said she told her brother she was going to be away for a week or so, and the Matherley family had no sons listed in the 1880 census. If a son were born following this census, then Willie's brother would have been younger than eight years old. Further complicating matters, as in the case of the Mayhews, the Matherley family surname does not correspond very well with "Matthews."

Finally, there is the James Mathews family of Jackson Township. Daughter Luz would have been twelve, and Maud age ten in 1888, with son Claud age eighteen and Glenwood nine. Their father, although born in Indiana (like A. Mayhew) could also have gone on a cattle drive from South Texas to Caldwell. In 1880 James Mathews was a hay loader, but he too could have changed professions to become a ranch hand. However, although not improbable, both Luz (the more likely candidate of the two Mathews daughters to be Willie) and Maud (like Gyeie Mayhew) would still seem to have been a bit young to travel alone from Caldwell, Kansas, to Clayton, New Mexico, in 1888 as Willie did.

Of course, it is also possible (but rather unlikely) that federal census takers did not include the family of Willie Matthews in their 1880 tabulation for residents in Sumner County. However, an examination of the census count for that county reveals that it seems very thorough (it even includes farm and ranch hands, railroad workers, and other types of laborers). Perhaps, too, the Matthews family did not reside in Sumner County in 1880, but they probably did, if what Willie Matthews told Samuel Dunn Houston was correct about her father living there in the 1870s as well as in 1888.

Other explanations are also possible. After Willie returned home from her trail drive with Houston, perhaps she married and moved to another location. It is possible the Matthews family left Sumner County in search of other opportunities, especially as Willie's father seemed to be a typical ranch hand. The federal government was opening to additional settlement the Cherokee Outlet in present-day Oklahoma, a horse ride of just an hour or less from Caldwell. Thousands of land-hungry pioneers rushed in to establish new homesteads in the area. The Matthews family could easily have been one of those families, or, if she married, Willie and her new husband might have gone there themselves.

In the end, none of the evidence or speculation is enough to verify the identity of the elusive Willie Matthews. And so she must remain the rather unusual young woman and probably the only one on the western frontier who rode astride her horse some two hundred fifty miles to successfully masquerade as a cowboy for nearly four months on a big cattle drive headed north.

NOTES

1. Thomas Ulvan Taylor, *The Chisholm Trail and Other Routes,* 121–22, 124–25, 127–29, 131, 134; Samuel Dunn Houston, "When a Girl Masqueraded as a Cowboy and Spent Four Months on the Trail," 75–77; Jane Graham, interview, July 23, 2003; U.S. Bureau of the Census, 1920, Kansas, vol. 16, enumeration district 92, sheet 4, line 11.

2. Houston, "When a Girl Masqueraded," 74.

3. Ibid., 75–77.

4. Linda Peavy and Ursula Smith, *Frontier Children,* 107.

5. Joyce Gibson Roach, *The Cowgirls,* 15.

6. Samuel Dunn Houston, "A Drive from Texas to North Dakota," 4.

7. Wayne Gard, *The Chisholm Trail*, 190, 211–12, 259.

8. Melvin Shafer and Della Shafer, *Milam Cemetery, Sumner County, Kansas, Tombstone Inscriptions; Tombstone Inscriptions: Goodell Cemetery;* and Elaine Clark, *Corzine Cemetery, Sumner County, Kansas, Tombstone Inscriptions.*

9. U.S. Bureau of the Census, 1880, Sumner County, Kansas, enumeration district 202, 203.

10. B. Byron Price, "Introduction," *Trail Drivers of Texas,* xi.

BEN (BENNIE) McCULLOCH EARL VAN DORN MISKIMON

MRS. WILLIAM ANDREW MISKIMON

James L. Coffey

AMERICANS ARE A GREAT PEOPLE FOR HAVING DREAMS. This is as true now as it was in our past. In the mid-nineteenth century, many boys dreamed of becoming a cowboy. Girls wanted to be a cowboy's sweetheart, and a dauntless few even imagined themselves as a cowgirl. But in those days women were not encouraged to attend school, they did not ride astride, and they certainly would not have been seen in trousers, so those fantasies were best kept under their bonnets. Still, a few, like Bennie Hughes, had the dream and dared to live it. Despite changes in the times and in fortunes, Bennie lived life the way she wanted to, and hers was a remarkable one.

With strong ties back East, her family was well established in Texas. Her parents, John and Emily Trimmier Hughes, moved from South Carolina to Texas in the 1830s. Bennie's mother, Emily, descended from Colonel Obidiah and Lucy Stribling Trimmier, prominent figures in South Carolina both during and after the Revolutionary War. Obidiah was a member of the Cincinnati Society, an organization established by George Washington for war heroes. It was on the Trimmier's porch, family legend has it, that the group that grew to become the Southern Baptists had its start.[1]

John Hughes married Emily Trimmier on December 31, 1839, and eventually moved to Whitesboro, Texas.[2] Initially, the town had little to recommend it. The tiny village, originally known as Warpath, was located about fifteen miles from Sherman, in western Grayson County. In 1861 it could not have been considered much of a boomtown since only fourteen families lived there. The attraction was not the slowly growing town but rather the land—gently rolling plains with live oak motts and grass that fed the buffalo and promised to also feed the new settlers' cattle. Following the precedent established in Texas when it was still part of Mexico, settlers grazed a portion of the land they claimed and farmed the rest. After the Civil War, Whitesboro began to grow and took on a rowdy life of its own. Because so many people, mostly men, came to the area, the few women there were prohibited from going to town on Saturday evenings because shootings were commonplace.[3]

Figure 38.   Bennie Miskimon in sunbonnet on horse. Courtesy of the
West Texas Collection, Angelo State University, San Angelo, Texas.

John Hughes built the first frame house in the county, as if to say, "I am going
to be one of the people who will be here for some time." He divided his time between ranching, growing an orchard, running a mill, and raising a family.[4] Eventually twelve children sat at John and Emily's table, making it clear that the Hughes
family had come to stay.[5]

Grayson County, like much of North and East Texas, was divided over the great political and economic issues of the time, and, when the talking ended, the fighting that became the Civil War began. Grayson County was a staunch Confederate area whose residents fully supported the new state's position on slavery. The bloody prince of the borderlands, William Clark Quantrell, visited Grayson County often, and the area provided a number of volunteer and regular units that were fed into the meat grinder of national madness. At least two of the Hughes sons were old enough to fight: James, born in 1845, and William, born in 1843. An examination of records listing the Confederate units shows a James Hughs (Hughes) serving with Company A of the Texas 34th Cavalry and a William Hughes in Company I of the same unit.[6] While it is conjecture that the Hughes family supplied these two sons to the Confederacy, it definitely provided two names for the little girl born on March 18, 1862, Ben McCulloch Earl Van Dorn Hughes.

Because of his military abilities and adventures, Gen. Ben McCulloch was known throughout Texas for more than a decade. He was a friend of David Crockett, and only a case of measles prevented him from joining Crockett at the Alamo. He scouted and led forces in the Mexican War and later became a U.S. marshal for the eastern district of Texas. His experience as an Indian fighter led him to a prominent position in the Confederate Army, where he was the first general appointed from the civilian ranks. He made a name for himself as a general who believed that his place was in front of his men; McCulloch even acted as a scout to see with his own eyes what the situation held in store for his troops. He was still out in front as a high-ranking scout when he was shot at the battle of Pea Ridge in Arkansas. McCulloch's commanding officer was a watercolor-painting ex-Indian fighter named Earl Van Dorn. Van Dorn had a mixed reputation as a Confederate general. He was eventually shot, not by a Northern soldier, but by a Southern doctor who believed that his wife and the general were involved in adult mischief.

It is possible that John Hughes, hoping that his next child would be male, chose for Emily's newborn baby the names of two prominent Confederate generals with whom his sons had ridden. John showed the same single-mindedness in baby naming that he had shown in homesteading. Once he had an idea, he stuck with it. Thus, in a spasm of patriotism, he named the baby that was born on March 18, 1862, Ben McCulloch Earl Van Dorn Hughes. It apparently made no difference to anyone that the baby was a girl, not a boy. Fortunately, someone in the family shortened that name to Bennie, or Bennie E, and she was known by this nickname for the rest of her life.

The end of the war brought depression and financial hardship. People had little money and little hope. Texas got dragged back into the Union and was occupied by Federal forces, and a generation of young men looked for their future. In a land dominated by agriculture, the financial situation now dictated that economic changes had to occur. Texans needed money and needed it quickly to feed their families and rebuild their lives. The young men began to search for jobs. In the brush country and bottomlands, they found cattle running wild, livestock that had been abandoned by their owners during the war. As one of the early cattlemen described it, they had to find a way to "connect the four dollar cow with the forty dollar market."[7] With no railroad to transport the animals, the solution was simple: A few men on horseback would walk several hundred cattle eight hundred miles or so to the railroads for shipment back East.

The idea of trailing the cattle to market originated in the days of the Spaniards, when the earliest vaqueros trailed cattle to Louisiana. However, "going up the trail" suddenly caught the imagination of several thousand young men in Texas, and they created a new and enduring icon: the American cowboy.

The people in Grayson County heard the stories and watched the herds and cowboys go northward. Bennie Hughes observed the birth of the cowboy and made it her dream. When the Hughes family moved from the treasured frame house out onto the prairie, the fantasy became hers. She and her siblings were dropped into the middle of Texas ranch country, and the expectation was that the children worked. Bennie later recalled that "We had a ranch of 1000 acres on Red and Little Wichita Rivers, and six large farms. We also had access to the open range for cattle and horses to roam."[8]

Bennie loved life on the ranch, especially working with the stock. She was a small girl with long dark hair worn in a knot at the back of her head.[9] For the children, it was a life that demanded much and delivered an equally large portion of good fortune. Bennie experienced a ranching way of life that found its way into novels, and some of her experiences read like something out of Mark Twain. One such incident, involving a fawn, introduced Bennie to the cattle business: "One day during a round-up the cowboys found a fawn . . . [and] they brought it to me. This was my favorite pet. I would sleep and eat with it."[10] Bennie soon discovered that fawns grow up and are not the sweet needy pets they once were. They become deer that love to eat, and this one spent considerable time investigating John Hughes's orchard. John was trying to get started in the produce business, and for a short time he had an orchard poacher.

"One morning father said, 'Ben, I'd like to swap you out of that deer.'"

Ever the trader, Bennie responded the way she must have heard him make a deal a hundred times.

"What have you got?"

He said, "I'll trade you that little speckled heifer for him."

Bennie reasoned that if her papa had the deer, she would still be able to play with her destructive pet, so she struck the deal. Shortly afterward, she was sent away from home for a few days and, upon her return, found that some changes had taken place. First, her former pet had become a quick meal for the family and hired hands, and her heifer had given birth to a calf. "This was how I got my start in the cattle business."[11]

The cattle business was not the only enterprise in which she found herself. Family records do not record the death of her father, John, but Bennie's stories indicate that she began to work and supplement the family finances when she was quite young. In 1871, with the orchard thriving and the half-tame deer no longer a problem, she went into the fruit business. Because the town was growing rapidly, the possibilities for enterprise were extensive. "I was a fruit peddler and I wasn't but nine years old either. . . . I would gather the fruit and carry it to the courthouse." There, she claimed, "Old Judge Harris was my helper. . . . He would help sell it."[12] Still, the idea of the cattle business was never far from her mind. "I kept saving my nickels and dimes and every time I got enough to buy a dogie, I bought, 'cause it took dogies to make cows. I just kept this up until I got a start."[13]

It was all about getting a start. Brother Jack (John) had moved to Stephens County, and there were trips back and forth between the home place in Grayson County and Jack's new ranches in Jack and Stephens counties. Bennie, like other young people of the time, assumed adult responsibilities early in life.

In 1876, at fourteen, Bennie experienced her first trail drive, not north to the railroad markets but southeast to better pastures. She and her sister Betty (Malvina) took part in a short drive to move about four hundred head of stock from Jack County to Stephens County.[14] The trip might have taken only three days, but that was ample time for several cow-herding adventures.

Cattle, like other animals, can remain calm for long periods, or they can be jolted into movement by the most ordinary thing. Too little water, too much water, lightning, the movement of a rattlesnake through the grass stubble, or the quick snap of a dust devil can instantly turn a relatively organized trail drive into chaos. Most likely the thought of a stampede was far from Bennie's mind that morning. "We rode along and began to get hungry. In them days we had to find a place suitable to stop our cattle before we could stop and eat."[15] A single cow can start a stampede—its head jerking around, eyes wide with the shock of a noise or movement that has invaded the morning stillness. When one cow moves, the stock around it also moves and communicates the feeling of unrest to the others. Stampedes rarely happen when they are expected.

"We unmounted our ponies and made a fire and put our coffee in a skillet to parch; it sure was smelling good, I heard a noise, looked up, and yelled, 'Stampede!'"[16]

The movement was so swift that in a moment the morning silence was filled with noise and dust. Everyone knew the herd had to be halted before it scattered into the brush or over the open plains. The only way to stop the herd was to get in front and turn the leaders, gradually forcing the frightened animals into a circle, slowing the rush, and finally bringing them to a standstill.

"We sprang on our horses and galloped around and around until we got them under control."[17] The idea of racing to the front of a panicked herd was an act that gave even veteran cowmen pause, but Bennie and Betty made it. For girls used to riding sidesaddle, the task of working cattle at a high lope was probably not so difficult, but, for an observer, the sight of the young women with skirts whipping in the wind and bonnets flying by the strap as they quirt their horses, stretching to reach the leaders of the run, was a memorable one. However, no one was watching this horserace; no one other than Bennie recorded it in words, and she told the story only rarely.

With the stampede safely stopped, everyone's mind turned back to breakfast. When Bennie described the sight they saw upon their return, she recounted a childhood story in which two stuffed animals tear each other into small pieces. "It was like the old tale, Gingham Dog and Calico Cat; there was no sign of fire, coffee nor skillet left."[18] If the close call with the stampeding cattle had frightened the cowgirl, she gave no sign of it. "The remainder of the journey was very pleasant," Bennie recalled.[19]

Life on the ranch may have been idyllic for children, but the adults constantly struggled to make payments, wrestled with markets that changed abruptly, and coped with weather that seemed to consistently prove difficult. The panic of 1873 showed the interdependence of the economy and the financial institutions on the East Coast, even for people on the Texas frontier. The panic was initiated by the failure of the Jay Cooke firm of investment brokers. Before it was all over, the New York Stock Exchange had closed for ten days, and several major companies were forced to shut down. When credit dried up in a number of states, including Texas, bank failures occurred. The panic cost Texas drovers more than two million dollars.[20]

While some of the smaller ranchers were able to ride out the panic, a number of people who were cattle rich on existing credit went broke. The reality was clear: Ranching meant not just finding water and fighting off outlaws; ranching was also business. This was a cruel awakening for many in Texas. Adults struggled with an increasingly complex business world, and children, protected by their parents, played at being adults.

"I kept adding to my herd, riding the range and cutting out cattle until I had a nice business. When I was seventeen years old, I bought and sold cattle like a man."[21] The literature of the cattle business is replete with stories of cowboys in their late teens working up a herd in this fashion; however, examples of young women following this pattern are very few. To take care of her cattle, Bennie probably ran her stock with that of her brothers, helping on moves to new grazing pastures with water. Nonetheless, life was not all work; she also found time for fun.

The most common form of entertainment on the frontier was dances or "soirees," which were held at a centrally located house. Usually the furniture was moved out to a porch or a shed to allow enough room inside for the dancing. Almost every cow camp had at least one fiddle player, who was sometimes accompanied by a harmonica or guitar player. Pianos and piano players were rare but were found in some locales and added a great deal to the festivities. Dances did not occur often, so, when they did, families attended with all of the children and the hired hands. The merriment lasted far into the night since everyone expected breakfast for the survivors in the morning. Children were generally bundled up in quilts and blankets and placed on pallets laid on the porch, which allowed for another bit of frivolity. Older children frequently moved the babies or traded quilts, so that when early leavers reached home, they might discover that they had picked up the wrong baby when leaving.[22] Bennie loved the dances, especially those held at the home of Jim Loving, a son of pioneer trail driver Oliver Loving.

Bennie grew into a young woman who was easily noticed, regardless of her financial prospects. She was small and thin and had long hair, piercing eyes, and a ready smile. She certainly did not look as tough as cattle work had made her. She loved to dance, and young women who enjoyed dancing with cowboys were at a premium in cattle country.

"We would ride fifteen miles to his house to a dance. The fiddlers would get better all the time and [at] times we would gallop home in early morning."[23] It may have been at one of these events that she met Will Miskimon. William Andrew Miskimon was born in Clinton, Missouri, on April 1, 1859, the son of a general mercantile storeowner.[24] While it is not clear what the attraction was when they met in Jacksboro, it is evident the two young people felt a definite attraction.

While Bennie maintained for years that Will was not a cattleman, there is a persistent family story that he was a horseman who knew and appreciated good horseflesh, and he undoubtedly appreciated the young woman with long hair who rode and traded cattle like a man. It is not known how long the couple courted, but they eventually decided to marry. The exact date of the event is uncertain. Bennie said "When I was nineteen years old I married W. A. Miskimon," which would have been 1880.[25] However, a family document states the wedding occurred January 7, 1883, when she was twenty-one.[26]

After moving to a ranch seventeen miles south of Jacksboro, Bennie and Will went into the cattle business. Will's widowed mother had remarried to a doctor named Kelley, and it is possible that they worked for the Kelleys. They might also have worked either on property they leased or on land that was controlled by Bennie's brother Jack, who ranched in the county.[27] In any event, they could not have picked a worse time to enter the cattle business. Beginning in 1883, the Great Plains and Texas began to experience one of the cyclical periods of summer drought and severe winter weather that plagued the area. The winter of 1885–86 was bitter cold and hit Texas hard. Cattle died by the thousands, and the sale price was dramatically affected. Cattle that had been worth $30 a head were sold for $8–10 each. The bad weather continued, and, by the winter of 1886–1887, many of the major cattle companies had closed, and the cattlemen sold out.[28]

Bennie and Will dug in their heels, intending to wait out the awful run of weather. Business was bad, and even though it was hard to raise cattle, they did have an opportunity to start their family: Alvin Andrew Miskimon was born on October 13, 1883. "We had a mighty hard time, lots of cattle, and dry weather. The severe drought had caused all the water holes to sink and all wells to dry up. I strapped the baby on my back, papoose style, and would walk a mile or two for water. The wild hogs rooted in the low places, and water would come up in small holes. With my baby on my back and a tea cup in my hand I would dip water here and there until I filled my buckets and carry the weary load home."[29]

Bennie developed the attitude that many women on the frontier adopted: They would not be stampeded by adversity. Seeking work off the ranch, Will went as far as Missouri on one occasion, perhaps to sell stock. Although the drought eased somewhat, it became obvious that their future was not going to be realized in Jack County, but Bennie was ready to go. "I didn't stay out of the saddle long. I began riding the range again when my baby (papoose, I called him) was quite small."[30] Bennie and Will pooled their resources, possibly an inheritance from both families, and decided to move to Tom Green County.[31]

Tom Green County was a large area in west central Texas. The county was drawn without a northern border, which resulted in an area spread over sixty thousand square miles from which, over time, sixty-six counties were formed. It marked the northern edge of the Texas Hill Country and the beginning of the plains and was inhabited by Jumano Indians, although the Lords of the Plains, the Comanche, visited it with grim regularity.

Fort Concho was established as a civilizing force in the area and remained the center of military authority. Across from the garrison in an area originally known as "over the river" was a rough-hewn collection of saloons, bordellos, and meager shops. (Cattlemen ran stock in the surrounding open country and "over the river," which gradually became a magnet for enterprising men on both sides of the law.) After several years, technology snaked through the area as barbed wire began to close the open range. This innovation brought with it ownership, frustration, and grief as a region that the drovers had controlled became constrained by wire and law. Disputes cropped up so often that fence cutting became a felony, causing some adjustments in attitude. The last of the big stock gatherings on open grazing land took place in 1886. When the Santa Fe Railroad arrived in 1888, the need to trail the herds to the railroads at Colorado City ended. Civilization had arrived. "Over the River" became Santa Angela, which then became San Angelo, as people and the post office slurred the name to a more Anglicized, yet incorrect, version of the chosen name for the county seat.

Bennie and Will, with help from his parents, decided to stake their future on ranching in West Texas. Along with a baby, five hired hands, a thousand head of cattle, and three hundred horses, Bennie and Will set out to move from Jack County to Tom Green. It is not clear whether their son Alvin was on the trail drive; he may have traveled separately with his grandmother, Mrs. Kelley. Bennie had driven cattle before, but this was the trail drive she would talk about for the rest of her life.

"We started to Tom Green County, September 1, 1889. We had about 1000 head of cattle and 300 head of horses. I had five cowboys to help, as I've said, my husband wasn't no cowman, couldn't ride nor cut out cattle, so he wasn't much help."[32] Despite this rather harsh characterization of Will, family stories relate that he was certainly a horseman. He handled horses well and took the horses for the remuda ahead to await the cattle herd at various points en route. On a drive, cowboys generally used eight to ten horses, allowing for remounts and substitute mounts, which left nearly two hundred horses and a considerable number of cattle to move the two hundred miles.

At the time, Texas was crisscrossed with a number of army trails laid out to provision the outlying garrisons, as well as other trails dating back to the Spanish era. They remained in use for years, and some became the basis for modern highways. Bennie was not very specific with regard to the route the drive took, but a few clues help us to speculate. She mentioned Graham City and a crossing at the Brazos River. One might ask why they trailed west when their destination lay due south of Jacksboro. This was probably to catch the crossing of the Brazos on the old Fort Belknap–Fort Graham road, about ten miles northwest of Graham City. This route would put them on the old supply road between Fort Belknap and Fort Phantom Hill, which led to Fort Griffin. From Fort Griffin there were two routes to the south: One, the old road used by the army to reinforce and supply the southern forts, veered westward; the other was the Butterfield Stage road, which took a slightly more easterly route. The Butterfield route would have taken them down the Clear Fork of the Brazos, affording water and some grazing until they made the long drive across Taylor County to Fort Chadbourne and then on south, crossing Coke County to the west of San Angelo, where the ranch was located.[33] Finding the trail was a lot easier than moving the cattle along it.

Many of the old trail drives could be considered miles measured in misery. This one was no exception. "I had five cowboys to help. We got as far as Graham City when the rain poured down."[34] The downpour slowed an already tedious process to a crawl. "We spent the night there [Graham City] and went on alright. When we neared the Brazos River, I told my husband to see if the river was up too much to cross with the horses."[35] The Brazos had a number of crossings that enabled traffic to cross over safely, but, with the recent rain, not all of them would be safe. After determining that he himself could cross, Will went back to bring Bennie up to get her opinion on whether the cattle could make it to the opposite bank. "He didn't know nothing about cattle," she would say later.[36] It was late in the day, much too late to try to cross the large number of cattle. Will and some of the hands moved the horses across and corralled them on the other side.

Bennie recalled the toll the rain and weather took on the men: "Me and the boys were to hold the cattle. We drove them down to the river and camped with intentions of pushing them across the next morning. The cowboys were from the malarial country and when they got cold and wet they took chills. I got on my horse and logged the wood up, built a fire for the sick boys and made blankets down, the poor boys with high fever and me with the cattle. That was one awful night, trying to hold the cattle with the wolves howling and the panthers and boys sick. I stayed on my horse, rounding the cattle, keeping them down."[37]

For the twenty-seven-year-old cowgirl, the night must have seemed interminable, but it did pass, and in the morning things looked brighter. "The boys were better next morning and pushed the bellowing herd across the swollen stream."[38] They rejoined Will near a shack where he had spent the night with the horse herd. We have no way of knowing how animated the conversation was between the two when Bennie described her night in the rain and Will described his night in the hut. "We got breakfast ready and ate and stood around the fire until we dried out, as we were submerged in the Brazos."[39] After everyone's clothes had dried, they headed south.

The old Butterfield Stage road did not bring them especially close to a town. They were twelve miles south of Throckmorton and ten miles west of Abilene. The country began to change slightly, from the open plains to prairie that was enhanced by low hills and clumps of mesquite and live oak. The farther south they rode, the more open the country became, with heavy buffalo grass and clusters of mesquite and red and shinnery oak. What Bennie's exact role was on the drive is fairly clear from her reminisces. She "cowboyed" on some pretty salty horses, which accounted for one of her slight injuries on the drive. Somewhere along the way she lost her hat and, while chasing cattle through the brush, left hairy reminders of her run. "The boys laughed and told me they could track my route by my hair hanging on the bushes."[40]

Bennie makes no mention of a chuck wagon, so we can only guess about how they ate. It was not unusual for a small outfit to use a "chuck mule," a hardy animal that carried a pack frame piled high with food, cooking utensils, and a heavy cast iron skillet or a dutch oven. Mealtime came about regularly, but the fare was monotonous. Usually they were limited to sourdough bread and coffee, supplemented only rarely with fresh beef and canned goods purchased when passing close to a town.

Bennie's destination was Red Creek, a small collection of settlers and ranches about four miles northeast of San Angelo. When she saw the country, Bennie was impressed: "We came to Red Creek which looked very desirable for camping. There was plenty of water and fresh tall grass."[41] The country was still open in this area, so the cattle business was a very mobile one at that time. Cattle strayed while searching for grass and water, but the cowboys kept them from drifting too far from the central area of the ranch. This changed somewhat when barbed wire went up. The Miskimons now found time for Will to build. In the latter part of 1889 he constructed a house on a town lot in the northern part of San Angelo, which Bennie had picked up herself. "I traded a little old red bull calf for that lot."[42] It looked as though their luck had changed.

What brought the Miskimons to Tom Green County was the grazing land. The state of Texas had appropriated land around the state to support public schools. As settlers poured into the newly opened west, the land was sold, and the funds went into the permanent fund to support schools in each of the many Texas counties. The land Bennie and Will found was on the old San Saba school land grant in the northern part of the county. In June of 1890 Will's mom, Mrs. Kelley, closed a deal for 946 acres on Red Creek in the school land grant.[43] A few short years later, Bennie and Will agreed to take over the note for this acreage, which they did officially in October 1893.[44]

Bennie thought of her father and remembered her family's dreams on their home place back in Grayson County. She realized then that land was the key to survival. In August of 1891, she purchased a tract of 109 acres on Red Creek for $485.75.[45] The land adjoined the original section and a half that Will's mother had purchased the year before. She bought the property in her own name, a habit she followed for the rest of her life. In January of 1893 and October of 1894, she began to buy land in town, not far from the original house Will built. Again she bought it "out of her separate property," meaning that she was the sole owner.[46] While it is impossible to know when the idea came to her, it quickly became apparent that she had her eyes on property that she could rent out. Once cattle or land was sold, it was gone, but rent something and you own it forever. While her eyes were on the future, her primary concern was the ranch.

"Ranching business looked fine, my herd had increased so much and water was plentiful. I bought old man Seymour's cattle and horses in 1893. We had such a great herd I sure 'nough did have to ride, rope and cut out cattle, but they never got too tough for me."[47]

Bennie's love for horses was unmistakable, and she did not back away from riding or breaking them herself. "In that Seymour bunch I bought, I found a frisky little horse. I called him Ned. I put a hacka-more [sic] on his nose and mounted him. He made a paw at the sun and fell backward in the cow disposal that was about knee-deep. It was easy to slide off at the side since I rode a side saddle. I did the same act three times and the fourth was a successful attempt. I rode old Ned until I thought he would fall for punishment. This really made a fine pony."[48]

Bennie, Will, and their son, Alvin, settled into life on the ranch working the cattle and enjoying the new people they met. In the style of ranch folk of that time, people were not turned away if they showed up at dinnertime. "We enjoyed helping cowboys: our house was always open to them. Boiled beef, red beans and good black coffee brought many a cowboy our way. They showed their appreciation by rounding up my cattle any time they found them on the range, and returned them safely."[49]

For Bennie, however, life was changing. She was a witness to the end of an era, the days of the open range. Change came from the new technology and the arrival of the railroads. Barbed wire held the cattle in big pastures, and five men could work the same stock that a few years before might have taken fifteen. The livestock no longer drifted as far south as the Devil's River, so many of the cowboys were laid off during the winter. Since windmills now pumped water, the cattle could be kept in one place. By the winter of 1890, just after Bennie and Will arrived, men looked for jobs just to hold on. Cowboy Ben Mayes was forced to work for a dollar a day, greasing windmills and skinning cattle that had died over the brutal winter. He summed up that experience in one memorable line: "If you never skinned a dead cow, you had better let it alone."[50] This was Bennie's life, for better or for worse, and the "better" part of it was so wrapped up in the "worse" that sometimes it was difficult to tell the difference.

Despite Bennie's optimistic view, the severe weather cycles returned. The years 1892 and 1893 both saw decreasing rain. "I knew something had to be done."[51] In January Bennie had purchased another lot in San Angelo, apparently outright, and while this may not have put a strain on the budget, the dismal cattle business demanded that money be brought in from some other source. "I was pretty much of a business woman, as well as a cow puncher. I really had a credit rating with Dunn and Bradstreet as good as gold. I wrote in and had supplies sent down to open a dress shop. I got my goods on a ninety-day plan and I did a good business."[52] By May 6, 1893, she had transformed herself into "B. E. Miskimon, Fashionable Milliner and Dressmaker," with an added attraction: "Call and see our new styles of Hats."[53] The dresses and hats Bennie sewed and sold provided the income that allowed the ranch to scrape by for another few years. That income was made with the help of San Angelo's well-known "personal services industry."

Prostitution in the Concho Valley was one of the few constant-growth enterprises. Drinking, whoring, and gambling were the primary cultural attractions for the city that for years was known as "the Pearl of the Conchos."[54] Most of the bars, saloons, and male-oriented businesses were focused on a strip along Concho Street, with the majority of brothels located in the one hundred block of West Concho. The ladies were encouraged to stay in that area, and "decent women" did not venture there. The working ladies who wanted fashionable attire contacted Bennie in some way, and she developed a system for taking their orders and delivering the hats. Although a respectable woman could not easily move in and out of the "zone," Bennie found a young African American boy who could.

Using a delivery boy, Bennie "would send pictures and scraps of material like my dresses were, and they would choose what they wanted. The negro [*sic*] boy would fill their order. They bought hats the same way, by pictures."[55] If Bennie was concerned about the source of the dollars, she got over it. "Their money was a good as anyone else's and they had a lot of money. I kept the ranch out of debt and that was my motive."[56]

Bennie's dressmaking ended when the rains came. "I sold my business, and had $500.00 in cash and $300.00 in merchandise that I sold to an Ozona merchant. The drought was over, and our ranch out of debt. I went back to the ranch where I belonged, to roam and ride with the cows and horses."[57] Although the drought was temporarily broken, it became clear that ranching was still in for a hard time.

Easter of 1894 was on March 28, and that date was remembered for many years because of a common and dreaded happening: the late "blue norther." Conventional wisdom in West Texas says that spring has not arrived until the mesquite trees bloom. In 1894, the bony limbs of the mesquite rose into the air as if praying for the warmth of spring, but there was one final visitor. Fueled by gusts of arctic air, the Easter norther tore through the plains country. Thunderstorms turned to sleet and hail and ended the promise of springtime. It also ended the dreams of many ranchers. The storm that tore through the countryside nipped the fruit trees, chilled the bones of the souls caught out in it, and killed cattle with an efficiency more deadly than a slaughterhouse. When spring finally arrived, Bennie and Will looked out at a ranch that had not only seen better days; it also had possibly seen its last days.

"I knew something had to be done."[58] Bennie's response to trouble on the ranch was to go work, so she went back to town. While she worked hard to bring in money, she kept up a steady trade in property and objects, trying to save the ranch and raise their son, Alvin, who was an only child at this time and as such was doted on by his parents. He learned "cowboying" from both of them and worked with his father, Will, who found jobs as a carpenter. He inherited a strong work ethic from his parents. If people didn't work, things didn't happen. Alvin, Bennie was sure, was going to achieve the success that seemed to be eluding them. Will also began to survey, laying out streets and lots for both San Angelo and nearby towns. All of this effort might have paid off except for another unanticipated event.

From late 1894 into 1895 Bennie leased and managed the Nesbitt Hotel.[59] The establishment was in the 100 block of West Harris, very close to the collection of property that Bennie was buying and within a few blocks of the house that Will had built. In January of 1895 she purchased another lot, but fate and biology intervened: Bennie found she was pregnant. She continued to work as long as she could, and their daughter, Dewey, was born in the hotel May 5, 1896.

With the loss of Bennie's income, the joy of a new child was tempered by the July foreclosure on Red Creek Ranch, signaling the end of their ranching dreams. Bennie somehow managed to hold on to the 109 acres she had purchased separately from Red Creek Ranch in 1891, so they still had some land and could continue to keep animals. "After we got established again we began to gather stock around us."[60] While the family was seemingly getting back on its feet, Bennie nearly became a victim of violence, the kind that seems so commonplace today.

It was probably in 1898, when Will was away moving a herd of horses to be sold, perhaps to the army, that Bennie decided to make the ride with him. She accompanied Will as far as Abilene and then returned home. When she arrived at the ranch, it was dark and she was tired.

"I was so tired I lay down on the porch to sleep. Bang! I hear a noise and got up and a man was trying to break in the back door. He knew my husband was gone. I rushed in and got my shot gun. I had no ammunition but bluffed the coward. I went through the house to the back door and [I] knew the old sneak. At the point of my shotgun I told him to get going. He had driven his wagon near my house and put his little girl to sleep under the wagon. He rushed back and put the mules in a high lope. I told him if he stopped before I heard him cross the four-mile hill I would follow him and kill him. He really went over that hill in a hurry."[61] Bennie obviously had a reputation for being a woman of her word.

The first years of the new century found Bennie's life filled with routine daily chores. Will, who continued to work as a surveyor in and around San Angelo, began spending time at the Arc Light Saloon. The Arc Light, a well-known tavern considered by many to be a "model drinking place" was a favorite of his.[62] He enjoyed the life he had and loved cold beer. It has been alleged that some of the twisting streets in San Angelo may have been laid out by Will after one of his visits to Tom McCloskey's establishment. At one time in San Angelo history, citizens made an attempt to set up a local prohibition on liquor. Even though Bennie could not legally vote, she found a way to make certain that her views were known. She gave Will what some called a "quietus pill," a precursor of the modern sleeping pill, which ensured that he slept through the election and did not vote. When later owners of the Arc Light sold the place and the furnishings in it, Bennie bought at least two of the marble-topped tables or bureaus. She commented that it was to be sure that the owners could not change their minds and reopen: no furniture, no saloon.[63]

When she was not trading for property or chasing off attackers, Bennie spent her time mothering Alvin and Dewey. Alvin was her first born and the central figure in what was the greatest tragedy of her life. He developed into a confident young man with good construction skills. Will and Alvin had built houses in San Angelo, and Alvin did fine woodwork. When he was sixteen, he left home to find work and found it building the framing for mines in Mexico.

Alvin was the baby of Bennie's youth. She had carried him on her back to search for water, she had taught him to be the cowboy she had imagined he wanted to be, and she stood aside when he built houses with his father and found his own love in the mines of Mexico and the Southwest. Without a great deal of formal education, Alvin had parlayed his business acumen and hard work into positions that began to bring him prosperity. He started as a mine framer, using the abilities he had acquired with Will to shore up the interior of the mine shafts and provide structure to the crumbling tunnels that snaked under the ground of Mexico and Arizona. He owned partnerships in at least three mines and wanted to get into the gold-assaying business. In an economy built on gold, the person who established the purity of the ore was the final authority; the assayer's decisions determined whether a mine became an investment that would pay off or turn back into merely a hole in the ground.

In a letter to Dewey, Alvin related that he wanted his mama and papa to move to Arizona.[64] On two occasions, possibly in 1903 and 1906, Bennie and Dewey went to Arizona by train and spent most of the summer with him. Alvin was in Bisbee, Arizona, during the first visit, and on the second he was in Globe. He hoped the family would join him in Globe, but his death ended that dream.[65]

Alvin told his family that he had developed a system that would improve the field assaying. He said the process looked promising, and he was prepared to build his future on it. On December 17, 1910, a deadly encounter in an alley in Globe left Alvin and his wife dead and many unanswered questions for the family.

Bennie was deeply affected by Alvin's violent death in the shooting. The baby she called Papoose became not the hero she wanted him to become, but a tragic figure whose final moments remain a mystery. Bennie never accepted the confused and contradictory version of the crime that she was told. She spent time and money trying to determine the exact circumstances surrounding the incident but found no final answer she could live with. Without that explanation, there was no finality for Bennie. She visited Alvin's grave each day for most of the year following his demise. While the tragedy of Alvin's death consumed her, the delight she took in his life gradually gave her new strength, and after a time she got on with her own life.

Bennie's daughter, Dewey, grew up and married a young man named Louis Kleitches from Karpenision, Greece. Louis had lived in a number of places before San Angelo, but it was there he made his home. He met Dewey Miskimon, courted her, and married her on July 31, 1918. Shortly afterward, Bennie, making one last major purchase of land, bought a tract facing what is now Nineteenth Street in San Angelo. She was no longer a rancher, but she did have property scattered all over the county almost in the same way her family had cattle scattered in pastures in years gone by. She spent these years overseeing her rental property.

Her place on Nineteenth Street was special. It was nowhere as big as the homes outside of town, but it gave her and Will a place to keep livestock of some sort

Figure 39.   Bennie and Will Miskimon at home north of
San Angelo. Courtesy of Louise Johnson, Bronte, Texas.

almost until the end of their lives. Here Bennie played out the role that her family
remembers the most, that of grandmother.

Bennie and Will lived with the joy of grandchildren the way many people do—
spoiling them, leaving them with bittersweet memories, and perhaps seeing them
as the link to the future, the ones to take life's dreams farther than they themselves
had. Bennie was famous with her grandchildren for at least three special foods
she made: teacakes, nutmeg-spiced cake, and smothered chicken.[66] While Bennie
cooked, Will delighted in taking the three little girls for rides in a single-horse
buggy, which he later replaced with a Dodge touring car. As they passed through
town, he drove and sang the old outlaw ballads such as "Sam Bass," which recounts
the death of that legendary desperado. The grandchildren, Norma Joe, Melba, and
Louise, recall Bennie singing while she churned butter, softly pounding the dasher
to the rhythm of "After the Ball Is Over" and "Annie Rooney." The cowgirl had
come a long way, and the old days were gone; they had slipped away before anyone could even notice their passing.

It is impossible to say how many old friends visited with the Miskimons in the
quiet days of the 1930s, but the number dwindled each year. If Bennie had regrets
about the ups and downs of her life, she kept them to herself, the way a cowboy
does. "I've had many trials and tribulations, but I own a good country home now
and lots of chickens and stock, four lots in Westland Park, and all the west end of
block P, on West College Avenue. My one daughter, her husband and children are

here with me. I am 'bout as happy as most people of my age. . . . I'm still working hard as a cow man."[67]

For Bennie, the dream of becoming a cattle queen in West Texas was shattered by the demons of reality: drought, debt, and death. She had continued to modify her aspirations as she matured and times changed around her. The big ranch was gone; the small place with chickens, a few goats, and cows remained. She was not herding cattle but managing rental properties instead. While she did not end her life on a ranch surrounded by property and children, her granddaughters inherited her dream and carried it forward. One of them managed to live out the vision of life on a ranch.

Late in life Bennie told of an early morning ride with a favorite horse named Silk Stockings: "We called [him] Silk Stockings, because of his nice stocking legs. The owner of his mother once said, 'She's as fine as split silk.' One morning I wanted to ride [him]. I knew I couldn't mount him by myself. I carried him to the Wagon Yard, for the cowboys to hold while I mounted him. I was riding with my new side saddle, handmade, that cost me near a hundred dollars. When Silk leaped for one of the boys, he threw the hacka-more [sic] at him and it wrapped around my waist, just as I was trying to mount. Well that horse pitched me as high as the courthouse and ran through a fence. He tore my fine saddle into strings. From then on I rode a man's saddle."[68]

Even though Bennie does not mention it, she caught Silk and rode him. From that day on, she may have ridden a man's saddle, but she had done a cowboy's job her whole life. She approached living the way she did her horses. She had to learn to master both of them. Her dreams changed from being the part owner of Red Creek Ranch, to milliner, to landlord, to grandmother, but what remained steadfast was her approach to life. Just like she did with her horses, she had to ride it out or quit. And she never quit on anything.

On February 14, 1940, at the age of seventy-seven, Bennie died of cancer. Her final days were spent in her daughter's home on the land Bennie had purchased fifty years before. Will followed her into death six months later, on August 16, 1941.

NOTES

1. Norma Joe Williams (granddaughter of Bennie Miskimon), "Miskimons," in *Tom Green County: Chronicles of Our Heritage*. Additionally she wrote articles about the family that were published while she was editorial page editor for the *San Angelo Standard Times*.

2. Melba McCormick (granddaughter of Bennie Miskimon), family genealogy.

3. "Whitesboro, Texas," *The New Handbook of Texas Online*.

4. Ruby Mosley, "I'm a Cowgirl: Mrs. Ben McCulloch Earl Van Dorn."

5. Hughes family Bible, 1977. In 1977 Melba McCormick identified the Hughes children

as William Thomas, born June 13, 1843; James, born Oct. 14, 1845; Isabel, born Oct. 14, 1846; Martha, born Jan. 18, 1848; Regina, born Jan. 18, 1851; John William, born Jan. 2, 1852; Melvina, born Dec. 12, 1854; Mary, born Sept. 26, 1856; Sara, born May 28, 1858; Hiram Herschel, born Aug. 31, 1859; Bennie, born Mar. 18, 1862; and Emma, born Dec. 25, 1865.

6. Ron Brothers, "Confederate Soldiers of Northeast Texas." It is unconfirmed that the names in the list are actually the brothers of Bennie Hughes. For a number of the young men listed, no ages or other identifying data are included. The strongest indicators are the spellings of the one name "Hughs," which is the way the family name is spelled in the 1870 census and the fact that both are listed as members of the 34th Volunteer Cavalry Regiment. Perhaps one brother had a better education than the other. Spellings notwithstanding, John Hughes had a strong connection to the war and to two of its leaders. This connection is obvious in the name given to his daughter.

7. "Butler, William G.," *The New Handbook of Texas Online.*

8. Mosley, "I'm a Cowgirl: Mrs. Ben McCulloch Earl Van Dorn," 2.

9. Louise Johnson (granddaughter of Bennie Miskimon), interview with author, San Angelo, Tex., Oct. 10, 2003.

10. Mosley, "I'm a Cowgirl: Mrs. Ben McCulloch Earl Van Dorn," 2.

11. Ibid.

12. Ibid.

13. Ibid.

14. Johnson interview. Louise Johnson identified Betty as the sister who made the drive with Bennie.

15. Mosley, "I'm a Cowgirl: Mrs. Ben McCulloch Earl Van Dorn," 2.

16. Ibid.

17. Ibid

18. Ibid.

19. Ibid.

20. James Cox, ed., *Historical and Biographical Record of the Cattle Industry and the Cattlemen of Texas and Adjacent Territory,* 93.

21. Mosley, "I'm a Cowgirl: Mrs. Ben McCulloch Earl Van Dorn," 2.

22. Ripp Martin, interview with author, Dec. 26, 1973. Ripp was a cowboy and sheriff in Kimble County, Texas.

23. Mosley, "I'm a Cowgirl: Mrs. Ben McCulloch Earl Van Dorn," 3.

24. Williams, "Miskimon," *Tom Green County: Chronicles of Our Heritage.*

25. Mosley, "I'm a Cowgirl: Mrs. Ben McCulloch Earl Van Dorn," 2.

26. Hughes family Bible. It is difficult to reconcile the differences in the two stories. The interview with Ruth Mosley was conducted around 1931, when Bennie was in her seventies, and it is possible that she simply forgot some pertinent information.

27. Johnson, interview. Jack Hughes ranched at a number of locations in Stephens and Jack counties, and it is probable that the young couple moved onto a place owned or leased by Jack while they were learning the cattle business.

28. The winter had an unexpected impact on the world of art. A businessman from Helena, Montana, wrote a neighbor, Jesse Phelps, to inquire about the status of his herd, which was wintering near Phelps's OH Ranch. Phelps wrote back a brief letter and had it illustrated

by a young man who was working on the OH. The drawing, variously called "The Last of the 5,000" and "Waiting for a Chinook," shows a bony steer, tail turned to the wind, waiting for the inevitable end. The steer died, the herd disappeared, and the young man became immortal. Charles Russell became the preeminent interpreter of the cowboy in art during the early twentieth century, based initially on this famous drawing.

29. Mosley, "I'm a Cowgirl: Mrs. Ben McCulloch Earl Van Dorn," 4.

30. Ibid.

31. Johnson, interview, Oct. 10, 2003.

32. Mosley, "I'm a Cowgirl: Mrs. Ben McCulloch Earl Van Dorn," 4.

33. J. W. Williams, *Old Texas Trails*. Williams includes numerous details about the old trails. The folding map that serves as the end piece of the book shows the direction of the Butterfield Stage route and the forts that the Miskimons passed.

34. Mosley, "I'm a Cowgirl: Mrs. Ben McCulloch Earl Van Dorn," 4. Graham City, now known as Graham, was 28–30 miles from the starting point south of Jacksboro.

35. Ibid.

36. Ibid.

37. Ibid.

38. Ibid., 5.

39. Ibid.

40. Ibid.

41. Ibid., 6.

42. Ibid.

43. Tom Green County, land records, book 2, 418.

44. Ibid., confirmed in Johnson, interview.

45. Tom Green County, land records, book 5, 428. In Johnson, interview, Louise Johnson commented that Bennie and Will kept at least part of their money separate.

46. Tom Green County, land records, book 7, 514.

47. Mosley, "I'm a Cowgirl: Mrs. Ben McCulloch Earl Van Dorn," 6.

48. Ibid.

49. Ibid.

50. Ibid., 93.

51. Ibid.

52. Ibid.

53. *San Angelo Standard,* May 6, 1893, 3, col. 9.

54. The story of the San Angelo brothels never has been completely told. An informant told the author that one reason the story remains untold is that several of the ladies married very well "outside of the house" or inherited a great deal of property from their grateful gentlemen friends. The obituary of one lady, "Honey," states that she was carried to her final resting place in 1953 by at least one prominent lawyer and banker.

55. Mosley, "I'm a Cowgirl: Mrs. Ben McCulloch Earl Van Dorn," 7.

56. Ibid.

57. Ibid.

58. Ibid.

59. Williams, "Miskimon," *Tom Green County: Chronicles of Our Heritage.*

60. Mosley, "I'm a Cowgirl: Mrs. Ben McCulloch Earl Van Dorn," 7.

61. Ibid.

62. John A. Loomis, *Texas Ranchman,* 48. Loomis was a wealthy New Yorker who moved to Tom Green County in the 1890s. Jack Spicer, the African American horse breaker, worked for him for many years.

63. Johnson, interview, Oct. 10, 2003.

64. Ibid.; see also Alvin Miskimon, letter to Dewey Miskimon, 1909. Louise Johnson has several letters that her Uncle Alvin wrote to her mother, Dewey, who was then about twelve or thirteen years old.

65. Johnson, interview, Oct. 10, 2003; Alvin Miskimon, letter to Dewey Miskimon, 1909.

66. Norma Joe Williams, "The 19th Street Lot Also Houses Memories," *San Angelo Standard Times,* May 12, 1984. When interviewed in 2003, Louise Johnson told a number of stories about her grandmother Bennie, but one of the funniest was one of the shortest. I asked, "Did she cook anything else?" Her reply came back with a grin, "Nothing you could eat."

67. Mosley, "I'm a Cowgirl: Mrs. Ben McCulloch Earl Van Dorn," 10.

68. Ibid.

Epilogue

THE STORIES PRESENTED IN THIS BOOK describe only a few of the many women on the Texas frontier who worked cattle, drove herds to new pastures, and took livestock up the trail. Future scholars and students will add to the historical record with many more stories about the women of the cattle empire. The well-known Henrietta King of the King Ranch was known as a cattle woman even in her day. She paid off the family debt and expanded the ranching enterprise to make it the premier cattle estate it remains today. Mrs. J. B. Irving of Alpine, Texas, became a member of the Old Trail Drivers Association. On March 11, 1915, the *San Antonio Express News* reported that "she rode over the trails in 1890 with her husband, Joe Irving, going the entire distance in the saddle."[1] Sources also suggest that a Mrs. Lovelady of San Antonio went up the trail. Laura Hoover, a pioneer of Ozona, Texas, told a WPA writer that, when she left Kimble County with her husband and a herd, he thought she could not manage two babies, the team, and her rifle, so he hired a boy to drive the wagon. When the boy put the collars on the team backward, she had him sent back home, knowing that she could successfully manage the team, the babies, and everything else herself. She told of helping her husband with the roundup and the branding.[2] Martha Rabb of the Coastal Bend area was another cattle woman, yet these stories remain untold. The women of Texas were involved in the cattle industry although certainly not in the visible and prominent way of men.

It is difficult to find the Hollywood myth of the romantic cowboy twanging his guitar beside a herd of longhorns in the lives of these women, who were surrounded by cattle. When frontier women went to Hollywood, they became Dale Evans, in need of rescuing, or the pioneer wife and mother in *Little House on the Prairie,* baking bread over a wood stove. These women created their own myths, none of which fit the reality of the Texas cattle women. The new challenges and struggles of the West forced women to adapt the Victorian code of their times to fit a new reality. And some, like Lizzie Williams and Willie Matthews, just plain did not fit. The adventuresome spirit and skills of Willie Matthews, who disguised herself as a cowboy and corralled the remuda for Samuel Dunn Houston, serve as a reminder that some women will always find ways to be more than society expects (and often more than it wants) from its women.

Mary Austin Holley, writing in 1836, stated that living in the "wild country of Texas forms the character of great and daring enterprise" and that "it is not uncommon for ladies to mount their mustangs and hunt with their husbands, and with them to camp out for days."[3] This was certainly true of these women, who bucked the social norms as they lived their lives trailing cattle, whether sitting in a buggy (Mary Bunton), driving a wagon (Molly Bugbee), or riding sidesaddle (Bennie Miskimon). From the fragments of their lives it is clear that for the most part these cattle women were just ordinary frontier women trying to cope with their new reality of the West. They found strength in their faith in God, and none saw their lives as anything special, except perhaps Harriett Cluck, but only when the reporters called and told her she was. However, for those looking back into history, these women validate the importance of ordinary lives. The courage of Margaret Borland endures, and the spunk of Willie Matthews is instilled in each of us. Cornelia Adair's pure delight in viewing the buffalo and Mary Bunton's joy in gazing at the nighttime constellations on the open range offer us new insights into the reality of a woman's view of the West.

NOTES

1. "Milling on the Old Cow Trail," 5.

2. Folkstuff and Range Lore, "Laura Hoover," American Life Histories: Manuscripts from the Federal Writers' Project, 1936–1940, http://memory.loc.gov/ammem (accessed Oct. 25, 2005).

3. Mary Austin Holley, *Texas,* 75.

Contributors

HARRIET L. BISHOP of Canyon Lake, Texas, earned a BS from the College of Agriculture at the University of Arizona. With her husband, who was in the U.S. Air Force, she has traveled all over the world. When he retired to Texas, they settled on a ranch and began raising cattle. She has worked as a medical social worker with the Texas Department of Health and, now retired herself, is researching her family history.

JAMES L. COFFEY holds a BS in education and history and an MEd in counseling. He is an education specialist in gifted and talented education with the Region 15 Educational Service Center in San Angelo, Texas. He is an avid amateur historian, and his writings include "Johanna July" in *Black Cowboys of Texas* and "Tom Three-persons" at www.texancultures.utsa.edu/hiddenhistory.

ANA CAROLINA CASTILLO CRIMM is a native of Mexico City, Mexico, and associate professor of history at Sam Houston State University. She has a BA in history from the University of Miami and a Ph.D. in Mexican Texas–Latin American history from the University of Texas–Austin, with additional studies in historic preservation. She is the author of *De León, a Tejano Family History;* editor of *Cabin Fever: The Roberts-Farris Cabin: A Campus, a Cabin, a Community;* and coauthor of *Turn of the Century Photographs: San Diego, Texas.*

PATRICIA A. DUNN is an education specialist with the Institute of Texan Cultures of the University of Texas–San Antonio, where she works with preservice and inservice teachers on multicultural education and the history and culture of Texas. Patti has a BA in history and an MA in bicultural studies and education from the University of Texas–San Antonio. She has worked as a reading and social studies teacher and as a historical interpreter at the Alamo.

LAURIE M. GUDZIKOWSKI has a BFA in painting and an MA in museum studies. She also holds a certification in modern art from Christie's in London. She is former director of programs at the Institute of Texan Cultures at the University of Texas–San Antonio, where she supervised the research and writing of numerous education specialists while developing exhibits highlighting Texas history and culture.

LISA A. NEELY of Kingsville, Texas, has been an archivist with the King Ranch since 1990. Lisa received a BA from Texas A&I University with specializations in history and English and an MA in history from Texas A&M University–Kingsville. She received the 1995 Graduate Paper Award from the Stormont Lectures on South Texas for "The Kingsville Good Government League, 1945–1949." Additionally, she wrote "Henrietta Chamberlain King: Religious Influences in Her Life and Work." At present she writes a column for the King Ranch quarterly newsletter, *Wellspring.*

MICHAELE THURGOOD HAYNES has worked as curator of history and textiles with the Witte Museum in San Antonio since 1995. She holds a BS in radio, television, and film, an MA in anthropology from the University of Texas–San Antonio, and a Ph.D. in anthropology from the University of Texas–Austin. Her publications include *Dressing Up Debutantes: Pageantry and Glitz in Texas* and "Coronation in San Antonio: Class, Family, and the Individual" in *Celebrations of Identity.*

ALLAN O. KOWNSLAR of San Antonio, Texas, is professor of history at Trinity University and a nationally recognized specialist in social studies curriculum. He received a Ph.D. from Carnegie Mellon University and was a Danforth fellow. He is editor and coauthor of a twenty-one-volume Honors World History Program for the Department of Defense Dependent Schools, as well as secondary textbooks titled *People and Our Worth, Discovering American History, World History: A Story of Progress,* and *The Americans: A New History of the United States.* He is a prolific researcher and author of Texas history, as well as the author of *Texas Iconoclast: Maury Maverick Jr.* and *The European Texans* in the *Texans All* book set.

SARA R. MASSEY is retired from the Institute of Texan Cultures of the University of Texas–San Antonio, where she developed award-winning instructional materials on Texas history. She holds a BS in science from the University of Colorado, an MA in American history from the University of Denver, and an EdD in curriculum and instruction from the University of Northern Colorado. She is the editor of *Black Cowboys of Texas,* winner of the 2000 T. R. Fehrenbach Award, and coauthor of *Turn-of-the-Century Photographs: San Diego.*

PHYLLIS A. MCKENZIE is a research associate with the Institute of Texan Cultures of the University of Texas–San Antonio, with responsibilities for researching and conceptualizing museum exhibits. Her primary area of expertise is Tejano identity and community. She has done extensive work videotaping interviews of migrant families in the South Texas borderlands. Phyllis holds a BA in history and archaeology from Cornell University, an MAT from the University of Idaho, and an MA in museum science from Texas Tech University. She is the author of *The Mexican Texans* from the *Texans All* book set and has presented numerous programs on interpreting controversial heritage and "The Mexican-American Community, 1880–1950."

JOYCE GIBSON ROACH of Keller, Texas, is a grand dame of Texas folklore. She edits anthologies, reviews books, and lectures on a variety of topics, but her passion is writing fiction and nonfiction about Texas and the Southwest. She has a BFA and an MA from Texas Christian University, where she taught in the English department, specializing in the Western novel and life and literature of the Southwest. She is a three-time Spur Award winner from the Western Writers of America, from which she received awards for *The Cowgirls,* "A High-toned Woman" from *Hoein' in the Short Rows,* and "Just as I Am" from *Women of the West.* From the Texas Institute of Letters she received a prize for *Eats: A Folk History of Texas Foods.* She is a fellow of the Texas State Historical Association and a member of the Texas Institute of Letters. In between all of her projects, she volunteers at her grandson's school library and the National Cowgirl Museum and helps work the family ranch in Wise County.

LOU HALSELL RODENBERGER of Baird, Texas, is professor emeritus of English at McMurry University in Abilene. She holds degrees in journalism and English and received a Ph.D. in English and philosophy from Texas A&M University. She is coeditor of *Listen Up: Stories by Texas Women Writers* and editor of *31* by Lawrence Clayton. In 2002 she was a guest at Laura Bush's White House symposium on Women of the West and won the Mrs. Percy Jones Award for her article in the journal of the West Texas Historical Association. Beginning as a society editor with the *Kerrville Times,* she has received numerous honors, including outstanding faculty member at McMurry University.

BRUCE M. SHACKELFORD of Boerne, Texas, is an independent consultant on Texas ranching history and Native Americans of the Southwest. He has designed and written numerous exhibits for museums in Texas, including "Thundering Hooves: Five Centuries of Horse Power in the American West" and "God, Gold, and Glory: The Conquistadores in the Americas," both for the Witte Museum in

San Antonio; and "American Indian Artists: The Avery Collection and the McNay Permanent Collection" for the McNay Art Museum in San Antonio. He holds a BFA from the University of Texas–Austin and an MFA from the University of Oklahoma. He served as curator and director of the Creek Council House Museum in Okmulgee, Oklahoma. As a recognized appraiser of western artifacts, he makes regular appearances on the PBS program *Antiques Roadshow.* His writings include "Bose Ikard" in *Black Cowboys of Texas,* as well as an informative chapter in *Navajo Saddleblankets.*

JAMES M. SMALLWOOD of Gainesville, Texas, is a retired professor of history from Oklahoma State University. With a Ph.D. in history and political science from Texas Tech University, he has published *Time of Hope, Time of Despair: Black Texans during Reconstruction; A Century of Achievement: Blacks in Cook County, Texas;* and *The Indian Texans* in the *Texans All* book set. While he has previously focused his research on African American Texans, he is currently working on *The Unforgiven: Lyndon B. Johnson—Neo-Populist, Southern Dissenter, American Nationalist.*

BILL STEIN of Columbus, Texas, is director and archivist at the Nesbitt Memorial Library. He is founder and editor of the *Nesbitt Memorial Library Journal,* a local history journal, which was published from 1989 to 2001. He is also founder and organizer of the annual Lee Quinn Nesbitt Symposium on Texas history and culture and designer of the Nesbitt Memorial Library's website, which contains thousands of pages of material on local history. His publications include a detailed, chronological history of Colorado County through 1883, serialized as "Consider the Lily: The Ungilded History of Colorado County." An avid scholar of history, Stein has made presentations such as "Colorado County Protects Womanhood: The Murder of Geraldine Kollmann and the Subsequent Lynching of the Accused" at the Stormont Lecture at Victoria College in Victoria, Texas, and "Life in Abasement: Slavery in Colorado County, Texas."

JEAN A. STUNTZ is assistant professor of history at West Texas A&M University in Canyon, Texas. After earning a law degree from Baylor University Law School, Jean went on to receive an MA and a Ph.D. in history from the University of North Texas. She combined her knowledge of the law and history in her thesis, titled "The Persistence of Castilian Law in Frontier Texas: The Legal Status of Women," and her dissertation, titled "His, Hers, and Theirs: Domestic Relations and Marital Property Law in Texas, 1750–1950." She won the H. Bailey Carroll Award from the Texas State Historical Association for the best article in 2001. She has made numerous presentations, including "Women and the Law in San Fernando de Bexar" and "Texas Indians and the Spanish Legal System, 1492–1821."

FRANCES B. VICK of Dallas, Texas, is former director and cofounder of the University of North Texas Press and founder and president of E-Heart Press. She is currently a publishing consultant. She holds a BA and an MA in English from the University of Texas–Austin and Stephen F. Austin State University, respectively, and received an honorary Doctorate of Humane Letters from the University of North Texas. She taught English at Baylor University and Stephen F. Austin State University, among other institutions, before beginning her publishing career. She has published 190 books in her twenty years of publishing. She has written introductions and chapters for *Texas Women Writers* and *The Family Saga,* a Texas Folklore Society publication. In addition, she has contributed articles for the *Alcalde,* the *Dallas Morning News,* and the *Proceedings of the Texas Philosophical Society.*

Bibliography

MANUSCRIPTS AND DOCUMENTS

"Amanda Burks, East to West," Manuscript fragment, n.p., n.d.

Anderson, Viola. Manuscript of interview with Grace Bunce Wilson. Summer 1932. Kearney, Nebr. In possession of Harriet L. Bishop, Canyon Lake, Tex.

Ashley, Linda. Librarian of the General Society of Mayflower Descendants. Letter to Allan O. Kownslar, June 5, 2003.

Bennett, Theresa. "Lizzie E. Johnson Williams: Cattle Queen and Financial Wizard." History 4328: Trans-Mississippi West since 1803. Southwest Collection, Texas Tech University, Denton, Tex., Spring 1977.

Bierman, Mary Margaret. "A History of Victoria, Texas." M.A. thesis, University of Texas–Austin, August 1948.

Borland, Margaret A. Estate. *Victoria County Probate Minutes,* vol. A-3, 396, 430; vol. 4, 108–10, 117–18. Victoria County Courthouse, Victoria, Tex.

Bugbee, Helen Francis. "Story of Thomas Sherman Bugbee and Mary Catherine Dunn Bugbee." Manuscript. 1915. Bugbee File. Panhandle Plains Historical Museum, Canyon, Tex.

Bugbee, Thomas Sherman. Estate. Deceased. Probate will. December term, 1925. County Court, Donley County, Tex.

———. Last will and testament. June 18, 1919. Donley County, Tex.

Bunton, James H. Death certificate. Bureau of Vital Statistics, Texas Dept. of Health, Austin.

Bunton, Mary Taylor. Death certificate. Bureau of Vital Statistics, Texas Dept. of Health, Austin.

Cemetery Marker. Rachael Starlin Perry Hanson. Valley View Cemetery, Garden City, Kans.

Cluck Family Bible Records. Cluck Family File. Georgetown Public Library, Georgetown, Tex.

Comanche County. Deed Records. Office of County Clerk, Comanche County Courthouse, Comanche, Tex.

———. Mark and Brand Records. Book A. Comanche County Courthouse, Comanche, Tex.

———. Tax rolls. 1867–1904. Comanche Public Library, Comanche, Tex.

Compiled Service Records of Confederate Soldiers Who Served in Organizations from the State of Texas. National Archives microfilm publication 323, rolls 45, 48.

Cranfill, J. B. Papers. Center for American History, University of Texas–Austin.

Cunningham, Carrie Holmsley. "Historical Record of the Holmsley Family." Unpublished, c. 1958. Comanche Public Library, Comanche, Texas.

Deed of Sale. Copy executed September 16, 1904, by José J. Martínez Días. Translated by Ricardo Trayas Bazán y Olazábal. Johnson Institute Files. Special Collections, A. Frank Smith Jr. Library, Southwestern University, Georgetown, Tex.

Dobie, Dudley Richard. "The History of Hays County, Texas." M.A. thesis, University of Texas–Austin, 1932. Cited in *Kyle (TX) News,* Apr. 20, 1928.

El Paso and Southwestern Railroad. Transit permit for the corpse of H. G. Williams. July 26, 1914. Johnson Institute Files. Special Collections, A. Frank Smith Jr. Library, Southwestern University, Georgetown, Tex.

Franklin, Louisa. "Letters of William F. Burks." Texas History term paper. Texas A&I University, Kingsville, Tex., 1979.

Hardy, Milton H. Estate. Victoria County probate minutes, vol. 2, 178–89; vol. A, 681; vol. A-2, 68. Victoria County Courthouse, Victoria, Tex.

Hays County. Deed Records. Book 66. Office of County Clerk, Hays County Courthouse, San Marcos, Tex.

———. Mark and Brand Records. Hays County, Book 1, January 26, 1858. Hays County Clerk, Hays County Courthouse, San Marcos, Tex.

Heffernan, John. Estate. Victoria County probate minutes, vol. 3, 199–200. Victoria County Courthouse, Victoria, Tex.

Holmsley, James. Papers. "Essay on Juan Nepomuceno Almonte," n.d. Center for American History, University of Texas–Austin.

———. Military records. Papers. Center for American History, University of Texas–Austin, c. August 1861–April 1862.

———. Promissory notes. Papers. Center for American History, University of Texas–Austin, 1871–1872.

Hughes Family Bible. 1977. In possession of Melba McCormick, Midland, Tex.

Johnson, Miss Lizzie. Teacher certificate. Johnson Institute Files. Special Collections, A. Frank Smith Jr. Library, Southwest University, Georgetown, Tex.

Johnson, John H. Letter of certification for Bachelor of Arts diploma, January 11, 1862. Johnson Institute Files. Special Collections, A. Frank Smith Jr. Library, Southwestern University, Georgetown, Tex.

Mayes, Ben C. "Jack Miles Takes a Bath." In Ben C. Mayes, "The Tom Green County Cowboy." Manuscript, West Texas Collection, Angelo State University, San Angelo, Tex., c. 1941.

———. "The Tom Green County Cowboy." Manuscript, West Texas Collection, Angelo State University, San Angelo, Tex., c. 1941.

McArthur, Daniel Evander. "The Cattle Industry of Texas, 1685–1918." M.A. thesis, University of Texas–Austin, 1918.

McCormick, Melba. Family genealogy. Unpublished manuscript. Copy in possession of Jim Coffey, San Angelo, Tex.

Mullins, Marion Day, comp. "Houston County Texas Tax List: 1838." http://www.rootsweb.com/~txhousto/census/1838taxlist.htm.

Nueces County. Deed Records. Office of County Clerk, Nueces County Courthouse, Corpus Christi, Tex.

Parish, David W. "Cornelia's Worlds: A History of Geneseo, 1850–1900." Unpublished, n. d.

Perry Family Bible. In possession of Max Warlow, Gillette, Wyo.

Perry, Maine. Cemetery Records.

Richter, Esther. "Women in Texas: 1821–1860." M.A. thesis, St. Mary's University, San Antonio, 1943.

Round Rock, Tex. City council minutes, May 11, 2000.

Shelton, Emmett. "Statement concerning Elizabeth E. Johnson Williams." March 30, 1946. Women's Collection, Texas Women's College, Denton, Tex.

Shelton, Mrs. John E. "Statement concerning Elizabeth E. Johnson Williams." File. Center for American History, University of Texas–Austin.

Snyder, Dudley Hiram. Papers. Center for American History, University of Texas–Austin.

Standefer Bible Records, Israel. Standefer Family File. Center for American History, University of Texas–Austin.

Sturcken, Johnye C. "Amanda and William Franklin Burks: A Nueces County Partnership." Literature and Language term paper. East Texas State University, Commerce, Tex., n.d.

———. "Amanda Nite Burks, Willie Baylor Bell, and J. Frank Dobie: A Brush Country Friendship," Literature and Language term paper, East Texas State University, Commerce, Tex., n.d., 1.

Taylor, Thomas Ulvan. Papers. Center for American History, University of Texas–Austin.

Tom Green County. Land records. Books 5, 7, 11. Tom Green County Courthouse, San Angelo, Tex.

Townsend, E. E. Reminiscences of Alpine, Tex. Unpublished. Files of Mody C. Boatright. Copy in Joyce Gibson Roach Papers. Special Collections, Alkek Library, Texas State University, San Marcos, Tex.

Travis County. Mark and Brand Records.

U.S. Bureau of the Census. 1850. Madison County, Tenn.

———. 1860, 1870, 1880, 1900, 1910, 1920. Comanche County, Tex.

———. 1910. Crockett County, Tex.

———. 1850. Denton Count, Tex., 108.

———. 1880. DeWitt County, Tex.

———. 1860. Dripping Springs, Hays County, Tex. San Antonio Public Library, San Antonio.

———. 1860. Hays County, Tex., 11.

———. 1870. Johnson Institute, Hays County, Tex., microfilm, San Antonio Public Library, San Antonio, 10.

———. 1870. Precinct One, Seguin, Guadalupe County, Tex.

———. 1870. Mason County, Tex., 4.

———. 1860, 1870. Palo Pinto County, Tex.

———. 1850. Kent, Pulaski County. Texas State Library and Archives, Austin.

———. 1850, 1880. Travis County, Tex. San Antonio Public Library, San Antonio, Tex.

———. 1920. Population. Kansas. Vol. 16, Enumeration District 92, sheet 4, line 11.

———. 1880. Population. Sumner County, Kans., Enumeration Districts 202, 203.

———. 1850, 1860, 1870, 1880. Victoria County, Tex.

———. 1850, 1860, 1870, 1880. Williamson County, Tex.

———. 1960. Young County, Tex.

Victoria County. Marriage records, vol. 1, 1838–1870. Victoria County Courthouse, Victoria, Tex.

Warner, Phebe Kerrick (niece of Mary Ann Goodnight). "Mary Ann Goodnight." Manuscript. Panhandle-Plains Historical Society, Panhandle-Plains Historical Museum, Canyon, Tex. n.d.

Williams, H. G. Estate. "Deceased Exhibit with Application to Sell." Johnson Institute Files. Special Collections, A. Frank Smith Jr. Library, Southwestern University, Georgetown, Tex.

Williams, Lizzie E. Johnson. Death certificate. Bureau of Vital Statistics, Texas Dept. of Health, Austin.

———. Estate. "Inventory and Appraisement." Probate File 5915, Travis County Court. October 1924. Woman's Collection, Texas Woman's University, Denton.

———. "Memory." Unpublished poem. n.d. Johnson Institute Files. Special Collections, Southwest University, Georgetown, Tex.

Williamson County, Texas. Death records. Book 2, Office of County Clerk, Williamson County Courthouse, Georgetown, Tex.

———. Deed Records. Office of County Clerk, Williamson County Courthouse, Georgetown, Tex., book 14, 451; book 15, 536; book 18, 643; book 24, 36; book 27, 382; book 33, 504; book 34, 145.

———. District court records. Civil case file 1456: *Joel Sutton v. George W. Cluck;* civil cause file 5404: *George W. and Harriett L. Cluck v. Houston and Texas Central Railroad;* civil cause file 5405: *George W. Cluck v. Houston and Texas Central Railroad Company;* civil cause file 5818/5819: *George W. Cluck v. Houston and Texas Central Railroad Company,* including statements of John G. Townes, James A. French, and J. B. Martin. Office of County Clerk, Williamson County Courthouse, Georgetown, Tex.

———. Mark and Brand Records, vol. 1. Office of County Clerk, Williamson County Courthouse, Georgetown, Tex.

———. Tax rolls. 1860, 1861, 1862, 1863, 1864, 1865. Office of County Clerk, Williamson County Courthouse, Georgetown, Tex.

Vandale, Earl. Collection. Center for American History, University of Texas–Austin.

INTERVIEWS AND CORRESPONDENCE

Bishop, Harriet L. (granddaughter of Viola Anderson). Interview by Laurie Gudzikowski. October 10, 2003. Canyon Lake, Tex.

Burks, William F. Letters to Amanda Burks: April 6, 1862; September 10, 1862; October 5, 1862; October 9, 1862; October 26, 1862; December 10, 1862; March 6, 1865; March 19, 1865; March 30, 1865; August 21, 1866; July 22, 1867; November 21, 1868; May 21, 1869; May 25, 1869; June 11, 1869; December 21, 1875. Amanda Burks File, Research Library, Institute of Texan Cultures, San Antonio, Tex.

Britt, William (great-nephew of William and Amanda Burks). Telephone interview by Lisa Neely. August 20, 2003.

Franklin, Louisa (great-great niece of William and Amanda Burks). Interview by Lisa Neely. August 22, 2003. Cotulla, Tex.

Graham, Jane. Interview by Allan Kownslar. July 23, 2003. Frontier Times Museum, Bandera, Tex.

Hagler, Tina. Deputy clerk, Donley County, Tex. Letter to Allan O. Kownslar, May 19, 2003.

Holmsley, T. H. Letter to Mrs. M. Holmsley, Comanche, Tex.; written while Holmsley was in Parral, Chihuahua, Mexico. March 23, 1892. James Holmsley Papers. Center for American History, University of Texas–Austin.

Johnson Institute Files. Letters. Special Collections. A. Frank Smith Jr. Library, Southwestern University, Georgetown, Tex.:

Thomas Johnson (father) to Lizzie Johnson (daughter). February 9, 1860.

William H. Day (suitor) to Lizzie Johnson from Mountain City, Tex. October 4, 1864.

J. H. J. (John Hyde Johnson) to Dear Sister (Lizzie Johnson) from Austin, Texas. October 4, 1866.

J. H. J. (John Hyde Johnson) to Lizzie Johnson. March 5, 1867.

J. H. J. (John Hyde Johnson) to his sister Em (Emma Johnson), from Day's Mills, Montgomery County, Texas, July 6, 1867.

Charlie (C. W. Whitis) to Lizzie Johnson. September 15, 1869.

W. H. Day to Jno H. Johnson from Drover's Cottage, Abilene, Kans. October 14, 1869.

Charlie (C. W. Whitis), from Austin, Tex., to Lizzie E. Johnson at Parson's Seminary, Tex. February 14, 1870.

Lizzie E. J. (Johnson) to Dear Brother (John H. Johnson) from Parson's Seminary. June 26, 1870.

Emma (Johnson) to My Dearest Friend, from Mountain Home, Tex. January 24, 1871.

Charlie (C. W. Whitis) in Austin to Lizzie E. Johnson at Parson's Seminary, Tex. March 3, 1871.

J. H. (John Hyde) Johnson to his sister Lizzie Johnson, from Chattanooga, Tenn. August 16, 1873.

Catharine Johnson to Emma, from Austin. June 23, 1879.

H. G. Williams to Mrs. H. G. Williams from Pueblo, Colorado. September 23, 1884.

Johnson, Louise. Interview by Jim Coffey. October 10, 2003. Bronte, Tex.

Martin, Ripp. Interview by Jim Coffey. Audiotape in possession of Jim Coffey. December 26, 1973. San Angelo, Tex.

Miskimon, Alvin. Letter to Dewey Miskimon. 1909. In possession of Louise Johnson, Bronte, Tex.

Pastor in Comanche, Texas. Letter to Mrs. Holmsley and Mrs. Harris in Fort Worth. May 6, 1898. James Holmsley Papers. Center for American History, University of Texas–Austin.

Schmitt, Cyndie Shelton (granddaughter of Emmett Shelton, who was the nephew of Lizzie E. Johnson Williams). Interview by Sara Massey. October 9, 2003. Austin.

Stavenhagen, Jean. Chair, Donley County Historical Commission, Clarendon, Tex. Letter to Allan O. Kownslar, July 15, 2003.

Stillwell, Hallie. Alpine, Tex. Letter to Joyce Roach, March 12, 1971. Joyce Roach Papers. Special Collections, Alkek Library, Texas State University–San Marcos.

Wilson, Grace Bunce. Letter to Harriet L. Bishop, July 2, 1957.

Wilson, Jesse Harris (granddaughter of Viola Anderson). Interview by Harriet L. Bishop. October 9, 2003.

BOOKS AND ARTICLES

Abbott, Edward Charles ("Teddy Blue"), and Helena Huntington Smith. *We Pointed Them North: Recollections of a Cowpuncher.* New York: Farrar and Rinehart, 1939.

Abbott, Shirley. *Womenfolks: Growing Up Down South.* New York: Ticknor and Fields, 1985.

Acheson, Sam. "C. C. Slaughter Helped Create City." *Dallas Morning News* (July 15, 1966).

Adair, Cornelia. *My Diary: August 30th to November 5, 1874.* Austin: University of Texas Press, 1965.

Adams, Ramon F. *Come and Get It: The Story of the Old Cowboy Cook.* Norman: University of Oklahoma Press, 1952.

Alley, Jack. "Fifty-four Years of Pioneering on the Plains of Texas." *Lubbock Daily Journal,* various issues, 1932.

Allison, Julie. "Preserving Spirit of Chisholm Trail: Pioneer Woman Remembered by Family and Community." *Round Rock Leader* (June 12, 2000), Section C, 1.

American Indians: The Reservations. Alexandria, Va.: Time Life Books, 1995.

Anderson, Adrian, Ralph A. Wooster, Arnoldo De León, William C. Hardt, and Ruthe Winegarten. *Texas and Texans.* Columbus, Ohio: Glencoe/McGraw-Hill, 2003.

Baker, D. W. C. "The Yellow Fever in Texas in 1867." In *A Texas Scrap-book, Made Up of the History, Biography, and Miscellany of Texas and Its People.* 1875. Reprint, Austin: Texas State Historical Association, 1991.

———. *History of Travis County and Austin, 1839–1899.* Waco: Texian Press, 1963.

Baker, Peggy M. "A Woman of Valor: Elizabeth Warren of Plymouth Colony." *Mayflower Quarterly* 69(2) (June 2003): 214–19.

Ballard, C. F. *The Family History and Genealogy of Cecil Raymond Ballard and Maurice (Bradford) Ballard, 1734–1975.* Seguin, Tex.: Country Printer, 1979.

Barkley, Mary Starr. *A History of Central Texas.* Austin: Austin Printing Co., 1970.

———. *History of Travis County and Austin, 1839–1899.* Waco: Texian Press, 1963.

Barnes, Lorraine. "Aged Central Texas Woman, Once a Fighter of Indians, Reads Tales of Adventure." *Austin Statesman* (April 15, 1931), 1, 13.

Bauer, Grace. *Bee County Centennial, 1858–1958.* Beeville, Tex.: Bee County Centennial, 1958.

Biographical Directory of the Texan Conventions and Congresses 1832–1845. Austin: Book Exchange, 1941.

Bloomingdale's Catalog. N.p., 1886.

Botkin, B. A., ed. *A Treasury of Western Folklore,* rev. ed. New York: Crown, 1975.

Bridges, Clarence Allen. *History of Denton, Texas, from Its Beginning to 1960.* Waco: Texian Press, 1978.

Brown, Dee. *The Gentle Tamers: Women of the Old Wild West.* Lincoln: University of Nebraska Press, 1958.

———, and Martin F. Schmitt. *Trail Driving Days.* New York: Scribner, 1952.

Brown, John Henry. *Indian Wars and Pioneers of Texas.* Austin: State House Press, 1988.

Browning, James A., and Janice B. McCravy. *A Complete Guide to Hunter's Frontier Times.* Austin: Eakin Press, 2000.

Brownlow, Kevin. *The War, the West, and the Wilderness.* New York: Knopf, 1979.

Bunton, Mary Taylor. *A Bride on the Old Chisholm Trail in 1886.* San Antonio: Naylor, 1939.

Burks, Mrs. A. "A Woman Trail Driver." In *The Trail Drivers of Texas.* Vol. 2: 1920–1923, compiled and edited by J. Marvin Hunter. 1924. Reprint, New York: Argosy-Antiquarian, 1963.

"Burks, William Franklin." *New Encyclopedia of Texas,* vol. 4. Dallas: Texas Development Bureau, 1931.

Burnet, Georgellen. *We Just Toughed It Out: Women in the Llano Estacado.* Southwest Studies Series 90. El Paso: Texas Western Press, 1990.

Burns, Mamie Sypert. *This I Can Leave You: A Woman's Days on the Pitchfork Ranch.* College Station: Texas A&M University Press, 1986.

Burton, Harley True. "A History of the JA Ranch." *Southwestern Historical Quarterly* 30(2) (Oct. 1927): 105–108.

"C. C. Slaughter." *Cattleman* 45 (March 1959): 13–14.

Campbell, Heather Green. "The Yellow Pestilence: A Comparative Study of the 1853 Yellow Fever Epidemic in New Orleans and the Galveston, Texas, Scourge of 1867." *East Texas Historical Journal* 37(1) (1999): 23–28.

Campbell, Lizzie. "Katherine De Lorme." *Frank Leslie's Illustrated Newspaper* 592 (February 2, 1867): 317.

Campbell, Randolph B. *Gone to Texas: A History of the Lone Star State.* New York: Oxford University Press, 2003.

Cardiff, Irma Brown. "Cedar Park Woman Tells of Adventures of Early Texas Days." *Austin Sunday American–Statesman* (October 9, 1932).

Carroll, H. Bailey, and Milton R. Gutsch. *Texas History Theses: 1893–1951:* A Checklist of the Theses and Dissertations relating to Texas History Accepted at the University of Texas. Austin: Texas Historical Association, 1955.

Cashion, Ty. *A Texas Frontier: The Clear Fork Country and Fort Griffin, 1849–1887.* Norman: University of Oklahoma Press, 1996.

Catlin, George. *Letters and Notes on the Manners, Customs, and Conditions of the North American Indians,* vol. 2, letter no. 41 (The Great Comanche Village). New York: Dover, 1973, 53–56.

Cattleman. Obituaries. 43(9) (February 1946): 77–78.

"Celebrate Golden Anniversary Here: Children and Relatives Gather in Honor of the Fiftieth Wedding Anniversary of Mr. and Mrs. T. S. Bugbee Today." *Clarendon News* (August 17, 1922).

Clark, Elaine. *Corzine Cemetery, Sumner County, Kansas, Tombstone Inscriptions.* Wellington, Kans.: Chisholm Trail and Genealogy Center, 2000.

Clarke, Mary Whatley. *A Century of Cow Business: The History of the Texas and Southwestern Cattle Raisers Association.* Fort Worth: Evans Press, 1976.

———. *The Slaughter Ranches and Their Makers.* Austin: Jenkins, 1979.

———. "When Willie Matthews Went up the Trail." *Cattleman* 45(12) (May 1959).

Clark, Sarah Wood. "Beautiful Daring Western Girls: Women of the Wild West Shows" (1985; reprint, Cody, Wyo.: Buffalo Bill Historical Center, 1991). Booklet.

Clayton, Lawrence. *Contemporary Ranches of Texas.* Austin: University of Texas Press, 2001.

Coffey, Jim. "Johanna July: A Horse-breaking Woman." In *Black Cowboys of Texas,* edited by Sara R. Massey. College Station: Texas A&M University Press, 2000, 73–84.

Cox, James, ed. *Historical and Biographical Record of the Cattle Industry and the Cattlemen of Texas and Adjacent Territory.* 2 vols. 1894. Reprint, New York: Antiquarian Press, 1959.

Cranfill, J. B. "Mind My Babies and I'll Fight These Rustlers: That's Cry of Texas Woman on Chisholm Trail." *Dallas Morning News* (April 25, 1937).

Comanche Chief (May 28, 1881).

Comanche Chief (March 1933), 5.

Crawford, Ann Fears, and Crystal Sasse Ragsdale. *Women in Texas: Their Lives, Their Experiences, Their Accomplishments.* Burnet, Tex.: Eakin Press, 1982.

———. *Texas Women: Frontier to Future.* Austin: State House Press, 1998.

Crimm, Ana Carolina Castillo. *De Leon: A Tejano Family History.* Austin: University of Texas Press, 2004.

———. "Mathew 'Bones' Hooks: A Pioneer of Honor." In *Black Cowboys of Texas,* edited by Sara R. Massey. College Station: Texas A&M University Press, 2000, 219–46.

Cross, Cora Melton. "Early Texas Cattle Industry." *Frontier Times* 5 (September 1928): 476–81, 486.

———. "J. B. Slaughter, of Post, Travels Last Long Trail." *Frontier Times* 6(5) (February 1929): 194–97.

———. "William B. Slaughter, Trail Driver of 1866." *Frontier Times* 6(11) (August 1929): 465–69.

Cruz, Gilberto Rafael, and James Arthur Irby. *Texas Bibliography: A Manual on History Research Materials.* Austin: Eakin Press, 1982.

Dale, Edward Everett. *Frontier Ways: Sketches of Life in the Old West.* Austin: University of Texas Press, 1959.

———. *The Range Cattle Industry: Ranching on the Great Plains from 1865 to 1925.* Norman: University of Oklahoma Press, 1960.

Dallas Morning News (July 15, 1966).

Dary, David. *Cowboy Culture: A Saga of Five Centuries.* New York: Knopf, 1981.

Davis, Graham. *Land! Irish Pioneers in Mexican and Revolutionary Texas.* College Station: Texas A&M University Press, 2002.

Davis, William C. *The Civil War: Brother against Brother.* Alexandria, Va.: Time Life Books, 1983.

"Death Takes Woman Who Managed Ranch for Half Century." *Cotulla Record* (September 18, 1931).

Dellagana, W. A. Letter to Alma Miles. April 11, 1900. Reprinted in *San Angelo Times* (May 5, 1900).

Dobie, J. Frank. *Coronado's Children.* Austin: University of Texas Press, 1978.

———. *Cow People.* Austin: University of Texas Press, 1964.

———. *The Mustangs.* Boston: Little, Brown, 1952.

———. *Some Part of Myself.* Boston: Little, Brown, 1967

Dorchester, E. D. *Trails Made and Routes Used by the Fourth U.S. Cavalry under Command of General R. S. MacKenzie in Its Operations against Hostile Indians in Texas.* Freeport, Tex., 1927.

Douglas, C. L. *Cattle Kings of Texas.* 1939, 1968. Reprint, Austin: State House Press, 1989.

Doyle, D. K. "Mrs. Holmsley Went up the Chisholm Trail." *Frontier Times* 4(10) (July 1927).

Dubbs, Emanuel. *Pioneer Days in the Southwest from 1850 to 1879: Thrilling Descriptions of Buffalo Hunting, Indian Fighting and Massacres, Cowboy Life and Home Building.* Guthrie, Okla.: State Capital Company, 1909.

Dunham, Curtis. "La Salle Woman Queen of Trail Drivers." *Cotulla Record* (June 16, 1923).

Early, Dudley. "Austin Woman Recalls Chisholm Trail." *Frontier Times* 27(2) (November 1948): 83.

"Early Settlers' History in Brief: Some Early Day History in an Appreciation of Mr. and Mrs. T. S. Bugbee." *Clarendon News* (August 17, 1922).

"East to West: Reminiscences of Mrs. Amanda Burks, Pioneer Woman and One of La Salle's Largest Ranch Owners." *Cotulla Record* (May 3, 1924).

"El Camino Real to Duval County." *El Mesteño* 5(1) (Winter/Spring 2002).

Elliott, Claude. *Theses on Texas History.* Austin: Texas State Historical Association, 1955.

Emmons, David M. "Constructed Province: History and the Making of the Last American West." *Western Historical Quarterly* 25(4) (Winter 1994): 437–59.

Exley, Jo Ella Powell. *Texas Tears and Texas Sunshine: Voices of Frontier Women.* College Station: Texas A&M University Press, 1985.

Ezell, Camp. *Historical Story of Bee County, Texas.* Beeville: Beeville Publishing, 1973.

Fehrenbach, T. R. *Lone Star: A History of Texas and the Texans.* New York: American Legion Press, 1983.

Flanagan, Sue. *Trailing the Longhorns: A Century Later.* Austin: Madrona Press, 1974.

Flannery, John Brendan. *The Irish Texans,* 2d ed. San Antonio: Institute of Texan Cultures, 1995.

Forbis, William H. *The Cowboys.* Rev. ed. Alexandria, Va.: Time Life Books, 1978.

Foster, Pearl O'Donnell. *Trek to Texas.* Fort Worth: Branch-Smith, 1966.

Fox, Lorena Eillyer. "Hattie Standefer Cluck." In *A Legend Collection,* edited by Ellen Seals. Austin: Anderson Mills Gardeners, 1981, 43–44.

Gard, Wayne. *The Chisholm Trail.* Norman: University of Oklahoma Press, 1954.

Garden City (Kans.) *Telegram* (April 3, 1999).

Garrett, E. "Two Years after Death: School Teacher Amassed Fortune" [Austin newspaper, 1926?]. Elizabeth Johnson File. Center for American History, Austin.

Givens, Murphy. "A Wool-buying Town: Texas' Biggest Wool Market Was Concentrated on Chaparral." *Corpus Christi Caller-Times* (September 3, 2003).

Gordon, Clarence W. "Report on Cattle, Sheep, and Swine, Supplementary to Enumeration of Live Stock on Farms in 1880." *Report on the Productions of Agriculture: Tenth Census,* vol. 3. Washington, D.C.: Department of the Interior, 1881. Excerpt in David Dary, *Cowboy Culture: A Saga of Five Centuries.* New York: Knopf, 1981.

Graham Leader (February 16, 1877).

Grimes, Roy, ed. *300 Years in Victoria County.* Victoria, Tex.: Victoria Advocate Publishing, 1968.

Guide to Spanish and Mexican Land Grants in South Texas. Austin: General Land Office, 1988.

Guimarin, Spencer. "The Rise and Fall of a Town." Paper submitted for History 121, Southwest Texas State Teachers College, San Marcos, Tex. From "Hays City—Fact or Fiasco." *Wimberly Mill* 3(14–16) (January 1969, February 1969, March 1969).

Haley, J. Evetts. *Charles Goodnight: Cowman and Plainsman.* 1936. Reprint, Norman: University of Oklahoma Press, 1949.

————. *George W. Littlefield: Texan.* Norman: University of Oklahoma, 1943.

————. "Historic Saddle Is Saved," *Cattleman* 13 (Jan. 1927): 30.

————. *The XIT Ranch of Texas and the Early Days of the Llano Estacado.* Norman: University of Oklahoma Press, 1953.

Hall, Martin Hardwick. *The Confederate Army of New Mexico.* Austin: Presidial Press, 1978.

Hamner, Laura Vernon. *No-gun Man of Texas: A Century of Achievement, 1835–1929.* Amarillo: Self-published, 1935.

————. *Short Grass and Longhorns.* Norman: University of Oklahoma Press, 1943.

Handbook of Victoria County. Austin: Texas State Historical Association, 1990.

Harris, William Foster. The Look of the Old West. New York: Viking, 1955.

"Haunted House." *Frank Leslie's Illustrated Newspaper* (February 9, 1867).

Hawkins, T. T. "When George Saunders Made a Bluff Stick." In J. Marvin Hunter, *Trail Drivers of Texas.* Austin: University of Texas Press, 1985, 390–96.

Haxton, Annie Arnoux. *Signers of the Mayflower Compact.* Baltimore: Genealogical Publishing Co., 1968.

Hébert, Rachel Bluntzer. *The Forgotten Colony: San Patricio de Hibernia: The History, the People, and the Legends of the Irish Colony of McMullen-McGloin.* Burnet, Tex.: Eakin Press, 1981.

Heritage Division of Comanche County, Texas. *Patchwork of Memories: Historical Sketches of Comanche County, Texas.* Brownwood, Tex.: Banner, 1976.

Hill, Robert T. "No Cowboy Was Ever Caught Wearing a Nightie." *Dallas Morning News* (August 28, 1932), section 4, 2.

————. "Prof. Johnson Removed Youth from Temptation." *Austin Daily Tribune* (June 14, 1941).

Holden, W. C. *Espuela Land and Cattle Company.* Austin: Texas State Historical Association, 1970.

————. "First Settlers at Jacksboro." *Frontier Times* 9(4) (January 1932).

Holley, Mary Austin. *Texas.* 1836. Reprint, Austin: Steck, 1935. Excerpt in David Dary, *Cowboy Culture: A Saga of Five Centuries.* New York: Knopf, 1981.

Houston, Samuel Dunn. "A Drive from Texas to North Dakota." *Frontier Times* 3(7) (April 1926).

————. "A Trying Trip Alone through the Wilderness." *Frontier Times* 1(6) (March 1924).

————. "When a Girl Masqueraded as a Cowboy and Spent Four Months on the Trail." In *The Trail Drivers of Texas.* Vol. 2: 1920–1923, compiled and edited by J. Marvin Hunter. 1924. Reprint, Austin: University of Texas Press, 1985, 75–77.

Hunter, J. Marvin. "Drank the Blood of a Lobo Wolf." *Frontier Times* 15(8) (May 1933).

————. "Mrs. Goodnight's Saddle." *Frontier Times* 4 (January 1917): 8.

————, comp. and ed. *The Trail Drivers of Texas.* Nashville: Cokesbury Press, 1925.

————, comp. and ed. *The Trail Drivers of Texas.* 2 vols. 1924. Reprint, New York: Argosy-Antiquarian, 1963.

————, comp. and ed. *The Trail Drivers of Texas.* Austin: University of Texas Press, 1985.

Hunter, Lillie Mae. *The Book of Years: A History of Dallas and Hartley Counties.* Hereford, Tex.: Pioneer Book Publishers, 1969.

Irwin, Mary Ann, and James Brooks, eds. *Women and Gender in the American West.* Albuquerque: University of New Mexico Press, 2004.

"J. M. (Monty) East, Native Texan, Won 'North of 36' for Houston; Has Been Picturesque Figure in Films." *Houston Chronicle* (September 7, 1924).

Jenkins, John Holland. *Cracker Barrel Chronicles: A Bibliography of Texas Town and County Histories.* Austin: Pemberton Press, 1965.

———, ed., *Recollections of Early Texas: The Memoirs of John Holland Jenkins.* Austin: University of Texas Press, 1958.

Jensen, Joan M., and Darlis A. Miller. "The Gentle Tamers Revisited: New Approaches to the History of Women in the American West." *Pacific Historical Review* 40(2) (1980). Reprinted in Mary Ann Irwin and James F. Brooks, eds. *Women and Gender in the American West.* Albuquerque: University of New Mexico Press, 2004, 9–36.

Johnson, Susan Lee. "'A Memory Sweet to Soldiers': The Significance of Gender in the History of the 'American West.'" *Western Historical Quarterly* 24(4) (November 1993): 495–517.

Jordan, Terry G. *North American Cattle-ranching Frontiers: Origins, Diffusion, and Differentiation.* Albuquerque: University of New Mexico Press, 1993.

Journals of the Convention Assembled at the City of Austin on the Fourth of July, 1845, for the Purpose of Framing a Constitution for the State of Texas. 1845. Facsimile reprint, Austin: Hart Graphics, 1974.

"Juan Rodriguez Kills Big Panther on La Motta Ranch." *Cotulla Record* (December 6, 1922).

Kane, Joseph Nathan. *Facts about the Presidents.* New York: H. W. Wilson, 1993.

"Kate Medlin's Story." *Los Angeles Times* (January 6, 1907).

Kavanaugh, Thomas. *Political Power and Political Organization of Comanche Politics, 1786–1875.* Ph.D. diss., University of New Mexico, Albuquerque, 1986. Cited in Linda Pelon and Tabbe Pete, "Comanche Women: Power and Influence," http://www.web-access.net/~hdo/features/women.htm.

Kelly, Leo. "Up the Trail in '76: The Journal of Lewis Warren Neatherlin." *Chronicles of Oklahoma* 66(1) (September 1988): 22–51.

Kenner, Charles. "The Origins of the 'Goodnight' Trail Reconsidered." *Southwestern Historical Quarterly* 77(3) (January 1974): 390–94.

King, C. Richard. "Margaret Borland." *Texana* 10 (1972): 321–25.

King, Dick. "The Businesswoman of Comanche County." *Cattleman* 65(4) (September 1978): 48, 54.

———. "Two Austin Women and the Chisholm Trail." *Cattleman* 62(6) (November 1975): 562–70.

King, Evelyn. *Women on the Cattle Trail and in the Roundup.* College Station, Tex: Brazos Corral of the Westerners, 1983.

"Lady Inez, or the Passion Flower, an American Romance." *Frank Leslie's Illustrated Newspaper* (January 12, 1867).

Lamar, Howard R., ed. *The New Encyclopedia of the American West.* London: Yale University Press, 1998.

Lanning, Jim, and Judy Lanning, eds. *Texas Cowboys: Memories of the Early Days.* College Station: Texas A&M University Press, 1984, 210–17.

Larson, Charles P. "The Children of Pocahontas." In *American Indian Fiction.* Albuquerque: University of New Mexico Press, 1978, 17–33.

Lea, Tom. *The King Ranch.* 2 vols. Boston: Little, Brown, 1957.

Lewis, Willie Newbury. *Between Sun and Sod: An Informal History of the Texas Panhandle.* College Station: Texas A&M University Press, 1976.

"Local Deaths: Mrs. Lizzie E. Williams." *Austin American* (October 10, 1924), 2.

Lodge, Henry Cabot. "Cross-country Riding in America." *Century* 32 (July 1886), http://cdl.library.cornell.edu.

Loomis, John A. *Texas Ranchman.* Chadron, Nebr.: Fur Press, 1982.

Luchetti, Cathy, and Carol Olwell. *Women of the West.* New York: Orion Books, 1982.

Ludeman, Annette Martin. *A History of La Salle County: South Texas Brush Country, 1856–1975.* Quanah, Tex.: Nortex Press, 1975.

Madray, Mrs. I. C. *A History of Bee County.* Beeville, Tex.: Bee-Picayune, 1939.

Malone, Ann Patton. *Women on the Texas Frontier: A Cross-cultural Perspective.* El Paso: Texas Western University Press, 1983.

Maret, Elizabeth. *Women of the Range: Women's Roles in the Texas Beef Cattle Industry.* College Station: Texas A&M University Press, 1993.

Massey, Sara R. "The Other Cowboys." *Insight.* Newsletter of the Educational Service, Texas State Historical Association 11 (Winter 1997–1998), 2.

Masterson, V. V. *The Katy Railroad and the Last Frontier.* Norman: University of Oklahoma Press, 1952.

Matthews, Sallie Reynolds. *Interwoven: A Pioneer Chronicle.* 1936. Reprint, College Station: Texas A&M University Press, 1993.

McBeth, Harry Leon. *Texas Baptists: A Sesquicentennial History.* Dallas: Baptistway Press, 1998.

McDaniel, Marylou, ed. *God, Grass, and Grit: History of the Sherman County Trade Area,* 2 vols. (1945; reprint, Hereford, Tex.: Pioneer Book Publishers, 1971; Seagraves, Tex.: Pioneer Book Publishers, 1975).

McMurtry, Larry. *In a Narrow Grave.* 1968. Reprint, New York: Touchstone Press, 2001.

McWhiney, Grady, and Forrest McDonald. "Celtic Origins of Southern Herding Practices." *Journal of Southern History* 41 (1985).

Menn, Alfred E. "She Was a Pioneer." *Farm and Ranch* 54(12) (June 15, 1935), 28.

Miles, Mrs. Jack. "Folkstuff and Range Lore." American Life Histories: Manuscripts from the Federal Writers' Project, 1936–1940. Library of Congress Online, http://memory.loc.gov/ammem, s.v. "Mrs. Jack Miles." Also in *Texas Cowboys: Memories of the Early Days,* edited by Jim Lanning and Judy Lanning. College Station: Texas A&M Press, 1984, 210–17.

"Milling on the Old Cow Trail." *San Antonio Express News* (March 11, 1915), 5.

Monday, Jane Clements, and Betty Bailey Colley. *Voices from the Wild Horse Desert: The Vaquero Families of the King and Kenedy Ranches.* Austin: University of Texas Press, 1997.

Moneyhon, Carl. *Republicanism in Reconstruction Texas.* College Station: Texas A&M University Press, 1980.

Moreley, Agnes. *No Life for a Lady.* Boston: Houghton Mifflin, 1941.

Morris, Leopold. *Pictorial History of Victoria and Victoria County: Where the History of Texas Begins.* San Antonio: Clemens, 1953.

Mosley, Ruby. "I'm a Cowgirl: Mrs. Ben McCulloch Earl Van Dorn." American Life Histories: Manuscripts from the Federal Writers Project 1936–1940, http://memory.loc.gov/ammem/, s.v. "Ruby Mosley." Also in *Texas Cowboys: Memories of the Early Days,* edited by Jim Lanning and Judy Lanning. College Station: Texas A&M Press, 1984, 199–205.

"Mrs. Araminta Holmsley." Obituary. *Cattleman* 19(11) (April 1933): 27.

"Mrs. Harriet Cluck Dead." *Williamson County Sun* (March 4, 1938), 5.

"Mrs. Jack Miles Rites Set." *San Angelo Standard Times* (July 30, 1958).

"Mrs. Kreisle Passed Away Friday Night." *Victoria* (Texas) *Advocate* (Mar. 31, 1929).

"Mrs. Minta Holmsley Buried at Oakwood." *Comanche Chief* (March 10, 1933).

"Mrs. T. S. Bugbee Dead at Home." *Clarendon News* (December 20, 1928).

Murrah, David J. *C. C. Slaughter: Rancher, Banker, Baptist* (Austin: University of Texas Press, 1981).

Myres, Cindi. "Pioneer Cattle Queens Rode the Trail." *Cattleman* (September 1995): 100–104.

Myres, Sandra L. "The Ranching Frontier: Spanish Institutional Background of the Plains Cattle Industry." In *Essays on the American West,* edited by Harold M. Hollingsworth and Sandra L. Myres. Austin: University of Texas Press, 1969, 19–39.

Nunn, Annie Dyer. "The Dyer Brothers, Leigh and Walter." In *Randall County Story,* compiled by Mrs. Clyde W. Warwick. Hereford, Tex.: Pioneer Book Publishers, 1969.

———. "She Saved the Buffaloes." Unknown newspaper, n.d., section 7, 2, 8.

Oberste, William H. *Texas Irish Empresarios and Their Colonies: Power and Hewetson, McMullen and McGloin.* Austin: Von Boeckmann-Jones, 1953.

O'Connor, Louise. "Henrietta Williams Foster, 'Aunt Rittie,'" In *Black Cowboys of Texas,* edited by Sara R. Massey. College Station: Texas A&M University Press, 2000, 67–72.

Officer, Helen Francis. "Sketch of the Life of Thomas Sherman Bugbee, 1841–1925." *Panhandle Plains Historical Review* 5 (1932).

"Old Settlement Is Paid a Visit: Col. Bugbee Makes Settlement in Hutchinson County in 1874." *Clarendon News* (August 24, 1922).

Padgitt, James T. "Colonel William H. Day, Texas Ranchman." *Southwest Historical Quarterly* 53(4) (April 1950): 347–66.

"Party in San Angelo." (San Angelo) *Standard* (January 22, 1887).

Peavy, Linda, and Ursula Smith. *Frontier Children.* Norman: University of Oklahoma Press, 1999.

Peña, José Enrique de la. *With Santa Anna in Texas: A Personal Narrative of the Revolution,* trans. and ed. by Carmen Perry. College Station: Texas A&M University Press, 1975.

"Pioneer Resident Counts Incidents of Early History." *Waco Sunday Tribune-Herald* (April 20, 1930).

"Pioneer Woman Buried Sunday: Resident of Clarendon since 1897, One of First Women in Panhandle." *Clarendon News* (December 27, 1928).

Pool, William C. *A Historical Atlas of Texas.* Austin: Encino Press, 1975.

Porter, Kenneth W. "Negroes and Indians on the Texas Frontier, 1834–1874." *Southwestern Historical Quarterly* 53(1) (July 1949): 151.

Porter, Millie Jones. *Memory Cups of Panhandle Pioneers.* Clarendon, Tex.: Clarendon Press, 1945.

Potter, Jack Meyers. *Cattle Trails of the Old West,* compiled and edited by Laura R. Krehbiel. Clayton, N.Mex.: Laura R. Krehbiel, 1939.

"Prairie Dogs and Rattlesnakes." *Frontier Times* 8(10) (July 1931): 444.

Price, B. Byron. Introduction. *Trail Drivers of Texas,* comp. and ed. by J. Marvin Hunter. 1924. Reprint, Austin: University of Texas Press, 1985.

Pyne, Frederick Wallace. *Descendants of the Signers of the Declaration of Independence: The New England States,* 2d ed., vol. 1, Rockport, Maine: Picton Press, 1990.

"Queen of the Trail." *Frontier Times* 9(3) (December 1931).

"Queen of Trail Dies Age 92." *Cotulla Record* (n.d.).

Raht, Carlysle. *Romance of the Davis Mountains.* El Paso: Rahtbooks, 1991.

Rasch, Phillip J. "Murder in American Valley." *English Brand Book* 7(3) (April 1865).

Rawick, George P., ed. *The American Slave: A Composite Autobiography.* Westport, Conn.: Greenwood Press, 1979.

Richardson, Rupert N. *The Frontier of Northwest Texas, 1846 to 1876: Advance and Defense by the Pioneer Settlers of the Cross Timbers and Prairies.* Glendale, Calif.: Arthur H. Clark, 1963.

———, Adrian Anderson, Gary D. Wintz, and Ernest Wallace. *Texas: The Lone Star State,* 8th ed. Upper Saddle River, N.J.: Prentice Hall, 2001.

Riley, Glenda. "Annie Oakley: Creating the Cowgirl." *Montana* 45(3) (Summer 1994): 32–47.

———. *The Life and Legacy of Annie Oakley.* Norman: University of Oklahoma Press, 1994.

———. *Women and Nature.* Lincoln: University of Nebraska Press, 1999.

Roach, Joyce Gibson. *The Cowgirls,* 2d ed. Denton: University of North Texas Press, 1990.

Robertson, Pauline Durrett, and R. L. Robertson. *Cowman's Country: Fifty Frontier Ranches in the Texas Panhandle, 1876–1887.* Amarillo: Paramount, 1981.

Rodenberger, Lou. "West Texas Pioneer Women: 'The Wilder, Stronger Breed.'" In *West Texas Historical Association Year Book* 77 (2001) and the *Haley Library Newsletter* 23(1) (Spring 2002): 1, 8–10.

Rogers, Mary Beth, Sherry A. Smith, and Janelle D. Scott. *We Can Fly: Stories of Katherine Stinson and Other Gutsy Texas Women.* Austin: Ellen C. Temple, 1983.

Rollins, Phillip Aston. *The Cowboys.* New York: Charles Scribner's Sons, 1922.

Roosevelt, Theodore. "Cross-country Riding in America." *Century* 32 (July 1886), http://cdl.library.cornell.edu.

Rose, Victor Marion. "Some Historical Facts in Regard to the Settlement of Victoria, Texas." *Daily Times Press* (Laredo) (1883). Reprinted as *A Republishing of the book most often known as Victor Rose's History of Victoria,* edited by J. W. Petty Jr. and Kate Stoner O'Connor. Victoria, Tex.: Book Mart, 1961, 131.

San Angelo *Standard.* May 6, 1893, 3, column 9.

———. March 26, 1887. Article about wedding of Alma and Jack Miles. Microfilm, West Texas Collection, Angelo State University Library, San Angelo, Tex.

San Antonio Express (March 19, 1932).

Sandoz, Mari. *The Cattlemen: From the Rio Grande across the Far Marias.* New York: Hastings House, 1958.

Sands, Kathleen Mullen. *Charrería Mexicana: An Equestrian Folk Tradition.* Phoenix: University of Arizona Press, 1993.

Santa Fe Daily New Mexican (April 14, 1884).

Savage, Candice. *Cowgirls.* Berkeley: Ten Speed Press, 1996.

Scarbrough, Clara Stearns. *Land of Good Water: Takachue Pouetsu, A Williamson County, Texas, History.* Georgetown, Tex.: Williamson County Sun Publishers, 1973.

Seagraves, Anne. *Daughters of the West.* Hayden, Idaho.: Wesanne Publications, 1996.

Sears Roebuck Catalog, 1897.

"Services Held for Mrs. Miles." *Clay County Leader* (July 31, 1958).

"Services Today for Jack Miles, Pioneer Cowboy, Peace Officer." *San Angelo Standard Times* (December 14, 1944).

Shafer, Melvin, and Della Shafer. *Milam Cemetery, Sumner County, Kansas, Tombstone Inscriptions.* Wellington, Kans.: Chisholm Trail History and Genealogy Center, 2000.

Sharpe, John M. "Experiences of a Texas Pioneer." In *The Trail Drivers of Texas,* comp. and ed. by J. Marvin Hunter. Nashville: Cokesbury Press, 1925.

Sheffy, Lester Fields. "Thomas Sherman Bugbee." *Panhandle Plains Historical Review* 2 (1929).

Shelton, Emily Jones. "Lizzie E. Johnson: A Cattle Queen of Texas." *Southwestern Historical Quarterly* 50(3) (January 1947): 355–62.

Shipman, O. L. *Taming of the Big Bend: A History of the Extreme Western Portion of Texas from Fort Clark to El Paso.* Austin: Von Boeckman-Jones, 1926.

Simpson, Charles. *El Rodeo.* London: Bodley Head, 1925.

Slatta, Richard W. *Cowboys of the Americas.* New Haven: Yale University Press, 1990.

Slaughter, Mrs. W. B. "My Experience on the Trail." In *The Trail Drivers of Texas.* Vol. 2: 1920–1923, compiled and edited by J. Marvin Hunter. 1924. Reprint, New York: Argosy-Antiquarian, 1963.

Smithwick, Noah. *The Evolution of a State, or Recollections of Old Texas Days,* edited by Alwyn Barr. 1900. Reprint, Austin: W. Thomas Taylor, 1995.

Sonnichsen, C. L. *Cowboys and Cattle Kings.* Norman: University of Oklahoma Press, 1951.

Sperry, Kip. "New England Sources at the Genealogical Library in Salt Lake City." *NEXIS: Newsletter of the New England Historical Genealogical Society* 3(5) (October–November 1986).

Stallard, Patricia Y. *Glittering Misery: Dependents of the Indian Fighting Army.* Norman: University of Oklahoma Press, 1992.

Stanton, Elizabeth Cady. *Eighty Years and More: Reminiscences, 1815–1897.* Boston: Northeastern University Press, 1993.

Steffen, Jerome O. *Comparative Frontiers: A Proposal for Studying the American West.* Norman: University of Oklahoma Press, 1980.

Stephens, A. Ray, and William M. Holmes. *Historical Atlas of Texas.* Norman: University of Oklahoma Press, 1989.

Stocking, Hobart Ebey. "Thomas Sherman Bugbee." *Clarendon* (Texas) *News,* centennial edition, 1982.

Stovall, Frances, Dorothy Wimberley Kerbow, Maxine Storm, Louise Simon, Dorothy Woods Schwartz, and Gene Johnson. *Cedar Springs and Limestone Ledges: A History of San Marcos and Hays County.* San Marcos: Hays County Historical Commission, 1986.

Strasser, Susan. *Never Done: A History of American Housework.* New York: Pantheon Books, 1872.

Stuntz, Jean A. "Spanish Laws for Texas Women." *Southwestern Historical Quarterly* 104(4) (April 2001): 543–59.

Sullivan, Dulcie. *The LS Brand: The Story of a Texas Panhandle Ranch.* Austin: University of Texas Press, 1968.

Surdam, David. "The Antebellum Texas Cattle Trade across the Gulf of Mexico." *Southwest Historical Quarterly* 100(4) (April 1997): 477–92.

Taylor, Thomas Ulvan. "An Airplane Trip over the Chisholm Trail." *Frontier Times* 16(11) (August 1939): 467–71.

———. *The Chisholm Trail and Other Routes.* San Antonio: Naylor, 1936.

———. "Honeymoon on the Old Cattle Trail." *Frontier Times* 14(1) (October 1936): 1–4.

———. "Johnson Institute." *Frontier Times* 18(5) (February 1941): 224–25.

———. "The Stork Rides the Chisholm Trail." *Frontier Times* 14(2) (November 1936): 51–55.

The Texas Almanac for 1871, and Emigrant's Guide to Texas. Galveston: Richardson, 1870.

"Thomas Sherman Bugbee Is Buried." Obituary. *Clarendon News* (October 22, 1925).

Thompson, Karen Ruth. *Historical Williamson County, Texas: A Pictorial History, 1848–2000.* Austin: Nortex Press, 2000.

Thonhoff, Robert H. *San Antonio Stage Lines.* El Paso: Texas Western Press, 1971.

Tombstone Daily Prospector (May 16, 1887).

Tombstone Inscriptions: Goodell Cemetery. Wellington, Kans.: Chisholm Trail History and Genealogy Center, 2001.

Tyler, George W. *The History of Bell County.* San Antonio: Naylor, 1936.

Tyler, Ron, editor-in-chief. *The New Handbook of Texas.* 6 vols. Austin: Texas State Historical Association, 1996. "Angelina County," "Apache Indians," "Banquete," "Beeville," "Bosque County," "Brown, John Duff," "Bryan," "Buffalo Hunting," "Bugbee, Thomas Sherman," "Canadian River," "Carpetbaggers," "Ciboleros," "Civil War," "Coahuiltecan Indians," "Coleman, Mathis, Fulton Pasture Company," "Corpus Christi," "Crockett," "Cuero," "Davis, Jefferson," "Dobie, J. Frank," "Dove Creek, Battle of," "Dyer, Leigh Richmond," "Ford, Colonel John Salmon 'Rip,'" "Folk Medicine," "Fort Worth," "Galveston," "Goodnight, Charles," "Goodnight College," "Goodnight, Mary Ann Dyer," "Goodnight, Tex.," "Goliad," "Gone to Texas," "Houston County," "Indianola," "International-Great Northern Railroad Company," "JA Ranch," "Jonesville," "Mexican War," "Nueces County," "O'Loughlin, Thomas," "Quarter Circle T Ranch," "Quitaque Ranch," "Rockport," "San Patricio," "Shoe Bar Ranch," "Slaughter, George Webb," "Slaughter, William Baxter," "Texas and Southwestern Cattle Raisers' Association," "Texas Revolution," "Tilden," "Tom Green County," "Trail Drivers Association," "Treaty of Guadalupe Hidalgo," "Trinity River," "Waul's Texas Legion," "Webb County."

———. "Welcome to the 108th Annual Meeting." Annual conference program, March 2004.

U.S. Federal Census Indexes 1855–1925. Kansas.

Vestal, Stanley. *Short Grass Country.* New York: Duell, Sloan, and Pearce, 1941.

Victoria (Texas) *Advocate* (March 31, 1929).

"W. B. Slaughter." Obituary. *San Antonio Express* (March 29, 1929).

Wakefield, Robert S. "Family of Richard Warren." *Mayflower Families through Five Generations,* vol. 18, part 1. Plymouth, Mass.: General Society of Mayflower Descendants, 1999.

Waring, Margaret T., and Samuel J. C. Waring. *Comanche County Gravestone Inscriptions,* vol. 1. 1976. Reprint, Comanche County, Tex., 1984.

Warner, Phebe Kerrick. "The Wife of a Pioneer Ranchman." *Cattleman* 7(10) (March 1921): 65–71.

Watson, Elmo Scott. "To Save Famous Goodnight Herd of Buffalo." Unknown newspaper, n. d., J. Evetts Haley Collection, Haley Memorial Library, Midland, Tex.

Webb, Walter Prescott. *The Great Plains.* New York: Grosset and Dunlap, 1931.

Wells, Eulalia Nabors, comp. *Blazing the Way: Tales of Comanche County Pioneers.* Private publication, 1942.

Wheat, Jim, comp. *Postmasters and Post Offices of Texas, 1846–1930.* Garland, Tex.: Self-published, 1974.

Wichita Beacon (June 4, 1873; July 9, 1873).

Wichita City Eagle (July 10, 1873).

Wightman, Marj. "Stones of Memory Fall, but Legend of Lizzie Lives." *Austin American Statesman* (March 20, 1960).

Wilhelm, Steve. *Cavalcade of Hooves and Horns.* San Antonio: Naylor, 1958.

Willey, Kenneth L., ed. *Vital Records from the Eastport Sentinal [sic] of Eastport, Maine, 1818–1900.* Camden, Maine: Picton Press, 1974.

Williams, Blaine T. "The Frontier Family: Demographic Fact and Historical Myth." In *Essays on the American West,* ed. by Harold M. Hollingsworth and Sandra L. Myres. Austin: University of Texas Press, 1969, 46–65.

Williams, Denise. "Generous Gifts Ring in the New Year for Chamber." *Intercom Newsletter.* Round Rock, Texas, Chamber of Commerce (January 2000), Section 1, 4.

Williams, J. W. *Old Texas Trails.* Austin: Eakin Press, 1979.

Williams, Norma Joe. "Miskimons." *Tom Green County: Chronicles of Our Heritage.* Abilene: H. V. Chapman, 2003.

———. "The 19th Street Lot Also Houses Memories." *San Angelo Standard Times* (May 12, 1984).

Winegarten, Ruthe, ed. *Finder's Guide to Texas Women: Celebration of History Exhibit Archives.* Denton: Texas Women's University, 1984.

———. *Governor Ann Richards and Other Texas Women: From Indians to Astronauts.* Austin: Eakin Press, 1993.

———. *Texas Women: A Pictorial History: From Indians to Astronauts.* Austin: Eakin Press, 1985.

Wolff, Henry, Jr. "Up the Trail, but Not Forgotten." *Victoria* (Texas) *Advocate* (April 7, 1996).

"Woman Who Pioneered in West Texas Dies." *Frontier Times* 10(10) (July 1922).

Woodman, David, Jr. *Guide to Texas Emigrants.* 1835. Reprint, Waco: Texian Press, 1974.

Wooster, Ralph A. *Civil War Texas.* Austin: Texas State Historical Association, 1999.

Worcester, Don. *The Chisholm Trail: High Road of the Cattle Kingdom.* Lincoln: University of Nebraska Press, 1980.

Wormser, Richard. *The Iron Horse.* New York: Walker, 1993.

Wyatt, Tula Townsend. *Historical Markers in Hays County 1907–1976.* Austin: Hays County Historical Commission, 1977.

Zlatkovich, Charles P. *Texas Railroads: A Record of Construction and Abandonment.* Austin:

Bureau of Business Research, University of Texas–Austin; Texas State Historical Association, 1981.

INTERNET: SITES AND E-MAIL

Agricultural Bulletin. North Dakota State University, http://www.ext.nodak.edu/extnews/newsrelease/back-issues/000433.txt.

"Amnesty Proclamation." Atlas Editions: Civil War Cards, http://www.wtv-zone.com/civilwar/amnesty.html.

Brenner, Paul. "The Covered Wagon." *New York Times Film Reviews Online,* http://movies2.nytimes.com/gst/movies.html?v_id=11314.

Brothers, Ron. "Confederate Soldiers of Northeast Texas," http://gen.1starnet.com/civilwar/allsold.txt (accessed October 25, 2005).

"Cattle and Cowley County Cattle Drives, 1876–1880." *Traveler* (May 24, 1876), http://www.ausbcomp.com/%7Ebbott/Subjects/cattle.htm (accessed December 1, 2005).

"Chisholm Trail." Oklahoma Historical Society Encyclopedia, http://www.ok-history.mus.ok.us/enc/chsmtrl.htm.

Chisholm Trail, http://www.onthechisholmtrail.com/cti_info.html.

Erickson, Hal. "*North of 36,*" "*The Texans.*" *New York Times Film Reviews Online,* http://www.movies2.nytimes.com/gst/movies/movie.html.

Franklin, Louisa, and Margaret Sturges (great-great nieces of William Burks and Amanda Burks), e-mail correspondence with Lisa Neely, September 14, 2003.

Folkstuff and Range Lore. "Annie Hightower," "Laura Hoover," "Mrs. Ben McCulloch Earl Van Dorn," "Mrs. Jack Miles," "Mrs. Kate Longfield." American Life Histories, Manuscripts from the Federal Writers' Project, 1936–1940, http://memory.loc.gov/ammem/.

Givens, Murphy. "Year of the Yellow Fever." Radio column (July 12, 2003), http://www.caller.com/ccct/opinion_columnists/article/0,1641,CCCt_843_1260198,00.html.

———. "The Yellow Hand of Death." *Corpus Christi Caller-Times* (July 15, 1998), http://www.caller2.com/mgivens/150798.htm.

Green, William Elton. Curator of History, Panhandle-Plains Historical Museum, Canyon, Texas. E-mail correspondence with Frances B. Vick. September 4, 2003.

Henley, Susan Rektorik. "Yellow Fever in Texas during the 1900s." Originally published in "The Storyteller's Notebook," *Český Hlas/The Czech Voice* 17(2) (May 2002), http://www.angelfire.com/tx5/texasczech/Stories/Storyteller/Yellow%20Fever.htm.

"History of Paramount Studios." *Paramount Studios,* http://www.paramount.com/studio/history.htm.

"History of the JA, the Ritchie Family, and the JA Family." JA Remuda, http://www.ranches.org/JAranch.htm.

JA Cattle Company. Records, 1813–1994 and undated. Southwest Collection, Texas Tech University, http://swco.ttu.edu/Manuscripts/jacc32.htm.

Jefferson County, Tennessee. Genealogy and history, http://www.tngenweb.org/jefferson/.

Johnson, Carole M. "Emerson Hough's American West," http://www.lib.uiowa.edu/spec-coll/Bai/johnson.htm.

Leffler, John. "La Salle County, Texas, History," http://www.reynoldsrecords.com/texas/lasalle_history.html.

"Livingston Lindsay to Pease, October 9, 1867." Introduction. Texas State Library and Archives Commission, http://www.tsl.state.tx.us/governors/war/pease-lindsay-1.html.

"Lonehand Western: Journal of the Old West," http://www.lonehand.com/chuckwagon_central.html.

Malthy, W. H. *Advertiser* (Corpus Christi), extra edition (August 14, 1867). Corpus Christi Public Library, http://www.library.ci.corpus-christi.tx.us/oldbayview/yellowfeverarticle.htm (accessed December 1, 2005).

McCoy, Joseph G. *Historical Sketches of the Cattle Trade of the West and Southwest.* Kansas City, Mo.: Ramsey, Millett, and Hudson, 1874. Kansas Collection Books Online, http://www.kancoll.org./books/mccoy/.

New Handbook of Texas Online, The. "Adair, Cornelia Wadsworth," "Bosque County," "Butler, William G.," "Camp Colorado," "Caprock," "Carpetbaggers," "Carter, TX," "Cattle Trailing," "Cedar Park," "Comanche County," "Epidemic Diseases," "Guajoco," "Hardin, John Wesley," "Holmsley, James Monroe," "Howard Associations," "Old Stone Ranch," "Reynolds Cattle Company," "Reynolds, George Thomas," "Slaughter, William Baxter," "Whitesboro, TX," http://www.tsha.utexas.edu/handbook/online.

"Notes on Early Residents of Victoria—Milton Hardy, Excerpted from 88th Anniversary Edition of *Victoria Advocate,* September 28, 1934." Victoria County Genealogical Society 9, http://www.viptx.net/vcgs/hotels.html (accessed Sept. 25, 2003).

Oglethorpe County, Tex. Archives. http://www.roadsidegeorgia.com/county/oglethorpe.html.

Parish, David W. Historian. E-mail correspondence with Frances B. Vick. April 21, 2003. Geneseo, N.Y.

Shackelford, Bruce. E-mail correspondence with Joyce Gibson Roach. October 10, 2003. Boerne, Tex.

Spurlin, Charles. Victoria, Tex. E-mail correspondence with Phyllis McKenzie, May 15, 2003; May 20, May 27, and June 8, all in 2003.

"Taming of the Shrew." http://www.arkangelshakespeare.com/tamingshrew-1.html.

"Texas Chisholm Trail." Sundancer's West, http://www.sundancerswest.com/texaschisholmtrail.htm.

Tubbs, Sandy, transcriber. "Houston County, Texas, 1840 Tax Roll." Entry #198 and #256, http://www.rootsweb.com/~txhousto/court/taxro112.html.

———. "Houston County. Republic of Texas, 1846 Poll Tax List for Houston County," http://www.rootsweb.com/~txhousto/census/polltax1846.htm.

———. "1850 Houston County, Texas Census," http://www.rootsweb.com/~txhousto/census/1850cen3g.htm.

"Tuberculosis." On-line Medical Dictionary, http://www.cancerweb.ncl.ac.uk/cgi-bin/omd?tuberculosis.

U.S. Bureau of the Census. Houston County, Tex. 1850. 676, http://www.rootsweb.com/~txhousto/census/1850cen3g.htm.

"Vignettes of Victoria County—Hardy, Mr. and Mrs. William, extracted from *Victoria Advocate* Historical Edition, May 1968." Victoria County Genealogical Society, http://www.viptx.net/vcgs/vignette.html.

"White County, Arkansas," http://www.rootweb.com/~arwhite/.

Wolff, Henry, Jr. "Some Movers and Shakers of Early Victoria: Evergreen Cemetery Tour," s.v. "A. B. Peticolas," "Margaret Heffernan Borland," and "Victor Marion Rose." Victoria County Genealogical Society, http://www.viptx.net/vcgs/evergreencem.html; http://www.viptx.net/vcgs/evergreencem2.html.

Woods, Dee. "Yellow Fever Killed Many Early Settlers: John Dunn Recalls When He Took Down with Dread Disease." *Corpus Christi Caller* (July 7, 1939). Corpus Christi Public Libraries, http://www.library.ci.corpus-christi.tx.us/oldbayview/yellowfeverarticle2.htm (accessed December 1, 2005).

"Yellow Fever." Encyclopedia.com. *Columbia Encyclopedia,* 6th ed., 2003, http://www.encyclopedia.com/printable.asp?url=/ssi/yl/yellowfe.html.

"Yellow Fever Accounts from the *Daily Ranchero,* Brownsville." Corpus Christi Public Libraries, http://www.library.ci.corpus-christi.tx.us/oldbayview/yellowfeverranchero.htm (accessed December 1, 2005).

Index

Numbers in **boldface type** refer to captions.
For individual cattle brand names *see* "brands." For individual cattle trails *see* "cattle trails."
For individual counties in Texas *see* "Texas counties." For individual Forts by name *see* "forts."
For individual railroads by name *see* "railroads." For individual ranches by name *see* "ranches."

A. J. Fimbel, Saddlery, **9**
Abbott, Shirley, 250n.14
Abilene, Kansas, 68
Adair, Cornelia Wadsworth Ritchie (Mrs.
   John George Adair), **4,** 15, 83, 139, 140,
   148–162, **149,** 158, 159, 282; on buffalo
   hunt, 152–53; as business manager of JA,
   157, 159–60; on cattle drive to Palo Duro
   Canyon, 154–56; childhood of, 148, 150–
   151; and love of horses, 152, 160
Adair, John George, 138–40, 151, 153; as
   cattle investor, 154–57, 159; personality
   of, 151, 196
Adair Brokerage, 154
Adams, Ramon F., 245
Adobe Walls, Tex., 83
Alamo, 95, 166, 263
Albany, Tex., 44, 46
Alley, Jack, 171
Amanda Burks School, 61
Amarillo, Tex., 161
American Life Histories collection. *See* Fed-
   eral Writers' Project of the Works Pro-
   gress Administration
American Revolution, 6
American Valley, Tex., 171

Anderson, Ellen Viola Perry Wilson (Mrs.
   Nels Louis Anderson), **4,** 207, **208,** 218,
   218n.1; on cattle drive, 213; childhood of,
   208–13; as cook, 213–14, 216–17; home-
   steading hazards, 215–16; and loneliness,
   215; marriage(s) of, 212, 217; as seam-
   stress, 216;
Anderson, Florence, 217
Anderson, Gladys, (Mrs. Charles Harvey),
   217, 218
Anderson, Mabel, 217, 218
Anderson, Nels Louis, 216, 218, 218
Anderson, Viola. *See* Anderson, Ellen Viola
   Perry Wilson
Anthony, Susan B., 20, 175
Arc Light Saloon (San Angelo, Tex.), 274
Arkansas River, 43, 44;
Arkansas River Bridge, 105
Austin, Tex., 26, 191
Austin Statesman, 72
Austin Sunday American–Statesman, 73,
   76n.3, 77n.16
Azusa Church (Denton County, Tex.), 33

Bailey, Joseph Martin, 243
Bailey, Martha Elizabeth, 243

ISBN-13: 978-1-58544-543-1
ISBN-10: 1-58544-543-6